Education and Psychology of the Gifted Series

James H. Borland, Editor

RECOMMENDED PRACTICES IN GIFTED EDUCATION

A Critical Analysis

Bruce M. Shore
Dewey G. Cornell
Ann Robinson
Virgil S. Ward

TEACHERS COLLEGE PRESS

Teachers College, Columbia University
New York and London

Research grants in support of the preparation of this work were gratefully received from several sources. Bruce M. Shore was awarded research grants from the Social Sciences and Humanities Research Council of Canada, the "Challenge" summer employment program for students of the Ministry of Employment and Immigration of Canada, the "FCAR" Research Program of the Ministry of Education of the Province of Quebec, and the Social Sciences Research Grants Subcommittee of the Faculty of Graduate Studies and Research at McGill University. Dewey G. Cornell received a Summer Research Award from the Curry School of Education at the University of Virginia.

Published by Teachers College Press, 1234 Amsterdam Avenue
New York, NY 10027

Library of Congress Cataloging-in-Publication Data

Recommended practices in gifted education : a critical analysis /
　　Bruce M. Shore . . . [et. al.].
　　　　p.　　cm. —(Education and psychology of the gifted series ; 7)
　　Includes bibliographical references (p.　　) and indexes.
　　ISBN 0–8077–3084–X
　　1. Gifted children—Education—United States.　I. Shore, Bruce M.
　II. Series.
　LC3993.9.R44
　371.95—dc20　　　　　　　　　　　　　　　　　　　　　　　　　91–4331

ISBN 0–8077–3084–X

Printed on acid-free paper

Manufactured in the United States of America

98 97 96 95 94 93 92 91 8 7 6 5 4 3 2 1

Contents

Series Editor's Foreword

This is a very important book. It is no exaggeration to state that the publication of *Recommended Practices in Gifted Education: A Critical Analysis* is a landmark in the history of the field of the education of the gifted. This work promises to change, and to change fundamentally, the way we think about and educate gifted children.

What makes the publication of this book a seminal event is the fact that, at long last, a group of prominent scholars has subjected the various beliefs that undergird practice in our field to careful and rigorous scrutiny. Numerous assertions that, through repitition, have been accorded the status of truth have, in most cases for the first time, been evaluated with respect to the degree and nature of support that can actually be found for them in the research literature. The importance of this undertaking can scarcely be overstated. It establishes an empirical base for our field and provides the means necessary to raise the field out of the realm of hype and near superstition into that of scholarly practice.

Reading this volume, one learns quite a bit about our field, some of it not very encouraging. One realizes, for example, that the education of thousands of gifted children has been predicated upon some beliefs that have no logical or empirical support. One is also reminded that we have neglected one of our basic obligations as a professional field, to undertake the research necessary to separate practices that are effective from those that are ineffective or even harmful. This has placed us in a difficult position and at times made the field vulnerable to the hard sell and the passing fad.

But there is good news implicit in the publication of this book as well. The very fact that this laborious but necessary analytical and evaluative undertaking has finally been accomplished is testimony to changes within the field of the education of the gifted, changes that bode well for our collective future. This is symbolic of a coming of age in this field, a passage from a period characterized by great energy and enthusiasm—but also, too often, a lack of critical discernment—to one of greater maturity and higher professional standards.

I have been excited about the prospect of publishing this volume as part of the Teachers College Press *Education and Psychology of the Gifted Series* since it was first proposed to us a few years ago. I am quite proud to be associated, in a very small way, with its production. It is a pleasure for me to be among the first to thank Bruce M. Shore, Dewey G. Cornell, Ann Robinson, and Virgil S. Ward for one of the most impressive and valuable pieces of scholarship that our field has yet seen. We, and untold numbers of gifted students, are in their debt.

JAMES H. BORLAND, EDITOR
Education and Psychology
of the Gifted Series

Foreword

This is a unique book that will make an important contribution to both theory and practice in the field of gifted education.

The education of the gifted has a long history which, until relatively recently, has been entirely too atheoretical. There has been a good deal of research reported over the years but, for the most part, it has driven neither theory nor practice to any great extent. It is generally agreed that the first large-scale program for academically able children in the U.S. was initiated in the St. Louis Public Schools 1868. Students were promoted first on a semiannual, then on a quarterly, and finally on a five-week basis. The motivation for Superintendent William T. Harris's program was two-fold—to permit brighter learners to move through the grades more rapidly and to reduce the size of classes in the early grades. Similar administrative procedures were soon established in other schools, most involving some kind of flexible promotion, ability grouping, or both.

In 1920, the National Society for the Study of Education published its nineteenth yearbook, under the title *Classroom Problems in the Education of Gifted Children* (Bloomington, IL: Public School Publishing). The yearbook's editor, T. S. Henry, noted that "Many cities and towns are already making special provisions for gifted pupils, either by schemes of flexible grading, or by special rooms or classes for them, and others are definitely planning to make such provisions as soon as it may be possible or feasible" (p. 9). The volume concluded with a set of no fewer than 18 recommendations "concerning the organization and conduct of special rooms for gifted children" (p. 112). Among the recommendations were the following:

> The enrollment of a special room for gifted pupils should represent a selection of approximately the top ten per cent of the ordinary school population in the grades which are to be represented.
>
> Health should be an important factor in the selection of the pupils.
>
> The method of selecting gifted pupils should be by mental tests, *not by teachers' estimates of the pupils' ability or estimates by school administrators from school marks*. [Emphasis added]

The teacher of a special room for gifted children must possess a large fund of general information.

The teacher must have had adequate foundation in the theory and practice of education.

The teacher must be characterized by energy, enthusiasm, and an inspiring personality.

In the special room for gifted children, drill should be decreased by about 50 per cent.

Likewise, explanation should be reduced about 50 per cent in amount, and needs be given in much less detail than to ordinary pupils.

Emphasis should be placed upon the development of the pupils' initiative.

Instruction should be as much as possible by broad, underlying principles, rather than by detached facts.

If any of the pupils in the special room seem to be developing egoistic tendencies, the teacher should apply the 'social check.' ["This can often be done by comparing the work of the child who needs to be thus corrected with that of some other pupil of superior, or at least equal, ability in that particular line."]

The teacher of a special room for gifted children should be allowed wide latitude in modifying the course of study to fit the purpose of the room and the needs of the pupil. (pp. 113–118)

Some of the wording of these recommendations may seem archaic today, but it is not unlike that of many directives which currently guide practice in the field of gifted education.

At the time the NSSE yearbook was published, research on the gifted was about to begin. Terman's Genetic Studies of Genius were initiated shortly thereafter and, in fact, the yearbook introduction mentions Terman and cites him as the person "to whom we owe the term 'gifted' as the standard designation of children of supernormal ability" (p. 9). There was already a growing body of literature, as evidenced by the bibliography in the NSSE's twenty-third yearbook, which followed in 1924 and was titled *The Education of Gifted Children* (G. M. Whipple, editor). The 453 items in the annotated bibliography of that volume consist primarily of descriptions of "the supernormal child" and of school practices. Incidentally, the title of Terman's 1906 article, "Genius and Stupidity" in the *Pedagogical Seminary* (entry 371), apparently said it all because no annotation followed.

I begin this foreword with the brief historical perspective because, in some ways, the pattern established by these early NSSE yearbooks of making recommendations based essentially on experience has continued through the decades. Thus, when the authors of this book point out in their Preface that they undertook the project because of their "deep concern that gifted education was enjoying a renaissance, but that very little attention was being devoted to research which would support the choices being made in policy, identification, pedagogy or family practice," they underscore a real need if the current revival is to have any lasting effect on the field. As they put it very well, "Strongly held opinions are insufficient in an era of accountability. Failure to make use of objective evidence will undermine credibility and render the field vulnerable to repeated waning of public support."

In this work, they have reversed the usual approach of deducing defensible practice from theory and have instead begun with "what educators of bright children are most widely advised to do, and [examined] research and theory from the practitioner's perspective." They acknowledge the fact "that empirical research is not the only legitimate support for an educational practice. . . . [that] there are also cultural, moral, religious, ethical, safety, and legal reasons (among others) for the educational choices we make." But, their focus is on the empirical research support for practice as an important resource needed to do better planning for the gifted.

The authors have identified 101 recommended practices in gifted education chosen from 100 books and "discuss the sources of the advice to carry out each practice, the research—especially empirical research—which supports or refutes each practice, the implication of the state of knowledge for practice, and the research still needed to strengthen our knowledge base." This is a tremendous undertaking which the authors have successfully carried out. They have grouped their practices into eight sections around the topics which are familiarly used in the field of gifted education.

What makes this book so unique and important is that no other publication in the field of gifted education has attempted such a comprehensive, challenging task. Everyone involved in teaching, administering, parenting, policy-making, research or program planning will find this book an invaluable, practical resource. This is not a book designed for "airplane reading." Instead, it is one which those who are involved in identifying and nurturing talent potential will want to read, reflect upon, and return to over and over.

A. HARRY PASSOW
Jacob H. Schiff Professor of Education
Teachers College, Columbia University

Preface

This book examines the research support available for widely recommended practices in gifted education. The practices were selected from 100 books on giftedness, gifted education, and the development and rearing of bright children. We discuss the sources of the advice to carry out each practice, the research—especially empirical research—that supports or refutes the practice, the implications of the state of knowledge for each practice, and the research still needed to strengthen our knowledge base. The main part of the book is a compendium of supported (and not so well supported) practices, perhaps best thought of as a field guide to practices and needed research.

We address this book to teachers, consultants, administrators, and program planners, who need to know the extent to which specific practices are defensible. It is intended equally for parents, school-board members, leaders in parent, professional, and advocate organizations who want to be able to judge what is available, to choose wisely from the menu of what is not offered in their schools, and to be knowledgeable about good practice in general. The volume is well suited as a textbook in graduate research seminar courses and as a supplemental text in survey courses on giftedness. Finally, we hope this volume will be useful to researchers. In this category we especially include teachers, counselors, psychologists, sociologists, subject-matter specialists, and others who are enrolled in graduate programs and are looking for project or dissertation topics with practical value and that which can build meaningfully on existing knowledge. We include faculty members interested in giftedness, from any discipline, who may have been involved primarily in training but now may be interested in developing a research theme with practical focus. Career researchers whose work is ongoing and theory-driven will benefit from being able to identify areas of application to which their work is relevant. Scholars new to gifted education may find opportunities to apply their expertise to important questions that need answers.

We began this project with deep concern that gifted education was enjoying a renaissance, but that very little attention was being devoted to research that would support the choices being made in policy, identification, pedagogy, or family practice. Strongly held opinions are insufficient in an era of accountability. Failure to make use of objective evidence will undermine credibility and render the field vulnerable to waning public support.

Nearly all previous comprehensive work on gifted education began with theory from which defensible practice was deduced. We reversed this, beginning with the practices so that the work would be immediately relevant to practitioners. Research and practice in education must contribute to each other; they are part of a two-way relationship. Beginning with theory was not serving this relationship well. Present theory cannot account for all current practice, and all current practice cannot be defended in terms of current knowledge. There is a need to look at what educators of bright children are most widely advised to do, and to examine research and theory from the practitioner's perspective. We have reached out to wide-ranging theory and research to see which of those practices are defensible on this basis. This simultaneously widens and focuses the theoretical base for gifted education as well as the list of practical questions that need research support. We hope to narrow the research-practice gap by involving practitioners in determining the research agenda and encouraging them to become stakeholders in that research.

We fully recognize that empirical research is not the only legitimate support for an educational practice. Although this book concentrates on such research, there are also cultural, moral, religious, ethical, safety, and legal reasons (among others) for the educational choices we make. Social justice, national, or world vision also can justify educational action. Our purpose is to present the empirical research support for major practices in the field because that evidence is important and not readily available. Each individual must then make the best possible informed decision, weighing all the evidence.

Our thinking about this book began some nine years ago. It grew out of the work of the Knowledge Production and Utilization Committee of The Association for the Gifted (TAG). This committee was proposed by Virgil Ward. From 1978 to 1982, with Ward in the chair and Bruce Shore and Hans Jellen among its members, it sponsored several symposia and paper presentations on the state of knowledge in gifted education. In 1982, Virgil Ward nominated Bruce Shore to assume the chair.

Ann Robinson was recruited on the basis of her work with Bruce Shore on the Evaluation and Research Committee of the National Association for Gifted Children, of which she is still an active member. Dewey Cornell became known to us through a presentation he made at the 1981 Fourth World Conference on Gifted and Talented Children in Montreal; one of Bruce Shore's graduate students (Marcella Grenier) had become interested in family variables related to giftedness and prompted our contact. The present project was proposed by Bruce Shore in 1983 as a new committee mandate. Hans Jellen withdrew from the project in 1985 while fulfilling a Fullbright Fellowship in Europe.

This is a coauthored work, not an edited collection of papers. We have all commented extensively upon the draft parts prepared by others, and then again upon the edited whole, especially Chapters 1 through 8 that form the heart of this document. We have been pleasantly surprised at the consensus we have forged in creating this work. We avoided identifying specific sections with individual authors. We all read and contributed freely to each other's drafts yet miraculously are all still on friendly speaking terms! As our work drew to a close and we had to decide which practices were supported and which not, we engaged in increasingly frequent phone calls, facsimile messages, and express mail to find the right words for our collective ideas.

That all being said, we cannot promise you the Truth. We have managed to get the four of us to agree, more or less, but the goal in this work is a moving target. If this volume is successful, the target will move even more quickly. Assuming we have succeeded in defining the state of knowledge at this time, we hope this work will become out of date. Indeed, the more quickly our work is out of date, the better for the field. This does not mean our efforts need be forgotten nor lack lasting impact. We hope their impact will be to provide a benchmark by which progress in future research and practice can be assessed and to help steer the field toward increasing its knowledge base and moving toward recommended practices that have better support than the ones we find today.

You do not have to agree with us for our work to have been successful. We will be happy if our efforts help you make a defensible decision in the education of a bright child or help you ask a good question about bright children and their needs at school or at home; if they prompt you to go about answering that question through research; or if they motivate you to report your practical or theoretical work in a suitable public forum. We will be especially pleased if this work enables and encourages you to forge links between research and practice, to be the reflective practitioner or concerned researcher, one in touch with the other. The ultimate beneficiary must be the child.

Finally, we would like this volume to be the beginning of a dialogue. At the end is a short feedback form that may be photocopied and sent to us. We will undertake to find ways to add your input to what we have written. We have taken an initiative but dare not insist upon the final word.

Acknowledgments

We were greatly helped by many marvelous people, to whom we are extremely grateful.

We must begin with successive Executive Committees of The Association for the Gifted (TAG), a division of the Council for Exceptional Children. TAG provided us with a forum, as its Knowledge Production and Utilization Committee, to interact on the development of the idea for this book with many of the leaders in the field at semi-annual board meetings and to share its progress with wider audiences at major conferences in plenary meetings and workshops. The confidence and opportunity we enjoyed were essential to completion of this volume, which will also serve as the report of our committee. We hesitate to call it a "final" report, because we hope this is a marker for the beginning of a process of linking practice and research in gifted education, not an end. To all our colleagues in TAG, singly and collectively over more than a decade, a special thank you!

At the University of Arkansas at Little Rock, Barbara Abney, Kathy Briggs, Sperry Davenport, Fredericka Douglas, Barbara Herring, Constance Meyer, Tonya Moon, Jaime Rollans, and Mary Kathryn Stein helped us with extremely competent bibliographic and preparatory work on this book. They and other students in the graduate seminar on giftedness provided valuable "consumer feedback" as final parts of the text emerged.

At the University of Virginia, students in courses on the educational psychology of giftedness offered provocative questions and insightful debate on the various practices reviewed in this book. We especially thank Scott Hunsaker, Mary Landrum, Helen Nevitt, and Shula Ramsay.

At McGill University, where the first drafts of the recommended practices were extracted from the texts, the general literature was searched and entered into a data base, and the contributions from all the authors came together, there were many who assisted. Sheila Glazer was involved throughout the production of the book, convening meetings to review the contents of every text, making materials accessible, moving bibliographic work along, and ensuring that the first author knew what was happening as all the pieces started coming together at an ever faster pace in the last year. Carole Ann Kleivstul and Barbara Koester helped the authors stay in touch with each other, assuring the postal services of two countries a fiscal surplus. Preparatory and bibliographic work, complemented by informed critique of our ideas, was performed most competently by Elaine Coleman, Josie Gambino, Ronald Janusaitis, Cindy Kaizer, Tanya Karabian, Carolyn Kato, Elsa Lo, Kathryn Macdonald, Laurie McMurdo, Irene Rapaport, Alan Romano, Angela Smailes, and Anasatassos Tsiamis. McGill colleagues F. Gillian Rejskind and Lannie S. Kanevsky were generous in their advice and support, and especially in the lending of books from their personal collections.

We also thank Hans G. Jellen, a member of the TAG committee while the project was in its early stages of conceptualization, for his ideas and support, John F. Feldhusen of Purdue University for his encouragement of this project and the inclusion of a report in progress in a symposium series supported by the State of Indiana, and A. Harry Passow of Teachers College, Columbia University, for his encouragement and honoring us with the foreword to this work.

Although expressions of thanks are normally directed outward, we have experienced an unusual collaboration in producing this volume. We four have never before worked together on a project; we came together specifically to produce this volume, and we all met together only once over eight years. We learned immeasurably from each other in the accomplishment of the group mission, not the least when we disagreed with one another.

Finally, each of us benefited immensely from the support and tolerance of our families. This is always the greatest burden in such an undertaking as ours, especially as deadlines approach (and pass!) and the share of family responsibilities is distorted for a while. With much love and thanks, we acknowledge everything from the patient listening to tolerance for tying up the family computers, to Bettina Shore, Nancy Cornell, Tom Stanley, and Alyne Ward—very special people!

RECOMMENDED PRACTICES
IN GIFTED EDUCATION
A Critical Analysis

Introduction

This book examines the state of research-based knowledge underlying gifted education, primarily from the perspective of educational practice. We identified recommended practices in textbooks on gifted education and giftedness, and, for each of these practices, present the following:

1. Examples of how the practice has been proposed in the literature
2. Research addressing the practice and a conclusion regarding its support or refutation
3. Implications of the state of knowledge for the implementation of each practice
4. Suggestions for research needed to improve the knowledge base for gifted education

In this Introduction, we describe how the work was done and provide some examples of how this book and its results may be useful. In Chapters 1 through 8, we offer detailed analyses of the 101 practices that we identified as recommended in the textbook literature on giftedness. Finally, we offer some general conclusions about the state of the knowledge base.

We hope this work will promote a systematic development of validational research on practices in gifted education and, toward this end, a greatly needed dialogue between practitioners and researchers as well as improvements in the educational choices we make in the education of exceptionally able children.

The Need for the Work

This is not the first examination of the state of the art in gifted education, but it is original in viewing gifted education from the practitioner's perspective. The most familiar of previous efforts are general textbooks. Each varies in style and focus, ranging from curriculum to child development to philosophical and research underpinnings. Another type is the edited volume of expert reviews on specific topics, in the form of yearbooks, conference proceedings, and independently prepared anthologies. There is also a growing number of volumes that address specific topics in the education or development of the gifted. Many or all of these types do a fine job of providing suggestions for good practice based on a theoretical perspective, and they are cited extensively in this book. Our goal is to complement these works. Indeed, they are the starting point for our work.

There has been a great deal written about giftedness and gifted education. The vast majority of this writing has, however, been descriptive and prescriptive. Research support for the advice offered has been rare. K. B. Rogers (1989) conducted a citation check on 2,680 different titles selected from major data bases and concluded that, from 1975 to 1986, only 32% of all the citations were reports of research. She found that curriculum issues dominated the nonresearch literature and that research addressed primarily student characteristics and identification. A large but unspecified number of the research titles were produced as dissertations meeting graduate degree requirements. It is quite typical for many of these people, upon graduation, to respond to the urgent need for the provision and supervision of services and not make further research part of their careers. There have also been relatively few university positions in the field where such research could be done; many college and university posts are seen by their institutions as training positions without time, reward, or other priority for scholarship. Together, this suggests the absence of programmed, systematic research on key issues in gifted education, notably curriculum and pedagogy.

Carter and Swanson (1990) confirmed and extended Rogers's conclusions. They examined all the journals on giftedness and several general educational research journals from 1972 to 1988 and used the *Social Sciences Citation Index* to identify 1,700 articles focusing on giftedness. Through several steps they identified a list of frequently cited authors and papers. Even among these prominent articles, 29% were data-based, compared with 24% of a randomly selected control sample of papers. Similarly derived figures for papers on learning disabilities from prominent authors showed 78% were data-based versus 62% for papers selected randomly. Furthermore, 57% of the prominent papers (versus 67% of the controls) on giftedness were applied. They concluded, therefore, that publications on giftedness are primarily non-data-based and address practice. They further observed that only half of even the prominent articles based their ideas on research or theory.

These studies support our impression that the literature on gifted education is replete with unsubstantiated general advice. One consequence of such a situation is that educational practice does not advance as quickly as it should. Passow (1986b) pointed out the limited advances in advocated practices between National Society for the Study of Education yearbooks two decades apart (N. B. Henry, 1958; Passow, 1979) and later repeated the observation (Passow, 1989) that research on adapted education for bright students was rare.

To redress this serious deficit Carter and Swanson (1990) suggested:

> An analysis of the gifted literature would provide insight into the quality of the database, as well as the discipline's current trends, future directions, and potential for development. To our knowledge, such an analysis of the gifted literature has not been conducted—probably because the task is so overwhelming. (p. 116)

We are pleased to present a first approximation of such an overwhelming task and hope that it provides some of the anticipated insights!

The Idea of Recommended Practices

The K. B. Rogers (1989) and Carter and Swanson (1990) studies pursued journals as the most likely place to look for research on gifted education. We decided that books were more likely than journals to contain prescriptions for action, especially as the principal journals in the field are increasing the amount of research they publish. We have also selected books over other media because of the status they retain in our educational system, because of their role in integrating knowledge in a field where scholarship is diffuse and poorly supported financially, and because of their widespread availability and durability. Indeed, some rather durable books with highly contestable advice are often readily available, more so than the latest professional journals in which the same advice may be coming under critical examination. We have made the pragmatic decision that the knowledge base is not merely the assemblage of the best information on the topic but the information that is widespread and most accessible to a concerned parent or teacher.

There are five important elements to our notion of a recommended practice. First, it refers to specific advice, for example, in the form of "do," "don't," or "should" statements. Second, it signals a level of agreement in the field that is somewhat narrower than what is represented by the word *standards,* which are fewer, formally endorsed by some organization (e.g., Association for the Gifted, 1989), and designed to form the basis for some process of certification or accreditation. Recommended practices, on the other hand, comprise the considered advice of experts and persons actively involved in the field. Third, recommended practices are broad enough to be generic, for example, proposing the use of IQ tests but not necessarily promoting a particular one, or suggesting the study of historical figures but not particular persons except as examples. They are approximately at the level of section headings or margin summaries in a textbook. Nevertheless, they unavoidably vary quite widely in breadth and could easily be combined or divided to create a somewhat longer or shorter list. Simply put, some are necessarily more profound, others more trivial. They share a common origin. Fourth, they should not be taken too literally or narrowly. This field presents many semantic problems, and we have tried to focus on matters of substance. Recommended practices should first and foremost be viewed as hypotheses— tested or untested—that are visible in the field. Fifth, in using the term *recommended practices* to describe these suggestions, we are not endorsing or recommending these practices, nor, necessarily, the books from which we gleaned them. Rather, we are reporting and reviewing what is recommended by the authors of the books we examined.

We are following an applied direction. Formal research that is based on well-developed theory and models, and that is designed to increase our knowledge of gifted education in relation to other knowledge, accounts for a very small portion of the literature on giftedness. A relatively small number of researchers in an equally small number of universities are involved in ongoing research, but few direct links can be drawn among these various efforts. This makes it extremely difficult to define a knowledge base in terms of action derived from tested theory or models. On the other hand, there is a large and growing amount of program activity, and there is an accompanying urgent need for practitioners to be able to assess the support for the programs they propose.

The Process

Although our procedures have the aura of a scientific exercise about them, they necessarily entail a large number of reasoned but subjective decisions. If we are to use books as the beginning of our data base, which books? How will we recognize a recommended practice when we find one? How will we state it succinctly? These and many other issues are addressed briefly, we hope in just enough detail that our effort will be understandable, useful, and reproducible. A reader eager for the results should feel free to jump ahead and around the reviews of practices that follow.

Choice of the Books

The first step was to identify the list of books to be examined for recommended practices. These should be regarded as a form of representative sampling. We decided that 100 books would be credible. As we moved through the second half of that number, we added very few recommended practices to the list and therefore did not feel compelled to add more books for review.

We selected the books because of their availability (not necessarily only in the United States), our respect for the reputations of the authors, and the advice given us by colleagues, students, and respondents to reports of our work at conferences and meetings. We purposely sought a diverse collection of books. We have new and old titles, American, Canadian, European, and a few others. A small number are not written in English, and several offer opposing positions or advice.

Our final list of authors and titles is given at the end of this Introduction. Many of these books are edited collections of chapters or papers by diverse authors. In Chapters 1 to 8, we cite the authors of the parts of these volumes. Full references to all the books and papers are available in the References at the end of the volume.

There might be value in seeking external validation of our choice of volumes. It is apparent to us that one criticism could be about our choice to sample books over a wide span of time. The newest books, but for two new editions that were published during our work (and we updated all our citations), are from 1985 and 1986 when this part of the task began. On the other hand, a sampling of recommended practices only from the latest books might not be as representative a sampling of the knowledge base, and older books are in school and district libraries. We have taken account of this problem by ensuring that the additional references consulted in the course of our analyses were up-to-date. We have been able to ensure that many 1989, 1990, and "in press" books and other publications were included. We began with what is now an older bibliography, but the contents of Chapters 1 through 8 are as up-to-date as possible.

We used the literature to validate our selections further. Torrance (1986) reported an informal survey of university teachers concerning the leading textbooks in the field. Only one title (on creativity) from his list of nine is not in our list. His references were the 1981 third edition of Barbe and Renzulli (1975), the earlier editions of B. Clark (1988), the earlier edition of Gallagher (1985), Gowan, Khatena, and Torrance (1979a), Khatena (1982), Maker (1982a), Maker (1982b), Sellin and Birch (1980), and Tannenbaum (1983).

Maddux and Candler (1985) assessed the readability, interest, and coverage of 13 college texts on gifted education. Their selection was based on ready availability. Every one of their titles is on our list: These include all the ones listed by Torrance (1986) except Gowan et al. (1979a) plus George, Cohn, and Stanley (1979), Laycock (1979), Newland (1976), and Whitmore (1980).

Finally, Breiter (1989) conducted a systematic survey of 62 instructors in 57 universities, who taught 182 courses on giftedness. Their text selections were tabulated and the eight texts most often reported (from Breiter, 1988 — the original presentation version of this paper, which was shortened for publication) were listed. One was on creativity. Six others are on our list: the second edition of B. Clark (1988), the first edition of Davis and Rimm (1989), Gallagher (1985), Maker (1982a, 1982b), and Swassing (1985a). We did not include Renzulli (1986a), though he was well represented in our list; this volume is similar in intent to Maker (1982b), and it was used in preparing Chapters 1 through 8. Breiter (1988) also identified 11 titles used as supplementary or optional texts, 8 of which are on the above list, and only 2 of which are not cited at all in this book. Our nearly complete inclusion of the books referred to in these three references assured us that we had made a suitable selection. Because our use of the books was cumulative, the additional titles might enrich and further validate the sampling of recommended practices but would probably not have a substantial effect on our results.

Selection of the Recommended Practices

A team of the first author, a research assistant, and several graduate students read several books simultaneously and met weekly, comparing notes in an attempt to agree on (1) what we meant by recommended practice in terms of specificity, and (2) what recommended practices were advocated in a particular book. After about six weeks we agreed on the wording provided in the table of contents and used as headings in Chapters 1–8. As new recommended practices were derived and edited, they were compared with others on the list. Coauthors were kept informed and contributed ideas and practices along the way. There is undoubtedly variation in specificity, but we found the list as finally constructed to be useful for the task at hand. Through active discussion, even debate, we reached consensus on the list of recommended practices derived from each book; errors of omission with regard to any one book were unlikely to be serious because there was much repetition among the books. Related to this, we have chosen only a few of the selections espousing the recommended practice; authors of these works, however, are not to be associated uniquely with these practices, and, actually, in many cases the authors are in turn reporting or summarizing the advice of others. We also acknowledge that the original authors may have changed their minds on certain issues since the cited works were published; we chose good statements of the practices and do not intend to punish the messengers. Our citations indicate merely where a reader may locate the advice in the available literature so as to be able to verify that we are representing it accurately and fairly. Indeed, in a few cases we noted the disavowal rather than the advocacy of particular practices.

Detailed records were kept on each book, including the pages on which the recommended practices were mentioned. This information was entered in a computer data base that enabled us to access and cross-list the contents by author or book with a list of recommended practices addressed by each or, more usefully for our purposes, by recommended practice. At the conclusion of this stage of our work, we had a list of 121 recommended practices.

We then pared the list to 101 during the writing of the reviews. In some cases we discovered that the literature addressing several practices was the same and they should be treated together, or, in others, that we could achieve some economy by combining them. As with the 100 books, there was nothing magic about the number 101, but as it approached, the opportunity to achieve a degree of symmetry in a work so open-ended was rather tempting.

We hoped the list of 101 recommended practices would stand, at least for a while, as a broad and representative survey of standards for the field of gifted education. This is an ambitious goal (we hope not a presumptuous one), and it is likely that there are recommendations that we have not included. (We point out the opportunity to add these or relevant research on the feedback form at the end of this book.) Such omissions were largely unintentional; that is, we overlooked the recommendations in our review of the literature. However, some were intentional, when the source was other than a book on our list, when we could find no discussion beyond a single statement of a practice, or when it was too general or too narrowly focused in scope or application. Some recommendations were subsumed by broader or more general ones; some represented a veritable family of related recommended practices. The 101 statements are certainly not of equal weight and type.

Once the basic list of recommended practices began to emerge, we grouped them into related sets. The chapter and section titles of general textbooks on giftedness were used as guidelines for these headings. It is clear from the following list that the assignment of some of the recommended practices is somewhat arbitrary; some fit in more than one category, and some badly in any. Nevertheless, we found it most useful to conceptualize the practices in four main groups with several subgroups. For simplicity we have used only the eight numbered subgroup headings for our text chapter titles. The four groups were useful in gaining an overview of the material we had gleaned. These headings were also adjusted as the work progressed:

Noncurricular Issues
    1. Advocacy and Administration
    2. Identification and Assessment

Curricular and Teaching Strategies
    3. Curricular and Program Policies
    4. Advice to Educators
Family, Counseling, and Personal Adjustment
    5. Advice to Parents
    6. Advice to Professionals
    7. Social and Emotional Adjustment
Special Groups
    8. Special Groups

As with the choice of texts, we pondered the need for validation of our list of recommended practices. Ideally, readers should recognize our list as the practices they have encountered or struggled to implement in their work. These data were not available at the outset, but another researcher, exposed to our work at a conference, conducted such a useful study (D. C. Armstrong, 1987, 1988, 1989) based on an early draft of our list of recommended practices. She also cited an independently produced list of bright children's ideal program components (Sellin, 1988), all of which were included in our list. These studies are described more fully below and indicate that the practices we have identified from books are reflected in opinions held not only by educators but by the students themselves.

It is probably impossible to arrive at a definitive list of "recommended practices." Others might reasonably differ with respect to wording, number, division, or grouping. However, to become obsessed with this issue would detract from the substantive task at hand. Once our list was "good enough" to be useful and defensible, it was not productive to invest further in refining it.

Supporting Literature and Reviews

The next major step was the cross-referencing of journal articles and other materials. To produce this part of our final report we examined every issue of the main journals and magazines dealing primarily with giftedness from 1975 to 1987, checking every article and cross-referencing each to the relevant recommended practices. Between 1987 and the end of 1989, additional material was selectively added. The periodicals included were *Gifted Child Quarterly, Journal for the Education of the Gifted, Roeper Review, Gifted Education International, Gifted International, Gifted Children Monthly,* and *Gifted Child Today* magazine (and, where applicable, their predecessors with slightly different titles).

We conducted an ERIC search for the same 12 years under the key words "gifted" and "giftedness" through journals other than those listed above and generated several thousand abstracts in hard copy. Those reporting research addressed any of the recommended practices were also added to our cross-referenced data base. This turned out to be a smaller number of references than from the "gifted" literature, which is consistent with Carter and Swanson's (1990) observation that general research journals contain few studies about gifted education as opposed to the nature of giftedness. As well, many ERIC documents were specific, project-oriented reports that did not present research.

We selectively included some of the hundreds of conference papers we have collected over recent years, though many were published before we completed this work. It was informative to watch for them. As noted above, a large number of useful studies are contained in theses and dissertations. Owing to their relative inaccessibility, we have not included these in the list of books but selectively refer to a small number in the reviews of the recommended practices.

We then divided the recommended practices amongst ourselves according to interests and expertise and used the data base of references as the beginning point for examining the literature relevant to each. We did not limit ourselves to these references and sought to include the latest material wherever possible.

Next, we reviewed each recommended practice, indicating strengths and weaknesses in the knowledge base. Reviews also indicate suitable theoretical contexts for examining these questions and suggest research questions that might profitably be asked. It took us about a year to work out a standard format for the reviews, using a draft of one as a model, then just under a year to complete the rest and add our introductory and concluding observations.

A Practical Exercise

The task we have undertaken was not designed primarily to have a direct theoretical impact. It is intended to be a practical exercise, which, if it leads successfully to the systematic study of the issues we have highlighted, may provide better data than we now have for the building of models and theories about the education and upbringing of children. At this point, no single theory fully encompasses the range of practices we have listed. This volume can therefore be helpful to theorists in delineating the range of practical concerns theories must address.

The value of this work also lies in creating a framework in which practical research can be focused and related to a broader picture. The development of our knowledge about giftedness and gifted education is not greatly assisted by isolated, "one-shot" research. The traditional focus of theory-based research does not drive most of the investigations about gift-edness; whether or not it should is another matter, probably worthy of dis-pute. Answering the practical questions first is professionally and ethically defensible. Applied or practical research questions also need to be presented in a conceptual framework, related to other knowledge of that type, and driven by a need for the knowledge that is not relevant only to a local pro-gram. The present exercise is conducted in that spirit, and with the hope that an overview of recommended practices and theory will eventually converge.

How to Use This Book

We especially hope that this volume will generate attention to the state of the knowledge base in gifted education. This attention can be provided in many ways, some of which we have tried to anticipate.

Program Evaluation and Research Tool

Every program is accountable to its sponsors. Program organizers, administrators and teachers can use the content of this book to help evaluate the defensibility of existing programs and to assist in planning for new or expanded opportunities.

For the evaluation of existing programs, one can make a checklist of which of the recommended practices described in the volume are used in the program, and these can then be grouped according to the degree of support for such practices.

An example of this use was provided by D. C. Armstrong (1987, 1989; the 1988 thesis version was also summarized by Geffen, 1989). Arm-strong adapted an early draft of our list of recommended practices to create a checklist of 40 program characteristics. She prepared two sets of the state-ments on cards for 57 Grade-6 students. They were asked to sort the state-ments into categories of practices, those they considered most to least appro-priate. Then they were asked to sort the second set based on what they thought their teachers would consider the most to least appropriate. Using factor analysis to group the results, she found that the students identified four main elements of ideal programs for themselves: (1) advanced content, (2) based on their interests, (3) variety of cognitive and creative demands, and (4) active, process-oriented learning. D. C. Armstrong concluded that the children could distinguish important program characteristics and that these closely resembled the main program directions promoted in the litera-ture. The students also discriminated between their ideal and actual pro-grams, indicating that what they hoped for was not universally delivered.

We can now assess the students' preferences: The inclusion of advanced content (see recommended practice Nos. 28, 34, 37, and 39) has moderate to high support; responding to interests (see No. 39) is valid but applies to all children; varied cognitive and affective approaches (see Nos. 32 and 35) has moderate support; and process-oriented learning which recognizes their learning styles (see Nos. 34, 35, and 59) is also supported by research. Although students cannot be expected to be aware of a great number of recommended practices, they evidently exhibit good judgment!

Without the list, students in Grade 6 may have had difficulty being precise about what they sought in a program. A similar approach could use statements based on practices with various degrees of support. The outcomes of such students, soliciting ratings from students, parents, teachers, and others, could be used to assess and improve programs. A straightforward checklist of well-supported practices and those less well supported could also be used.

There are important limitations to be observed, of course. Because this volume lists only practices suggested in commonly available texts, other literature may well offer other supported practices or ones well adapted to local needs that should be tried on an experimental basis, even in the absence of prior information about their supportability. Our list of 101 practices is not intended to define the field fully and thereby stifle experimentation; rather, in this context, it is to help assure that programs include sufficient numbers of defensible practices. The prospect of adding experimental activities is most exciting. We hope that practitioners will invite researchers to work with them from the beginning so that their experiences, both the successes and the opportunities for improvements, can be shared with the field.

Program Planning and Advocacy

There are three direct applications to planning or promoting new or expanded opportunities for bright students. First, it seems reasonable to suggest that program developers begin by selecting recommended practices that are defensible and choose from them a variety that are appropriate to their local needs. Second, practices that appear to be less well supported should be avoided. The discussions in Chapters 1 through 8 also contain points that may be helpful when it is necessary to retain some practices with local appeal despite their lack of supporting evidence. Third, combinations of practices can be examined to avoid mutually contradictory situations, some of which were anticipated.

In addition, checklists of recommended practices could be used with teachers, parents, students, and program planners to ascertain their preferences as part of the program-planning process. Of course, these inputs cannot fully determine the planning because other information is also relevant, such as the extent of available resources and educational needs revealed by means other than expressions of preference.

The practices described in this book do not cover every good idea one might have, and a vibrant program should experiment with new ideas and document its successes and disappointments. On the other hand, there is a large enough number of defensible ideas reviewed in this volume to help a new program succeed, once the program needs are identified.

Validating Parallel Advice

We refer again briefly to D. C. Armstrong (1989). In a preliminary study, she asked health professionals to rate on a four-point scale the extent to which they agreed with each recommended practice (from a draft version of our list). This enabled her to assess the extent to which the counselors and others in her sample were aware of what textbooks advocated as good practices in the education of the gifted. In general, she found high levels of agreement with suitable practices. As well, she found that every one of these practices had a counterpart in Sellin's (1988) Leta Hollingworth Award-winning study, which elicited student comments about ideal programs (these data were made available to her by Sellin).

The *Standards for Programs Involving the Gifted and Talented* (Association for the Gifted, 1989) were developed independently of our work by members of a working group of The Association for the Gifted (TAG), a division of the Council for Exceptional Children (CEC), and appeared in print just shortly before this book was completed. The timing was just right for us to compare our conclusions with theirs.

The standards contain 35 recommendations grouped into four categories: Program Design Standards, Professional Development Standards, Assessment for Identification Standards, and Curriculum Design Standards. Of course, the standards project had a purpose different from that of the present work. The recommended standards were intended to

> describe the *minimum* characteristics that should be found in all programs serving the gifted and talented. . . . For new programs, they can be a guide for program development; for established programs, they can aid in reevaluating the policies and procedures already in place. (p. 4)

No effort is made to provide a rationale for the standards or to review research support for them. The purpose of the standards is to promulgate a definitive and prescriptive list of recommendations. We, on the other hand, do not endorse our list of 101 recommended practices. They were not "recommended" by us but by others; instead, we have simply examined the evidence in support of them.

Because of the differences in purpose between our more comprehensive list of recommendations and TAG's effort to define minimum program characteristics, we had no reason to expect perfect agreement between the two. In addition, our list uniquely addressed parental and developmental concerns and did not discuss the details of teacher education to the same extent TAG did in its standards. Instead, we expected that our own list would include the recommendations from the standards as well as additional recommendations that elaborate or go beyond those. As elaborated below, this proved to be the case. We were surprised and pleased with the degree of overlap between the two sets of recommendations. Most of the fairly broad and sometimes compound recommendations in TAG's standards are articulated in one or more of our 101 recommended practices. We also took the comparison one step further and attempted to gauge the research evidence in support of the TAG standards.

All but three of our 49 recommended practices dealing with Administration and Advocacy, Identification and Assessment, and Curricular and Program Policies found their counterparts in the TAG standards. The three that did not fit dealt with early admission (some support), voluntary participation, and the assessment of student interests (both lacking in research). All but three of our practices offering Advice to Teachers were included. Those missing were the use of peer teaching (some support), the study of historical figures (deemed suitable for all students), and concern for task completion (no research). As these categories are the major emphasis of the standards, the match is very good and provides evidence that we and they have reliably sampled the knowledge base for common understandings of what the field advises in educational practice.

It is also apparent that in contrast to the recommended practices we discerned and evaluated—which were, by design, relatively specific statements about practice—the TAG standards are very often compound statements. There is, as a result, considerable variance in the degree of support for nearly all of the TAG standards, which renders them extremely difficult to evaluate. It is necessary to divide them into sections in order to assess their validity as judged by the present volume.

Examination of the levels of support for the corresponding practices suggest that standards A5 (programs commensurate with abilities), C2 (assessment of potential as well as demonstrated abilities), C4 (using quantitative and qualitative data-collection methods), and D3 (curriculum matched to developmental levels) share some research support with their corresponding recommended practices. Standards A7 (blend of community and school resources) and D7 (experiential and interactive learning) appear to be appropriate to all children. The professional development standards and A2 (comprehensive, structured, sequenced programs) are neither supported nor refuted by adequate research. Finally, standard C8 (trained personnel in identification) is matched to the two disputed recommended practices from our analysis.

With this kind of approach, we can begin to evaluate existing support for the proposed TAG standards and, more importantly, to identify the kinds of research needed to validate them. We believe that evaluation through the recommended practices exercise is a highly practical means of analyzing educational policies and standards. Ultimately, confidence in any set of educational standards depends considerably upon the demonstrated effectiveness of the specific practices that underlie them. As William James (1978/1907) said in his classic work on pragmatism:

> There can *be* no difference anywhere that doesn't *make* a difference elsewhere—no difference in abstract truth that doesn't express itself in a difference in concrete fact and in conduct consequent upon that fact, imposed on somebody, somehow, somewhere and somewhen. (p. 90)

Guide to Needed Research on the Recommended Practices

The first way in which this book can be useful in supporting research is to encourage school districts, teachers and other professionals, college and university faculty members, and graduate students to undertake some of the research ideas outlined with each recommended practice in Chapters 1 through 8. This will help to fill the gaps in the applied knowledge base and ensure the development of the field on a practical as well as a theoretical level. Because these 101 recommended practices are widely available to practitioners and the "shelf life" of books with good advice or bad is, indeed, very long, it is extremely important to know with greater certainty the defensibility of practices. This "gap-filling" type of research is especially appropriate for professional educators who engage in graduate studies requiring a thesis or research project but who are unlikely to pursue continued career research. It is also very suitable for instructors in teacher-training programs for the gifted who find themselves heavily committed to professional practice but who would like to engage in systematic studies closely related to their interests and responsibilities. The book allows them to avoid isolated studies that do not contribute to a cumulative body of knowledge.

Research inspired by practical concerns is often weak theoretically, so it makes little contribution to our fundamental understanding of giftedness. Although we favor, in the long term, research driven or at least guided by theory, there is an enormous practical value to be gained from at least preliminary answers to very utilitarian questions. Just as research and practice can and should be guided by theory, so must theory be guided by reliable observations of relevant events. Our research-backed understanding of what works in gifted education is still limited, so studies concerned with practice should be pursued in order to make possible defensible statements about what events theories should explain.

Creating Links to Theory

This book does not evolve from a particular theoretical view of giftedness or gifted education. In this regard, it may be described as eclectic. It is also evident from the diversity of recommended practices reviewed that this leads to a rather imperfect collection of statements whose groupings are, to be impartial, rather arbitrary, even if these categories are common in textbooks and other compendia. There have been, however, several other attempts to generate sets of recommended practices based on sets of theoretically defensible premises. One example is the axiomatic, philosophical approach proposed by Ward (1961/1980). It is probably not a coincidence that two of Ward's former doctoral students (Renzulli and Jellen) have also tried their hands at comprehensive models. The Schoolwide Enrichment Model proposed by Renzulli (Renzulli & Reis, 1985) claims to be pragmatic but is strongly influenced by theory and research in educational and management psychology. Jellen (Jellen & Verduin, 1986) has pursued a more epistemological approach, imbued with strong sociopolitical assumptions.

It would be very interesting to examine in detail how the recommended practices derived from diverse approaches are similar or different. Other comprehensive views that could be part of such a comparison include those of VanTassel-Baska (e.g., 1989), who includes systematic guides to practice, and Maker, who has written several volumes of such scope (especially see Chapter 2 and Chapters 5 through 8), though they differ from the ones cited here in drawing more extensively and explicitly upon the ideas of many contributors. Passow (1989) cited several of historical importance in the field. Other writers have begun to advocate models based on revised views of what giftedness means, but the practical implications of their work for educators are only beginning to be explored (e.g., Gardner & Hatch, 1989).

Such an analysis is beyond the scope of this book, but the effort would make a useful contribution toward linking the knowledge base derived from a focus on practice with one built upon theory. The most important contribution of this book to theory building is that it has described the pedagogical and related activities whose success or failure theories of giftedness and gifted education should be able to explain. In the spirit of John Dewey, we see theory and practice as different approaches to the same phenomena. Excellent education for highly able students depends upon both. Excellence in education depends upon both.

Reviews of the Recommended Practices

Each of the reviews in Chapters 1 through 8 contains four parts: examples of sources for the practice, an analysis of current knowledge based primarily on research, a discussion of the implications for practice of the state of this knowledge, and suggestions for further research.

Often we must acknowledge that tired cliché of educational research: "More research is needed." We have tried to avoid repeatedly saying just that, but even the best supported of the practices has incomplete support. Support and refutation are relative, not absolute judgments.

We could not resolve the apparent problem that some of the advice given in the book literature is good general educational advice and probably aimed at extremely able students only because of heightened awareness of their need for good educational experiences. This may be an issue whose only resolution is to acknowledge that it exists; we try to deal with what is recommended, adequately differentiated or not. When the recommended practice is not uniquely appropriate for the gifted, this is noted in the review and in the Conclusion, where it is suggested that such shared interests with general education may have numerous advantages for all.

List of the 100 Books Reviewed

Alexander, P. A., & Muia, J. A. (1982). *Gifted education: A comprehensive roadmap.*

Alvino, J. J. (1985). *Parents' guide to raising a gifted child: Recognizing and developing your child's potential.*

American Association for Gifted Children. (1978). *On being gifted.*

Barbe, W. B., & Renzulli, J. S. (Eds.). (1975). *Psychology and education of the gifted* (2nd ed.).

Blanning, J. M. (1977). *Ideas for urban/rural gifted/talented: Case histories and program plans.*

Bloom, B. S. (Ed.). (1985). *Developing talent in young people.*

Boston, B. O. (Ed.). (1975a). *Gifted and talented: Developing elementary and secondary school programs.*

Boston, B. O. (1976). *The sorcerer's apprentice: A case study in the role of the mentor.*

Brandwein, P. F. (1955/1981). *The gifted student as future scientist.*

Callahan, C. M. (1978). *Developing creativity in the gifted and talented.*

Clark, B. (1988). *Growing up gifted: Developing the potential of children at home and at school* (3rd ed.).

Clendening, C. P., & Davies, R. A. (1980). *Creating programs for the gifted: A guide for teachers, librarians, and students.*

Colangelo, N., & Zaffrann, R. (Eds.). (1979). *New voices in counseling the gifted.*

Coleman, L. J. (1985). *Schooling the gifted.*

Conant, J. B. (Ed.). (1958). *The identification and education of the academically talented student in the American secondary school.*

Cornell, D. G. (1984). *Families of gifted children.*

Cox, J., Daniel, N., & Boston, B. O. (1985). *Educating able learners: Programs and promising practices.*

Cushenbery, D. C., & Howell, H. (1974). *Reading and the gifted child: A guide for teachers.*

Daniels, P. (1983). *Teaching the gifted-learning disabled child.*

Davis, G. A., & Rimm, S. B. (1989). *Education of the gifted and talented* (3rd ed.).

Delp, J. L., & Martinson, R. A. (1975). *The gifted and talented: A handbook for parents.*

Feldhusen, J. F. (Ed.). (1985d). *Toward excellence in gifted education.*

Flowers, J. V., Horsman, J., & Schwartz, B. (1982). *Raising your gifted child: How to determine, develop, and nurture your child's special abilities.*

Fox, L. H., Brody, L., & Tobin, D. (1980). *Women and the mathematical mystique.*

Freehill, M. F. (1961/1982). *Gifted children: Their psychology and education.*

Freeman, J. (1979). *Gifted children: Their identification and development in a social context.*

Freeman, J. (Ed.). (1985a). *The psychology of gifted children: Perspectives on development and education.*

Gallagher, J. J. (1979b). *Gifted children: Reaching their potential.*

Gallagher, J. J. (1985). *Teaching the gifted child* (3rd ed.).

Gallagher, J. J., Aschner, M. J., & Jenne, W. (1967). *Productive thinking of gifted children in classroom interaction.*

Gardner, H. (1983). *Frames of mind: The theory of multiple intelligences.*

George, W. C., Cohn, S. J., & Stanley, J. C. (Eds.). (1979). *Educating the gifted: Acceleration and enrichment.*

Gibson, J., & Chennells, P. (Eds.). (1976). *Gifted children: Looking to their future.*

Gold, M. J. (1965). *Education of the intellectually gifted.*

Gowan, J. C., & Bruch, C. B. (1971). *The academically talented student and guidance.*

Gowan, J. C., Khatena, J., & Torrance, E. P. (Eds.). (1979a). *Educating the ablest* (2nd ed.).

Hagen, E. P. (1980). *Identification of the gifted.*

Heller, K. A., & Feldhusen, J. F. (Eds.). (1986). *Identifying and nurturing the gifted: An international perspective.*

Henry, N. B. (Ed.). (1958). *Education for the gifted. 57th yearbook of the National Society for the Study of Education: Part II.*

Hill, M. B. (1967/1983). *Enrichment programs for gifted/talented pupils.*

Hoyt, K. B., & Hebeler, J. R. (1974). *Career education for gifted and talented students.*

Kaplan, S. N. (1974). *Providing programs for the gifted and talented: A handbook.*

Keating, D. P. (Ed.). (1976a). *Intellectual talent: Research and development.*

Kerr, B. A. (1985). *Smart girls, gifted women.*

Khatena, J. (1982). *Educational psychology of the gifted.*

Kramer, A. H., Bitan, D., Butler-Por, N., Evyatar, A., & Landau, E. (Eds.). (1981). *Gifted children: Challenging their potential—New perspectives and alternatives.*

Laycock, F. (1979). *Gifted children.*

Lindsey, M. (1980). *Training teachers of the gifted and talented.*

Maier, N. E. A. (Ed.). (1982). *Teaching the gifted, challenging the average.*

Maker, C. J. (1975). *Training teachers for the gifted and talented: A comparison of models.*

Maker, C. J. (1977). *Providing programs for the gifted handicapped.*

Maker, C. J. (1982a). *Curriculum development for the gifted.*

Maker, C. J. (1982b). *Teaching models in education of the gifted.*

Martinson, R. A. (1974/1975). *The identification of the gifted and talented.*

Martinson, R. A. (1976). *A guide toward better teaching for the gifted.*

Martinson, R. A., & Seagoe, M. V. (1967). *The abilities of young children.*

Miley, J. F. (Ed.). (1975). *Promising practices: Teaching the disadvantaged gifted.*

Miller, B. S., & Price, M. (1981). *The gifted child, the family and the community.*

Mitchell, P. B. (1981a). *An advocate's guide to building support for gifted and talented education.*

Mitchell, P. B. (1981b). *A policymaker's guide to issues in gifted and talented education.*

Moore, L. P. (1981). *Does this mean my kid's a genius? How to identify, educate, motivate and live with a gifted child.*

Newland, T. S. (1976). *The gifted in socio-educational perspective.*

Parker, M. (1975). *The joy of excellence.*

Passow, A. H. (Ed.). (1979). *The gifted and talented: Their education and de-*

velopment. 78th yearbook of the National Society for the Study of Education: Part I.

Passow, A. H. (1980a). *Education for gifted and talented children and youth: An old issue—A new challenge.*

Perino, S. C., & Perino, J. (1981). *Parenting the gifted: Developing the promise.*

Perrone, P., & Male, R. A. (1981). *The developmental education and guidance of talented learners.*

Polette, N. (1982). *3 R's for the gifted: Reading, writing, & research.*

Povey, R. (Ed.). (1980a). *Educating the gifted child.*

Reis, S. M., & Renzulli, J. S. (1985). *The Secondary Triad Model: A practical plan for implementing gifted programs at the junior and senior high school levels.*

Renzulli, J. S. (1975a). *A guidebook for evaluating programs for the gifted and talented.*

Renzulli, J. S. (1977). *The Enrichment Triad Model: A guide for developing defensible programs for the gifted and talented.*

Renzulli, J. S., & Reis, S. M. (1985). *The Schoolwide Enrichment Model: A comprehensive plan for educational excellence.*

Renzulli, J. S., Reis, S. M., & Smith, L. H. (1981). *The Revolving Door Identification model.*

Reynolds, M. C. (Ed.). (1962). *Early school admission for mentally advanced children: A review of research and practice.*

Roedell, W. C., Jackson, N. E., & Robinson, H. B. (1980). *Gifted young children.*

Roldan, A. H. (Ed.). (1985). *Gifted and talented children, youth and adults: Their social perspectives and culture.*

Rowlands, P. (1974). *Gifted children and their problems.*

Sellin, D. F., & Birch, J. W. (1980). *Educating gifted and talented learners.*

Shore, B. M., Gagné, F., Larivée, S., Tali, R. H., & Tremblay, R. E. (Eds.). (1983). *Face to face with giftedness.*

Smilansky, M., & Nevo, D. (1979). *The gifted disadvantaged: A ten year longitudinal study of compensatory education in Israel.*

Speed, F., & Appleyard, D. (1985). *The bright and the gifted.*

Stanley, J. C., George, W. C., & Solano, C. H. (Eds.). (1977). *The gifted and the creative: A 50 year perspective.*

Stanley, J. C., Keating, D. P., & Fox, L. H. (Eds.). (1974). *Mathematical talent: Discovery, description and development.*

Stein, M. I. (1981). *Gifted, talented, and creative young people: A guide to theory, teaching, and research.*

Sternberg, R. J., & Davidson, J. E. (Eds.). (1986). *Conceptions of giftedness.*

Swassing, R. H. (Ed.). (1985a). *Teaching gifted children and adolescents.*

Syphers, D. (1972). *Gifted and talented children: Practical programming for teachers and principals.*

Tannenbaum, A. J. (1983). *Gifted children: Psychological and educational perspectives.*

Tempest, N. R. (1974). *Teaching clever children 7–11.*

Terrassier, J. C. (1981). *Les enfants surdoués ou "la précocité" embarrassante.*

Vail, P. L. (1979). *The world of the gifted child.*

VanTassel-Baska, J. (1981). *An administrator's guide to the education of gifted and talented children.*

Vernon, P. E., Adamson, G., & Vernon, D. F. (1977). *The psychology and education of gifted children.*

Ward, V. S. (1961/1980). *Differential education for the gifted.*

Webb, J. T., Meckstroth, E. A., & Tolan, S. S. (1982). *Guiding the gifted child: A practical source for parents and teachers.*

Whitmore, J. R. (1980). *Giftedness, conflict and underachievement.*

Willings, D. (1980). *The creatively gifted.*

Witty, P. A. (Ed.). (1951c). *The gifted child.*

Woodliffe, H. M. (1977). *Teaching gifted learners: A handbook for teachers.*

CHAPTER ONE

Advocacy and Administration

<table>
<tr><td>1</td><td>

Continuous Government Support Should Be Solicited

</td></tr>
</table>

This recommendation addresses two issues, the need for government funds as a necessary condition for the existence of specific programming for highly able students, and the condition that these funds be continuous, not merely seed money or for special projects. Surprisingly, perhaps, the matter is controversial even among strong advocates of such services.

P. A. Alexander and Muia (1982) devoted a detailed chapter to the United States' history of legislation and funding patterns. The need for funding was accepted as a given. They also accepted without question that the process is competitive and provided specific guidance for pursuing these funds. D. M. Jackson (1979) also implicitly acknowledged the need for such funds but was critical of this categorical funding because it was not a steady source; programs incur considerable extra cost, and the budget should be in a block. Ontario's Minister of Education (Stephenson, 1983) described such a comprehensive system now in place in that province, wherein all special education funding, including that for the gifted, is provided to school boards based on overall enrollment, not on categorical identification of specific types of children or services. These funds may be used for direct services, administration, or whatever.

Whitmore (1980) expressed the most direct opposition to some of the assumptions contained in the arguments above, notably that extra funding is required to provide any level of services for the gifted. She suggested that the needs for continued cash are specific and limited to the cost of a district coordinator and the identification process:

21

The real reason for a lack of programming is a lack of commitment and awareness of the significant needs of the gifted. Federal leadership has been helpful in countering local apathy or denial of the special educational needs of the gifted. Continued and increased federal funding of state and local program development, research, and evaluation is needed. (pp. 407–409)

D. M. Jackson (1979) also acknowledged the lack of research funding as "the major lacuna of the federal effort" (p. 52).

Current Knowledge

The principal supporting literature calls for strong advocacy and lobbying. The basic questions have not been examined, and no one appears to have asked whether state or federal funds necessarily make a real difference, or what role the categorical or continuous nature of any funding might play. One study, however, reported useful data. Zettel (1979) presented extensive descriptive tables of the state funding and student participation across the United States in 1976–77. We selected three variables, the total of reported state and federal funds earmarked for the education of the gifted (48 states replied), the number of gifted children served in each state (32 replied), and the total school-age population (available for all 50). Because there are imprecisions in the reported data, we simply calculated the rank-order correlations for the three possible pairs of these variables, based on the information for the 32 states that indicated the number of gifted students served. The correlation between funding and number served was 0.57. Between funding and total student population (which is a direct result of total population and tax base), it was 0.63, and between total school population and the number of gifted students served, the correlation was 0.66.

State and federal funding seem to be moderately related to services being available, but causal effects are unclear. It could all be an artifact of district size and the tax base. A better understanding is obtained by examining large states. Larger states have larger educational budgets that more easily enable basic infrastructures to be put in place. One interesting observation is that the range of state funding was from $20 million to zero (in nine states). The first nine had over $1 million in that year: Pennsylvania, California, Florida, North Carolina, Georgia, Connecticut, Illinois, Virginia, Missouri. Nearly every one of these states also had, even in 1976, influential university-based advocates. Is there indeed some active, symbiotic link between a solid scholarly base and financial support? Perhaps Whitmore was correct as well in calling our attention to attitudes, because money alone does not explain the levels of activity. The same conclusion was reached in a review of general school expenditures in relation to pupil performance (Hanushek, 1989).

Implications for Action

A clear distinction should be made between temporary funds to initiate programs, additional funds to be sought outside, and expenses to be borne by the district, based on recognition that the gifted children are already there and that the district's responsibility is to allocate to them their share of the total budget, after allowing for common expenses.

Even for state and federal funds, there is so far only a modest indication that the amount of such funding affects the numbers of gifted children served; we know even less about the relation to quality of the services proffered.

Needed Research

First, there is a need for an extended analysis of updated data on state and local funding, such as the information collected by Zettel. The analysis should also consider the distribution of any federal funding, supplemented with information about the quality of the programs. Has more federal and state money led to more gifted children being served well? What other variables might be better related?

Second, there should be some analysis of differentiated budgeting: What sources should be tapped for what parts of the total costs? This needs to be combined with some critical self-appraisal in the field about the constant "at the trough" posture. Are funding agencies, private or public, impressed by an internal, up-front commitment to continuously support part of the activity as well as by an argument that well defends the need for additional funds only for special start-up costs and clearly additional operating expenses?

Third, what is the contribution of the research establishment to program funding? Is there a reciprocal support system? It may be the prestige of the university establishment as much as the conclusions of its scholarship. This would not explain, however, why Massachusetts was 37th in the list of funding of gifted programs and why the state did not even report how many students were served in 1976. The answer will not be a simple one.

Fourth, the U.S. Office of Educational Research and Improvement held a 1989–90 competition for a major research center or consortium. Will the establishment of a National Research Center on Gifted and Talented Children lead to significant changes in funding, funding policy, or services in the states or regions of the consortium universities (Connecticut, Georgia, Virginia, and Yale)?

Finally, are there lessons to be learned from funding studies in other educational sectors, with regard to both quantity and quality of services?

2 | Advocacy Is Needed to Encourage and Maintain Support

Intensive public relations activity is widely advocated on behalf of programs for the gifted, from local to federal levels, and in all phases of program planning (cf. Aubrecht, 1981; Lanza & Vassar, 1975; Lawrence, 1980). "The need for community understanding and support of what the schools are doing is fundamental. It must be sought and secured and maintained" (Havighurst, 1958, p. 392).

Current Knowledge

Several authors use language indicating the utility or desirability of such informational activities but not implying its necessity (Monson, 1984; VanTassel-Baska, 1981; C. W. Williams, 1958). In many cases there is a suggestion about the specific impact intended for this information, for example, in encouraging participation by students and families (Kough, 1958) or securing funding (Lawrence, 1980). Specific needs are clear in the cases of program options requiring community participation, such as mentorships (Mattson, 1979), and believable with regard to special groups such as the gifted learning-disabled (P. Daniels, 1983) or in cultures where strong negative stereotypes persist (Coker, 1983).

We located only one historical study that examined the funding or legislative history at school, county or district, state or provincial, or national levels, for the purpose of confirming the importance of such public relations efforts in the promotion and sustenance of programs. This was a fascinating history of the swings in public policy in the U.S.S.R. regarding programs for the gifted (Dunstan, 1978, 1983). There, and at that time, the major audience for lobbying was the elite of the scientific community, and support for programs and its withdrawal were portrayed in relation to changes in political influence of different groups. At a more anecdotal level, Stephenson (1983) referred to the role of Ontario parents' associations in developing legislation in that province. In an overview of programs in Canada, Maier and Shore (1989) suggested that intensive involvement and dedicated activity by a small number of concerned and persistent individuals were behind much activity. The role of national organizations in supporting the United States' "Javits" legislation in the late 1980s is well known among members, but the processes by which these influences were exerted, the targets of the lobbying, and where the efforts succeeded and where they fell short, have not been adequately documented.

That advocacy is necessary to either implementation or maintenance of all types of programs is not sufficiently supported. It may be important to the allocation of supplemental funding, but the appropriate spending of per capita or other funds already in the school system, and perhaps being dispensed inappropriately on behalf of very capable pupils, may be a subject open to discrete, private advice. The matter of funds and government support is addressed in recommended practice No. 1.

Implications for Action

When a specific contribution is to be sought from outside the school, suitable information about the program is clearly essential. Public information seems a very good idea when carefully executed, with an effective review process. We need research to verify this. P. Daniels (1983) and Monson (1984) provide sensitive advice about dealing with expert teachers who may be poor spokespersons, overeager parents who need to be contented with behind-the-scenes roles, and so forth. Mitchell (1981c) offers general guidelines.

As we have stated elsewhere, no activity should take priority over the resources needed to design and provide the best possible program.

Needed Research

The literature requires documented cases of the relative importance of public information programs to the development and maintenance of programs for the gifted. Comparisons are needed with programs where such procedures were not followed. International comparisons might be useful. Studies should focus at particular levels—for example, local or national—and on specific outcomes, from program initiation to legislation, funding, student pride, increased access to field trips, or apprenticeships. Overall, a historical, policy, and comparative approach to such research would be helpful.

3 | Administer and Fund Gifted Programs Separately

There are two issues here. The first is the matter of competition for portions of block funding with other categories of exceptionality:

> A better approach might place programs for the gifted in a separate category altogether, to compete equally with all other demands for educational re-

sources, and not just against programs for cognitively impaired children. (Keating, 1979, p. 187)

A related issue is whether or not the actual administration of services for the gifted and handicapped should be in the same hands. Except as tied to funding, books on giftedness do not address this.

Current Knowledge

Fichter (1987) cited data provided by O'Connell (1985) to argue that gifted programs have been better funded where they are under the auspices of special education, but the difference between these per-state figures would be eliminated if one ignored the two states with exceptionally high funding levels ($30 and $50 million each versus an average for all the others of about $7 million). The effect on local expenditures is also not known. We can conclude from his argument, however, that there is no evidence that financing or placing gifted programs in special education is, a priori, cataclysmic. Why each state made the decision it did would be illuminating.

We do not really know if it makes a difference where this budget line is placed. Possible effects on learning, the dissemination of innovative practices, staff qualifications, and so on, are not reported. A related suggestion is that "what is offered to the gifted and talented should be commensurate with what is offered to the students in other special education programs" (S. N. Kaplan, 1974, p. 12). No empirical support is offered for either proposal.

Implications for Action

Concentrate first on getting enough funding and personnel for a defensible program, whatever the source. Separate funding is not so much a scientific issue as a strategy for assuring adequate commitment by districts to gifted programs; this interpretation could be studied.

Needed Research

Experimental studies are not viable. Surveys or comparisons of historical case studies could be illuminating. Variables should include the location of budget lines and administrators in the organizational chart; the initiation, growth, types, and quality of programs; the source of initial leadership (in special education or outside); the variety and number of gifted students served; identification strategies in use; teacher training, certification, and background; the fate of budgets or programs in times of constraint; and others suggested by practice or theory. Control for the size of districts and when the programs began.

4 │ Coordination Is Required Between Grade Levels

The coordination of services across levels of schooling is strongly recommended by many authors (cf. Cox, Daniel, & Boston, 1985; Feldhusen, 1985b; Gold, 1965). Feldhusen (1985b) added that this would assure "a continuity of special experiences to foster their talent throughout the school years" (p. 179).

Two issues need to be resolved. First, is there a relation between the existence of such coordination and the availability, nature, or quality of programs? Second, if so, does such coordination lead to more services, appropriately paced movement through sequential curricula, greater fostering of talent, and the building upon curriculum from one level to another?

Current Knowledge

Silverman (1980) observed poor continuity from elementary to secondary levels. L. H. Fox (1976c) also raised the matter of the transitions to junior and senior high school as well as to higher education.

There is no research evidence or systematically documented experience to show that coordinated planning across levels achieves any of the desired or other benefits.

Implications for Action

Program planners should not hesitate to attempt such coordinated planning, but if one level or another is unable or unwilling to participate, begin anyway. Separate planning committees can establish liaison subcommittees, exchange documents, or have occasional joint meetings. A variety of arrangements would enrich the research opportunities for studying the impact of collaboration.

Needed Research

Case studies and correlational research in educational administration, evaluation, and policy studies are needed to verify this recommended practice. Given the number of other potential causes of good programs (e.g., inspired leadership within one level or another) and the near impossibility of conducting controlled experimental studies on this issue, there is a risk that this practice may be difficult to support empirically.

5 ## A Full-Time Coordinator Is Necessary

> It has been found that in states where the total time of at least one person is devoted to gifted education, far more students have been adequately served. What is true for state levels can be also said for local levels. Whatever monies are allotted to educating gifted students in your district would be best spent on a full-time person. (B. Clark, 1988, p. 188)

B. Clark went on to list an 18-point job description, but no support was offered for the opening assertion. Clendening and Davies (1980) suggested that a half-time coordinator is needed at the district level but full-time at what they called the regional level, that is, for a group of schools within a district. Newland (1976) proposed a ratio of one consultant (presumably full-time) for each 5,000 school children or 300 to 500 identified gifted children. Whitmore (1980) implied full-time district coordination.

Do better programs for student ensue when administrative responsibilities for programs for the gifted are full-time? Without being sure of the cause-and-effect relationship, a large program with part-time administration might eventually generate enough work to warrant a change to full-time administration. In such a case one could not assert that full-time coordination brought about the size or quality of the program.

Our focus will be on administrators directly involved in services rather than on state or provincial consultants.

Current Knowledge

Several authors have stated the need for local or regional coordination (Boston, 1975b; Cox & Daniel, 1985; Gallagher, 1979b; Marjoram, 1979) or proposed substantial lists of responsibilities for administrators of programs for able students (S. N. Kaplan, 1974; VanTassel-Baska, 1981) but none explicitly states that the positions should be full-time.

At the state level, cited here for contrast only, Cox and Daniel (1984) noted that 37 of 50, or 74% of the states, had full-time coordinators. They suggested that such coordination is prerequisite to the provision of comprehensive programming. In the "Richardson Study," Cox, Daniel, & Boston

(1985) made a similar assertion at the program level. They reported that 35% of exemplary programs that they described had designated coordinators, but a full- versus part-time breakdown was not given. That 65% of the exemplary programs did not have such administrative infrastructure was not explained and may contradict the state-level observation. Full-time coordination at the local and state levels is not supported by the data presented in the "Richardson Study."

The level of debate is well captured by Crutsinger (1980), who stated that a district's appointment of a full-time coordinator is an indication of administrative commitment to the mission. There is no empirical support for the assertion that full-time program administration is necessary, or superior, in assuring any particular level or quality of services to gifted children.

Implications for Action

Persons planning new programs should not defend the need for full-time administration on the basis of the superior level or quality of programs that will certainly follow. If, in the context of the usual administrative traditions of a district, the best way to fit the responsibilities into a budget structure is to create a full-time position, then propose to do so. Substantial job descriptions are provided in the references noted above and by Newland (1976). B. Clark (1988) cautioned that whatever one spends the money on should be defensible in terms of meeting the needs of gifted children in a planned and accountable manner.

In the absence of clear support or refutation for the "full-time" requirement for the administrator of a gifted program, one might consider the formula suggested by C. W. Williams (1958). To us it suggests a degree of trial and error. Administration "should be in the hands of one person who has been freed from other responsibilities to such an extent that the chances for success are favorable" (p. 164).

Needed Research

The first need is for historical studies that test the hypothesis that full-time coordination is prerequisite to the provision of comprehensive programming and to better programs that serve more children. These studies should present chronological charts of the development of programs and the time at which part- or full-time administrators were appointed. The nature and extent of other responsibilities need to be taken clearly into account. Comparisons with experience in special education might be helpful, where comparable numbers are involved.

Second, it would be interesting to carry out some comparative case studies that follow the evolution of new programs under different administrative models. A varied selection of situations for case study would be useful. Detailed reporting of the decision-making processes at the outset could provide some assurance that causal effects can be observed. Participants must not be informed that they are potentially part of a comparative study.

Third, would the appointment of a full-time coordinator be an indication of special commitment to gifted education or any more of a commitment than taking other steps? The measures of commitment would have to be developed, but such studies could ferret out important, practical information.

6 | Early Admission Is Appropriate in Specific Cases

> Early admission . . . seems to combine most of the favorable features associated with acceleration and to minimize the unfavorable features. (Birch, 1975, p. 308)

L. H. Fox (1977a) stated further that it "is particularly desirable for girls since later acceleration is less appealing to them. Early entrance to school is also likely to benefit the child from the educationally disadvantaged background" (p. 133). Newland (1976) suggested it is

> for the bright child of preschool age whose total psychological picture warrants it, and it must be perceived in terms of the kind of educational program into which he is to be admitted. (p. 239)

Several authors give equal consideration to early kindergarten admission (cf. M. C. Reynolds, 1962).

Current Knowledge

Much has been written about early admission. In the literature on giftedness, the commentary has been mostly positive. For an overview, one may peruse the concluding section of the chapters by Daurio (1979), H. B. Robinson, Roedell, and Jackson (1979), or chapter 5 in Gagné (1986), or any of the principal textbooks in the field.

Early admitted children experience substantial academic success throughout their careers (Hobson, 1963/1979). Because early admission is usually based on high IQ, this is not a surprise. Hobson (1962) pointed out that children more than a few months younger than the minimum age might perform worse initially. N. E. Jackson, Famiglietti, and Robinson (1981) noted that teachers, perhaps surprisingly, viewed early admitted children rather negatively. Repeated reference is made to social and emotional maladjustment problems, especially in early grades (e.g., P. J. Alexander & Skinner, 1981), but Holbrook (1962) noted that "it is scarcely safe to assume that these problems would have been diminished if the child had waited a year to enter; possibly they would have been more severe" (p. 39).

Although the above discussion may imply the need for flexible selection criteria, Wallis (1984) pointed out that a school district that made early admission more selective increased the success of its early entrants. This result, although valid, is also an artifact of the selection process: By narrowing the band of high IQs by which students were selected, greater academic success of these selected was assured, but the number of students who would have ultimately succeeded, but were then excluded, was also increased. Birch (1975) pointed out that, unlike other forms of provision for the gifted, the opportunity for early admission occurs only once in a lifetime. Should we intentionally take steps to reduce this opportunity?

Support for the recommendation is not universal. Maddux (1983) showed that a significantly larger proportion of children in gifted programs are born in the first third of their eligible year for admissions than in the last third. He pointed out that this is consistent with research on learning disabilities, which has shown that early admitted children were so identified significantly more often. Of course, children admitted near the end of their eligibility will be nearly a year younger than those admitted at the beginning. They would actually be accelerated by a year in comparison with children a few days or weeks younger who have to wait a year to achieve regular school entry. The older children in any grade may therefore have greater need of the special program. The difference Maddux reported is real, but it is not so clear that the data reveal a problem. Maddux's overall message is, however, reasonable: The focus should be on true individualization, not overly general rules.

There are serious criticisms of early admission in the general educational literature (cf. Cornell, Callahan, Bassin, & Ramsay, 1991). Concerns include the risks to later attitudes toward education and especially social and emotional development if children are pushed beyond their developmental readiness (Elkind, 1981, 1987). The most critical statement comes from Hedges (1977) who reviewed over 250 articles. He pointed out in great detail how many of the studies supporting early admission were badly done, badly interpreted, or both. It is difficult to reconcile the positive and negative judgments because studies and programs vary so widely in their selection criteria and in the quality of the programs to which the children are admitted.

The weight of anecdotal and survey evidence supports the recommendation that early admission is a viable program option, but only for carefully selected pupils whose social maturity matches their intellectual readiness.

Implications for Action

Early admission accelerates schooling without necessarily compressing it or removing the opportunity for enrichment. It avoids the social disruption of skipping but increases the need for schools to attend to suitable individualization of programming because it does not automatically entail simultaneous attention to pedagogical concerns. It is also expensive, because it nearly always requires individual psychological assessment.

Early admissions programs seem especially appropriate with children from 0 to 6 months younger than the minimum age. Assessment should cover academic, social, and emotional readiness, and account should be taken of size because it affects the ability to share some physical activities. As with all forms of acceleration, the child and the family should be willing participants, and ways must be built in to cope with the situation when it does not work for a given child; "failing" kindergarten by repeating it will find few supporters!

It is most important to consider what happens with the children once they are selected. A year's acceleration is not extraordinary. For a number of reasons, including moving across school jurisdictions where the school entry age differs by a few months, as many as 20% of university matriculants may be so accelerated (Glazer & Shore, 1984). There are easier and less expensive ways to save a year in a child's school career. Early admission may be especially suitable for girls, because girls might shun later acceleration but often show greater early readiness for school. It should include an outreach program for educationally disadvantaged, potentially gifted children and provide them with an extended, enriched start to their educational careers; conventional selection criteria need to be used with great care toward such a goal.

Needed Research

There appear to be five key questions that can still benefit from research on early admissions.

First, because of the preponderance of IQ testing in the identification of young gifted children, there is a need for studies that would make practice in this domain consistent with the advice concerning the use of multiple criteria in identification (see recommended practice No. 14). Part of this effort would address educationally disadvantaged bright children who might be well served by special programming in early school admission.

Second, are there long- or short-term negative consequences for children if an early admissions program is not provided or is canceled? As Maddux (1983) points out, parents might object and it would be very difficult to assign qualified children randomly to served and unserved groups. However, such studies are precisely what is needed, and one approach would be to create a program with exactly half the number of places one would hope to fill, but perhaps have a second group start at mid-year, and offer a lottery. Should the deception be unpalatable, parents might voluntarily collaborate. Wilmeth (1979) reported that a number of parents agreed to delay their children's entry to kindergarten for a year on the advice of a psychologist who reviewed screening information with them. The 25 children were later found to do better in school than children whose families refused the advice to wait. Such willingness, even to be assigned randomly, can be checked experimentally. If parents have any choice, there is always the possibility that their willingness to delay admission might be related to some other important variable, but it may be necessary to tolerate this design problem.

Third, the quantitative nature of many of the studies supporting early admission renders the topic eminently suitable for a series of statistical meta-analyses, in which a large number of related studies are combined to examine their cumulative effect.

Fourth, not all the families of children who might qualify for early admission seek it. Why not? How do the futures of these children compare with those of others? What distinguishes these families with respect to their child-rearing practices and educational preferences? Are there reasons other than to keep a more able younger child from imposing on the personal space of a less able older sibling?

Finally, considerable work is needed to clarify the kinds of differentiation that schools should provide. In what ways, if at all, is the optimal differentiated program for a gifted early entrant different from the program for a nonaccelerated student? Does this change between kindergarten and the end of high school? What is the balance between extra challenge in response to the child's abilities and extra help in response to the social, physical, and other limitations faced by early entrants?

7 | Participation Should Be Voluntary

W. C. George and Denham (1976) recounted that the success of accelerated mathematics classes for the gifted depended on appropriate identification of students and teachers and on voluntary participation by the students. Speed and Appleyard (1985) observed that "bright young people can benefit greatly from voluntary, flexible, and enriching experiences in their out-of-school hours" (p. 119).

A general recommendation covering gifted programs in regular school time was not found.

Current Knowledge

We located no formal research on this topic. J. C. Stanley (1976/ 1979a), the founder of the project about which W. C. George and Denham (1976) wrote, reported the same observation.

Implications for Action

In North America, where considerable choice exists in school programs, voluntary participation is normally presumed. Everywhere else in the world, students compete for access to such programs; the choice rests with the schools. Compulsory extracurricular activities are not unheard of. There is no research from which to advise about the value of choice, outside or within school hours.

Needed Research

It seems reasonable to ask to what extent voluntary participation is appropriate and makes a difference within school-based programs for the gifted. Many variables influence a decision to participate in or withdraw from a program for the gifted, and the reasons may change over time.

Although experimental studies are not possible, case comparisons of evolving voluntary and compulsory programs might be possible and informative. Such differing programs could be compared in terms of the satisfaction of parents, students, and other constituencies, as well as the extent to which they benefit deserving populations who might, to their own disadvantage, not elect to participate voluntarily. Adolescent females and other special groups might be among these.

It is important for any study to be clear about who is volunteering, parents or students, which will be at least partly related to the age of the student and the way decisions are made at home. Studies of volunteers in spare-time programs do not seem to be especially needed, because such participation would be an expression of rather high interest and assured success.

| 8 | **Acceleration and Enrichment Should Be Integrated** |

Nearly every book on gifted education stresses the need for the integration of acceleration and enrichment. Perhaps Keating (1979) stated it best:

> Good educational acceleration is always enriching . . . and solid enrichment programs always advance the student's learning of new and relevant material and are consequently accelerating. (p. 188)

Keating was careful to emphasize "good" enrichment and "solid" acceleration. Should an isolated or newly involved school with few resources for enrichment engage in acceleration alone in one form or another? Is enrichment that entirely ignores the official course of study (hence not acceleration of the school program) less useful? Must the two necessarily go hand in hand?

There is more than a semantic difference between "different" as implied by enrichment and "faster" or "more" as implied by acceleration. The merits of each alone are considered under recommended practice Nos. 28 and 29.

Current Knowledge

W. C. George, Cohn, and J. C. Stanley's (1979) review refers to but one experimental study by Goldberg, Passow, Camm, and Neill (1966), who concluded that combinations of enrichment and acceleration led to more successful learning than either alone. That conclusion is probably reasonable, despite limitations in the design. It leads us to ask, would two forms of enrichment or acceleration also be better than one alone? Cox, Daniel, and Boston (1985), Feldhusen and Kolloff (1978), and Lester and Schroeder (1983) came to the same question based on their observations of acceleration and enrichment programs. There is no body of research that considers alternative operational definitions of acceleration and enrichment and systematically examines whether individual students benefit more from different combinations of one from each list or one at a time.

Acceleration in some forms, such as grade skipping, is essentially inexpensive (though not when the loss of per-student revenue is considered), and enrichment at any level of sophistication is relatively expensive. The two together may allow a range of options at normal per-student costs. Accelerated curriculum versus accelerated students is not inexpensive, because more has to be taught in the same time, which is a type of enrichment. Maybe the real conflict is apparent only in the more clear-cut and extreme versions of the two approaches, which cannot be accomplished simultaneously. No wonder the issue is confused!

Finally, however effective acceleration might be, do we want to speed our students through the curriculum and on to university as soon as possible, or do we want to keep them at or close to chronological age level but expose them to a wider variety of subjects or deepen their knowledge of the subjects they study? Do students have preferences in this regard? Which institution, the high school or the college, is better able and more willing to ensure this enrichment?

Implications for Action

Virtually all standard textbooks and most supplementary materials provide advice on the implementation of enrichment and acceleration. There are no specific guidelines regarding their combination.

Needed Research

Two kinds of studies are needed. The first would identify specific types of enrichment and acceleration and create or seek out situations where they are in use alone or in combination. Do students fare better over the years when exposed to both enrichment and acceleration, or do some students need one and some the other, in varying combinations? Control conditions should also offer two forms of enrichment (e.g., independent study based on interests and career education) and two forms of acceleration (e.g., classes doing two years in one, and curricular compacting within the normal yearly progression). It is important to control for differences in student and teacher background, class size, grade, and subject (there has been an emphasis on mathematics, to date).

Policy studies are especially needed. How do administrators perceive the contrast between acceleration and enrichment? Do they recognize and are they influenced by the financial implications? It is important to get beyond the opinions of the people involved in studying these relationships, because, in the absence of hard data, administrators have little choice but to base their decisions on economics, public opinion, their own biases, and the concerns of the person or group of people to whom they are accountable.

9 | Teachers Should Be Specially Selected and Trained

This is one of the most often encountered recommendations in the literature, for example, by W. E. Bishop (1981), Gold (1979), Maker (1977), and Renzulli (1981). Seeley (1985) wrote, "Program administrators should expect that new personnel would be of high calibre, would most likely be experienced teachers, and certainly should be especially trained to work with gifted students" (p. 115). Gallagher (1985) suggested that administrators may also need some form of special training.

Current Knowledge

Does teacher training improve gifted education? This question was directly addressed in a review by Shore and Kaizer (1989).

First, untrained teachers overlook large numbers of students identified as gifted on the basis of IQ scores while incorrectly identifying others as gifted (Borland, 1978; Ciha, Harris, Hoffman, & Potter, 1974; Cornish, 1968; Jacobs, 1972). Gear (1978) showed that identification based on achievement and intelligence tests could be improved with specific training in gifted education terminology, definitions of giftedness, selection criteria, the role of intelligence tests in the selection process, and the characteristics of gifted children. Of course, teachers may be taking note of alternative qualities that are equally valid.

Second, trained teachers tend to be more supportive of gifted students and programs, and teachers without special training have been apathetic and even hostile (Jacobs, 1972; Sister Josephina, 1961; S. B. Thomas, 1973; Wiener & O'Shea, 1963). Rothney and Sanborn (cited by Martinson, 1972) found that untrained teachers believe "the gifted will reveal themselves through academic grades, that they need all existing content plus more" (p. 107). Teachers with more favorable attitudes might more likely pursue training; this needs to be explored.

Third, Martinson and Wiener (cited in Martinson, 1972) suggested that even capable teachers can improve their teaching skills through training. Shiner (1986) obtained similar results in an introductory course on giftedness, but neither study examined the ultimate impact on students. On the other hand, Ebmeier, Dyche, Taylor, and Hall (1985) demonstrated that classroom teachers with some in-service could achieve gains in student performance similar to those achieved by formally trained specialist teachers of the gifted. This may be regarded as positive or negative in terms of the recommended practice.

Most publications on this topic address models for teacher education (cf. Lindsey, 1980) and desirable characteristics and competencies of teachers of the highly able (see W. E. Bishop's, 1968, classic study, and Feldhusen, 1985d, for a summary of this genre of study). These depend heavily on assumptions that highly rated teacher qualities, selected or taught, will make a positive difference in the education of the gifted. This assumption is barely tested in the literature, which also does not distinguish between the selectable versus trainable characteristics. There has been a gradual shift in the literature from an emphasis on selection to certification (we thank Montreal educator Mary Xenos-Whiston for this observation), but no study has yet shown an advantage to either selection or training, or a combination, in achieving the best rated and most effective faculty. It is also not clear whether a suitable combination would add new skills or enhance those already present.

In summary, there is some evidence that teachers' performance can be enhanced in several respects. Students also express preference for certain qualities. However, there is little evidence for the ways in which these skills or characteristics are any less appropriate for any other student, for the differential impact of teachers with such characteristics, or for any advantages in selection versus training to obtain them. Borland (1989) argued strongly that the consideration of teacher traits was irrelevant and unsupported. In addition, if minimal training is effective, then this also suggests that the recommended practice is not well supported.

Implications for Action

Special selection of teachers based on preferred characteristics, or special training based on a priori training models, cannot be defended on the basis of empirical research to date. No harm will be caused by selecting or training teachers with skills and attitudes well matched to a program's goals and philosophy, except possibly to overlook a teacher with unexpected talents to offer.

Needed Research

More surveys of characteristics of successful teachers of the gifted, or a priori models of training, will not answer the questions that need investigation. The negative assessment of the state of research on this topic is warning that the selection and education of teachers must be a priority area for research.

We need to know which characteristics and competencies lead to benefits in students' learning (in any domain) and which are uniquely beneficial or necessary (not merely desirable or sufficient) for the highly able. How are these related to goals and philosophies of programs and to different desired outcomes? Are special populations of the gifted differently and more directly affected by these concerns? We also need to ask similar questions about the career lines of teachers in the field: satisfaction, longevity, burnout, and so on. Can training programs serve as effective self-selection processes? How do different models compare in achieving desired outcomes? What difference does an introductory survey course make, and so on?

Many of us share professional experiences that endorse the recommended practice; we need to document these. Given the strength of opinion on this topic, researchers should be alerted to design studies with adequate controls.

10 | Provide Consultant Services for Teachers

Newland (1976) envisioned the consultant as someone hired by the school administration to assist with program development and implementation. "Many teachers truly want to do things for children but, for one reason or another, just don't know how to proceed" (p. 194).

Gowan and Bruch (1971) viewed consultancy from a slightly different perspective, as

> more directly related to the teachers' needs for understanding gifted students. Since counselors and school psychologists are most often associated with the identification processes, their consultations with teachers about how to select gifted, talented, and creative students are important. (p. 30)

Current Knowledge

Although several models of program development imply the need for consultants (Davis & Rimm, 1989; VanTassel-Baska, 1981), we could locate no studies that addressed the role or needed qualifications of consultants. We therefore face a recommended practice not supported by research and for part of which there is an element of pessimism: The small amount of empirical evidence that exists on this question has reported that counselors and psychologists were relatively hostile toward programs for the gifted (Wiener, 1968; also see recommended practice Nos. 22 and 77). Not all individual counselors should be tarred by this same brush, but new data are urgently needed to support their participation in consultancy to teachers regarding the gifted.

Implications for Action

Securing support for teachers from knowledgeable consultants or district support personnel remains a defensible course of action only when a specific staff-development need is systematically identified. Noticeably absent is research to support the efficacy of one-shot outside consultancies in effecting school change. Within-school support from counseling and psychological staff as a matter of program design is also problematic. One should not overgeneralize: A contribution from an interested and knowledgeable counseling colleague, as from any other, should be eagerly welcomed.

Needed Research

Documentation is needed of staff-development consultancies that improve teacher skills or build schoolwide support for the teachers. These field reports should be preceded or accompanied by needs assessments of teachers providing different kinds of services for gifted pupils. It is important to demonstrate that these expensive personnel would enable teachers to improve the quality of their work, and do it better than other ways (e.g., conferences and workshops).

Case studies that investigate the specific ways school counselors may operate successfully as consultants would help to clarify the role of such support personnel in gifted programs. There is a definite need for replicating the Wiener studies in a variety of settings and taking into account the counselors' personal histories and their own backgrounds in the study of giftedness, in the light of needs assessments. Teachers are unlikely to be uniform in their needs nor counselors in their interests or ability to satisfy them. There are a small number of programs in North America that specifically train counselors to work with gifted students; it might be very helpful if graduates from these programs were specifically included in these studies. The role of counselors with respect to teachers must also be treated separately from the direct role of counselors and psychologists in working with gifted pupils (see recommended practice Nos. 67 and 77 through 79).

There is considerable interest in broadening identification models, not merely to wider varieties of psychometric tests but to cognitive or learning-based indices related to students' learning processes (see recommended practice Nos. 11 through 25). It may well be that teachers, consultants, and counselors can benefit from each other's experience and knowledge, and from additional input, under a program model that includes learning-based conceptions of giftedness.

Finally, it might be profitable to study the applicability to gifted education of the consultant-teacher model currently popular in special education.

CHAPTER TWO

Identification and Assessment

<table>
<tr><td>11</td><td>Systematic Identification Should Be Widespread</td></tr>
</table>

> We should seek on a widespread scale to identify in every school and community our gifted children and to provide for them the opportunities required for their full development. (Witty, 1958, p. 62)

C. W. Williams (1958) insisted on the additional word *systematic*.

Current Knowledge

The literature elaborates the advice. Reynolds (1962) warned that such selection procedures come with a price tag that may be beyond the means of some districts. We are elsewhere advised to place services to children first (see recommended practice No. 3).

Otey (1978) suggested that ignoring this advice would lead to overlooking many capable students. Any procedure will miss children to the extent that a relevant criterion is not used. One must also consider the risks of identifying more children and more types of giftedness than one can serve adequately, if not excellently. DeHaan and Wilson (1958) advised that,

> It is recommended that schools adopt both steps of identifying gifted children: that all children be systematically screened and that the selection be made on the basis of data obtained in the screening. (p. 167)

IQ tests have become the major screening device, and selection is indeed based on the results (Alvino, McDonnel, & Richert, 1981; Yarborough

& Johnson, 1983). DeHaan and Wilson might regret this narrow realization of their advice.

There has been no direct research to guide this recommended practice nor to show that it leads to more thorough and appropriate identification of highly able children.

Implications for Action

There is an insufficient knowledge base to insist that the implementation of this recommended practice in the form of a highly structured, formal testing program should be a high priority.

Needed Research

A serious need exists for applied research that examines the impact on selection of different types and levels of initial screening in relation to program goals. Can parent, teacher, and peer nominations as well as a review of student records be sufficient at the screening level? For which kinds of students and programs are more psychometric approaches suitable?

What kinds of available information are used in selection decisions where discretion is exercised? Are proactive identification methods more effective in selecting underserved populations of gifted children, or should one reduce the number of hurdles, to the point of an open door (see recommended practice No. 21 for an example of this approach)?

Research on a recommended practice demonstrates the advantages gained by respecting it or the deficits risked by ignoring it. Given the potentially high costs of testing, benefits should also be cost-effective.

12 | Identification Should Be an Ongoing Process

Among our selected texts were 22 calls for continuous assessment. Tannenbaum (1983) stated the overall case well:

> Identification should begin as early as possible in the child's life and go on as long as possible, because there are always opportunities for discovering new insights and correcting old errors of judgement. (p. 365)

Other writers essentially elaborate the opportunities and errors. For example, DeHaan and Wilson (1958) and Callow (1980) noted that new abilities and motivation become apparent in secondary school, and Laycock (1979) proposed that "Passage in and out of special programs should be routine to correct for test imperfections" (p. 169).

Current Knowledge

Laycock (1979) was correct that the unreliability of tests is a reason not to rely on a single administration. However, caution is required with his assumption that "underlying ability has not changed, but only the scores" (p. 169); this assumes that abilities are static, which is widely challenged.

This challenge comprises a second reason for continuous assessment: New forms of motivation and new abilities emerge over time (Callow, 1980; DeHaan & Wilson, 1958; Passow, 1979). Renzulli (1975b) advocated frequent assessments, especially for the disadvantaged, because "of the dynamic nature of abilities such as creativity" (p. 418). Contemporary research in cognitive psychology supports this dynamic view. Quite different processes may underlie similar performance by different age groups.

Third, Solano (1979) reminded us that the curriculum also changes as students move through school. Because selection procedures should relate to curricular experiences, identification processes that are part of an evolving program necessarily call for ongoing assessment so as to assure the best fit of students' needs to resources as the program changes.

The logic of these three reasons, however, is not supported or refuted by reports of specific implementation or systematic research on the topic.

Implications for Action

Laycock (1979) was the only writer to raise the possibility of removing a child from a special program as an outcome of declining scores on retesting. This would be poor practice: First, the satisfactory performance is more important than the prior selection device; second, because all tests are potentially unreliable, decisions with negative consequences should not be based on a single administration.

The search for students distinguished by new types of motivation, new or developed abilities, or potential enrollment in new curricula also implies continuous assessment, but using new procedures attuned to the new circumstances. It may be wise to risk error on the side of inclusion rather than exclusion, in order to assure the student of the most suitable education and to avoid litigation by disappointed parents who recognize the risk of error in decisions based upon test scores.

Needed Research

Although we are not in favor of identifying gifted and talented students exclusively on the basis of IQ and similar tests, it would still be useful to have some data on statistical regression toward the mean in such measures among identified gifted pupils, especially among those who are receiving high-quality services (and we acknowledge the vagueness of that category). It is conceivable that well-served gifted students might experience no such decline in test scores. It would certainly be desirable to be able to tell schools to spend money on teaching, not retesting, psychometrically identified bright children. Continued screening by every possible means among children who were not previously identified for special provisions is not contradicted.

Second, it would be useful to have survey data on the kinds of continuous assessment procedures in different jurisdictions and the reasons for the particular types of data sought. What decisions are made based on the data collected? What old errors are corrected? What new opportunities are discovered? Is there any relation between ongoing identification and other indices of quality in programs?

Third, some formal research may be useful in the development of models for a continuous assessment plan. What are the new abilities and motivation that are relevant in adolescence? How should they be assessed and in relation to what kinds of educational experiences and performance?

13 | Identification Should Be Made as Early as Possible

H. B. Robinson, Roedell, and Jackson (1979) proposed that:

> Early identification creates the opportunity for early intervention. The parent who is aware of a child's special abilities can plan intelligently for appropriate, challenging educational experiences. The educator who has direct information about a child's advanced abilities can develop programs geared to the child's actual level of competence rather than to a level calibrated on the basis of chronological age alone. Since intellectually advanced children have skills beyond those usual for their age, their educational needs are different—in some instances, radically different—from the needs of their same-age peers. (p. 141)

Martinson (1974/1975) pointed out that "Valid individual testing of potentially gifted children is possible from the kindergarten level onward" (p.

11). Callow (1980), referring to Tempest (1974), was concerned to avoid disenchantment with school, which can occur as early as 8 years of age.

The two key issues are: Can children be effectively located at early ages? If they are not, what negative outcomes might occur?

Current Knowledge

The importance of identifying gifted children early (usually defined as preschool or primary) has been increasingly discussed, debated, and investigated (Fatouros, 1986). Hollinger and Kosek (1984) noted that support is based on the premise that preschool and primary years are developmentally potent and sensitive to environmental influences. Objections to early identification focus on the means of identification for young children, the related issue of stability of intelligence, and concerns about labeling that result from identification at any age. We will discuss the concerns first and the evidence in support second.

Many researchers (even those generally in favor of the recommended practice) have cited the belief that instruments for measuring intelligence and other manifestations of giftedness are not reliable at early ages. In addition, the cost of individually administered assessment is prohibitive (Hollinger & Kosek, 1984).

A related issue is the stability of intelligence measures at early ages. One suggested solution is that global IQs are more effective in predicting the later progress of young children than are more specific ones (Laycock, 1979). The concern that those who may be identified early as being gifted may not be so considered later on was contested by Silverman (1986a), who pointed out that it is much more difficult on full-range individual IQ tests to obtain high scores by chance. Other considerations that may especially affect specific measures are uneven development over time and the validity of nonverbal and motor performance tests.

A second concern is "pushing." Elkind (1981) was probably the most vocal of the child developmentalists who decry family and school emphasis on early academic achievement. Although his cautions were not specifically tied to the early identification and labeling of giftedness, certainly they extend to this group of children.

Studies given as evidence to support early identification fall into three categories: (1) retrospective studies of gifted adults who have attained eminence or noteworthy achievement (Bloom, 1985; Pressey, 1955; Roe, 1953), (2) longitudinal studies of individuals identified as being gifted (Terman, 1925; Terman & Oden, 1947, 1959), and (3) studies of underachieving gifted persons (Shaw & McCuen, 1960; Whitmore, 1980).

Bloom (1985) investigated the characteristics and development of 120 individuals in the areas of music and art, athletics, and mathematics and science who had attained high levels of accomplishment in their fields. Small successes and the recognition, support, and encouragement of these successes by parents and teachers during elementary school years resulted in a spiraling of increased interest on the part of the child followed by increased support and encouragement by parents and teachers.

Earlier studies of precocious musicians and athletes and of eminent scientists by Pressey (1955) and Roe (1953) also documented the importance of family encouragement. In addition, Roe (1953) observed that if young scientists could investigate on their own, poor teachers did not seem to hinder them, whereas interested and helpful ones were beneficial.

The work of Bloom (1985), Pressey (1955), and Roe (1953) documented the importance of early support and encouragement from family and school. There is, however, no evidence that lack of early identification necessarily results in underachievement, and it may also be possible to identify successful adults who did not benefit from early support; this has not been documented.

In terms of the literature on underachieving gifted, Shaw and McCuen (1960) compared 168 high school seniors in the top 25% of achievement in their classes with below-average students. Male underachievers received more lower-than-average grades beginning in Grade 1; the grades decreased significantly at Grade 3 and continued to decrease through Grade 10. The female underachievers' performance actually exceeded the achievers' during the first 5 years of school and then began to decline at Grade 6, becoming statistically significantly lower at Grade 9.

Whitmore (1980) compared the effects of a special class on 29 underachieving gifted students to the performances of other underachieving gifted students who had not been so served. She found lasting desirable effects over time in both academic achievement and self-concept for the students who had been in the special class. Her study did show that intervention can ameliorate underachievement by bright students, but it did not show clearly that early identification and the provision of special services can prevent later difficulties in self-concept or achievement. Future research on this topic requires designs in which causal effects can be traced more clearly.

It is not at all well established that early identification is essential or even especially valuable to avoiding specific problems such as underachievement, or that it leads to or instructs more effective programming, even for children not at risk. The potential benefit of later intervention has not been studied adequately.

Implications for Action

School programs that place children in stimulating environments and establish a regular system of observation over a period of time are likely to be successful in locating bright children early, or whenever they need special services. Even if a causal link between lack of early identification and the development of underachievement in bright children is never clearly established, observing for the purposes of locating talent is a worthy and realistic goal for the early grades.

Needed Research

Studies that extend the Seattle Project's work on identification by parent and behavioral observation are needed (cf. H. B. Robinson, Roedell, & Jackson, 1979). For example, can protocols be developed that allow busy early childhood teachers to employ some of the methods undertaken by the clinicians in Washington State? To validate the use of protocols, later productivity rather than the scores of individually administered IQ tests would be appropriate as the criterion. In addition, are there ways to adapt the traditional preschool readiness screening so that it is calibrated for exceptional performance as well as traditional age norms?

It is also important to investigate the purported link between underachievement and the absence of early identification. Should a clear and directional causal link exist, it would be compelling evidence for the importance of early education provisions for the gifted.

Case studies and program reports where various forms of early identification have taken place should report what happened to the children over their academic careers and later. It is important to clarify what is meant by "early," because it can mean anything from preschool to mid-elementary grades.

---

14 │ Base Identification on Multiple Criteria

"If giftedness is defined broadly . . . then a broad identification program is necessary" (DeHaan & Wilson, 1958, p. 169). Some writers insist that broad identification is always necessary. Echoed by Swassing (1985b), Mitchell (1981c) stated, "No single criterion should be used in deciding which children will be included in a gifted and talented program" (p. 23).

Martinson (1974/1975) stressed the educational benefit of such a polyvalent approach: "Abilities should be identified not only in terms of IQ but also by descriptions of actual performance, special skills and talents so that teachers can offer meaningful education" (p. 3).

Current Knowledge

Whole models of identification and programming have been built around the idea of multiple talent or intelligence (cf. Gardner, 1983; Renzulli, Reis, & Smith, 1981; Taylor, 1978), and these report varying amounts of supporting research that is, in turn, not without controversy (cf. Jarrell & Borland, 1990; Jellen, 1985; Matthews, 1988; Renzulli, 1985).

At the other extreme, where there remains a greater attachment to IQ as the defining quality of giftedness, books make little mention of multiple criteria and do not hesitate to state unabashedly that gifted means an IQ over 130, or perhaps 120 with other considerations (e.g., Vernon, Adamson, & Vernon, 1977, p. 65). Vernon et al. did note, however, "that different indices of giftedness do not correlate very closely, and probably several such indices should be used rather than relying on any single one" (p. 104). This acknowledgment of multiple criteria is not the same as one based on a different conceptual base about the nature of giftedness.

Whatever is proposed, most students are still identified for participation in programs for the most able on the basis of IQ and achievement, and where multiple criteria exist, they are used as cumulative hurdles rather than alternatives (Alvino, McDonnel, & Richert, 1981; Jenkins-Friedman, 1982; Yarborough & Johnson, 1983). It has also been shown that students admitted by alternative multiple criteria may be the match of those identified by individual IQ tests and achievement. Shore and Tsiamis (1986) found that students admitted to a summer enrichment program on the basis of their own or their parents' interest equalled pupils chosen for their IQ and achievement on those and other measures. The seminal "Marland Report" (U.S. Commissioner of Education, 1972) was one of the first and most influential to propose alternative criteria, but it never made explicit that each of the six types of giftedness it recognized should be assessed in more than one way.

The idea of multiple criteria makes good psychometric sense. It reduces the risk of error, either missing a qualified child or, more grievously, wrongly excluding a child from special services. J. C. Stanley (1984), usually associated with the narrow use of the SAT-Mathematics test for selection, recommended that a variety of measures, general and specific, are needed to assure "a more democratic procedure" (p. 177).

The use of multiple criteria reduces the chance that a gifted child with specific disabilities or a history of underachievement will be ignored. It serves social justice by increasing the possibility of recognition to poor, minority, and other systematically different groups of children. Multiple criteria also favor selection for specialized programs where traditional scholastic prowess is not a priority, such as in the arts (Kavett & Smith, 1980). E. S. Fleming and Hollinger (1981) provided empirical evidence that multiple sources of data provided useful information that was not correlated with the data provided by grades and standardized test results.

Of course, opponents of the recommended practice will argue that if one does not get a high IQ, whatever the reason, one does not qualify to participate in any kind of special program.

Do we know that multiple criteria achieve their social and educational goals? Only partly, because alternative multiple criteria and corresponding differentiated programs are not generally available. Where programs have been built around such models as Renzulli's, the corpus of reported research does suggest that a variety of program outcomes can result, but the literature does not yet report the impact on the characteristics of populations served (cf. Renzulli, 1984b). To answer this question, we need to be mindful of the nature of the program offered and of the versatility of the system in dealing with more than one kind of giftedness. It also does not lend itself to small experiments; rather, it depends on large-scale implementation.

Implications for Action

It is necessary to be cautious about giving advice on a practice that is so heavily weighted by the expression of opinion. Those who have experienced great success in selecting a narrow band of highly able students on a single criterion, be it IQ, mathematics aptitude tests, or grade-point average, can point to their own successes and argue against the cost, complication, and dilution of standards implicit in multiple criteria. Advocates tend to place higher priority on the hope for personal and social benefits, as well as program differentiation. These are untested as yet. Finally, studies such as Shore and Tsiamis's (1986), if replicated, could be cited to suggest that the whole formal testing apparatus associated with the identification of gifted students is, to some extent, unnecessary.

The best advice at present is to start with defensible definitions of the populations to be served in one's context. If it is clear that there is support for more than one definition, hence more than one program strand, then multiple criteria are needed to identify the different kinds of children. For each type of giftedness, it is psychometrically defensible to propose more than one alternative criterion. It is important not to use overlapping criteria cumulatively.

Needed Research

Several kinds of studies are needed. Nearly all require the collaboration of school districts or laboratory schools.

The simplest need is for a solid base of information about attitudes toward this recommended practice. Second, it would be useful to check if we have made any progress since the early 1980s in closing the theory-practice gap, such as by replication of the Yarborough and Johnson (1983) study. Is there enough variation in practice to allow us to discern a relation between the different views of giftedness and the types of programs offered? Are a greater number of multidimensional programs present when there are multidimensional identification procedures in place?

Does the use of multiple criteria favor the more appropriate identification and education of children in particular program options? Does it lead to the more frequent identification of children from nontraditional backgrounds, who are poor, or who have been underachievers? Does an open door, as suggested by Shore and Tsiamis (1986), work as well in general practice as in the limited summer school in which they tried it? Does it better serve nontraditional populations?

15 | Use Standardized Identification Instruments

Should preference be given to standardized versus other measures?

> The major advantage of standardized tests is that they do yield comparable data for all students. . . . The major disadvantage of standardized tests is that they appraise the performance of an individual at one point in time. (E. P. Hagen, 1980, p. 40)

Chauncey (1958) noted that standardized tests complement other measures because they increase predictive ability, and they are relatively unaffected by disciplinary differences. He continued,

> If we are fishing for sizable intellectual talent, standardized testing will not single out the species or net the catch for us. But it will tell us which pools are likely to contain the "big ones." (p. 30)

Current Knowledge

The advice and the practice are ubiquitous. Yarborough and Johnson (1983) provided original data showing the three most widely used selection criteria for gifted students to be standardized achievement tests (93% of programs), individual IQ tests (73%), and group IQ test (61%). Auditions (10%) and demonstrations of talent (17%) were the lowest. There was no mention of student interest.

Whitmore (1985) has been one of the most persistent critics of what may well be excessive testing. Standardized tests are useful in identifying gifted underachievers, but, given the way test results are used (multiple hurdles rather than multiple windows), low or average achievement of gifted underachievers can be cited to deny them services. Jenkins-Friedman (1982) was one of the first to point out and object to the serial approach to the use of multiple criteria.

E. P. Hagen (1980) revealed the thinking behind strong advocacy of standardized testing: If the result is unsatisfactory, test again, rather than consider an alternative. Chauncey (1958), then president of the Educational Testing Service, was nevertheless more open to alternative data but still saw tests as providing the pool to which other criteria would be applied. The use of standardized tests also presumes that giftedness is either present or not; it is to be fished out, and identification is not for the purpose of fostering creativity and giftedness in these children with unique potential. E. P. Hagen (1980) concluded her book by reminding us of the declining predictive ability of any measure over time. Part of this decline is caused by the fact that the nature of the learning changes as one proceeds. The review of recommended practice No. 37 discusses goals for which standardized tests appear ill suited.

Implications for Action

If program goals can be identified that would be well served by the use of tests of any kind, then standardized tests could help select a suitable pool of candidates (cf. J. C. Stanley, 1984). Chauncey's (1958) argument that tests add significantly to the prediction from other methods applies equally in reverse: Other methods add to whatever tests can predict.

Standardized tests have a place, but there is little justification for their virtual monopoly in identification.

Needed Research

There is a need for studies that compare the educational, social, and other outcomes of selecting students for participation in different kinds of programs, based on standardized versus other criteria. Too often, in the past, such studies have been limited to comparing how many high-IQ children are identified by other means. What are the various cost benefits?

Standardized tests have been the benchmark against which other approaches have been judged. All need to be evaluated in terms of the quality of learning experienced by the pupils.

16 | IQ Is a Necessary Part of Identification

IQ is the most universally advocated and used criterion for the identification of giftedness. Although no author recommends it as the exclusive criterion for selection, many place it clearly first:

> No two gifted children are the same in their abilities, talents and personalities. Nevertheless, a very large proportion are distinguished from average children by virtues of superior general intelligence; and this can be measured fairly reliably. . . . (Vernon, Adamson, & Vernon, 1977, p. 101)

> The bottom-line instruments for confirming suspected brilliance are individual intelligence tests. (Davis & Rimm, 1989, p. 75)

When multiple criteria are suggested, IQ is usually among them, though normally with the advice not to reject a child because of low scores on IQ alone.

Current Knowledge

As discussed in recommended practice No. 14, from the point of view of the design of an identification program, IQ alone is not a sufficient operational definition of giftedness. The present question, as in the debate about IQ and creativity, is whether or not IQ is a necessary component of the identification of giftedness.

IQ-bashing is somewhat popular in the literature on giftedness these days. On the other hand, books and journals are replete with arguments that, despite their limitations and abuse, IQ tests should not be abandoned (Borland, 1986), because they are especially favorable to underachievers and unpopular children of various sorts, and because nothing better has been invented (Gallagher, 1985; Kaufman & Harrison, 1986). Compared with many other methods, IQ tests are far fairer than detractors would have us believe, largely because of their consistency. The problem lies in the misuse, not the use (Sternberg, 1986a). Treffinger and Renzulli (1986) provided examples of arguments for alternatives such as indices of creative productivity independent of IQ, but almost all of these alternatives are at least equally open to the insertion of the tester's bias or artifacts of the assessment situation (e.g., parents' financial status—poor children write fewer original computer programs because their parents cannot afford computers).

As Whitmore (1980) reminded us, one's definition of giftedness, or of a good gifted program, is inexorably tied up with the procedures used to identify gifted children. It is commonly understood that IQ tests measure certain intellectual skills or abilities that are related to success in some kinds of school learning; they were invented nearly a century ago to serve that purpose. A student with an extremely high score should be better at basic school learning. That we often set high cut-off scores for admission to programs but still advise administrators not to reject a child because of a low score—indeed, that is the law in some jurisdictions (Silverman, 1986a)—implies that we know more clearly what a high IQ means than we do an average or low one. Perhaps the presence of a high IQ indicates that the learner possesses more of some desirable quality, or possesses a purer form of it.

Such a notion was challenged by Freeman (1979, 1983). On the basis of an extensive field project, she found (not uncommonly) a high correlation between children's IQs and their homes' cultural milieux and provisions for scholastic success. Freeman's interpretation was original and perhaps provocative. She speculated that as IQ scores climb, especially well above 130, they must reflect an even greater amount of environmental experience and learning. Freeman concluded that if one wished to know more than such achievement, one could add a nonverbal IQ test or subtest to a battery to get some estimate of the ability underlying the learning, because nonverbal tests are less influenced by the highly verbal content of much learning. This is controversial advice. When a student is weak in the language of instruction, P. E. Vernon et al. (1977) recommended the nonverbal subtests on full-scale tests rather than separate measures such as the Raven. The subtests' relations to verbal ability are better understood, and partial comparability is possible with scores of students who have taken the performance and verbal sections.

The main point is not at all trivial: Giftedness feeds on its successes, and able children increase the gap as a result of their learning. They do not just learn more but also enhance their abilities as a result of their accomplishments. This is important support for the overall idea of differentiated educational experiences for the gifted.

Not to be misinterpreted, Freeman remains a defender of the use of IQ tests in identification, largely because of their psychometric strength and widespread interpretability among professionals, but she notes that what they measure at high levels is not innate ability but ability greatly shaped by enriched experiences.

So, is IQ a necessary part of the identification of giftedness? Perhaps we are coming to the point where, for each individual, it is not necessarily so, but in some cases it may be sufficient. There is, however, a useful place for IQ testing in an overall identification plan.

Implications for Action

IQ tests are among the most expensive identification procedures available. Perhaps when no other direct index leads to the identification of a child's high ability, the addition of an IQ test might be helpful. On the other hand, the costs of developing equally reliable and valid alternative measures is as serious a concern. Cost is not the only consideration.

The best advice is to choose identification instruments that are related to the specific demands of a program, for example, science performance and interest for an advanced science offering. IQ can be used when a more specific alternative is not available. An IQ alone below a cut-off should not be used to exclude a child from a gifted program if more specific information suggests inclusion. Once the child is admitted, performance is always more important than the entry criterion or score.

Such a strategy would be consistent with the most recent theorizing about the nature (or natures) of giftedness, but it does not throw the proverbial baby out with the bathwater. In the absence of any other data that are well linked to program goals and known opportunities for achievement in the learner's history, then a high IQ score, nonverbal or otherwise, is a "good thing."

Needed Research

What kinds of student populations would be selected by using IQ? If they were quite comparable with groups identified by alternatives, there would be a financial savings and much of the objection to IQ on the basis of social and other discrimination could be set aside.

Given the "staying power" and specific utility of IQ tests, it would be interesting to attempt to design studies to ascertain how the very learning that IQ is supposed to predict might enhance IQ itself. The studies would likely have to be of a cognitive nature; unlike most cognitive studies, they would need to take into account individual differences. They would certainly benefit from longitudinal designs, so the environmental histories of the subjects could be specified. What kinds of learning, at home or school, have effects on thinking processes and IQ? In consequence, what are the characteristics of programs that may be suited generally or uniquely to high-IQ children? If none is uniquely appropriate, the necessity for IQ in an identification plan would be reduced.

17 | Include Testing for Potential Giftedness

According to Gold (1965), the identification process in gifted education

> must also give attention to means of identifying abilities that are hidden by underachievement, lack of motivation and cultural handicaps. The identification program must supplement the customary testing devices with a broad exploratory program and with the sympathetic eyes of teachers who are alert to the faintest glimmer of potential. (p. 138)

Giftedness is not only revealed by performance but also by the potential for distinguished performance (Khatena, 1982; Maker, 1977; U.S. Commissioner of Education, 1972). Gagné (1985) suggested using the word *talent* for that which is revealed by accomplishments and *giftedness* for the broader notion, including potential.

This recommended practice is a specific example of multiple criteria in the identification of giftedness (see recommended practice No. 14).

Current Knowledge

The justification for this practice depends partly on one's definition of giftedness and partly on the nature of program offerings. If one offers master classes for instrumentalists, it makes sense to seek students with some degree of musical mastery rather than potential alone. Potential giftedness is not the same as an ability that exists but is overlooked because of unfair or inappropriate testing procedures. Of course, disadvantaged youth may be at risk from both perspectives (cf. Fuchs & Fuchs, 1989).

The literature deals mostly with the practicalities of measuring potential giftedness. Assessing potential is really deciding how one kind of performance can predict another, or how a small performance sample might predict a larger one. Whitmore (1985) reviewed several obstacles to the identification of potential (through IQ or otherwise), including the influence of school performance and test-taking skill on the scores, stereotypical expectations regarding overall excellence, developmental delays or handicaps, classroom behavior, and insufficient information about a child, sometimes resulting from the lack of opportunity for children to become known.

Should we include the search for potential or hidden giftedness? Current thinking in the field seems to be oriented toward an affirmative answer, when appropriate, but practice is lagging behind (cf. Cox, Daniel, & Boston, 1985, and recommended practice No. 14).

Implications for Action

One must first decide whether the services to be made available are appropriate for learners who are not already excellent performers in the area of interest. If the answer is yes, a variety of advice is available. For example, Whitmore (1985) suggested teacher observations, parent concern, and referral for special education services as sources of data about undeveloped talents. Cox et al. (1985) suggested motivating puzzles and games and paying "close attention to children's ability to use other symbol systems as well as the verbal" (p. 35). Blanning (1977) recommended several useful prompts in the search for potential ability, notably teachers' ratings of the following:

> Enjoyment of academic activities, persistence, responsibility and responsiveness, concentration, preference for challenge, reasoning ability, independence in work habits, questioning attitude, original thinking, and ability to express oneself orally and in writing. (p. 33)

Needed Research

Useful empirical research to support this recommended practice would follow up two groups of students in a variety of programs for the highly able. The control group of students would be those identified as meeting the specific prerequisites for performance required for entry. The experimental subjects would be children lacking the specific criteria but admitted because of some form of affirmative action program (not intended merely to compensate for test bias—that is another issue), a legal or judicial requirement, or even a real experimental curiosity on the part of the school. It would then be interesting to observe the relative performance of the two groups over a long term. Such a situation has occurred at Hunter College School in New York, where one of the conditions of public support was to serve the local community, which happens to be Harlem (R. F. Subotnik, personal communication, August 8, 1989). Until 1986 this took the form of admitting about 25 local children each year, based upon recommendations from community leaders, despite their lower entrance scores. Though no formal evaluation has been published, it appears that about half of the local children caught up at a remarkably rapid rate. This is good evidence of potential being realized under favorable conditions and in a manner equivalent to having had the specific entry requirements. It also appears that about half were not happy and some transferred out; this does not indicate intellectual inability to cope (also see recommended practice No. 92). We need formal studies of such experiments in more representative settings. It is important in each case to explain the definition of giftedness being assumed by the program serving as the experimental situation. It would be interesting to try to document the Hunter College experiment. Retrospective studies are difficult enough, but contact with former students should be by persons unaware of the purpose of the study.

| 18 | **Testing Instruments Should Have High Maximum Scores** |

> When one tests very bright students it is particularly crucial to use tests that have sufficient ceiling to differentiate among them. (Fox, 1976c, p. 39)

The same point was made by E. P. Hagen (1980), Laycock (1979), Vernon, Adamson, and Vernon (1977), and J. C. Stanley (1976), among others.

Current Knowledge

The basis for this recommendation is psychometric. J. C. Stanley, Keating, and Fox (1974), J. C. Stanley (1976), and Keating (1976b) elaborated on the need for discrimination among high-scoring children. First, children who "top out" on an easy test will have their abilities underestimated. Freehill (1982) pointed out that over a few years, as well, a child's IQ will likely drop on a test where a maximum score was attained.

Second, at extreme upper levels, even small percentile differences represent relatively large differences at the group level in the abilities being measured. Keating (1976b) explained this with an example:

> A 99th percentile score on the numerical subscale for sixth-graders was 40 or greater on a sixty-item test. One student got 58 right, another 40. Both were 99th percentile on in-grade norms, but the same raw score difference of 18 between 40 and 22 was the difference between a 99th and a 65th percentile score. (pp. 26–27)

Third, some measures such as IQ are composites of different subtests, and a low ceiling would make it difficult to adapt a child's education suitably. Keating (1976b) gave the example of two children who reverse each other's scores of 125 and 175 on verbal and performance parts of an IQ test. They both have IQs of 150, but they are very different in their needs. A test with a maximum score of 130 or so would not provide that information.

Finally, Keating (1974) observed that difficult tests work well with bright children. P. E. Vernon et al. (1977) noted that simpler group tests could be used in a preliminary screening to save the time and expense of more sophisticated measures as well as to avoid exposing less able children to unnecessarily difficult and possibly frustrating situations. Group tests identify fewer "false positives," but all tests identify "false negatives," that is, they miss children who would be identified as gifted by different criteria.

We want to be able to distinguish among gifted children as well as between them and others because each individual has a different pattern of abilities to be addressed. Only tests with high ceilings allow this differentiation. The greatest risk with such tests is the temptation to be extremely narrow or exclusive in the selection criteria. This is hardly discussed, and never from the point of view that less selectivity might be preferable. For a related discussion, see recommended practice No. 14, regarding the use of multiple criteria in identification. This recommendation is supported modestly, but one must not overgeneralize this conclusion to suggest that standardized tests are essential; rather, when they are justifiably used, they need high ceilings.

Implications for Action

Formal tests should have high maximum scores, and the average scores of exceptionally able persons should not be close to the maximum. In-grade achievement tests, group IQ tests, or other low-ceiling, group tests are defensible prescreening measures. See Fox (1976c) for suggestions about useful measures and P. E. Vernon et al. (1977) for several cautions about specific tests whose utility may be overestimated, notably nonverbal and factor-based tests. Their concern is partly over the adequacy of training in testing on the part of the people interpreting and using the results. The advice is controversial for people who advocate such instruments based on Thurstone's Primary Mental Abilities, Differential Aptitude Tests, or Guilford's Structure of Intellect model.

Needed Research

The need for high maximum scores on formal tests has a strong rationale. Programs that invoke difficult formal tests as a part of the identification of giftedness should use the information they obtain to individualize choices or offerings. If they do not, the information may be expensive and unnecessary. We also need to know what steps are necessary to increase the appropriate utilization of this information. Such research could use Study of Mathematically Precocious Youth (SMPY) program graduates. Observations of programs in action would be especially interesting.

It would be necessary to develop supplements to the users' manuals that would provide important information to teachers of the gifted. Psychometrists, psychologists, and counselors are widely trained to do this with regard to learning handicaps, but rare is the general testing course that addresses the special needs of the gifted.

19 | Past and Present Achievements Should Be Used

E. P. Hagen (1980) stated that "the best single predictor of future achievement is past and present achievement" (p. 34). Three decades earlier, Hobbs (1951) anticipated this advice: "An outstanding performance itself is one of the surest bases for predicting continued outstanding performance" (p. 173).

Renzulli, Reis, and Smith (1981) suggested that a student's becoming "extremely interested in or excited about a particular topic" (p. 36) would also be relevant information.

Current Knowledge

E. P. Hagen's (1980) observation reflects a well-known principle in psychoeducational measurement: The best predictor of future performance of any particular type is the most recent performance on a similar task. Brandwein (1955/1981) used this idea to develop several operational definitions of "high level ability in science" (p. 2), including publications or acknowledgments of contributions. Gold (1965) noted:

> The advantage of school grades over aptitude tests lies in the fact that they reflect a teacher's experience with a given student over an extended period. (p. 82)

Solano (1979) observed data in the SMPY program (cf. J. C. Stanley, Keating, & Fox, 1974) which partly contradicted Gold, namely, that "the old test scores proved to be considerably better predictors of success in the contest (SMPY) than were the current teachers' evaluations" (p. 93). The psychometric argument is clear and defensible. If one is looking for students who will be high achievers in a particular domain, then previous, especially recent, achievement in that domain will be an excellent predictor. There are, however, three limitations to this argument.

First, one must take care to define appropriate performance as the goal. For example, if the tests measure rote learning rather than the ability to think at high levels, they will not be the best predictors of such high-level or creative performance. Also, if the tests are universally easy for bright students, then the high correlations might be artifacts of this general ease rather than true measures of the connectedness of the performance.

Second, if the measures are statistically unreliable, then the ability to predict other performance will thereby be reduced ("attenuation" in statistics).

Third, the importance of potential is overlooked in such measures. Achievement is not an adequate solution to the dilemma of identifying gifted children, unless it includes opportunity to learn the target performance.

Implications for Action

A strong psychometric argument can be made for including achievement among the criteria for identifying giftedness. It must be applied carefully. A high score is good, unless the measures are facile or unreliable. A low score may indicate nothing if the child has not had a high-quality learning opportunity in the domain of interest. This addresses one of the conceptual strengths of Type I activities in Renzulli's (1977) Triad.

Where it is difficult to provide such opportunities, other indications of aptitude remain defensible.

Needed Research

It would be useful to have reports of achievement data in the identification of gifted students, especially based on tasks appropriate to the children and program involved, and including opportunities to acquire knowledge and skills.

Research is needed that delineates the balance needed between tests of achievement and aptitude in relation to opportunity. Renzulli's Type I Triad activities could provide a suitable basis for this research.

20 | Affective Talents Should Be Assessed

It is important to develop methods of detecting those who exhibit special gifts in such areas as the arts, music, mechanics, social relations, leadership and organization. (Bristow, Craig, Hallock, & Laycock, 1951, pp. 10–11)

The last three items are the most relevant here. M. Lewis and Michalson (1985) added that "a positive self-concept and good emotional adjustment may be important in predicting giftedness" (p. 44). Feldhusen (1986) similarly emphasized positive self-concept and motivation as key characteristics. Renzulli (cf. 1986b) suggested task commitment as a component of giftedness.

What is the justification for including affective variables and how can they be measured?

Current Knowledge

"Among the variables which are affective in nature are emotional responsivity, self-concept, and persistence/motivation" (M. Lewis & Michalson, 1985, p. 43). Haviland (1983) pointed out that affectivity is involved in virtually every item of the Bayley (1969) Scales of Infant Development, for example, in apparent interest, cooperation, and fear. She cited the Birns and Golden (1972) study, which showed that pleasure manifested by 18- to 24-month-old children significantly predicted Stanford-Binet scores at age 3, whereas early perceptual-motor skills were poorly correlated with later problem solving.

Beyond infancy, M. Lewis and Michalson (1985) summarized a variety of research affirming that gifted children's persistence and self-concept, especially academic, exceed those of other children and adolescents.

> Whether this focused behaviour actually produces giftedness or whether giftedness itself involves focused or directed behaviour remains undetermined. In either case, some motivational variable must play a crucial role in gifted development. (p. 45)

Tidwell (1980b) compared some 1,400 10th graders who had been identified as gifted using aptitude tests with another 202 who were selected by the forms of nomination. She found no differences between the two groups in self-concept, indicating that the level of self-image in gifted students was not necessarily tied to identification based on IQ.

Bloom (1985) recounted numerous examples of the importance of commitment in eminent achievement. Renzulli's widely promoted interest in task commitment as a component of a definition of giftedness has been criticized by Jarrell and Borland (1990), who argue correctly that Renzulli's original rationale for its inclusion is weak. The research mentioned above, and in the articles cited, provides better support; Jarrell and Borland are also correct in implying that the rationale for the three-ring model could be updated. Task commitment is a useful but not necessary index of high ability.

Good teachers spend a considerable amount of time helping children develop interest, commitment, persistence, honesty, loyalty, and caring. All these are worthy affective goals. Acquiring task commitment may also be a part of becoming more gifted and should be regarded as a suitable representative of the affective domain, not the totality (though it might subsume some other characteristics).

It appears that affective variables have a place in the definition of giftedness; consequently, they have a place in identification.

Implications for Action

The use of affective variables in an identification plan seems to be warranted, but it should be inclusive. Their absence should lead to the search for other strengths and provision of opportunities to develop the missing characteristics. Male and Perrone (1979) reminded us that economically disadvantaged children have often lacked such opportunities more than others.

Self-report questionnaires, teacher and parent observational scales, personal and academic self-concept tests, letters of reference, and previous performance (reported or in a portfolio of work), among others, can all serve effectively.

Needed Research

There are two gaps in the knowledge base. The first requires elaboration of the interaction between giftedness and affectivity over time and, within that, the impact of interventions addressing either the cognitive or affective components, or both. Is commitment, for example, a prerequisite or corequisite of the development of giftedness, variously defined?

Second, we need instruments that provide different kinds of data from a variety of sources, address different ages, and are not correlated with variables such as social competence.

21 | Nominations Should Be Considered

Unfortunately, there is a tendency to determine the educational needs of a child by examining an array of test scores with too much respect for their presumed objectivity, while perceptions and observations of parents and teachers are regarded as too subjective to be acceptable in decision-making. (Whitmore, 1985, p. 99)

Feldhusen and Baska (1985) and Khatena (1979) also advocated parent nominations. Khatena suggested this as a step prior to more formal screening, but Renzulli and Reis (1985) recommended that teacher nominations follow selection by tests so as to identify children missed. Appendices in Renzulli, Reis, and Smith (1981) and Martinson (1974/1975) contain suggested forms for identification by parents, teachers, and peers.

Current Knowledge

Published research on this topic nearly exclusively addresses teacher nominations. The benchmark study appears to be Pegnato and Birch's (1959) report that teacher nominations only partially overlapped selections based on general intelligence tests and were therefore poor selection devices. This study is widely cited and reprinted in several anthologies (e.g., Barbe & Renzulli, 1975).

Borland (1978) was one of the first to challenge the overgeneralization of the Pegnato and Birch (1959) results. He showed that if teachers were asked to rate the presence of specific indicators of giftedness, rather than general ability, their assessments correlated better with IQ itself. Teachers were better identifiers of underachieving high-ability children, a group that might be missed by other means. Denton and Postlethwaite (1984) obtained similar results in Britain, when teachers addressed specific subject matter. They concluded that checklists could be useful when they addressed present ability rather than future potential. In all cases, teachers were constrained by their ability to observe and get to know students.

Kirschenbaum (1983) reviewed the literature on nominations and concluded that teachers' nominations were especially useful for the identification of creativity. Rimm (1984) agreed.

Friedman, Jenkins-Friedman, and Van Dyke (1984) reported a study in which outstanding leadership was assessed through nominations by self, peers, and teachers. Self-nomination was found to be the best single predictor. This study was unique in addressing other sources of nominations. It prompts the question of what is more important, the process of nomination, or the existence of any sort of alternatives to tests.

Birch (1984), a quarter-century after the study with Pegnato, asked if there was any value in formal identification at all. Shore and Tsiamis (1986) collected a battery of test-based measures, from IQ and school performance to self-concept and locus of control, in Grades 4 to 8 pupils admitted to two summer programs for gifted students. In one program, there was a completely open door. In the other, children were admitted on the basis of either high performance or IQ. No significant differences were found on any of the measures between the two groups. This study suggested that "identification by provision" (a phrase we believe was originated by Tom Marjoram) may belong among nomination procedures based on student- and parent-generated information. However, the open door alone did not attract the expected number of hard-to-identify gifted pupils. Nominations from other sources might be useful here.

Limited research indicates that nominations can identify able children missed by tests and that children readily identified by tests might also be identified by focused nomination procedures, or even by their election of programs made available.

Implications for Action

Nomination forms and questionnaires should address specific characteristics or subject matter, and especially abilities not addressed by formal tests. Whether these procedures should precede or follow test-based procedures is an open issue.

Needed Research

Replications are needed of all the past studies. In addition, more sophisticated criteria are required. So far, studies typically compare selection using one criterion with another. What are the educational and later consequences of these decisions? Do able children selected by parent nominations do as well under the same optimal educational conditions as those selected by IQ tests?

There is a dearth of information on parent and peer nominations. To what extent does formal identification provide information beyond "identification by provision," and not only in summer programs?

What is the potential for nominations to identify children whose giftedness is in some way masked? Since nominations are at least partly based on social interactions, care should be taken to determine if there are gender or age differences in their use.

22 | Psychologists Should Participate in Identification

Seeley (1985) acknowledged the psychologist's role in assessment and went on to advocate a consultative role regarding programming. British authors Marjoram (1979) and Rowlands (1974) focused on the testing issue, in accord with the acknowledged status there of IQ tests in defining giftedness. Vernon, Adamson, and Vernon (1977), expatriate Britons with over a decade in Canada at the time their volume was published, partially assented to Seeley's (1985) view:

> It would be more satisfactory if trained psychologists were involved in the selection. The recommended procedure would be quite closely analogous to that used with seriously retarded or maladjusted, i.e, with other exceptional children. (pp. 116–117)

Is identification improved by the involvement of psychologists knowledgeable in the matter of giftedness?

Current Knowledge

The question needs some refining. Except for the ability to generate reliable IQ test results, it is not clear what expertise about giftedness psychologists bring to the identification process that is not available from other education professionals.

P. P. Brown (1987) specifically addressed this issue:

> The school psychologist, most importantly, can . . . evaluate the adequacy of an identification program by determining if it will select students who fit the district's definition of gifted. The school psychologist must also be sure that the district's identification program is ongoing and flexible. . . . The school psychologist [can] get the most mileage out of time spent in educating and supporting parents, i.e., parent consultation. (p. 28)

Although some of these roles may indeed be most appropriate to psychologists or counselors, many of them are likely the purview of the gifted program coordinator. There is evidence of negative attitudes on the part of some psychologists and psychometrists regarding the gifted (Deiulio, 1984; Wiener, 1968). If their main contribution is test scores, the importance of that contribution is to some extent challenged by a study that has shown that comparable groups of children, selected on the basis of IQ and school performance versus an open door, did not differ significantly on any of several measures of intellectual ability, including IQ (Shore & Tsiamis, 1986). These last studies cast some doubt on the recommended practice.

Implications for Action

There is no research evidence that psychologists, as a class of professionals, knowledgeable about giftedness or otherwise, directly enhance the identification process for gifted students. A variety of knowledge about identification, using many models, is widely available to teachers, parents, and others. Nevertheless a psychologist may be an extremely useful consultant in this process, especially where individual testing competence is needed. School districts should involve all available informed professionals and others in planning identification policy and practice. Special consideration should be given to the cost-benefits (in terms of program enhancement for the students) if direct, psychometric involvement is contemplated.

Needed Research

An important preliminary step is to identify the kinds of roles psychologists can play in the identification of gifted students, to list the knowledge and skills needed to exercise those roles, and to note other professional or lay groups to whom such expertise is or could be available. This process would allow one to suggest unique roles for psychologists.

Surveys comparing the levels of service and the populations served by groups of school districts making various uses of the services of psychologists in gifted education would be useful. The nature of the identification processes in use and their relations to the programs offered should be stated.

The suggestion that the school psychologist is especially valuable in parent consultation should be set in context. Is this what school psychologists do on the job in most districts, and how is this role coordinated with that of program directors?

23 Consider Cultural and Social Differences

Cultural and social differences present similar challenges for the identification of high-ability children.

> Gifted programs for culturally different youngsters must be suited to them, not merely offered on a take-it-or-leave-it basis, and not designed and implemented with only little deliberation about their psychological, cultural and linguistic characteristics. (Bernal, 1979, p. 397)

This is echoed by nearly every book on identification or education of the gifted (e.g., Baldwin, 1975; Martinson, 1975).

Current Knowledge

It is widely reported and well supported by several studies that the major impediment to the identification of giftedness in culturally and socially different populations is the overwhelming dependence on test criteria that call upon middle-class reading skills in the majority language (Baldwin, 1975; Chambers, Barron, & Sprecher, 1980; Cox & Daniel, 1985; Evans de Bernard, 1985; K. George, 1983; Tittle, 1979).

Chambers et al. (1980) compared Mexican-American gifted children with Anglo-Americans and found that identical verbally based instruments would not reveal them equally. Evans de Bernard (1985) suggested that Mexican-American children with incomplete mastery of English watched for familiar expressions in tests, whereas the tests were based on anticipating unfamiliar material. The children had capitalized on the strengths they had so far acquired. Measures are needed that also respond to that adaptiveness. With a similar population, DeLeon (1983) found that differences in cognitive style were culturally linked.

Butler-Por (1985) observed different constellations of abilities among three groups of Israeli children, and K. George (1983) suggested that differences in semantic and abstract processing distinguished Amerindian thinking.

Given the nature of these differences, it is not surprising that advocacy of culture-fair tests (e.g., Rimm, 1984; Swassing, 1985b) has not been successful (Tyerman, 1985). Emphasis on thinking processes in an area of the individual's competence may hold promise. Torrance (1980) summarized it well: "It is important to attend to those kinds of excellence that are encouraged and valued by the particular culture to which the person belongs" (p. 44).

Social and cultural differences exist. Identification of gifted children from these groups on an equitable basis is hampered by dependence on tests that ignore their intellectual strengths; these include tests of reading and language ability. Although the research in support of all these points is fragmentary, and worthy of replication, it is competently done. Social justice and good educational practice require that the recommended practice be heeded.

Implications for Action

There are three parts to a long-term solution. First, educators should be among advocates of social action that will reduce those differences that are the result of poverty and its correlates. A. Robinson, Bradley, and Stanley (1990) have demonstrated, for example, that purposeful search for capable black children and their inclusion in a rigorous mathematics program led to very satisfactory achievement. Other action includes promoting literacy and the accompanying intellectual and creative skills that foster good thinking as well as basic reading. Second, new measures or nomination procedures must be developed that are sensitive to children's intellectual and creative strengths. Third, among these new identification procedures should be alternatives that rely less on reading skills.

The literature offers several suggestions that are consistent with the current state of knowledge. For example:

1. Have available tests that are less dependent on English mastery (Cox & Daniel, 1985)
2. Seek a broad range and wide variety of high ability children, and do not label one group as *the* gifted (Cox & Daniel, 1985; Masten, 1985; Passow, 1975)
3. "Remember that discovering and nurturing talent are independent" (Cox & Daniel, 1985, p. 35)
4. Use a variety of identification procedures, tuned wherever possible to specific groups (Maker, 1983; McFarland, 1980; Torrance, 1980)
5. Among multiple criteria use best results; provide multiple opportunities for discovery, not multiple hurdles (Goldman & Rosenfeld, 1985; Passow, 1975)

A truly culture-fair test may be unattainable, but some nonverbal IQ tests (e.g., the Raven) are well suited to address areas of cultural strength. Where possible, Vernon, Adamson, and Vernon (1977) prefer the Performance subscale on tests such as Wechsler's over the Raven because of their greater interpretability. Baska (1989) suggested that it is better to lower the cut-off scores on existing measures than to seek alternate measures, because underrepresentation is not necessarily due to poor identification procedures but also to real deficits in learning and skills resulting from educationally deficient environments. Tests standardized within an underrepresented population help identify students who might especially benefit from special programming, but the ways in which their knowledge and skills need reinforcing will be better revealed through more broadly standardized assessment procedures.

Needed Research

We need to know more about the processing and cognitive differences that are related to specific cultures and the ones that arise from economic or social disadvantage. Emerging cognitive literature might provide clues about processes that reflect giftedness across cultural boundaries, as long as one examines content or circumstances that are valued in each group. The impact of literacy programs on screening outcomes also deserves investigation.

We should resolve the positions represented by Baska (1989) and Frasier (1989): Is the underrepresentation of minority students, blacks in particular, a result of biased selection or of educational deficits arising from both the home and early schooling? Research must avoid excluding children from potentially valuable services merely in the name of science. The success of children identified in different ways should be paramount.

24 | Selection Should Be Appropriate to the Program

This practice is so widely recommended that only a representative example can be cited here:

> It is essential to have a clear appreciation of the specific goals of and resources for any gifted program prior to the selection or development of identification techniques for that program. (Foster, 1979, p. 72)

Current Knowledge

If we seek to identify certain kinds of talents in children and youth, then it is reasonable to design programs that match these talents and their concomitant needs. The logic also works in the other direction. Schools may design gifted programs and subsequently identify students to be placed in them.

This practice is more than pragmatic, administrative guidance. Renzulli (1984c) elaborated:

> The way in which one views giftedness should be a primary factor in both constructing a plan for identification and providing services that are relevant to the characteristics that brought certain youngsters to our attention in the first place. (p. 163)

Rimm (1984) and Torrance (1980) have used the practice to defend a place for creativity in identification and programming. J. C. Stanley (1984) pointed out that IQ scores do not permit careful diagnostic-prescriptive programming for youths with highly specialized abilities in mathematics or other content domains. In each case, the authors pointed out that inconsistencies in identification and subsequent programming may result in all-purpose programs that do not match the needs, interests, or abilities of those served (Feldhusen, Asher, & Hoover, 1984; J. C. Stanley, 1984; Swassing, 1984). F. Williams (1978) further cautioned that gifted programs are vulnerable to discontinuation when the evaluation data do not reflect the link between identification procedure and the program services.

Although this practice is readily supported by thoughtful discourse, less attention has been paid to it empirically. Prediction studies are not common in the specialized gifted education literature. An exception is Julian Stanley's work with the Study of Mathematically Precocious Youth (SMPY) in which SAT scores were used to locate mathematically talented youths.

A. Robinson and T. D. Stanley (1989) examined the relationship between a composite identification variable and a problem-solving outcome measure. Their results indicated that the Raven's Standard Matrices and the composite mathematics scores on the Sequential Tests of Educational Progress (STEP) were predictive of outcomes. In a follow-up study of ethnic differences, the identification variable continued to predict performance, but rather less well for black students when compared with white students (A. Robinson, Bradley, & Stanley, 1990). The overall conclusions were that these specialized identification measures were successful in locating students who would profit from the program.

Implications for Action

Despite the lack of an extensive empirical knowledge base on this practice, educators should incorporate it as best they can in their program designs. On the other hand, until some of the unanswered research questions are dealt with, it is useful to retain some skepticism and flexibility. The link between service and identification should not be rigid when applied to individuals, where a rather wide range of data, including interest in the offering, may be at least as important as any test result. Well-tailored identification routines are intended to help find students for whom the offerings are especially suitable; they should not be used to exclude students identified in other ways.

Needed Research

Additional prediction studies beyond the content domain of mathematics are needed. Any attempts to relate the identification procedures to curricular offerings or to student performance in the program are welcome.

Does a program suffer if children are admitted who do not meet well-coordinated criteria? Is the quality of the program compromised by the presence of uninterested children or those who cannot comprehend? Are especially qualified children excluded owing to swollen enrollments? Do "off target" pupils enjoy it less, do less well, or otherwise not fit?

The broad interests of many bright children (see recommended practice No. 86) might render excessively narrow identification procedures unnecessary. The oft-cited SMPY program is a good example: Though the children are selected on the basis of extraordinary mathematical talent, and the initial services are directed toward mathematics, the students have been remarkably successful in a wide range of university programs (cf. W. C. George, Cohn, & Stanley, 1979, and other titles in that series).

| 25 | **Fair Grading Practices Should Be Employed** |

"Gifted students in pullout classes often encounter grading practices that penalize them for missing class sessions while they attend their special class" (B. Clark, 1983, p. 466). Gowan and Bruch (1971) pointed out another abuse:

> The grading practices in honors courses, for example, should not penalize students by grading on a curve. If students would have made A's and B's for their efforts in regular classes, they should not be graded at a lower rate in honors groups. (pp. 27–28)

Reis and Renzulli (1986) suggested that if students demonstrate mastery of the regular curriculum, they should be given an A for that part of it. In contrast to formal grading, they proposed product assessment with descriptive feedback.

Current Knowledge

Fair grading is crucial for all learners at all times. The extent of grading malpractice for exceptionally capable students is not reported in the literature. It is primarily limited to recommendations that alternative practices be used to remove the punishing aspects of grading (B. Clark, 1983; Gowan & Bruch, 1971), descriptions of nongraded approaches (Jackman & Bachtold, 1969), and the development of guidelines for evaluations other than grading (Griffin, 1975; Maker, 1982b). More general works on grading, intrinsic motivation, and the unreliability of grades are also relevant but they apply to all students and are too extensive to be reviewed here (cf. Cornfield, Coyle, Durrant, McCutcheon, Pollard, & Stratton, 1987).

Schilling (1986) reported that gifted students were more likely to express worries about getting poor grades. W. H. Clark and Hankins (1985) compared 162 pairs of gifted and nonidentified elementary students and found the gifted worried more in general about their education.

Implications for Action

Punitive grading practices should be avoided. One step would be to respect the confidentiality of formal grades. Zeller (1990) has assembled useful advice on this practice:

> The final grade:
> Must fairly reflect the composite strength of the student using the work of an average student as a benchmark;
> Must contain fair mark value for enhanced learning beyond the regular program;
> Should reflect the degree of success in meeting the revised program objectives as described in the most recently edited version of the individual education plan;
> Must yield a satisfactory ranking of the enhanced student among his or her non-enhanced peers. That is, they must be comparable and compatible with all other grades for the particular course involved. (p. 27)

Zeller continued with specific suggestions for collecting and using data in the presence of such a grading policy.

Needed Research

Evidence that teachers are applying punitive grades or are unwittingly providing disincentives for bright students to take challenging classes needs to be established beyond anecdotal reports. Observational studies conducted over weeks or months could correlate data with student outcomes. Laboratory-based scenario studies might be useful, examining teachers' responses to a description or videotape of a child leaving class for a special gifted program. Studies that compare the problems of gifted students with those of students who are removed from class for other kinds of special programs are also necessary.

Survey research, perhaps retrospective, is needed to establish the extent and consequences of these punitive practices; are they rare or common?

School districts that have implemented special grading provisions (such as grade weighting) for gifted students should be compared with schools that have not. Outcome variables might be continuing motivation for advanced classes and reports of satisfaction from the students, parents, teachers, and school administrators.

CHAPTER THREE

Curricular and Program Policies

| 26 | **Programs Should Be Part of Overall Individualization**

"Education of the gifted is one application of adapting programs to individual differences and needs" (Gold, 1965, p. 135). Coutant (1983) added:

> It is probably true that the more gifted and talented a person is, the more he may differ from others in both kind and degree. . . . [We should serve] students as individuals, making opportunities for them to follow their own interests, not grouping them at all unless they have similar interests. (pp. 142–143)

Current Knowledge

A considerable part of the literature on curricular planning and instructional design for the gifted addresses the matter of how to raise the intellectual level of content, not how to personalize it. In the last decade, U.S. federal and Canadian provincial legislation has addressed individualized instructional planning for exceptional students, mainly but not exclusively those with handicaps.

An underlying theme in this recommended practice is that gifted education should foster quality education for all, based at least in part on the unique needs of each individual (Freehill, 1961/1982; Jeter & Chauvin, 1982; Newland, 1976; Passow, 1979; Polette, 1982; Vernon, Adamson, & Vernon, 1977; C. W. Williams, 1958). Providing good programs for the gifted should not merely draw strength from the general program but also provide it. This was the theme of the Fourth World Conference for Gifted and Talented Children in 1981 and motivated the selection of featured presentations (cf. Shore, Gagné, Larivée, Tali, & Tremblay, 1983).

To date there has been no formal research on this question.

Implications for Action

Research does not guide action on this potentially important practice. Whatever the means, it is defensible on philosophical and developmental grounds to offer each child specific learning experiences for which she or he appears "ready."

Coutant (1983) reminds us of the power of student interests to motivate learning. It is not expensive to find out what student interests are, and one need not overturn the entire curriculum and school structure in order to begin. The role of the teacher is not thereby diminished; rather it is enhanced by the students' assumption of some responsibility for their own learning. If one accepts this recommended practice, then curricula that build in opportunities for fostering student interests are advised (cf. Maker, 1982b; Renzulli, 1986a).

Needed Research

First, we need large-scale survey research to determine the extent to which individualization of various types is practiced in both gifted educational and other settings. Second, we need reasoned discussion about a symbiotic relationship between the differential education of gifted children and that of others in the context of individualization. The concerns may be esoteric, such as differences in metacognitive components of mathematical problem solving, or they may be straightforward, such as overt student interests. The research should address the application of general individualization to the gifted and also the benefit to other students from pursuing such an approach with the gifted. There may be lessons to be learned for watching the progress and effects, both good and bad, of integration as a guiding principle in special education for learning-handicapped children. How well, for example, can the principle of individualization function under integration as a curricular model?

One problem with the concept of individualization is that it somewhat undermines the idea that the gifted by any definition constitute an educational group requiring specific services precisely because they are a special group. Might opting for individualized instruction detract from recent modest successes in encouraging differentiation for especially able students, mainstreamed or not? The pressure in special education is toward mainstreaming;

in gifted education it is in the opposite direction. Parke (1989) has attempted to describe how mainstreaming and gifted education might coexist.

Finally, which types of individualization (e.g., acceleration, grouping, independent inquiry) produce greater achievement and satisfaction with which kinds of students?

27 | Intervention Should Be Adapted to Levels of Giftedness

Passow (1980b) urged that we provide

> experiences which are appropriate and adequate in terms of each student's unique nature and needs. Appropriateness and adequacy can be judged only in terms of clearly defined goals for students with various kinds and degrees of giftedness. (p. 36)

Gallagher (1985), McDonald, Moore, and Freehill (1982) and Webb, Meckstroth, and Tolan (1982) suggested that diversity within and between individuals increases with ability. There may be an "optimal" IQ range of 125–145 or 155 that favors excellent school performance, but needs become much more idiosyncratic at higher levels. Gallagher pointed out that an IQ of 180 will normally appear once in a million cases. One should not expect schools to be able to adapt easily to such children.

Current Knowledge

There is little research on levels of giftedness other than with regard to IQ.

Concepts such as multiple intelligences (Gardner, 1983) and components of intelligence (Guilford, 1967, 1977; M. Meeker, 1969) involve specific types of intelligence overlapping as little as possible with each other and appear to warrant specific curricular provisions. We are aware of no specific curricula that are differentiated as to level on any of these notions, though Hudson (1968) suggested different career orientations of young people differing in levels on convergent and divergent ability tests.

The nonacademic curriculum has been addressed. Reflecting upon his clinical experience with children and families, Dishart (1983) suggested that the universal need of all gifted students, "and to a large extent in proportion to the degree of their giftedness, is other gifted children, chronological peers who have approximately similar degrees of giftedness, preferably in related fields or areas" (p. 29). Citing Hollingworth and Tannenbaum, B. Clark (1988) proposed that "the more highly gifted the child, the more the risk of social maladjustment and unhappiness increases" (p. 139), but Grossberg and Cornell (1988) pointed out that this relation is still debatable. Whether or not Dishart's suggestion is the medicine for this ailment is not confirmed by any formal research.

The state of knowledge about this recommended practice is tentative. There are concerns, based largely on clinical psychological experience, about children with extremely high IQ scores; the clinical origins of these data render suspicious the attention to adjustment problems. There is virtually nothing about levels of giftedness on other indices, such as creative productivity, leadership, or cognitive-processing perspectives, to mention just three. The nature of potentially needed adaptations to levels of giftedness is not extensively elaborated.

Implications for Action

The level of the child's giftedness, in comparison with that of other children also deemed gifted, is not clearly established as the rationale for curricular adaptation. Whatever criteria for the identification of giftedness one employs, for the sake of the psychological well-being of the children, there seems to be valid (but unsystematically reported) clinical evidence for being alert to interpersonal adjustment among those who are exceptionally high on criteria such as IQ.

We suggest caution in heeding this recommended practice, even while the question is further studied.

Needed Research

Every aspect of the recommended practice needs examination. What does level of giftedness mean for indices other than IQ? What kinds of provisions are advocated and defensible for different kinds of extreme giftedness? Which ones actually make a difference in the scholastic, vocational, or personal lives of these children? Should regular curriculum be adapted or totally replaced?

Are maladjustments and unhappiness general phenomena of highly gifted children of all types, or only of those with high IQ? Are peer relations a key to resolving such problems? Does it matter whether or not appropriate educational services are being provided to a particular child? Such research may require the pooling of data from several counselors or clinicians working with gifted students and their families.

The observation that variability is extreme among highly gifted individuals is contrary to psychometric predictions that, when one restricts the range of scores, the variability should decrease. It would be useful to explore this question on a variety of types of giftedness. It is important to the consideration of whether or not highly gifted individuals can be discussed as a group. Confirmation of at least two levels requiring differential treatment would comprise support for the recommended practice and then justify exploration for possible finer discriminations.

It may be that every child needs a combination of group-oriented and individualized interventions, and the more unusual the nature of any child, the more the balance shifts toward the individual. Theory would be well served by research on this question.

28 | Acceleration Should Be Used

No single recommendation has been stated more often in one form or another for example, by B. Clarke (1988), Feldhusen (1985b), and J. C. Stanley (1976/1979b), and as follows:

> Solid research shows that mathematical talent and foreign language ability can be most economically developed through an accelerated mode. (VanTassel-Baska, 1985, p. 50)

> It is appropriate at any age, in any type of program, although its effectiveness increases as the child becomes less dependent on seeing the same faces in the same classroom every day. (Gutteridge, 1984, p. 118)

There is consensus that acceleration is not for every gifted child, though some will support it for the most gifted students. There is universal endorsement that acceleration in some form should be one of the services in any program for the gifted.

Current Knowledge

Unless accompanied by other action, acceleration has little effect but to shorten the number of years a child spends in school. This can be good in itself, depending on the quality of instruction in the extra years spent in school. It is also relatively easy to implement.

Hundreds of studies have been published on the topic. We will refer only to some of the best summaries. B. Clark (1988) provided a good rationale for considering acceleration and a compact review of research. Daurio (1979) also reviewed the research extensively. Gallagher's (1985) summary is shorter but important because it makes the distinction between the benefits of acceleration itself and the acceleration of content (one could cover a wider range of content more quickly but not finish formal schooling any earlier). Most of the benefits arise from the increased curricular density. J. A. Kulik and C. C. Kulik (1984) conducted a meta-analysis of 26 controlled studies in which elementary and secondary accelerated students were directly compared with comparable nonaccelerated students. They found that accelerants moved ahead of nonaccelerants by nearly a full grade level and did not differ significantly in achievement from older, gifted nonaccelerants. Petersen, Brounstein, and Kimble (1988) showed that adolescents taking college-level courses demonstrated substantial, long-term knowledge gains, and career thinking and educational plans were influenced by the experience.

Gagné's (1986) thorough review of acceleration for the gifted concluded that it works and that it does no general harm, academic or social. Reported social problems would likely have been present or even worse without it. Yet, acceleration is avoided by some educators and families, even though it allows some students to progress at their own, faster rate. Brody and Fox (1980) found a social benefit: Girls benefited to at least an equal measure as did boys.

While the academic benefits of acceleration are clear, parents and teachers alike often express concerns about the impact of acceleration on the student's social and emotional development (Southern, Jones, & Fiscus, 1989). Although many authors point out the lack of evidence that acceleration has a deleterious effect on affective adjustment, a recent review of literature (Cornell, Callahan, Bassin, & Ramsay, 1991) points out that most previous studies were not designed to assess the specific effects of acceleration on affective adjustment. For example, many studies fail to use appropriate control groups or to assess student adjustment both before and after a period of acceleration, using standard, well-validated adjustment measures. Several well-designed studies (Klausmeier & Ripple, 1962; Obrzut, Nelson, & Obrzut, 1984) did find evidence of social immaturity among some accelerated elementary school students. Cornell et al. (1991) specify what is needed to establish that acceleration does not have an adverse impact on social or emotional development.

The evidence is overwhelming that acceleration in some of its many forms should be included in any comprehensive set of services for the gifted (also see Southern & Jones, 1991). As in any provision, when it comes to deciding on the best services for a particular student, the needs, interests, strengths, and weaknesses of the individual are the most important information.

Implications for Action

There are many forms of acceleration. Some are easier to implement than others, for the school or the individual. G. F. Lewis (1984) offers advice that seems to be generally useful:

> Each highly intellectually gifted child is likely to need radical acceleration in some area(s) at some point in his or her school career. Each of these children will need attention to other methods of delivering services, as well. (p. 135)

Renzulli's (1977) caveat is useful to the implementation of acceleration in any program for the gifted:

> When youngsters have simply been enrolled in advanced courses without any concern for the other important dimensions of the learner, then everyone ends up marching to the tune of the same drummer, albeit a faster beat. (pp. 15–16)

Acceleration is economical when relatively undifferentiated, and it can serve relatively large groups of children. Grade skipping is the most economical, though in excess it can affect a school district's external funding sources. Compression of several grades into fewer years can be quite expensive when it implies segregated groups on a full-time basis.

Negative consequences are apparently rare when acceleration is conducted well, but there will undoubtedly be individual cases, or badly conceived applications, where some negative consequences might ensue (children exposed to work beyond their ability, disrupted social relationships, excessive parental or self-imposed pressure). It would probably be wise for counselors at all levels through university to be alerted to these consequences, their causes, and remedies.

Gagné (1986) provided a good summary of key advice. First, students should be clearly interested in accelerating, show evident talent in the area of acceleration, and be socioaffectively mature. The other criteria are of lesser priority. Parent agreement is strongly advised, but their active support is not. Students need not have model attitudes in general, and age is important only in the consideration of early entry. Acceleration of cohorts of children can help avoid social difficulties. He also stressed the need to sensitize everyone concerned to the value of acceleration; the facts are not always enough.

Acceleration may operate on a smaller scale than the number of years pupils spend in school. It can mean taking less time to cover the general curriculum, in any of a number of ways, including rapid pacing (see recommended practice No. 62).

Needed Research

The most important research problems are not how to accelerate (there are dozens of good ways) or whether or not it is good for gifted children (it is, in many cases). We need a good collection of studies on the contradiction between intellectual support for acceleration and emotional rejection. What is needed to reconcile these positions? What legitimate objections to acceleration are obscured by current knowledge or opinions?

Some details need study. Is group acceleration better? Is it enough for parents to say "go ahead"? Does it matter when grade skipping is carried out, and how much preparation is needed before one proceeds confidently?

Also, there is no general agreement on which subjects beyond mathematics and second languages are well served by acceleration. There is no consensus regarding the importance of self-motivation, age or grade level, the need for accelerants to be highly gifted, or the long- or short-term nature of the compression. Studies should examine academic and other outcomes, include control groups of nonaccelerated peers, and take into account the nature of the learning environment provided. How can acceleration and the other pedagogical needs of the gifted (see recommended practice No. 37) be satisfied simultaneously?

Policy studies are needed. How might schools and districts assure that they simply do not lose per-student funds when they accelerate students? How might the economic benefits of saving some years of schooling among certain groups of pupils be used to support a range of services for gifted students?

29 | Enrichment Should Be a Program Component

Enrichment is the most commonly reported provision for gifted children. Although nearly every book on giftedness mentions the topic, most give it only cautious approval. A person new to the field might be puzzled by the gap between its ubiquity and its advocacy. B. Clark (1988) noted this limited endorsement:

> It must be well planned, and enhanced by other modifications, or it will meet few of the gifted students' needs. . . . Enrichment in many classrooms often means just more work, sometimes more of the same work. (p. 202)

An ocean away, Povey (1980b) made the same observation: "Enrichment programs should be more radical than just more and more work of the same nature" (p. 21).

Hill (1967/1983) supported enrichment and defined four elements, each of which is reflected in at least two specific practices reviewed in this volume:

1. Increasing ability to analyze and solve problems (see recommended practice Nos. 46, 59)
2. Developing profound, worthwhile interests (Nos. 51, 64)
3. Stimulating originality, initiative, and self-direction (Nos. 56, 65, 83)
4. Increasing social consciousness (Nos. 44, 48, 73)

In gifted education, the term *enrichment* is probably most closely associated with Renzulli and his colleagues. Renzulli (1977) was explicit in defining enrichment as those activities that are based in large measure on student interests and learning styles. Renzulli and Reis (1985) later added further precision by referring specifically to advanced-level activities. Relatively undifferentiated use of the term *enrichment*, such as B. Clark, Hill, and Povey warned against, should not be confused with Renzulli's use of the word.

Current Knowledge

Passow (1958) remarked on the dearth of research on enrichment three decades ago, and the situation has changed little. We do have the findings of several careful observers of the field. In their major survey of exemplary practices, Cox, Daniel, and Boston (1985) noted: "A program of enrichment in a classroom frequently lacks clear goals, adequate substance, and carefully planned teaching strategies" (p. 141). Students were typically involved for fewer than 3 hours a week. Although nearly two-thirds of the schools they studied reported having formal enrichment programs, they considered only 16% to be substantial in terms of enrollment, time, suitability of materials, and content. The term had very different meanings across school boards.

J. C. Stanley (1979a) is well known as a critic of enrichment. Typical of his opinions are these:

> The more relevant and excellent the enrichment program, the more it calls for acceleration of subject matter or grade placement later. Otherwise, it just puts off the boredom a while and virtually guarantees that eventually it will be more severe. (p. 235)

Perhaps the earliest warning of the difficulties inherent in the notion of enrichment came from Ward (1962). He wrote,

> The concept of "enrichment" as a means of providing for gifted children has . . . been proven in the usual instance to be a bullwark behind which scarcely anything desirable has in fact transpired. (p. 53)

A few studies of enrichment in its various forms have been conducted under the rubric of program evaluation. Worcester (1979) reviewed that literature extensively and reported that enrichment programs are widely successful. Criteria ranged from expressions of satisfaction from parents, children, and teachers to performance improvements. Indeed, all program evaluations in the literature tend to be positive. First, such evaluations are almost never independent—the program promoters report their success. Second, failures are unlikely to be either reported or, if submitted, published.

Any provision that takes a child beyond what might normally have been encountered in school or outside is enrichment. Used as anything more than the title of a program (a valid use), and without more precise methodological and goal statements, the term itself is not very helpful.

Implications for Action

Enrichment is an important objective to all students. We do not advocate that programs for the highly able not be enriched; rather, we assert that the word *enrichment* adds nothing new, unique, or specific to the education of highly able children. Educators need to be more specific when detailing and labeling such practices for classroom use.

There is a tendency in the educational literature on giftedness to discuss enrichment and acceleration as though they were opposites. As discussed in recommended practice No. 28, acceleration comprises many specific procedures that are potentially compatible with almost any educational program, so long as it is appropriate for the child. Equally, other specific provisions (future focus on the curriculum, career thinking, research skills, etc.) are also enrichment. As Gold (1965) stated, "What counts ultimately is what happens to the bright youngster and what he is stimulated to do by himself" (p. 138).

Needed Research

This discussion highlights a striking need in scholarship on giftedness, one that lies at the root of our motivation for preparing this volume. We lack a richly developed body of reasoned conceptual terminology, such that dependable research can be undertaken and the outcomes entered into a reliable and relatively enduring science of differential education, which, in turn, will support and encourage all the arts and skills that able and understanding teachers can use. *Enrichment* is not, at this time, part of this terminology, but a number of enriching and defensible pedagogical practices most certainly should be.

Because of the appeal and popularity of enrichment as a basis for serving gifted pupils, it might be appropriate for professional groups to attempt to develop guidelines or standards for what might be called enrichment in the context of gifted education. It remains to be determined whether just a few curricular ideas can supplement all the things one might do, such as most of the recommended practices reviewed here, or whether the majority of the recommended practices should simply be labeled as enrichment. It is an attractive concept and a term that appeals to many people who find the word *gifted* discomforting. To search for consensus about specific meanings and to validate these meanings against practice and program improvement would be a suitable extended project for a team of researchers.

30 | **Ability Grouping Is Appropriate**

There is a strong integrationist movement in special education. Should educators of exceptionally able students relent on their interest in services that sometimes involve segregation?

> All gifted students need to interact with those who can challenge them. For the highly gifted, ability grouping would justifiably comprise the major part of their educational experience. (B. Clark, 1988, p. 199)

> But they need even more to be with those who share their excitement, who can follow their ideas, who understand and accept their way of learning, who may even outstrip them. (Laycock, 1979, p. 124)

> The strongest argument for some form of grouping is the need to provide contact with children who are more likely to be understanding and accepting. (Woodliffe, 1977, p. 9)

The important questions are: Do segregated gifted students achieve better? Do they benefit socially? What are the effects on the pupils from whom they are segregated? These are more important issues than whether people like ability grouping, or whether it is administratively convenient.

Current Knowledge

B. Clark (1988), Laycock (1979), Passow (1958), and Woodliffe (1977) summarize the rationale for grouping, the arguments against, and research. There is some, but not consistent, research evidence that congregating gifted pupils, in and of itself, improves their academic progress. Laycock (1979) summarized Swedish studies that showed that work in arithmetic, English (as a second language), and reading improved for grouped gifted children. He also reported a well controlled Swedish study with random assignment in which the segregated gifted pupils did better than integrated gifted pupils in academic achievement and their awareness of civic equality and individual value.

Meta-analyses of 25 studies on ability grouping concluded that bright students improve their performance in separate classrooms and within-classroom programs (Kulik & Kulik, 1987, 1991), but that comprehensive ability grouping has little or no effect on achievement of the general student population (Kulik & Kulik, 1987, 1991; Oakes, 1985; Slavin, 1987a, 1988).

B. Clark (1988) proposed that concomitant program adjustments were needed for academic gains. It is not clear that the program adjustments required the grouping. "Narrowing the ability range *per se,* without specifically designing varied academic programs for the various ability levels, does not result in consistently greater academic achievement" (Goldberg & Passow, 1962/1980, p. 81; also cited at length in B. Clark, 1988).

Few studies have examined program effects on affective development, despite its influence on learning and achievement (B. Clark, 1988; Tannenbaum, 1983). Two reports found positive effects on student attitudes toward learning from separate classroom placement (Enzmann, 1963; Tremaine, 1979). Kulik and Kulik (1991) observed that only 6 of the 25 studies in their meta-analysis included a measure of affective development (self-esteem). This was too few to yield persuasive findings, although four of the six studies did find more positive self-esteem when students were grouped by ability rather than placed in regular classrooms.

O'Shea (1975) described a 1957 study by Horace Mann in which high mental age children spent half the day in segregated groups and half in home rooms and responded to sociometric questions about including and excluding other children in several activities. Positive choices were overwhelmingly for other part-time segregated children, and so were the rejections. O'Shea recounted similar observations made about children moved into such groups by Hollingworth (1926). Woodliffe (1977) informally reported a 5-year follow-up survey of 750 graduates of part-time segregated students. Students greatly enjoyed the separate class, though there were mixed judgments of their prior experiences in regular classes. However, Woodliffe observed,

If a homogeneous class is set up, changes must be made in the curriculum or there will be no significant change in the children's performance. (p. 18)

Separate grouping enhances the self-concept and social situation of gifted pupils. Laycock (1979) related variable effects on nonsegregated students in the Swedish and other studies. No negative effects seem to have been reported, until an experimental study by Dar and Resh (1986). More able students benefited from segregation, but less able students lost more. In integration, the less able students' gain was greater than the more able students' loss. Goldberg and Passow (1962/1980) found different effects in different subjects, with the presence of the most able group almost always benefiting (but never harming) the least able, sometimes raising (e.g., in science, and in social studies when less able students were also present) and sometimes lowering (e.g., in arithmetic, and in social studies when less able students were absent) performance for the above-average group. Bracey (1987) summarized studies that showed similar social disadvantages for the less able groups: They were given less opportunity for self-directed activity, received more criticism (but not less praise), and generally had a less warm socioemotional climate in which to work. These deficits were less for low groups in socioeconomically favored schools. Veldman and Sanford (1984) found similar academic outcomes. All students do better in high-ability classes; the less able respond more to class norms. At the extremes of ability, segregation clearly enhances achievement, but this is undermined by other negative effects.

Perhaps ability grouping bestows an implicit label (see recommended practice No. 88). Segregation is good for the gifted and possibly bad for some others, but the negative effects are sometimes stronger. This presents a serious moral dilemma. Adequately serving the more able student's need for intellectual peer contact may be accompanied by an educational disservice to slightly less able students. This is one of the two main objections to ability grouping for the gifted; the other is that they might develop élitist attitudes, but this has not been supported. It seems that the children most negatively affected might be those just missed in selection for special classes. Ability grouping itself may not cause the negative effects but rather applying too strict a cut-off, resulting in children's needing differentiated services in some subjects but not getting them.

Implications for Action

Useful practical suggestions on the implementation of ability grouping within classes, by class, or at the school level are given by B. Clark (1988), Laycock (1979), and Woodliffe (1977).

First, there is no evidence that full-time segregation accomplishes the benefits of ability grouping more effectively than part-time. Second, identification procedures should be inclusive and one should err, if one must, on the side of providing differentiated service for too many rather than too few students. Third, highly cumulative subjects such as languages and mathematics may be the most appropriate for ability grouping. These are subjects in which grouping is routine in almost any classroom (cf. Passow, 1958). Fourth, to achieve maximum academic benefit, grouping in academic subjects should be accompanied by curricular adaptation.

Finally, when anticipating benefits to be achieved by grouping, also specify the potential risks, then double-check that the benefits cannot be provided by another mechanism (partially heterogeneous groups, tutoring, mentoring), and that procedures could be put in place to overcome the negative consequences, such as intentionally planning some joint activities. Equally, if advocates for the gifted do not insist on ability grouping, they are entitled to be assured that the benefits are provided in other settings.

Needed Research

Goldberg and Passow (1962/1980), Dar and Resh (1986), and the Swedish work described by Laycock (1979) are some of the most sophisticated examples of research on educational provisions for the gifted. They need to be replicated and extended. Future research must separate administrative devices from the curricular adaptations and transformations they make possible.

One puzzle in the research base is how to reconcile the Goldberg and Passow results, for example, with those of Dar and Resh: Are the negative effects of ability grouping a consequence of poor identification procedures and excessively rigid "in or out" boundaries on services? Some of the positive effects for the gifted may be the result of pedagogical adjustments in response to the concentration of interest and drive. For example, teachers could raise the level of expectations. We also need research on the specific conditions under which negative consequences arise from ability grouping.

Finally, the research base would benefit from more precise data on different school organizations (single class versus rotary), subject specialists for young learners, and different subject matter in terms of the structure of knowledge in the discipline. Procedures intended to reduce the negative consequences without losing the benefits need to be validated.

31 | Curriculum Should Be Multidisciplinary

This is the fourth of Feldhusen's (1985a) four key elements in differentiated education for the gifted: "Their view of the world, school, learning, and studies should be interdisciplinary" (1985c, p. 181). The other three are acceleration of regular content (see recommended practice No. 28), fast pacing (No. 62), and in-depth study (No. 64). It is also one of the central principles endorsed by VanTassel-Baska (1985). She and others credit Ward (1961/1980) for conceptualizing the importance of this objective. This recommended practice complements part of No. 64, which addresses in-depth study.

Current Knowledge

This recommended practice is supported by a strong rationale, some indirect research, and virtually no direct research, though this may very well be worth pursuing. The rationale begins with Ward's proposed general principle that differential education for the gifted should address universal perspectives (see Ward, 1985, for a summary), including study of "the common assumptions underlying different scientific and social theories" (p. 9). This was an implicit model, to use Sternberg and J. E. Davidson's (1986) useful label, not yet supported by an array of direct empirical evidence but compelling enough to become a keystone of nearly every proposal on curriculum design for highly able learners. Additional support came from Torrance (1979a), who restated the observation that many gifted children are multi-talented. Callahan (1985) purported that gifted children can see relationships among fields of knowledge more easily. Torrance and Reynolds (1979) added that career interests of very bright people often have interdisciplinary components; school curriculum should therefore provide opportunity to strengthen the intellectual skills involved.

Some indirect research support is provided by Landau (1979). She argued that:

> Thinking becomes more and more creative as one succeeds in discovering mutual relationships between data which seemingly have nothing in common, as one relates data pertaining to different disciplines while dealing with one problem, and as one reorganizes and expands the categories of environmental data. (p. 155)

This is easily defended by contemporary cognitive research. More able learners connect new learning to more prior knowledge, access that learning in unique ways (Krutetskii, 1976; Larkin, McDermott, Simon & Simon, 1980), and create more elaborate relationships among key concepts (Donald, 1983; Rabinowitz & Glaser, 1985; Shavelson, 1974).

Several authors have elaborated on this recommended practice. First, Kersh and Reisman (1985) pointed out that only the student can do the integrating. Educators can make the components available to learners, but understanding is constructed by the learner, not imposed. Second, VanTassel-Baska (1985) suggested that interdisciplinary study has to be built on solid disciplinary or multidisciplinary knowledge. The connections among these are the interdisciplinary knowledge. This is consistent with Kersh and Reisman's (1985) view, except that it incompletely explains how effective learning can take place in a subject where students have very little prior knowledge on which to build. At the frontiers of knowledge pursued by advanced scholars, the need for a multidisciplinary approach may be obvious, in order to make sense out of unfamiliar events. The young learner may be in a comparable situation, but this has not been studied directly. The widespread interest in "whole language" curriculum reflects this different view; one can at least begin to exercise the processes underlying high-level creative endeavors from a basis of little specific knowledge. Both can then grow.

One study provided indirect support for the idea that young learners are able to engage in high-level learning without the advantage of an extensive knowledge base in a traditional discipline. Schermerhorn, Goldschmid, and Shore (1975) prepared unfamiliar grade-level readings in probability for groups of students at intervals from grade 1 through university graduate studies. The youngest students were read to. Students were tested on their understanding of the basic knowledge after initial reading; after preparing questions for a partner that would elicit discussion about the main ideas in the text; and again after engaging in discussion with a partner based on each other's questions. Part of the exercise included training the learners to ask "high-level" questions, questions that required more than basic knowledge or comprehension. There was an increase in performance following each step at all ages. Engaging in the process of verifying if a learning partner understood key concepts (defined by the question asked) led to superior learning by the asker in statistics-ignorant first graders and also among university research students drawn from a statistics course. Can the knowledge base and the processes underlying asking creative or other kinds of high-level questions be developed simultaneously? This is one of the most important parts of the present recommended practice and requires further investigation.

We are left with a recommended practice with considerable appeal, but there is a need for direct research support.

Implications for Action

With regard to Kersh and Reisman's (1985) suggestion that the learner must make the ultimate integration, we stress the "ultimate." Students themselves cannot be expected to be either disciplinarians or interdisciplinarians, which means that their involvement in the design or evaluation of multidisciplinary curricula should be phased in carefully, and probably not compulsorily. On the other hand, it can be expected of teachers that they will be able to create these curricular experiences. These must be within their personal ranges of expertise.

Kersh and Reisman (1985) propose several steps to develop interdisciplinary curricula. Their most important suggestion is to begin from one's own area of strength (and, by implication, to have one or more!), to reach out for expertise in areas to be linked, and to base initial curricula on searches for what they call "symmetry, patterns, constraints and variations, and transformations" (p. 155). These refer to sets of ideas that have counterparts in the two domains, to analyzing the ways one has to limit or expand ideas from one domain to make the connections to another, and making the connections.

Goldberg, Passow, and Lorge (1958/1980) suggested that a good pedagogical approach to introducing interdisciplinary thinking can be through seminars organized around themes such as great issues, problems, or people. This is worth verifying.

Needed Research

The ideas raised by Landau (1979) are especially worthy of study with highly able and control samples: Are the very able especially apt at relating diverse knowledge, perhaps in original ways? Do they organize their own knowledge in different ways? Does this categorization and organization resemble the knowledge structures of novices versus experts in the cognitive literature? What pedagogy develops these kinds of thinking?

Second, what are the advantages and disadvantages of multidisciplinary study versus a traditional curriculum in providing a suitable knowledge base for later intellectual activity?

Third, how may bright children be especially well served by multidisciplinary and interdisciplinary studies, and to what extent? Does multitalent or multipotentiality facilitate such study? Are career interests or opportunities related?

Fourth, to what extent can inexperienced or young learners engage in multidisciplinary study or in the kinds of thinking that are appropriate to it, while they still may know very little about the topic—in other words, how much within-discipline knowledge does one have to have before embarking on the creative and multidisciplinary parts of knowledge creation?

32 | Stress Affective as Well as Cognitive Growth

The admonition to attend to affective as well as cognitive growth is ubiquitous and is addressed to both educators and parents. As proposed by Tannenbaum (1983),

It is necessary for all gifted children to concentrate as seriously on the affective domain . . . as they do on the cognitive. (p. 439)

J. P. Parker (1989) elaborated the ways in which the two domains fit together in a specific educational setting:

It is not possible to cover adequately such historic events as the Boston Tea Party and the Emancipation Proclamation, or such concepts as apartheid, genetic engineering, and substance abuse, without allowing students to explore their attitudes, beliefs, and concerns on these questions. (p. 104)

Thus, in addition to the emotional adjustment of gifted children, this practice also touches on the issues of social responsibility and values as a part of the affective development of the gifted. Wolf and Stephens (1985) suggested these were especially important in gifted education, because

gifted students are more likely to achieve positions of power and influence as adults; . . . The importance of these skills for the gifted lies in the assumption that the gifted have the potential to make significant contributions to society and to their own personal development. (p. 80)

Current Knowledge

This is a practice widely espoused in general education. However, in terms of personal adjustment issues, gifted students, no less than others, appear vulnerable to suicide, delinquency, and dropping out (Lajoie & Shore, 1981).

For our purposes, the affective domain may include self-concept, motivation, emotional responsivity, and social relations. Related concepts are humanistic values and moral reasoning. Several recommended practices in this text review each of these topics thoroughly; for example, see No. 19, which is an examination of the affective talents included in the identification of the gifted, and Nos. 48, 81, 83, 84, 85, and 86, which address humanistic values, intrinsic motivation, personal independence, self-concept, leadership, and the development of interests, respectively.

Most closely related is the discussion concerning the account that should be taken of gifted students' physical, social, and emotional limitations in recommended practice No. 82. In view of the extensive coverage elsewhere in this volume, a detailed review is not presented here.

Implications for Action

Failure to develop positive self-concepts and intrinsic motivation are problems for some gifted youth, most notably underachievers. The potential for bright people to occupy positions of power is also a good reason to attend particularly to affective development with such persons.

Good citizenship, humanistic values, moral reasoning, and leadership are goals of virtually every educational system. Not to include them for the gifted would be indefensible. On the whole, this practice applies to all children. This does not diminish its importance to gifted children. It simply places part of the responsibility on the shoulders of general education, which should not assume that the most able will take care of themselves in this regard.

Needed Research

Creating or maintaining conditions likely to cause dysfunctional emotional, social, or moral development or purposely stressing cognitive gains at the expense of affective growth cannot be done in school programs simply to validate this recommended practice experimentally.

A more fruitful line of inquiry might be to examine the conflict possible for many gifted and talented youth: individual development versus social responsibility. To what extent do bright youths feel they should develop their talents for the good of society or as a part of their personal growth and satisfaction? Are these two orientations in conflict? Have talented young people reconciled them? If so, how?

33 | Materials Should Be High in Quality and Reading Level, Require Complex Verbal Responses, and Avoid Repetition

This recommended practice is a composite drawn from several sources; it overlaps to varying degrees with Nos. 34, 37, and 42. The particular emphasis on teaching materials deserves separate mention. The general principle, notably regarding "equipment and materials beyond that practicable or essential for children in the average range of intellectual ability," was first explicitly stated by Ward (1961/1980, p. 99). Barbe and Malone (1985) offered the early reading skills of many young gifted children as a rationale for avoiding repetition. Cushenbery and Howell (1974) addressed the issues of level and broad interests, with particular focus on secondary schooling. Tempest (1974) observed that students least in need of repetition are most likely to have to endure it. Most of what has been written about this topic deals with literature.

Current Knowledge

There is little that might be described as research on this recommended practice. McCormick and Swassing (1982) conducted a U.S. national survey on reading programs for the gifted, and respondents regarded access to high-quality literature as an important feature. Several studies (cited by Barbe & Malone, 1985, and Cushenbery & Howell, 1974) noted the early reading and wide interests of many bright children.

Implications for Action

These skills are elaborated in the discussion of recommended practice No. 37. A long out-of-print series of textbooks that apply the needed principles are represented by the first volume of the *International Encyclopedia of Unified Science* (Neurath, Carnap, & Morris, 1955), first copyrighted in 1938, notably in the contributions *Foundations of Biology* (by Mainx, 1955) and *The Conceptual Framework of Psychology* (by Brunswik, 1955). The works guide the student on the path of original inquiry in the discipline rather than through a carefully arranged summary of the organized conclusions of the subject matter. This is an important quality to look for in any instructional materials.

General literature is addressed by several authors, such as Witty (1971), Cushenbery and Howell (1974), Baskin and Harris (1980), Polette (1982), and Pennington (1984).

This practice has an appealing rationale and likely represents good judgment, but it has a weak research base.

Needed Research

The ultimate test of the appropriateness of instructional materials is in the attainment of the intended objectives. These objectives are not always clear. It would be useful to select a few specific domains and key characteristics (e.g., fostering independent enquiry, developing literary appreciation, being enjoyable to use, avoiding repetition) by which to compare a variety of materials. These need not be limited to texts; there are also computer software, construction kits, workbooks, films, videotapes, and workshops. Well-controlled studies would be easy to construct.

Attention should be directed to determining for whom this recommended practice is appropriate; it may have broad applicability.

34 | Provide a Qualitatively Different Curriculum, at Least Part-Time

The expression "differential education for the gifted" was coined in the late 1950s by Ward (1961/1980). The idea has been crucial to the growth of support for this recommended practice. As Maker (1982a) began her book on curriculum development,

> The most basic principle underlying curriculum development for the gifted is that the experiences for these children must be qualitatively different from the basic program provided for all children. (p. 3)

The nature of these qualitative differences is elaborated in dozens of the other recommended practices in this volume. What distinguishes this recommendation from these others is the issue of time. How much of a gifted student's educational career should be differentiated? This question is not addressed clearly in the literature, and the phrase "at least part of the time" is our advice. Here are some statements that suggest it:

> What is necessary and sufficient for the nongifted is necessary but *insufficient* for the gifted, who need more and different learning experiences commensurate with their potentialities. (Tannenbaum, 1983, p. 461)

> Programs for the gifted and talented should provide for . . . activities involving interaction with both gifted and nongifted students. (Passow, 1981, p. 100)

These statements suggest a connection between the gifted and regular programs (Massé & Gagné, 1983).

Current Knowledge

The first part of this recommended practice does not lend itself to empirical inquiry. Such evidence is available for several of the ways in which education can be differentiated for exceptionally able learners, according to their exceptionalities, and these are reported elsewhere in this book.

Ward (1961/1980) provided an extensive conceptual framework supporting the need for differentiated curriculum. Maker (1982a) offered a table (cf. pp. 8–17) that summarized the personal and social characteristics of gifted children, backed by references, and her suggestions about how the content, process and method, product, and learning environment should be adapted to provide an appropriate distinct curriculum. Each of the 296 marks in the 925 cells of the resulting grid suggests a curricular adaptation (e.g., variety of content, group interaction, suitability of a real audience) necessitated by a particular characteristic. However, only the list of characteristics is largely research-backed; some of the characteristics would today be regarded as stereotypical, and the supporting studies vary widely in quality. The recommended action is conceptually sound and worthy of detailed study, but to study these adaptations requires an updated rationale for each, plus their implementation. Our discussion of recommended practice No. 46 adds cognitive material not available when Maker wrote her book.

The question of how much time to devote to differential education has not been the subject of empirical research, but it is addressed by research on ability grouping (see recommended practice No. 30 for details). These studies fall into two groups. Both show advantages for more able students, but some reveal no ill effects on other students whereas others report negative consequences. Do the benefits arise from the increased social contact with intellectual peers, the curricular adaptation that may be more readily provided, or some other quality of the grouping, such as the underlying recognition?

Case reports from the literature on counseling gifted students (e.g., Perrone & Male, 1981) repeatedly point out the harm done to many students who are inadequately served.

Overall, we have strong faith, a good argument, and growing research evidence at more specific levels that very able children do need a qualitatively different education, reflected in the curriculum. We also have the suggestion that this differentiation must be applied at least part of the time, but we have only indirect research to guide the application of this principle.

Implications for Action

Such a pedagogical approach should indeed be used. It is consistent with most of what we are learning about the nature of giftedness and creativity in learning. Applicability to regular programs is an open question.

A basic principle is that the provisions must be unique (Ward, 1961/ 1980). This is not achieved by merely (1) requiring more of the same kinds of learning, (2) displacing the same kind of learning activities downwards in the age-grade school organization, or (3) advancing the child across one or more grades or subject areas. The failure of these practices when implemented as mere administrative arrangements is neither difficult to understand nor to state: The essential properties of the curriculum and pedagogy are in the main not adapted to the intellectual and other needs of the children. What is needed is curricular transformation as distinct from curricular transportation. This major distinction involves all manner of related changes in program and curricula, including those that are part of the general enjoinder to bring about qualitative differences. Examples include teaching children to think, teaching on higher planes of cognitive process, employing language and logic of a nature abstracted from everyday experience, and the like. All of these measures should entail, but frequently do not, appropriately transformed text and reference materials (see recommended practice No. 33). Ward (1981) urged care in differentiating curriculum:

> Equally mandatory are cautions that in the gradual development of increasingly pertinent processes, no *abusive* practices be allowed to creep in. Bright youngsters are being unwittingly subjected in today's heightened pressures to requirements and expectations some of which unquestionably serve to defeat their intended purpose, rather than to support it. . . . Practices are likely to be inherently wrong if they lead to avoidance on the part of able youngsters and their parents, and if they require work in amount or kind which is not positively attractive in immediate nature and purposeful in ultimate objective. (p. 74)

The concept of punishment introduced above refers to such practices as increasing the burden of teacher-assigned homework for bright students, lengthening the school day or week, or using lunch hours or recess to provide compulsory extra class time, and grading work "on a curve" even though all the students would be "A" students in the regular program.

Needed Research

The validation of the general call for a differentiated curriculum will come from study of other recommended practices taken together. Additional support could be gained from enquiries into the specific recommendations for differentiation suggested by Maker (1982a). The key questions in each case are: Does this adaptation improve the situation for a gifted student? Is it different from what is provided in the regular program? Is it inappropriate for the regular program? A general question that needs to be examined in a large number of program implementations is whether this curricular differentiation accomplishes more than is accomplished by the underlying administrative arrangement alone. For example, does a special mathematics course achieve more than what mere grouping of these same students might have accomplished?

We need specific research on the question of time. Virtually all of the curricular proposals can be carried out in some form in a range of time from one period a week, through more substantial part-time provision, or in completely segregated settings. How much time is needed for a program to work? This question is probably less important pedagogically than politically and socially, because there will always be concern about risks to gifted children served and to those not served, gifted or otherwise. Attention to affective variables is important in all such research.

35 | **Take Learning Styles Into Account**

"Certain classroom environments, modes of teaching, and educational materials might influence different types of learners in different ways . . ." (P. A. Alexander & Muia, 1982, p. 220). Cox, Daniel, and Boston (1985) advised, from their observations of superior gifted programs, "Develop teaching strategies that are appropriate to the learning styles of able students . . ." (p. 155). Interests and learning styles are also central to the Triad/Revolving Door Model (Renzulli & Reis, 1985).

Even though attention to learning styles is fundamental in the individualization of instruction, are learning styles of the gifted as a group different from those of other learners? As individuals, do they also differ from each other in ways that are different from the ways other children vary? Finally, does attending to these differences make any difference in outcomes?

Current Knowledge

Recognition of learning-style differences among gifted children, and between them and others, should be placed alongside other variables in the personality, abilities, and experiences of the learner that also affect attitudes and approaches to classroom activities. Scruggs and Mastropieri (1984) correctly pointed out that

> investigations have referred mostly to self-reported preferences for external environmental variables such as light, color, and sound. What we are concerned with are internal learning characteristics, that is, how gifted students learn and whether this learning process may differ from that of average learners. (p. 183)

Between a learning style based on environmental preferences and one based on internal learning is the style characterized by self-reported preferences for particular instructional situations. We will consider selected reports of all three types of learning styles, in turn, with respect to the three questions that preceded this brief examination of the literature.

Dunn and Griggs (1985) recounted over a dozen studies of learning styles in gifted children.

> Among those traits that tended to characterize the gifted's styles are (a) independence (self-learners); (b) internal or external control; (c) persistence; (d) perceptual strengths; (e) nonconformity; (f) task-commitment; and (g) high self-motivation. . . . Although gifted youngsters preferred to learn alone rather than with heterogeneously grouped classmates, they learned best with their *true* peers, other gifted children. In addition, their attitudes toward learning were significantly more positive when engaged in problem solving and rote memory tasks with other gifted in the same program than when they were mismatched with nongifted youngsters. (p. 43)

Environmental preferences may still operate at the individual level, but they did not appear unique for the gifted. They may be related to improved achievement and attitudes, and fewer discipline problems.

Boultinghouse (1984) reported that gifted children differed from nongifted in rejecting peer teaching (she did not ask students whether they liked being the peer teacher, however) and excessive teacher talk. The gifted preferred "independent, divergent, student-controlled activities" (p. 209). The gifted also displayed greater variance in distinguishing between likes and dislikes. Goldberg (1986) found examples in previous studies of performance differences that could be explained by differences in group versus individual assignments, the pace of the class, or its theoretical versus practical orientation.

Several studies have attempted to show that there are systematic thinking differences between gifted and nongifted learners that have pedagogical consequences. These include the use of more complex strategies and the spontaneous production of strategies (Scruggs & Mastropieri, 1984), flexibility of strategy, and the use of metacognitive processes (Shore, 1986; Shore & Dover, 1987). R. R. Daniels (1986) found processing differences among gifted children using the Meeker Structure-of-Intellect materials, but, as in so many studies of giftedness, there was no nongifted control group.

We have not considered a fourth category of differences often labeled *brain hemisphericity* (see Chen, 1981; B. Clark, 1985; F. A. Karnes, McCallum, & Oehler, 1985). It might explain something about performance related to learning styles, but brain-function differences themselves are not learning styles.

The state of knowledge appears to be that (1) gifted students as a group may indeed differ from the nongifted on some dimensions of learning style, (2) gifted students may differ among themselves in degree and ways that the nongifted do not, and (3) there may be differences in outcomes to be gained from attention to these differences. The evidence so far is fragmented, variables differ widely from study to study, and the research varies in design quality, but the overall consistency among the results is important.

Implications for Action

Take learning styles into account, but be careful not to rely on a single understanding of what learning styles are. Environmental, pedagogical, and cognitive differences are among those now apparent. Gardiner (1983) offers an example of the implementation of Dunn's environmental model; Colon and Treffinger (1980) illustrate how to fit learning styles into an instructional model, as do Renzulli and Reis (1985).

Questions should still be raised about the impact of program differences among schools (highly disciplined or less formally structured around electives) and curricular content (more mathematics and physics or less, and what kind, maximal emphasis on writing, a balance of fine and performing arts).

Finally, attention to learning styles is not a sufficient definition of a gifted program. Programs must be built around suitable content well taught (Gallagher, 1976) and adapted to "the very characteristics which led to the students' identification as talented" (Goldberg, 1986, p. 46).

> It is impossible for teachers to accommodate all students' learning style preferences on all occasions. [However], unless at some point in the school day or week the teachers are organizing activities that accommodate the varying learning style preferences of their students, it is not likely that a comprehensive individualization program is actually taking place. (Renzulli & Reis, 1985, p. 202)

Needed Research

Rigorous empirical enquiry into the truth of this general assertion appears largely unnecessary. If the injunction were investigated, it would be with respect to specific subquestions. For example, some replication and extension of work showing group differences between the gifted and others would be welcome. Second, our understanding of within-group differences is not as secure; it would be useful to take variables from reports of significant group differences and examine them to see if the dissimilarities within the gifted group are different from those observed among other children. Third, the outcomes question has barely been studied; again, variables examined in the first two groups of studies should be central to these so that some cohesion may ensue among the reports.

In addition, this topic could benefit from an overall synthesis or theoretical treatment. We need to direct our attention to the validation of the program and curricular developments that should follow.

36 | Gifted Children Need to Set Long- and Short-Term Goals

> Gifted children, like most others, must learn the skill of goal setting. They must learn to set tentative, attainable, short-term goals, as well as long-term goals. . . . The intellectual abilities of gifted children . . . allow them to comprehend and use these mental approaches early in life. (Webb, Meckstroth, & Tolan, 1982, pp. 72–73)

Cushenbery and Howell (1974) also referred to bright children's ability to cope with goal setting as a part of taking responsibility for an increasing portion of their own learning. Passow (1980b) related this to the pursuit of special interests (see recommended practice No. 39), and E. S. Fleming (1985) to career thinking.

Current Knowledge

Wesolowski (1982) offered a rationale for this recommended practice:

> When we ask gifted students what they want to know, we often find they are unable to articulate questions in such a way that answers may be derived. That's why we need to help gifted students learn to state their own real educational objectives. . . . As students develop their own objectives, they begin to realize what is possible within their resources. They gain better understanding of themselves. (pp. 32, 33)

There is some concern that bright students may have difficulty establishing goals. In the review of recommended practice No. 49, the importance of career education—certainly an important long-term goal—it is noted that students regard this part of their education with the greatest favor, which indicates consistent priority setting in their thinking about what school has to offer them. J. L. Hoffman, Wasson, and Christianson (1985) reported a school program for bright underachievers in which one of the first assignments was to write down five things they would want to change about themselves. They obtained 79 varied items easily categorized by topic and recognizably distinct with regard to the long or short term. This suggests that if one sets the task in an appropriate way, bright students can generate many goals at various levels. It was not clear, though, if these expressed goals played any role in these children's actions.

There is no empirical literature, however, that tells us that engaging explicitly in goal setting has any particular beneficial effect, in general, or specifically for the gifted. The little evidence reported does not directly support or refute the recommended practice.

Implications for Action

Goal setting, short and long term, can be a useful part of the individualization of instruction based on student interests.

It is not clear to what extent or in what ways attention to goals should be different for exceptionally able and other children; neither is it apparent whether or not it is necessary to differentiate between long- and short-term goals.

Needed Research

To what extent do highly able children organize their lives around goals, and how well they can articulate them? How much help do they need in either? Do they differ in these regards from others?

---

37 | Employ Professional End-Products as Standards

The development of persons who may become producers of and contributors to existing knowledge must begin with at least some experience in an instructional model that provides young people with an opportunity to experience the *modus operandi* of the first hand inquirer. (Reis & Renzulli, 1985, p. 7)

Although this assertion was made in the context of secondary programs, Renzulli (1977) earlier defined enrichment for any level as "activities in which the youngster becomes an actual *investigator* of a *real* problem or topic by using appropriate *methods of inquiry*" (p. 29). Maker (1982b) elaborated Renzulli's idea as follows: "The products expected from gifted children should resemble the products developed by professionals in the discipline being studied" (p. 6).

Current Knowledge

Renzulli's suggestion that emulating professional thinking is a step toward standards of excellence has been examined in the literature. Haensly and Roberts (1983) sent questionnaires to professionals in different fields, asking

1. Where they got the inspiration for their ideas (most often from within, sometimes from others)
2. If they needed new skills to pursue their new ideas (nearly always yes)
3. The nature of the intended product (a moving target in many cases, or one whose use changes)
4. The value of persistence to their success (nearly universal)
5. Obstacles met (money, time, and others) and how they were met (time management to humor)
6. The role of the intended audience (integral)

The authors extrapolated the results to the education of the gifted: The six headings corresponded well with the prescription offered by Renzulli for implementing his proposal, namely, addressing real problems and real audiences, going beyond given information (such as provided by an encyclopedia), and incorporating suitable evaluation. It is not clear how broadly this result could be generalized.

Starko (1988) compared students with 4 years' experience in a Renzulli-inspired program with students who had no special services. She reported that creatively productive activity outside school, impact of such activities on career thinking, school attitude, and (with hints of metacognitive knowledge) insight into personal strengths and weaknesses were all statistically significantly enhanced by the participation.

Tannenbaum (1981) suggested that with curricula that extend beyond the ordinary, the gifted are capable of making original contributions to knowledge. He later added that "the world of ideas is changing and new disciplines deserve attention especially from those who are equipped to contribute to these realms of knowledge" (1983, pp. 465–466).

From a more general perspective, it is relevant to cite Bruner's (1960/1963) "central conviction":

> Intellectual activity anywhere is the same, whether at the frontier of knowledge or in a third-grade classroom. What a scientist does at his desk or in his laboratory, what a literary critic does in reading a poem, are of the same order as what anybody else does when he is engaged in like activities—if he is to achieve understanding. The difference is in degree, not in kind. The schoolboy learning physics *is* a physicist, and it is easier for him to learn physics behaving like a physicist than doing something else. The "something else" usually involves the task of mastering . . . a "middle language"—classroom discussions and textbooks that talk about the conclusions in a field of intellec-

tual inquiry rather than centering upon the inquiry itself. Approached in that way, high school physics often looks very little like physics, social studies are removed from the issues of life and society as usually discussed, and school mathematics too often has lost contact with what is at the heart of the subject, the idea of order. (p. 14)

The literature supports this recommendation, philosophically and anecdotally, though (with the exception of the Starko study) the evidence is empirically weak.

Implications for Action

This recommended practice addresses the nature of assignments given to and taken on by students. It is not restricted to level or discipline. Examples of how to implement it are provided by Renzulli and his coauthors in several publications—Reis and Hébert (1985) offer a very useful example of the application to a history program. Maker (1982b) provides a useful observer's summary. This practice is not dependent on the implementation of any other part of Renzulli's model of either enrichment or identification. For example, as of 1988, every New York State student from Grade 3 to 12 is required to complete at least one extended, interdisciplinary project every year, with the use of computers encouraged from Grade 7 up (Ambach, 1984).

One of the most important corollaries of this recommended practice may be that teachers need experience with this process in order to be sensitive to the challenges faced by students.

Needed Research

A good start would be a replication of Haensly and Roberts (1983) study, with detailed supporting data. The study could also look at processes used by students who are involved in such learning, from those reminiscent of creative problem solving to cognition.

Medium and long-term follow-up of students exposed to such curricula would provide important evidence about the attainment of the overall goal: Producing knowledge producers. Such studies should include a control group of equally able students from similar situations whose "gifted programs" were more conventional in their assignments. For example, do students having had such quasi-professional experiences in high school, earlier or later, more easily define thesis topics if and when they ever become graduate students? Do they more often pursue research training and careers? Do they think or behave differently in school or outside? Do they understand better how knowledge is created and disseminated? Starko's (1988) study is a good example of such needed work.

Can this objective be adapted for a wide range of abilities at different grades? What are the underlying intellectual abilities and skills needed to perform well in such learning situations? To what extent can these be taught, and how? Are they related to "creativity"?

38 | Combine Individual Programming With a Common Curriculum

> As with all students, the gifted and talented need to be provided with both general and specialized education. If the emphasis is on general education, including the acquisition of foundational skills, knowledge, and attitudes on which specialized talents can be developed, then content and methods should aim at broad understandings and meanings plus depth of insight into basic processes and resources. Specialized education, on the other hand, should provide for immersion into deeper, more intensive, and possibly more accelerated experiences in the students' special areas of talent. (Passow, 1979, p. 449)

> Even though individualization is a laudable idea, one might point out that the conventional class instruction for at least part of the time is not only less costly, but also helps in conveying to all children a common core of fundamental skills which they require in our culture. (Vernon, Adamson, & Vernon, 1977, p. 179)

B. Clark (1988), Freehill (1961/1982), and Marjoram (1983), among others, have made similar statements. There is a parallel between the advice contained here and that regarding attention to abstract concepts versus basic (see recommended practice No. 42). In both cases, the literature advises special curricular adaptation but not at the total expense of core or common material.

Current Knowledge

There is no empirical research on this recommended practice. Maker (1982a) elaborated two points related to Passow's:

> One is the overall degree of individualization for all children, the other is the number and type of curricular modifications made for gifted students. If, for

instance, the overall philosophy is that of providing for individual differences in learning rates, interests, and achievement levels, these modifications will not need to be made for the gifted program. (p. 128)

Renzulli and Smith (1980) emphasized that even the common core of a program should be adapted to the needs of highly able students. C. L. Lewis and Kanes (1979) provided an interesting example of the use of Individual Educational Plans (IEPs) based on the idea that "the IEP is a reflection of the modifications necessitated by the unique learning needs evidenced by the student" (p. 62). Another was offered by Fearn and Owen (1984): Their study was uncommon in having used Structure of the Intellect (SOI) (Meeker, 1969) testing materials as criterion measures for intellectual growth but not for teaching the target performance.

Perhaps the best reason we can offer for following this recommended practice is that it is so sensible professionally, because, as Passow (1979) has also said, it can be applied to all children. Common sense can be and is occasionally overruled by controlled scientific investigation; but wholesale experience among professionals in any field can, in the long haul, offer a reasonably secure recourse—as long as the practice it advocates remains open to confirmation or refutation as research progresses.

Passow (1983) suggested four curriculum components that need to be addressed: general education, specialized education, subliminal or covert education (covering growth arising from the general educational environment), and educative settings (regarding socialization). Each needs to be adapted to the special needs of the gifted, but the specialized curriculum especially needs to be defensible. There is insufficient evidence that combining individual programming with a common curriculum leads to adequate differentiation on any of Passow's four curricular elements.

Implications for Action

Although this recommended practice does not have explicit support with regard to the specialized education of the gifted, it remains defensible as a benefit to their general education and the education of all students. A major reason is that an individualized part of the curriculum can address student interests (see recommended practice No. 39), which are often quite different from the norm, and provide opportunities for mentorship (No. 55), individual exploration in the arts (No. 43), and independent study (No. 65), to cite a few ways in which this recommended practice can be implemented.

Adopting the practice will require creating time in the students' academic life. This can be accomplished by curricular compacting or rapid pacing (see recommended practice No. 62).

B. Clark (1988), Maker (1982a), Renzulli and Reis (1985), and many other authors provide a great number of ideas for combining individualized and common curricula.

Needed Research

This recommended practice is, in one sense, a restatement of the rationale for individualizing the curriculum and, as such, is defensible on grounds of common observation and logic. It also fits well with societal acceptance of a balance between collective and individual needs, though there may be a favoring of one or the other in different places and at different times.

Nevertheless, careful analyses of the outcomes of its implementation, such as reported by C. L. Lewis and Kanes (1979) and Fearn and Owen (1984), are always useful, especially as they are conducted in varying settings, with different ages, and so on. As well, there are certainly settings where this advice is ignored, on the grounds that the school believes it has a strong common curriculum that, in the judgment of its parents and staff, best serves the needs of all its students, be they diverse in abilities or not. Where these programs serve a wide range of students, their success would be evidence against this recommended practice. Such schools should be sought out and involved in comparative research. Special schools for gifted children, public or private, are not appropriate for such a study because they have implicitly adjusted some parts of the curriculum (at least the setting). The questions to be asked in each case are:

1. Has the school implemented a curriculum that combines individualization and a common curriculum?
2. Are bright students particularly well served by this arrangement? In what ways and to what extent?
3. Are any students adversely affected by this curricular arrangement? What can be done to avoid or ameliorate the problems?

Data should be collected before a program is in place, then again after a period of implementation. The combination of curricular activities needs to be made available to students of a wide range of abilities. Preferably, such studies should be conducted in classes or schools where gifted students have not yet been identified or separately served, and where high socioeconomic status and other favoring variables do not effectively reduce the range of outcomes that can be observed.

39 | **Systematically Assess Student Content Interests**

Student interests are the cornerstone of Renzulli's (1977) influential Enrichment Triad Model. He makes it clear that his focus on student content interests represents an assumption on his part, though he informally reports the importance of interests in program evaluations he has conducted:

> An almost universal finding in the evaluation work I have done in numerous programs for the gifted has been that the greatest source of student satisfaction almost always resulted from the students' freedom to pursue topics of their own choosing in a manner with which they themselves felt most comfortable. (p. 16)

Renzulli and Reis (1985) later restated the practice in terms of goals:

> One goal is to peak interests that students may already have and focus these interests into more specific areas that students may investigate or pursue. The second major goal is to develop interests in students who do not seem to exhibit any initiative, motivation, or predetermined interest in a topic or area. Therefore, we highly recommend assessing the interests of all students. (p. 60)

Roberts and Wallace (1980) and VanTassel-Baska (1985) are among the other supporters of the need to assess student interests in gifted programs.

Current Knowledge

There is little organized evidence to support or refute this practice. Goldberg (1986) cited a study by Thelen (1967), conducted at the University of Chicago Laboratory School: The school authorities

> released six outstanding sixth grade achievers from their regular school work during the last month of school to investigate independently a subject of their choice (and their teacher's approval). Three of the students turned out original, worthwhile work and found the experience highly rewarding. The other three, equally bright and academically successful students, did not do too well. It turned out that two of the students in particular needed a group setting in order to be productive. (Goldberg, 1986, p. 45)

This is a thoroughly inadequate research design, but it does offer support for Renzulli's claim that interest alone is insufficient. Group settings may offer more help getting organized, planning the project, and the like. In addition to determining interest, a teacher should also attend to the conditions under which individual students learn well.

Implications for Action

The balance between interest-based activities and an imposed curriculum was discussed in recommended practice No. 38. Assessment of interests appears to be a reasonable and economical way to address the individual curriculum. Extensive advice on collecting these data is offered by Renzulli and Reis (1985), among others.

Should one do so? We do not have answers based on studies that compare the long- and short-term outcomes of interest-based versus prescribed curricula. Such comparisons are complicated by the difficulty of categorizing as "imposed" those fixed curricula from which creative teachers make a variety of side trips based on student interests. As L. J. Coleman (1985) suggested, "Instructional activities should provide opportunities for exploring interests, discovering new interests, observing the differences between people, and interacting with other children" (p. 204).

Needed Research

The first type of needed study would be to identify a large number of programs that vary in the types and amounts of interest-based activities offered, the extent to which they may systematically assess student interests, the use of alternative sources of information to individualize activities, and the commitment of the staff to such curricular activities. Then some suitable outcome variables, such as student and other persons' satisfaction and the quality of the products, should be identified and the relation described between the assessment of interests and the kinds of benefits their recognition is intended to foster. Do students prefer or do better in portions of their programs that arise from a central curriculum than they do in those based on their interests? Is the relationship linear, or is some optimal amount of attention to interest best?

The relation between interests and motivation and the undertaking of in-depth individual or team projects could be studied on a smaller scale in individual studies. Is formal, systematic assessment of interests superior to informal judgments set during instruction or other encounters?

Does this recommended practice facilitate the development of new, productive, student interests, or does it build only on existing interests? It would be useful to search the literature thoroughly, e.g., the ERIC Documents records, for examples of programs and implementations. It might be possible to apply some summary statistical procedures to these reports.

Finally, is this recommended practice uniquely applicable to the gifted? Given an equivalent fixed curriculum, more able students might have or create more time to explore areas of interest, but does it benefit the more able to a greater degree or in different ways than it benefits students at large?

40 | Broad Curriculum Choice Should Be Available

Two ideas, "breadth" and "choice," recur with great frequency in the literature, but there is controversy. Here is an overview of the variety of replies one will encounter.

The exhortation to cast off traditional education and introduce wide student choice was exemplified by Caudill (1977)—"What can they study? Anything" (p. 93)—and Kaplan (1974): "The goals and/or objectives of the program should outline the possibilities for learning while allowing students to pursue individually what they wish to learn and do" (p. 28).

A less radical position was taken by Ehrlich (1981), Gold (1965), Maker (1982a), and VanTassel-Baska (1985), who strongly endorsed breadth or scope but did not make a great issue of choice, Gold in particular calling for "guided choice" (p. 147). Passow (1979) and Renzulli and Reis (1985) pointed out that there are different kinds of choices, for example, within a course, above and beyond a course, or between an advanced or regular course.

The Europe-based International Baccalaureate offers choices, but from among a very limited list of traditional subjects. As described by its North American director, "The program is a new application of general education theory which has been extolled and opposed for centuries" (Nicol, 1983, p. 432). This is the normal pattern for the education of able students throughout most of the world beyond North America. Marjoram (1979) pointed out that student choice eats away at breadth because students might choose not to take important subjects (the American literature on gifted girls and mathematics reveals the realization of this concern—see recommended practice No. 101). He added (Marjoram, 1983) that breadth in compulsory courses keeps the real choices of adult life open to students, though gifted students should have the option of adding additional courses. This approach acknowledges the second role of schooling beyond the learning itself, namely, the credential its successful completion provides. Why else bother with certificates and diplomas?

There is widespread agreement that a student expressing interest in a topic should be encouraged to pursue it and, indeed, that the opportunity to do so promotes interest. There is no agreement that breadth is important if it means nontraditional courses. There are contrasting opinions as to who should be making the choices: students, parents, or curriculum planners at local and higher levels.

Current Knowledge

Breadth (as well as depth) is discussed philosophically by Ward (1961/ 1980), but his admonition to include all the chief branches of knowledge may be interpreted broadly by some and narrowly by others. What to do is mostly a question of educational philosophy and policy. How to do it best is more amenable to empirical comparison, in this case.

There is no replicable evidence that gifted students are happier, learn more content or intellectual skill, generalize better from school learning, or anything else because they have exercised broader curricular choice at school.

Implications for Action

Exercising choice is an important skill which can be developed from breadth of curricular experience. Gifted programs should pursue both breadth and choice, but the state of the art leaves entirely open whether we provide the choice through the academic curriculum, extracurricular activities, student politics, sports, or whatever, and also who should decide what should be studied. While some authors implied that curricular choice should be absolute, most endorsed the opportunity for students to pursue topics of interest to them.

Needed Research

First, what are the benefits to be gained by students' exercising choices of different types: what to do at all, whether or not to take an optional course specifically designed for the gifted, to take an additional course, or to exercise topical interests within a course? Outcome variables should include basic knowledge, intellectual skills, attitudes, and—if the researchers can wait long enough—some follow-up later in the learners' lives.

Second, how broad is broad? Does breadth defined in terms of being able to study nontraditional courses have different effects on the students than breadth gained from the in-depth study of a small number of subjects? Will the high school student who experiences 10 hours a week of compulsory English literature over 4 or 5 years be missing something that an educational cafeteria has provided, or vice-versa? How might one assure that comparisons are based on equally inspired teaching in both cases, including relating specific learning to broader contexts?

A useful start might be to interview students who have experienced both regimes and solicit their opinions.

This recommended practice may not be fully confirmed or rejected on the basis of empirical data. The pursuit of an epistemological solution might be worthy, and Ward's axiomatic approach provides a useful prototype for this kind of exercise, though the language of that earlier work might be different if it were written today. Jellen and Verduin (1986), for example, have attempted this in relation to ideals of a democratic society. Depending on the premises one accepts, the variety of outcomes may still be large.

41 | Curriculum Should Be Future-Oriented

Torrance (1979b) has consistently been the strongest proponent of this practice. Bleedorn (1979) specifically addressed the curricular topic of future studies:

> Future Studies deals largely with uncertainties and emphasizes open-ended questions and divergent-thinking processes. Its natural link with intellectual challenge for Gifted and Talented children and youth is unmistakable. (p. 120)

A personal theme mentioned by several authors is that career education (see recommended practice No. 50) is future-oriented and forms a bridge between personal relevance and societal focus (E. S. Fleming, 1985). A third perspective is perhaps best described as therapeutic. Landau (1976) has argued that gifted children's views of the future are relatively pessimistic, and that this is a reason to address these concerns in school.

Current Knowledge

Several studies provide evidence that gifted children do think naturally about the future. In addition to Landau's concern that this may be in the form of a burden, Torrance, Bruch, and Goolsby (1976) reported interesting anecdotes of interviews with children. Wooddell, Fletcher, and Dixon (1982) conducted a formal experiment that did not have many significant results but that should be replicated. Their results, uniformly in the same direction, suggested cognitive and affective gains from participation in the curriculum. Even exposed to the same future-oriented curriculum as the gifted students, the nongifted children did not equal the performance of the control group of gifted children who did not participate in the program.

P. G. George and Gallagher (1978) reported an interesting comparative study that confirmed that gifted students were more pessimistic about the future, but their thinking also reflected more attention to possible solutions, whereas the less able comparison group focused on the problems. We did not find research that explored bridging the topic through career exploration, though it is discussed by Seif (1981) and Torrance (1978).

These studies lend the promise of support for the inclusion of a future-studies element in gifted education. The research literature is small and experimentally weak, but it points consistently in the same direction and is consistent with other supportable recommended practices (e.g., on creativity, high-level thinking, and career thinking).

Implications for Action

A future orientation would bear upon the history of the issue or problem at hand, and forward, extracting potential implications for the future (should present or alternative conditions prevail). Interesting possibilities for curriculum development arise. In current events (e.g., social issues such as race relations, criminal justice, "sunbelt" or "silicon valley" economic opportunities for families), one can address the forms that the problem has taken in the past, here or elsewhere in the world, how these manifestations have changed over time, and how they might look in the next 10 or 20 years. Technological and scientific events and processes—acid rain, ozone destruction, off-shore oil drilling, food supply, medical epidemics—similarly have their own stories to tell.

Futures study provides opportunities for interdisciplinary work (see recommended practice No. 31), the introduction of abstract ideas (No. 42), individualization (Nos. 26 and 38), varied methodology such as sociodramatic play and sociodrama (Torrance et al., 1976), and uncommon content, for example, the technology of peace (Joseph, 1983). With younger children, personal and family history provides a starting point.

Needed Research

Studies such as that by Wooddell et al. (1982) need to be refined and replicated in order to confirm the differential effect and appropriateness of future-oriented curricula at different age and ability levels and with different subject matter. It would be useful if the P. G. George and Gallagher (1978) study could be replicated in a curricular context, not merely as a survey. The bridge between the focus on self through careers and on the larger questions of society and knowledge needs to be explored. What preparation, if any, do teachers need to function well and to help children function well in this interdisciplinary context?

Finally, what relationships exist between the ability to do very well in a curriculum that features a future orientation and a definition of giftedness based upon various intellectual skills, e.g., creativity, abstract thinking, other high-level thinking processes, and high performance in particular subject matter? Future studies also provide a potentially valuable context in which to study the interaction of prior knowledge and intellectual processes (including creativity).

42 | Emphasize Abstract and Basic Concepts

This is a specific case of curricular differentiation for the gifted (recommended practice No. 34). Gallagher (1985) wrote:

> Since the gifted child has demonstrated manifest ability to handle a complexity of ideas far beyond his chronological age, it is natural to assume that schools sensitive to this problem will make a genuine effort to modify the content reaching these students to stress the greater complexity and higher levels of abstraction that they can comprehend. (p. 72)

Maker (1982b) made a similar assertion:

> The major focus of discussions, presentations, reading materials, and lectures in a gifted program should be on abstract concepts and generalizations. (p. 3)

Maker regarded basic facts as illustrative of abstract ideas. Freehill (1961/1982) concurred: "There should be opportunity for thorough learning of basic concepts and fundamental skills but not mere extensions in amount" (p. 226).

Current Knowledge

There is no question about the greater capability of gifted students (according to most definitions of giftedness) to be able to use abstract concepts. A curriculum that addresses this ability is therefore desirable and, if beyond the abilities of other students, differentiated.

A meta-analysis of several studies on the use of abstract or high-level questions showed that they facilitate learning in more able students (Redfield & Rousseau, 1981). Other research has reported that they did not (Winne, 1979). One study found that both lower and higher order questions were necessary (Evertson, Anderson, Anderson, & Brophy, 1980). These studies differed methodologically, and the relative impact of higher or lower order questions also has socioeconomic correlation. The different results do not indicate a controversy in the field; rather they point out the need for carefully controlled experimental studies.

The need for a focus on abstract or high-level concepts is not unambiguously established.

Implications for Action

There is every reason to attend to abstract thinking but also to recognize that it is almost certainly an insufficient curricular modification on its own and sometimes inappropriate or too difficult—for example, in difficult new subject matter where concrete examples or physical manipulation may be necessary for initial understanding, and with children who have not had adequate prior experience with abstract concepts.

Attention to the level of abstraction in discussions, written material, classroom questions, assignments, homework, and lectures, is suitably given in taxonomies such as Bloom's, covered in nearly every general text on the gifted, or guides to asking high-level questions, such as presented by Woodliffe (1977) or Taba (1975) (and summarized by Maker, 1982b).

The general curriculum assures children mobility, across school systems should the family move and between the special and regular curriculum should such a change become desirable for any reason.

Needed Research

To what extent is abstract thinking a curricular objective rather than a characteristic skill of bright students? It is necessary to be more precise about the nature of the learning being undertaken. There may be a difference, for example, between new learning of unfamiliar material and the elaboration of a secure knowledge base in a subject.

Also, is this an appropriate goal for the large majority of students? It may vary according to socioeconomic status, the nature of the assignment (cf. Maker, 1982b), ability level, and prior knowledge.

43 | **The Arts Should Be Included**

Seeley (1989) captured both the practice and the underpinnings of this practice's rationale.

> An arts curriculum is essential for the talented development of children with high potential, whether artistically gifted or academically gifted. It heightens sensitivity and creative ability. It provides emotional outlets and a medium for expression that words and numbers cannot. The arts also provide a new means of understanding and explaining complex phenomena of human endeavor and human motivation. (p. 302)

Others have also supported the inclusion of the arts in programs for the gifted (Feldhusen & Robinson, 1986; Lanza & Vassar, 1975; Marjoram, 1983). The cultural merit of including the arts is not at issue, merely research that supports their special inclusion or adaptation for bright students.

Current Knowledge

The arts generally include the visual arts, music, dance, theater, and creative writing. Ostensibly, their importance is highlighted by the inclusion of visual and performing arts as one of the areas in the United States Office of Education (U.S.O.E.) categorical definition of giftedness (U.S. Commissioner of Education, 1972—the "Marland Report").

The widespread lip service paid to this recommended practice is not reflected by an extensive knowledge base reporting either the incidence or the effectiveness of arts programming for the gifted. In their survey of program effectiveness, Weiss and Gallagher (1982) did not mention the arts at all. In the "Richardson Study," Cox, Daniel, and Boston (1985) found most of the exemplary programming for gifted students in a small number of specialized high schools and academies; F. A. Karnes, Chauvin, and Trant (1984a) found that outstanding students in such programs had distinctive personality profiles. It is likely that the arts as a component of the differential education of the gifted suffer from the same difficulty the arts in general education do—they are considered a frill.

Arts advocates have concentrated, perhaps in response, on establishing a strong rationale for their inclusion in the curriculum. J. P. Parker (1989, see p. 261) summarized and documented the arguments for inclusion of the arts in a differentiated curriculum for the gifted. For example, she reported Gowan's (1984) argument that the study of art and music stimulates creativity. She cited others who suggested the arts offer a means of self-expression, enhance the self-concept, and increase the skills of observation, abstract thinking, and problem analysis (Krippner & Blickenstaff, 1970; Szekely, 1981; R. M. Williams, 1977). Dorn (1984) commented that the arts provide an important window to understanding other cultures.

The rationale that addresses the unique needs of the gifted most directly was advanced by G. Clark and Zimmerman (1984), who examined the research on talented adult and child artists and concluded that superior performance in the visual arts requires above average intelligence and extended training.

Most of the data-based research related to this practice focused on the characteristics of talented musicians and artists and on the factors that contributed to the realization of their capabilities (Bloom, 1985; G. Clark & Zimmerman, 1983; Getzels & Csikszentmihalyi, 1976; Lark-Horovitz & Norton, 1959). Much of the work is retrospective, anecdotal, or built on case studies. One exception is an attitudinal survey of students attending the New Orleans Center for the Creative Arts (Kaufmann, Tews, & Milam, 1985). The importance of family support and teachers, mentors, and extended opportunities for practice is repeated across much of this literature.

Another body of literature relevant to the question of how the arts curriculum should be differentiated for the gifted is the debate between the creative expressionists and the art-as-a-discipline schools of thought. During the child-centered education movement of the last five decades, the value of art as creative expression led to unstructured pedagogy. It was deemed appropriate to lay out materials and let children experiment. Formal art instruction was viewed as adult interference. In contrast, the art-as-a-discipline school of thought, which has regained popularity in recent years, suggested that the visual arts require instruction and intellectual activity as well as emotional response and experimentation. G. Clark and Zimmerman (1984) pointed out that the early work on talented visual artists and Bloom's (1985) more recent investigations of sculptors and concert pianists support the value of extended instruction in the development of artistic potential.

Implications for Action

Despite the lack of empirical evidence supporting arts programming for the gifted, it is defensible on philosophical and aesthetic grounds both here and in general education. VanTassel-Baska (1989) noted that it is difficult to discuss how one might differentiate the arts curriculum for the gifted when many schools provide so few opportunities in the arts: There is simply nothing to differentiate.

G. Clark and Zimmerman (1984) suggested that the best course of action is to provide the talented child with the same kinds of tools and resources used by adult artists. Because adult artists work in many media, this encourages exploration.

G. Clark and Zimmerman (1984) and Szekely (1981) also advocated a problem-solving approach to the arts for the gifted. Influenced by the art-as-a-discipline school of thought, G. Clark and Zimmerman stated that a visual composition is the artist's solution to a problem. Therefore, an arts curriculum organized around problem solving (and its partner, problem finding) rather than around traditional foci of different media (drawing, painting, sculpture) is more defensible for the gifted student.

There are published reports of specific programs that provide guidance to the educator interested in the artistically gifted student (Galbraith, 1985; Wenner, 1985).

Needed Research

We need a status study of the incidence and types of arts programming for the gifted currently in place. Using the G. Clark and Zimmerman survey (1984) as a foundation, one might simply describe the location and kinds of arts programs that exist beyond specialized arts high schools and academies attached to adult arts institutions. Locating and describing programs at the elementary level would be particularly helpful. These studies should report how the arts are accommodated (compacting other subjects, extending the day, etc.) and what additional resources are provided.

Second, studies of curricular content and adaptations in arts programs would be useful. Marjoram (1983) noted that in the performing arts, the physical development of the child and the availability of private tutoring often affect the degree of talent displayed by the young dancer or musician. However, talented young visual artists have flourished within the public school arts curriculum. Case studies of programs that nourish such talent would contribute to the applied knowledge base.

Third, what is the impact of such programs on artistically and generally gifted students? This might be examined first through retrospective research but also through longitudinal studies (for which Getzels & Csikszentmihalyi, 1976, is a good model).

Finally, it is important to establish how art experiences for students with general or artistic abilities should be different in kind or extent from experiences in the arts for all students. How can educators recognize when this differentiation is required? What is the role of interests? A useful research program would compare the artistic expectations, processes, and products among regular classes, special art classes, and specialized schools; between generally talented and artistically talented students; and among generalist

teachers, art education specialists, and active artists, with or without specialized training on giftedness. Ethnographic methods would be appropriate.

44 | Include World Affairs and a Global Perspective

B. Clark (1988) stated that curriculum for the gifted "should provide
learning experiences for students to address the unresolved issues and problems of society and apply personal and social data to analyze, clarify and
respond to such issues and problems" (p. 286). Gallagher (1985) recommended the development of a sense of one's relationship with the environment and with fellow citizens, whereas Cox, Daniel and Boston (1985)
stated emphatically that "our very survival depends on intelligent leadership
that understands other cultures and speaks their languages" (p. 57).

Current Knowledge

World affairs is generally the purview of social studies. Both Gallagher
(1985) and Kaplan (1979) emphasized the importance of social studies to
the gifted. Kitano and Kirby (1986) contended that the human interactions
and institutions studied impact upon any gifted individual's activities regardless of the field of study ultimately chosen. They remarked that there appear
to be two major contrasting approaches to social studies education: the social
science approach and the social studies approach. In the social science approach, the curriculum consists of the content and investigative methodolo-
gies of the various social science disciplines (e.g., sociology, anthropology,
political science, and economics), consistent with the recommendations that
gifted students become firsthand inquirers (see recommended practice
No. 37).

By contrast, the social studies approach focuses on broad themes such
as change, interdependence, and resolution of conflict, congruent with the
recommendations of many educators that curriculum for the gifted emphasize broad themes and issues. Kaplan (1979) proposed an integrated social
studies curriculum for gifted elementary students structured around central
themes.

There is not a clear preference for either the social science or the social
studies approach. The issue is philosophical rather than empirical. Neither
the social studies nor the social science approach seems to have first claim on
world affairs.

Nillissen (1987) found that the major obstacles were lack of funding coupled with the idea that international studies and foreign languages are educational frills. Only a small percentage of Illinois school districts gave special attention to the teaching of international concepts. Stephens (1986) examined the status of international education in the sixth-grade classrooms of Ohio public schools. Only 18% of 237 randomly selected schools referred to international education.

The literature does mention materials with world-affairs content: an honors social studies course incorporating the study of cultural universals for Grades 8–10 (Clendening & Davies, 1983); an integrated English and social studies unit for Grade 7 (Maker, 1982a); and a modified world-history course (Lasher, 1986). A program developed for students of Hunter College Elementary School also used an interdisciplinary approach (Seldman & Spain, 1983) for an in-depth study of the Aztec and Mayan Indians using a variety of resources such as *National Geographic* materials and museum resources. An evaluation reported by Seldman and Spain (1983) revealed that the overall program expanded the students' knowledge of the history of the Americas and gave the students additional insights for drawing comparisons between cultures.

World affairs are often implicit in future studies. There is a basic human need to have some image of the future in order to have a confident basis for present actions (Plowman, 1980). The Center for Global Futures in the Burris Laboratory School at Ball State University serves students in Grades 5–12 and is an example of a future-studies program with an international focus. Credit classes, pull-out classes, and seminars focus on issues and aspects of global futures, while emphasizing active student involvement and the tailoring of courses and seminars to the needs of the gifted (Kolloff, 1983). Whether interwoven into the curriculum or presented as a separate course, global futures are seen to offer exciting opportunities to encourage analysis and creativity (Becker, 1982).

The assumption that gifted students, as likely leaders of the future, need opportunities to study world affairs is reasonable and logically consistent. How the study of world affairs should be differentiated for the gifted is less obvious. Differentiation appears to be only generically addressed in the form of higher order thinking skills and abstract thinking. Neither question has been the object of formal study beyond reflection.

Implications for Action

Social justice demands that all the citizenry should have opportunities to inform themselves of world affairs.

Currently, the best course is to make the study of world affairs available to gifted students through whatever general program options are in place in the school. Specialized secondary social studies courses, seminars, or journalism clubs are likely vehicles. At the elementary level, teachers could infuse world affairs in the grade-level social studies curriculum, and gifted facilitators might use world affairs as the impetus for individual investigations and projects.

Needed Research

Studies are needed on existing curricula and programs to evaluate their effectiveness. It is important to develop concise definitions of what constitutes "world affairs." Sometimes referred to as "global education" or "global studies," interventions vary widely in scope—ranging from enhancing leadership skills and developing an appreciation for cultural differences to futures studies, peace education, and ethics.

Equally important is an examination of the attitudes of educators toward global studies, to determine its value relative to the overall curriculum and the gifted curriculum in particular. Dirkes (1981) states that society turns to the gifted for solutions concerning social welfare, environmental protection, and world peace. To what degree do educators and administrators share his viewpoint, and how will that viewpoint drive the curriculum? What kinds of issues can be dealt with and by whom? In the United States, some schools have dropped or avoided world affairs and global education in the face of a paper entitled "Blowing the whistle on global education" (cited in Wronski, Fair, Boyes, & Fullinwider, 1987). This paper charges that the global education movement is, in general, a reflection of the viewpoints of the political left. The problem may well be political as well as pedagogical.

45 | Microcomputers Should Be Included

Trifiletti's (1985) chapter was the first in textbooks on gifted education to specifically advocate the use of microcomputers with the gifted, in a variety of uses from programming to applications.

> Gifted children who program computers must teach the computer how to think and solve problems. In doing so, they gain valuable insight into their own thought processes. (p. 317)

As this practice is increasingly advocated, the types of uses need clarification. The presentation that follows draws heavily (sometimes verbatim) on the advice presented by Shore, Kanevsky, and Rejskind (1991), who strongly favor uses that address thinking processes that distinguish gifted persons, including creativity, metacognitive skills and knowledge, and exploration of high-level subject matter.

Current Knowledge

Some interesting theory is developing on this topic, but little empirical research is yet available.

Adults use microcomputers primarily for writing, information management, communication, and recreation. These allow extensive opportunity for creativity, exploring alternative ideas, and communicating with peers.

> What makes the computer stand out (among information technologies) is its ability to represent information in many different ways, and to switch instantly between alternative representations. (Shavelson & Salomon, 1986, p. 24)

Gifted people are generally good at problem solving, but they are notably good at problem finding (Getzels & Csikszentmihalyi, 1976). This involves asking questions rather than merely answering those to which others already know the replies.

This is compatible with characteristics of giftedness. Spreadsheets and databases allow different perspectives of data, if the user asks good questions. The computer nearly instantly recalculates data, rescales a drawing, reformats the text, or exposes alternatives in multiple windows. Time is redirected from recalculating, retyping, or redrawing the information needed to answer a single question to asking good questions; creativity becomes the primary activity. Such environments take account of cognitive skills in which bright people already excel or have high potential. Research also indicates that highly competent people, like experts, use more time planning solutions to complex tasks and less time actually executing them (Davidson & Sternberg, 1984; Lajoie & Shore, 1986; Ludlow & Woodrum, 1982). Computers capitalize on these types of thinking (cf. Olson, 1985; Shavelson & Salomon, 1985).

One study compared gifted and average-ability teams of students in the writing and execution of LOGO routines (Maniatis, 1983). The gifted students created more complex designs involving more turtle moves and subroutines. This study demonstrated that general software was used differently by gifted pupils and in ways consistent with cognitive qualities of giftedness.

Beasley (1985) proposed that "Computer literacy for the gifted differs from computer literacy for other students in the same ways that other aspects of curriculum for the gifted differ" (p. 157). He and R. A. Jensen and Wedman (1983) also endorsed the emphasis on high-level intellectual skills.

Consistent with early research, Kanevsky (1985) found no significant differences in basic mathematics learning among gifted students in computer-assisted or traditional methods, but within the computer groups, cooperative instructional environments seemed more appropriate for high-level, problem-solving activities. Koetke (1983) presented a similar bridge to offering advice on the use of microcomputers with gifted students:

> When dealing with the gifted student, learning to program simply isn't advanced—it's fundamental. Teaching the gifted to program is mostly a matter of providing resources; programming itself will not be a major challenge. . . . Once the gifted have developed their programming skills, however, they are prepared to undertake applications of their skills that can be correctly labeled "advanced." (p. 270)

We have a small amount of empirical evidence that bright students might use computers differently from others, but no evidence that they systematically do so. To the extent that computing as an intellectual tool might extend the performance of any computer user, we are not in a position to say that the use of microcomputers has a special place in gifted education; it may, if well done, have a special place in education for all.

Implications for Action

Computers in classrooms must extend quality curricula, not substitute for inadequate schooling. Olson (1986) noted, specifically, that "Computing is an extension of activities and competencies already well underway in literacy" (p. 24).

Good computing experiences are desirable for all children, and gifted children should share these, including ensuring interest and participation on the part of girls in what is often seen as a boys' domain. Many people fear computers; particular attention might be given to the control it can give over their learning and working situation (Dover, 1983). Software should be entertaining as well as informative. Computer experience also opens doors to employment or entrepreneurial opportunities. This is compatible with bright children's early propensity for career thinking (see recommended practice No. 49).

Try not to be drawn into hardware or software that is described as "easy" or "for children." Simple databases may not permit rearranging the means of input, or the format of reports. Low-level word processors frequently do not enable one to embed commands to turn on special printer features and do not produce accents or convert files so they can be exchanged; they may be slow or unable to combine files, move around text with ease, or produce a file more than a few pages long. Price is only a moderate guide to quality. Excessively "simple" programs do not give the user enough control. Adults may be afraid of complex programs, but bright children usually are not.

Be cautious of claims of "artificial intelligence" in software. First, such applications are at best primitive; some are total misrepresentations. Second, it is a bad educational goal to have the computer actually do what we want to teach: thinking. We want it to facilitate and enhance our thinking. Suhor (1986) observed that word-processing programs "cannot detect unwarranted leaps of logic, specific failures to provide appropriate information, or the need to anticipate an adversary's squelching argument" (p. 23). Much preferred is a real debating partner, on-line if necessary.

We are particularly attracted to the following advice by Dickson (1985):

> The use of microcomputers to enrich metacognitive awareness, social awareness, and competence in culturally valued productive symbol systems ought to have the highest claim on this precious resource in schools and homes. (p. 30)

One way gifted youngsters can distinguish themselves is in their potential to operate at the frontiers of knowledge in a subject of interest, in ways similar to experts. Metacognitive awareness is partly aided by tasks in which monitoring and self-evaluation are valuable. These include strategy games, writing, and drawing. Social awareness is enhanced in many ways: simulations of important social or political decision making, communications, electronic publishing, working with another person at the computer. Dickson's reference to "competence in culturally valued productive symbol systems" is relevant to more able people's facility with abstracts.

To know what a bright child should do with a computer, perhaps we should ask how a capable adult might take advantage of a computer environment. For example, a flexible database with graphic capabilities provides opportunities to change the representation of data (from one's stamp collection to reports on radiation leaks). A flexible word processor facilitates the review and revision of what one has written (so rarely done with a pencil), an attractive presentation of the results (in contrast to many gifted children's illegible handwriting), and the exchange of ideas (via a modem with an electronic pen pal).

Needed Research

Descriptive research, perhaps ethnographic, is needed on the uses of computers by children, alone and in class, and by adults. How do these uses correspond to experience and instruction? Can the use of microcomputers with the gifted have the indicated effects on thinking? Are these effects unique for the gifted? Can such microcomputing experiences enhance the intellectual abilities of children of different ability levels in different ways? Is programming fundamental? How much emphasis should be placed on adult-level application programs? Is the thinking of highly able students more similar to that of adult experts when engaged in working with a computer?

46 | Thinking Skills Should Be Taught

Nearly every writer on gifted education has commented on the importance of fostering clear, creative, critical thinking. VanTassel-Baska (1985) stated the general principle that

> development of process skills should be viewed as basic to their curriculum and begin as soon as they enter school. These "basics for the gifted" would reflect practice in the following skill areas:
> —critical thinking
> —creative thinking
> —problem solving
> —research
> —decision making.
> Each of these skills should be linked directly to a content domain. (p. 53)

Callahan (1985) narrowed the focus to "productive (creative), complex, abstract, and/or higher level thinking skills" (p. 195) in an attempt to specify how such training should be different for the gifted, and Freehill (1961/1982) anticipated that concern and suggested that gifted education implies "increasing awareness of the learning process on the part of the learner" (p. 157).

Current Knowledge

This recommendation is ubiquitous, but there is little research support for practices commonly implemented with the gifted or with others. Conference exhibits and educational publishers' catalogues are filled with assorted thinking-skills packages. There are workshops, summer institutes, and seminars devoted to these practices. Some, such as the Structure of the Intellect (SOI) (Meeker, 1969), de Bono's Cognitive Research Trust (CoRT) (de Bono, 1982; Maier, 1982), and Parnes's Creative Problem Solving (CPS) (cf. Maker, 1982b—especially see pp. 177–205), are extremely elaborate. Some, including Sternberg's (1986b), have a substantial research base. A much larger number have more intuitive origins; these are frequently linked to the development of creativity, but other types of skills are also represented.

Most major skills packages have a published literature illustrating their application with the gifted, for example, Maier's (1982) description of the use of CoRT at the University of Toronto Schools and reports in the SOI literature (Meeker & Meeker, 1986). In most cases the criterion for success in the training is progress through or within the levels of the particular program itself. As VanTassel-Baska (1985) observed, little in the research literature supports the generalization of thinking-skills training to specific domains.

One study (Baldwin, 1981) field-tested a program designed to teach high-level processes in the form of critical and constructive thinking. The study included independent administration of the materials to gifted and nongifted experimental and control groups. There were no differences between experimental and control groups at either ability level, and under both conditions the gifted students performed better than the controls. We laud the courage required to publish this study because it highlights most of the difficulties faced in such research. First, the main criterion, the Watson-Glaser Appraisal of Critical Thinking (Watson & Glaser, 1964), primarily assesses ability to recognize flawed arguments; this does not necessarily require the same skills as constructive and critical thinking. A more discourse-focused approach might have yielded positive differences. Second, the original training program may not have been effective. Third, the study applied the measures only to the post-test results, whereas interesting data might lie in differential gains resulting from exposure to good instruction. That suggests a fourth potential problem: One never knows how well one's instructions will be followed in the field. Nonetheless, we have one experimental study and the results are negative.

Little in the giftedness literature directly addresses the intellectual skills that define high performance. Such research is very recent (cf. Horowitz & O'Brien, 1985; Shore, 1986; Sternberg & Davidson, 1986), but it does indicate that there may be some ways that gifted persons differ from others in how they think. It is interesting that they appear to do so without special training, and that the value of training may be to improve the intellectual performance of all people, identified as gifted or not (cf. Ghatala, Levin, Pressley, & Lodico, 1985).

The ways more able people think differently from others was very nicely anticipated by Seiger (1984) in an article that, interestingly, makes no reference to the cognitive literature in which the research is appearing. He stated,

They need to be more than thinkers, they need to become thinking *strategists*—people who know when and how to use various thinking skills in particular, systematic ways in order to produce thought products of the desired quantity and quality for a given situation. (p. 186)

The skills to which Seiger referred are part of what is now called metacognition, which was first studied in cognitive research into expertise. Recent studies above have suggested that these skills are characteristic of the gifted as well, though experts may learn them and their history in individual gifted persons has barely been studied (Gardner & Hatch, 1989).

A major unanswered general question in cognitive science is the degree to which the intellectual skills are general or content-specific. D. N. Perkins and Salomon (1989) surveyed the literature on both sides of the issue and concluded that the two must in some way interact. Do they interact differently in the very able? Is there a different degree of dependence of one upon the other? Does this relationship vary across disciplines or for different intellectual skills?

In conclusion, there is little support for the widespread practice of teaching thinking skills as special curricula for gifted students. There is good and improving evidence for the soundness of the general principle if the focus is placed on the processes by which strategies are selected, planned, evaluated, and adjusted. Gifted students might be more able to think actively about their thinking, and curriculum can be differentiated to take that into account. Such extrapolations are, however, only beginning to appear in the literature, with one notable exception: Gifted children should be steered toward knowledge production rather than knowledge consumption (Polette, 1982; Renzulli, 1977).

Implications for Action

Specific thinking-skill training packages that arise from general practice and do not relate explicitly to ways in which more able children differ from others in their intellectual processes are not suitable curriculum for bright students.

Thinking skills should be regarded in terms of thinking strategies, and these processes should not be taught in isolation or artificial situations. They must be related to specific subject matter, because there appear to be subtle differences among domains in the kinds of strategies that are used to create new knowledge in them. Freeman (1985a) expressed it well:

Children should learn how to obtain information and put it into a form in which it may later be retrieved. This implies that they must have a full understanding of the material as well as the higher-level abilities to synthesize from it, and to follow through to novel understandings. Problem-solving skills should be built in to teaching in many subject areas, so that pupils are obliged to think for themselves. The skills of communicating what they have found are as important as the discoveries themselves, and should be taught and practiced in schools. (p. 17)

Use thinking skills or strategy training in the context of helping able and perhaps all youngsters experience the thought of an expert in pursuing new understandings (see recommended practice No. 37). There will be more than one means to this end. The goal is a large, adaptable repertoire of intellectual strategies related to and between domains of knowledge. Interdisciplinary activities might enable the comparisons of different strategies. B. G. Rogers (1983) offered some specific suggestions about the implications of metacognition for educating teachers, including avoiding isolated thinking-skill activities, encouraging self-inquiry and monitoring of one's thinking in the course of regular activities, and facilitating introspection about one's own learning processes. She points out that teachers-in-training are not always accomplished learners in this sense, and they need the experiences as much as the children they will teach.

This advice is highly speculative but also very suggestive of the research that needs to be done.

Needed Research

Theoretical work still needs to be done in educational and cognitive psychology, such as defining the level of understanding and skills needed in a discipline so as to begin to be able to ask good questions. The greatest practical need is probably to validate the advice just given in the previous section. There are some important considerations in the design of the studies. First, it must be shown that the training proposed is in some way more appropriate (and not harmful) for brighter students, for example, that it does not accomplish the same goals for others nor does it interfere with effective strategies the child may have already developed. Second, there must be experimental and control groups; it is not sufficient to show only that the procedures work for bright children. If they work equally for all children, then the advice belongs in the general educational literature, not the gifted literature.

It is important to explore the differences in the applications of such training in different single and interdisciplinary subject areas. There are opportunities for decades of curricular studies in virtually every domain.

Finally, what kinds of training do teachers in general and of the gifted need to be able to foster these types of intellectual processes in children?

47 | **Communication Skills Should Be Taught**

The special role of communication skills for highly able students is frequently portrayed in the literature. It is a multifaceted question. Two main sets of skills are encountered: academic communication in the form of good speech, writing, and understanding of verbal material, and social communication in the form of being able to interact effectively on general matters with adults and other young people. A third feature of communication has been receiving renewed attention, the acquisition of second languages (Feldhusen, 1985b; Tempest, 1974).

P. A. Alexander and Muia (1982) offered a typical argument for the academic skills:

> To function as effective communicators, gifted learners must possess many skills. They must be good listeners, attentive to the message being delivered. They must learn to question themselves and others about the information they encounter. Also, it is important that gifted students skillfully compare the ideas communicated with the knowledge that they already possess, carefully weighing one against the other. (p. 227)

Passow (1980b) regarded these abilities as "foundation skills for advanced, specialized endeavors" and "precursors to any original creative thought" (p. 26). From this perspective, communication skills are seen as part of a package of critical thinking skills widely advocated for the gifted (Goldberg, Passow, & Lorge, 1958/1980; Hill, 1967/1983).

Freehill (1961/1982) expressed the strongest links amongst these different facets:

> The gifted person . . . has a special need for communication skills, research skills, and group skills. He should be proficient in discovery, research, critical thinking, and persuasion. . . . The research and study skills are inseparably associated with the group and communication skills. (p. 249)

This association is visible in several areas of adult activity, as illustrated by Perrone and Male (1981):

> Cooperation and communication are commonplace among talented persons who focus on social and environmental problems. This is evidenced by the growth of research centers and "think tanks." (p. 41)

This emphasis on teamwork has been endorsed as well by Maker (1977) and Sellin and Birch (1980).

Current Knowledge

The journal literature on this topic offers a large number of program descriptions, for example, Dearborn (1979) on journal writing, Master (1984) on writing, and Swicord (1984) on debating. In much greater prominence than in the book literature are articles on second-language learning as curriculum for the highly able (e.g., Feldhusen & Hoover, 1984; Llanes, 1980; Rosenbusch & Draper, 1985).

We located but one experimental study. Stoddard and Renzulli (1983) compared bright students' writing samples before and after the students were exposed to specific training in writing skills and creative writing. One group was pulled out specifically for this program; the other received it within regular classrooms. Better quality writing ensued for all the students, but even more so for the in-class than the pull-out groups. It was not clear what effect overall grading or other practices might have played in this observation. In any case, this study indicated that these interventions can work.

There is one pervasive anomaly that should be pointed out. The need for guidance in interpersonal relations, discourse, argument, and the like, exists clearly in groups and classes where there is no prevailing extraordinary educational provision, as well as among the exceptionally able. There is no evidence offered that communications skills of all types, including second languages, are especially appropriate for the gifted or need to be specially adapted.

One suggestion of the special relevance of this recommended practice comes from P. A. Alexander and Muia (1982) concerning the comparison of old and new knowledge; this fits well with research showing that gifted learners resemble experts in their use of prior knowledge and its integration with new (E. B. Coleman & Shore, in press) (also see recommended practice No. 37). On the other hand, many of the proponents placed communication among critical-thinking skills, and the differentiated importance of these as curricula is not well substantiated (see recommended practice No. 46). Canadian second-language immersion programs began in the 1960s with selective admissions for more able students, and such criteria are sometimes still applied, but a large body of research has shown that students of all abilities learn more in this environment than they would by other means (Genesee, 1987). Is the premise underlying the proposals for social communicative skills that the intellectually highly able are deficient socially, or in special need of communication skills?

Overall, although there is evidence, and certainly testimony, that communication-skills programs work well with gifted students, the premise for using them is unclear. The term has several diverse meanings, and there is evidence that they are more aptly part of good general education.

Implications for Action

Communications skills in all forms are quite defensible as general curriculum. Their special applicability for the gifted is not supported by research.

Needed Research

This recommended practice needs to be examined in very fine detail. First, it should be studied within the separate categories of verbal and related skills, persuasive or social skills, and second-language learning.

Within verbal and related skills, some may be especially suitable for highly able children or especially within their abilities. These include such skills as judging the quality of arguments, organizing one's knowledge, and relating new learning to these structures. Interventions need to be studied one specific skill at a time. The extent to which these are foundation skills for more advanced and especially creative activity could be studied explicitly.

Social-skills training has hardly been studied at all, though there has been some interest in leadership as a curricular objective for the gifted (see recommended practice No. 85). Is one talking about remedial attention to perceived deficits among gifted children, or taking advantage of special assets, on a skill-by-skill basis? Possible relations amongst these abilities also need to be explored; studies of creative adults working collaboratively should be a part of this.

The second-language issue is clearer. The studies reported and reviewed by Genesee (1987) make it evident that similar instructional approaches can work well with children of different abilities and lead to considerable linguistic gains, commensurate with ability. Second-language programs (especially immersion, that is, the full school day spent in the second language) might be an impediment to the exploration of creativity and high-level performance until children master the second languages, and, even then, their homes and libraries may be ill-equipped in that language. These special considerations are worthy of study, more so than the overall argument that languages are especially appropriate curriculum for the gifted.

48 | **Humanistic Values Should Be Developed**

The preponderance of writing about gifted education has concerned scholastic performance.

> Talents anciently thought virtuous: the talent to love, to understand, to empathize, to be compassionate, to be of service to others. . . . They need as any other to be discovered and encouraged. (Getzels, 1981, p. 7)

Hoyt and Hebeler (1974) made a similar, if less impassioned, plea: "More attention must be given to those gifted in areas of leadership and humanistic development" (p. 58). Maker (1982b) strongly endorsed the recommended practice and cited Ward's (1961/1980) early advocacy for a moral and personal component in gifted curriculum. Maker also cited the relevance of Kohlberg's (1975/1978) work on moral development, though levels of moral development were not conceived in relation to intellectual or creative abilities.

Current Knowledge

Wolf and Stephens (1985) also cited Kohlberg's work and mentioned a study by S. Hoffman (1977) that showed modest relations between IQ and Kohlberg's stages, as also reported by Diessner (1983). In addition, they cited the first edition of B. Clark (1988) to the effect that "a sense of justice appears at an earlier age in gifted children and that they are often concerned with serious issues such as death, divorce, and world hunger in advance of their nongifted peers" (Wolf & Stephens, 1985, p. 84). Beyond this the journal literature deals primarily with advocacy for such curricula (e.g., Bear, 1983), occasional references to relevance to leadership development (see Lindsay, 1981b), and program ideas (e.g., Fantini, 1981; Lindsay, 1981a; R. G. Nelson, 1981).

Shore, Gagné, Larivée, Tali, and Tremblay (1983) presented five chapters under the heading "Giftedness Deflected," three of which discussed the susceptibility of gifted young people to delinquency. M. Parker (1983) claimed that gifted delinquents had strong survival instincts, and King (1983) showed that bright children in certain types of rural settings were at risk. On the other hand, Tremblay (1983) did not find differences in the nature of delinquency between high- and lower-IQ boys admitted for treatment. These studies marginally address a matter of humanistic development, but the outcomes are not consistent.

There is no convincing evidence that directly supports the recommended practice as particularly applicable to the gifted.

Implications for Action

The importance of humanistic development is indisputable, though the strength of the argument lies in our societal values, not in psychology or pedagogy, and not in gifted education. Our use of this term refers to valuing people and the things that are important to them, and being respectful of relationships among them; it does not presume any particular doctrine of humanism, secular or religious. Humanistic development belongs to the arena of good general education. Any program for gifted students that, in whole or part, removes students from the general program should include such a component, for the benefit of all children.

Societal attitudes and deeply rooted convictions being what they are, it is unlikely that genuine attainment of more enlightened understandings and uses can be developed immediately in all situations. Everyone might agree on the importance of being good and serving humanity, until one tries to define these terms operationally. On the side of reason lie compacted global interconnections and contacts through satellite television, travel, sports, the arts, and international student exchanges as well as the dramatic lessening of some tensions in the late 1980s between the Eastern and Western worlds. On the other side are disintegrating sociocultural value patterns, religious dogma, and personal avarice. Although it is not inappropriate to encourage the prospects of leadership in exceptionally able young people, this must be done along with the anticipation (and encouragement!) of understandings, conscience, and willingness on the part of the population at large.

Needed Research

Do some kinds of gifted children have special needs in this context? Are gifted children more at risk on some dimensions of humanistic development?

Can values be instilled at school, and will these values generalize beyond school in place and time? What other agencies are the desirable or necessary allies in this effort? Churches, community services to youth, neighborhood groups, television networks, the home? Further work would be welcome relating Kohlberg's ideas to questions of identification and programming with the very able. This would require careful and narrow definition of all terms and attention not only to total scores on tests but the processes by which able students approach the moral dilemmas, processes that might distinguish them from other learners. Finally, the impact of advocacy could be studied. This could be an interesting arena for the "gifted move-ment" to forge links with other educational concerns.

49 | Include Career Education, Especially for Girls

There is broad agreement on the need for career education for the gifted (e.g., B. Clark, 1988; Delisle, 1985b; E. S. Fleming, 1985; Hoyt & Hebeler, 1974). Several proponents refer to the particular needs of gifted girls (Frederickson, 1979; Harding & Berger, 1979) and specifically to math-ematical and scientific career opportunities (Fox, 1979a). Rodenstein, Pfle-ger, and Colangelo (1979) captured the overall sentiment:

> Gifted and talented students have career development needs that differ from other students'. Gifted and talented girls have career development needs dif-ferent from gifted and talented boys. (p. 389)

Current Knowledge

The overall need of the gifted (and other children) for career educa-tion is strongly endorsed, as well as the need for some differentiation of that component. Delisle's (1982b) longitudinal survey showed that the absence of such exposure led to later disadvantages for bright students in making satisfactory vocational decisions. B. Clark (1988) reported a study in which gifted students rated their career education as the most positive part of their high school experience, ahead of extracurricular activities, and far ahead of anything else, including the overall enrichment program (see p. 524). The most important elements distinguishing gifted children are their multiple in-terests (which make decisions harder) and their competence (which opens additional and rare work opportunities).

There is one partially dissenting voice. Howley (1989) suggested that young people are not ready to work out conflicts between what he called careerism (the drive for high pay and status) and intellectualism (more re-lated to seeking high satisfaction). The literature broadly supports the claim that many gifted people are unhappy with their work, whichever route they take. Perhaps his objection is to career education based on career choice above all. He might not object to career education that placed the emphasis on learning more about oneself, in the context of broad career awareness and keeping options open.

Although most authors argue that gifted girls need special attention in this regard (Fox & Tobin, 1978; Kerr, 1985), the essence of these arguments seems to be that girls and especially gifted girls have been disadvantaged in career opportunity, which is a function of society. Endless data support this view (Betz & Fitzgerald, 1987). On the other hand, the personal characteristics of gifted girls that may be relevant have not been studied as extensively. Some research indicates very similar career and family ambitions for gifted boys and girls, though there are some motivational differences to be resolved (Dolny, 1985), such as girls being more likely to discount their abilities, hence avoid certain occupations. Dolny's study was conducted in a highly selective school for academically gifted students; this might have influenced the results and limited their generalizability. Nevitte, Gibbins, and Coding (1988), however, noted that from among males and females already enrolled in undergraduate science, males were more likely to continue to graduate science studies, and, among females, the above average but not most outstanding undergraduates continued.

Implications for Action

Career education should be a central part of a comprehensive program of services for the gifted. It is relatively easy to implement, it should start no later than during preadolescence, and it should address a wide variety of occupations and the educational paths that lead to these choices (see Delisle, 1984, and most of the other references cited for many practical ideas). The program should take account specifically of multiple abilities, high levels of competence, and the considerable interest of these children in extended education; it should also consider the risks of young people leaping into specific career choices without gaining an understanding of their motivation, interests, and breadth of options. Attend explicitly to sex-role stereotypes in thinking about careers, involve appropriate role models especially for the girls (see recommended practice No. 53), and take care to deal diplomatically with cultural differences that may influence parental views in this regard. In many cases these parental views will take the form of limitations on occupations for females, and the goals of the school and expectations or traditions of the home will conflict.

Needed Research

Is it sufficient to offer gifted girls the same appropriate, high-quality career education as gifted boys, or do they require additional differentiation (also see our discussion of role models in recommended practice No. 53)? To what extent should career education have career choice as a goal?

Delisle (1985b) pointed out four research-worthy topics identified by E. L. Herr (1976):

1. Are there ideal careers for the gifted?
2. Might career education overemphasize society's expectations at the expense of fulfilling personal needs?
3. Can career education open doors for disadvantaged gifted children or those whose parents are strongly trying to guide their career choice?
4. What role can be encouraged for out-of-school apprenticeships?

Finally, there remains a need for research that examines the processes by which most able female students undertake advanced and nontraditional studies, e.g., in mathematics and science. Why do they avoid or persist in such studies and careers?

CHAPTER FOUR

Advice to Educators

| 50 | **Reading Should Be Highly Individualized** |

> The reading program should be highly individualized. With early and accurate assessment of children's abilities, the teacher can individualize the reading program for the gifted child. By analyzing his strengths and weaknesses in reading skills, the teacher may decide where he will profit from individual instruction. Each child should be permitted, indeed be encouraged to move ahead as rapidly as he desires and is able to proceed. (J. B. Nelson & Cleland, 1975, p. 446)

J. B. Nelson and Cleland also suggested that reading for the gifted should develop higher level thinking skills and extend interest in reading by gifted students. Similar recommendations were made by Cushenbery and Howell (1974).

Current Knowledge

Educators widely share the opinion that gifted reading programs are needed (Anderson, Tollefson, & Gilbert, 1985; Boothby, 1980; Dawkins, 1978; S. Jensen, 1979; Tresize, 1978; Witty, 1971). The provisions being made have been reported in at least two surveys.

McCormick and Swassing (1982) surveyed 149 school districts and found that most gifted reading instruction takes place within the classroom and is highly dependent on the interest and ability of the regular classroom teacher. The most frequently used program was Junior Great Books, which teaches students to apply higher level thinking skills to reading assignments. Mangieri and Madigan (1984) surveyed 150 school districts and found the focus of most programs was enrichment rather than individualized instruction. Basals were the primary means of reading instruction for the gifted, and most of it was done by classroom teachers untrained in individualized reading instruction for gifted readers. Dole and Adams (1983) found few differences between provisions for the gifted and developmental reading programs. Martin and Cramond (1983) found wide agreement that creative reading should be taught but that little such reading is experienced by students.

A few reports of the characteristics of effective individualized reading programs for the gifted are available. Stevens (1980) found interest level to be important in gifted readers' comprehension. Martin (1984) studied gifted students who had poor reading attitudes and found instruction could be improved if, among other things, these students were involved in selecting their reading material, time was taken to develop interest in the materials, and the attitudes and interests of the students were taken into account.

The literature does not make a strong case that bright students benefit uniquely from highly individualized reading or that special pedagogy is needed.

Implications for Action

Individualizing reading programs for the gifted is as useful as doing so for any children.

Some of the specific advice one finds are assessment of children's reading skills (Bonds & Bonds, 1983), flexible scheduling and clustering of precocious young readers (N. E. Jackson, 1988a, 1988b), and the use of trade books instead of basals (W. Brown & Rogan, 1983; Cushenbery & Howell, 1974). After reviewing several basal readers, Caldwell (1985) found there were no provisions made for early readers.

W. Brown and Rogan (1983) suggested that gifted early readers should be problem solvers, problem finders and evaluators, and that they should learn to use critical judgment. Criscuolo (1986) suggested activities that ask gifted students to rate the books they read critically. Biersdorf (1979) recommended having young gifted students read selections such as the "Clifford" books using literary analysis and critical judgment.

For older students, Cassidy (1981) proposed "inquiry reading" where students read while doing research on topics of interest. Boothby (1980) suggested using DRTA (Directed-Reading-Thinking-Activity) with gifted students.

Individualization of reading instruction is often hampered by the lack of expertise of many teachers with regard to children's books (Mangieri & Isaacs, 1983). However, several guides are available to books appropriate in different ways for gifted children (Flack & Lamb, 1984—gifted characters and activities; Mangieri & Isaacs, 1983—categories and grade levels; Vida, 1979—genres; Pennington, 1984—a rating scale; Schlichter, 1984—Types I, II, and III Triad). Pennington (1984) offered a useful scale for evaluating the appropriateness of books for use with gifted readers. A more recent text on reading for bright students (Halstead, 1988) offers suggestions for specific reading and complementary activities that are less dependent on series or packaged materials than those recommended by many others. Her recommendations are consistent with "whole language" curricula at the elementary level, because they suggest bridges between the reading program and other parts of the curriculum. Her literature selections are international.

Needed Research

Long-term studies should be undertaken to determine what differential effects individualized reading programs have on gifted readers. Beyond word knowledge and comprehension, studies should include reading interest, reading for recreation, and appreciation for books and literary pursuits.

Second, studies are needed that examine the components of individualized reading programs. When are critical and creative reading strategies most effectively introduced? How are research skills best integrated into the reading program? These might be accomplished by case studies of classrooms.

Third, comparative studies of the use of basals versus trade books with the gifted should be undertaken. Does the controlled vocabulary of basals suppress new word knowledge and depress motivation to read for pleasure?

51 | Extracurricular Activities Should Be Encouraged

Extracurricular activities are advocated as forms of enrichment of specific curricular (Allen, 1983; Gold, 1965) and social (Freeman, 1985b) needs of the gifted, such as meeting other people with whom they can identify. Also:

> Extracurricular activities can create opportunities especially for gifted children to explore new and challenging experiences, particularly if the group is small and the activities are unusual or the result of a teacher's enthusiasm or hobby. Often in this situation there are opportunities for the exchange of ideas in an informal atmosphere on a one-to-one basis, the chance to work in breadth and depth. (Roberts & Wallace, 1980, p. 130)

Equally important, though less often mentioned, are the needs of children simply to have fun, to choose their companions, and to engage in physical activities such as sport or games.

Current Knowledge

There is no direct research available on the desirability of extracurricular activities for the gifted, though there are reports of levels of participation. The only extensive research deals with accelerants, who may be a distinct category of gifted pupils. The results are divided between reports of no differences in extracurricular participation (Glazer & Shore, 1984; W. A. Herr, 1937; Klausmeier, Goodin, & Tuckla, 1968; Terman & Oden, 1947) and more participation by the accelerated (Hobson, 1963/1979; Keys, 1938; A. J. Miller, 1937; Wilson, 1951). Michael (1958) was correct that there is no evidence that capable students participate less in extracurricular activities. These data support the suggestion that the gifted may not be in any greater need of encouragement to take part in such activities than anyone else.

Implications for Action

Congdon (1980) wisely cautions that gifted children, like all others, need contact with other children and time and space to play, including the pursuit of hobbies. He suggests that "it is far more valuable to give *time* to children than to give *things,* and gifted children have a special need for time" (p. 152), especially from parents. Time is also relevant to their curiosity, question asking, and frequently lesser need for sleep. Of course, free time and extracurricular activities are not the same; a child may use free time for extracurricular activities. If some degree of participation in the latter is compulsory, we have a potentially very different situation.

Cushenbery and Howell (1974) offer several suggestions for extracurricular activities, which Compton (1982) suggests should be part of the regular school day.

It is interesting that British authors were especially visible in support of this recommended practice. It may reflect differences in expectations for the regular school program between Britain and North America.

Needed Research

We suggest that the various claimed advantages of extracurricular activities be examined. In addition, it would be helpful for schools and agencies now offering differentiated recreational activities for the gifted to document their work. We need evidence that these activities serve different needs in the gifted and others, and whether or not, given the choice, gifted students prefer and elect different kinds of activities. The extent to which participation is optional is relevant.

International comparisons of the role of extracurricular activities in the curriculum for the gifted would be useful.

52 | Continuous Program Evaluation Is Necessary

The essential point of this recommended practice is not merely that programs should be evaluated but that this evaluation should be an ongoing, dynamic practice:

> Evaluation should be an essential and ongoing part of total programming. (Renzulli, 1975a, p. 1)

> Before educators set out to collect and analyze information about their gifted programs, they must ask themselves exactly what it is they wish to know or want others to know about their projects. (P. A. Alexander & Muia, 1982, p. 280)

> Even after a program for the gifted has been established in a school, evaluation must be constantly undertaken in order to keep the program vibrant and ever improving. (Syphers, 1972, p. 60)

The knowledge necessary to support this recommendation is not the technical expertise involved in conducting evaluations. Rather, it is the question of whether the continuous conduct of evaluations of gifted programs leads to program improvement or any other benefit normally ascribed to evaluation, and whether the continuous nature of the evaluation is a critical element.

Current Knowledge

As in general education, the major purpose of evaluating programs for the gifted is to improve them (Callahan & Caldwell, 1983). The second purpose is to establish accountability on a variety of variables:

> Because gifted programs are not popular and probably never will be, they must be defended and promoted by solid evidence of gifted student growth, cost effectiveness, and positive ripple effects for all students throughout the school system. (Dettmer, 1985b, p. 146)

Unfortunately, there is little evidence that all the theory about formative evaluation (for improvement) in fact leads to improvement; in addition, many of the models of evaluation in general cannot be applied readily to gifted programs. There are three main reasons for this (Archambault, 1983; Renzulli, 1984a; Roedell, Jackson, & Robinson, 1980). First, the high-level and broad objectives of gifted programs are not readily assessed by procedures developed to assess the attainment of much narrower scholastic goals, and gifted programs frequently give priority to social, affective, and career objectives that require many years to assess. Second, usual statistical techniques do not deal adequately with scores at the extremes of what may (or may not) be a normal distribution. It is hard to demonstrate an achievement gain in raw-score terms for a child already at the 99th percentile on a measure. It is difficult to specify what kinds of gains one seeks and how to assure their statistical significance. In many cases such an approach is inappropriate or impossible. Third, because of these difficulties, limited funding, and the urgency felt to provide services, evaluation is usually added on rather than built into program design. Techniques have been demonstrated that use available data effectively. Kulieke (1986) showed that add-on evaluations revealed outcomes whose causes defied conclusions about what brought them about. T. D. Stanley and Robinson (1986) explained the use of routinely available data as the basis for program assessments, but these are still affected by the problems of the extremes of a distribution.

As P. A. Alexander and Muia (1982) observed, gifted programs are rarely evaluated, so we have no systematic data in the literature to show how evaluation, ongoing or not, can assist the development of programs for the gifted. Indeed, if such programs are unpopular and always under the budget microscope if not the scalpel, then potentially negative data might be suppressed. It would be useful to know if that kind of thinking played any part in the absence of evaluative data.

The recommended practice is neither confirmed nor refuted.

Implications for Action

Despite the limitations on knowledge, accountability requires that some program evaluation be conducted. Because there is no evidence in support of continuous evaluation, a cyclical plan may be defensible and less intrusive.

It is possible to determine the purpose of a program evaluation by the nature of the distribution of the results. If the principal audience is the participants in the program, then it is quite likely that the purpose is, indeed, program improvement. Specific advice on conducting evaluations of programs for the gifted is widely available and too voluminous to address here. All the sources mentioned so far contain useful and generally consistent, indeed overlapping, advice. To these can be added Carter and Hamilton (1985), Cox and Daniel (1985), Ganapole (1982), and Rimm (1982).

Evaluation results can also be used to satisfy a political agenda, worthy or otherwise. It is crucial to separate those procedures that best address opportunities for improvement from those that offer the chance to put the best foot forward, and the appropriate engagement of each. Formative evaluation emphasizes improvement in areas of weakness. Summative evaluation is often a more political exercise, for example, tied to funding, and it is proper, not deceptive, to assure that the relevant successes and strengths of the program are reported. An honest report will indicate areas that still need improvement, but it would be irresponsible to be excessively modest in the face of decisions to be based on merit.

More honest assessment of weaknesses may ensue when the formative portion can be conducted internally with a degree of confidentiality, and sufficiently before public evaluations so that the latter may report improvement in areas of weakness. Improvement cannot be demonstrated in one-shot evaluations.

Needed Research

One type of useful research would ask administrators, school-board members, and others to indicate (e.g., in a checklist) the kinds of information they would find interesting and useful about gifted programs in their jurisdiction as well as their views on the purposes for such evaluation. One could examine the consistency of the views expressed, which might allay some of the cynicism about this topic. Or it might reinforce it.

A second level of study requires the implementation of evaluation plans. It might be possible to identify a number of schools or districts that engage in occasional, ongoing, or some degree of program evaluation. An observational or participant-observational study could examine the likelihood that program improvement is an important outcome. The participants must not be aware that the latter goal is on the agenda, though they must be informed before results are disseminated. A parallel type of study could examine a number of randomly selected programs to determine if and how program-improvement decisions are made. This might be the most feasible of the studies, and it could be very revealing.

Finally, practitioners involved in programs could contribute most valuably by writing up descriptions of examples of program evaluations and improvement strategies, addressing the knowledge base for this recommended practice. It is certainly important to know if continuous program evaluation is necessary, or even useful. Theoretically, it could be, but the education of the gifted presents unique circumstances that are not dealt with in existing theory on evaluation.

53 | A Variety of Teachers Is Needed as Role Models

This recommended practice is adapted from Passow (1979): "Gifted and talented students need access to a variety of 'teachers'—instructors, mentors, counsellors, and role models" (p. 451). We focus on the need for the role models. The theme is widely echoed, for example, by Cox, Daniel, and Boston (1985), E. S. Fleming (1985), Foster (1985), and Gowan (1979a, 1979c).

Current Knowledge

Although expert endorsement is widespread and the sources are greatly respected, we found but one source of evidence in support of this practice.

This was the early work on the election of "fast math" classes and later acceleration by girls who scored high in the selection tests used in the Study of Mathematically Precocious Youth initiated by Julian Stanley. Gender and role modeling were important to girls' decisions in favor of further participation (see, e.g., Brody & Fox, 1980).

For hundreds of years, schools operated by the Jesuits recruited some of the most able students and moved up one instructor a grade at a time with his class. Although this practice challenges the notion of variety, it contains implicit endorsement of the importance of role models.

The power of role models is well established in social psychology. We do not know that they are important in different ways for the gifted, nor that greater variety is important.

Implications for Action

This advice is imperative only for gifted girls, regarding mathematics, science, and career thinking (Harding & Berger, 1979; Rand & Gibb, 1989); Rodenstein et al., 1979). Kerr (1985) even recommended all-girls colleges with high female-to-male faculty ratios. This recommendation seems to be an element of good general educational practice. Only potentially wider occupational interests and opportunities for very able children make it especially relevant.

Needed Research

There is a definite need for social psychological studies of groups or individuals that show that variety in adult contacts is important. Might the call for variety be a disguised call for quality? Increasing the range of contacts will increase the chances of encountering quality over the day, week, year, or lifetime. Is the need for variety, if true, related to or limited by different learning styles on the part of the students? Are gender differences persistent?

What uses do gifted children make of role models over their educational careers? Are these different from what other children experience? Are gifted children who do not experience such variety of role models disadvantaged in some way in comparison with gifted children who do have such opportunities, and how do both groups compare with average-ability control groups?

There is much opportunity for observation in different settings, simulations, and experimental interventions in the course of providing services. We suspect that this recommended practice will be confirmed only in very limited circumstances related to socialization (e.g., bright girls and mathematics, bright boys and librarianship). These specific applications need to be determined.

54 | Use a Variety of School and Community Resources

The challenge in this recommended practice is to identify its unique application to the gifted. Many books include advice on its implementation, several state the principle, and a few give hints as to its special role:

> Make use of community resources, including the private sector. (Cox, Daniel, & Boston, 1985, p. 155)

> Community organizations must work with the school to provide richer opportunities for the gifted. (Hobbs, 1951, p. 166)

> Educational services can be enhanced by community activities which are well designed. (Freehill, 1982, pp. 351–352)

> It is probable that the fullest development of the potential of gifted and talented persons cannot occur wholly within the confines of the school, since many of the resources needed are in the community and family. (Passow, 1979, pp. 451–452)

Current Knowledge

The rationale for including community contacts includes career awareness (Cox et al., 1985; E. S. Fleming, 1985), the exploration of leisure opportunities (Wolf & Stephens, 1985), overcoming shortcomings in the school environment (Freehill, 1982; Hobbs, 1951; Passow, 1979), and meeting the intellectual needs of the gifted, for example, by letting them play a role in the planning of their learning environment (suggested by Fox, 1979c) and helping them develop their broad range of interests and abilities (C. W. Williams, 1958). In each of these, it is possible that very capable students might differ from other pupils.

The journal literature adds other applications, such as developing knowledge, skills, and attitudes related to participation in society (Schug, 1981). Plese (1982) noted that community involvement provides positive publicity for schools and stimulates interest and further study.

We found no formal research in support of any of these connections, but several examples of successfully implemented programs are reported (Ambrose, 1980; Bogue & Wolf, 1985; Clendening & Davies, 1980; Colson, 1980; DeBrun & Schaff, 1982; Johnsen-Harris, 1983; F. A. Karnes & Collins, 1978; Kingsley, 1986; Pirozzo, 1985; Plese, 1982; Schug, 1981). *Roeper Review* features such reports on a regular basis.

Testimonials do not constitute substantive evidence. Some support lies in the observation that the gifted open doors for community experiences and the high-level learning many of these opportunities provide.

Implications for Action

It is important to match needs (e.g., career awareness, attracting resources not available in the school, providing opportunities to respond to specific abilities in a group of children) available to community resources. Several authors advocate an administrative structure to nurture the relationships that are created. Such services have the welcome potential for gifted programs to share their benefits with the entire school.

Needed Research

Elaborated reports or project case studies are needed that specifically address the ways in which bright students' particular needs or characteristics are well served by extended school and community involvement, for example,

1. Developing career awareness
2. Exploring leisure opportunities

3. Compensating for specific shortcomings in a school's environment
4. Developing advanced or complex skills and attitudes in leadership, citizenship, or participation in society
5. Stimulating interest and further study
6. Responding to multiple abilities and interests and distinct learning styles of bright students

55 | **Mentor or Apprenticeship Programs Should Be Used**

One adjunct program option you can make available for enrichment, which often provides acceleration, is a mentor's program that includes tutorials and internships. (B. Clark, 1988, p. 195)

The practice is widely supported. Many advocates regard it as an essential rather than an adjunct activity (American Association for Gifted Children, 1978; Feldhusen, 1983b, 1985d; E. S. Fleming, 1985; Gensley, 1979; Torrance, 1979a; Wolf & Stephens, 1985). Cox, Daniel, and Boston (1985) added that the special element of a mentorship is "a shared, long-term commitment on the part of the student and mentor to a particular tradition and by having as its goal the shaping of a student's life outlook" (p. 59).

Tannenbaum (1983) emphasized that "the range of abilities and interests of gifted children is so wide that the school is actually a restrictive environment for them" (p. 425). This is one indication of how this recommendation might be especially appropriate for the gifted.

Current Knowledge

The majority of references to this practice are program descriptions (Boston, 1975b; Edlind & Haensly, 1985). These comprise useful data (though the failed programs do not get written up), and there is some direct research summarized by L. Beck (1989). The main conclusions were generally endorsed: Mentorships lead to eager learning, positive self-image, and often a contribution to the community (Booth, 1980). Edlind and Haensly's (1985) review concluded that there are benefits in career and interest advancement, increases in knowledge and skills, development of general abilities such as leadership or social interaction, enhancement of self-esteem and confidence, establishment of long-term friendships with intellectual peers, and the facilitation of creative achievement. They also pointed out benefits for the mentor. VanTassel-Baska (1985) noted the special importance of mentorships (and their strong relationship to role modeling—see recommended practice No. 53) for gifted girls; she recommended mentors as one of the two key elements in programming for them, along with career education.

VanTassel-Baska (1985) and Bloom (1985) also pointed out that historical biographies of eminent persons frequently highlight the role of mentors in their development. There is little doubt of the value of the approach. There is less clarity about the intended clientele.

L. Beck's (1989) survey of mentorship participants confirmed that career development was most affected, especially for females. This was not correlated with academic gains. Different individuals attained different benefits.

Mentorships, in their various guises, are enjoyed and work well. They are adaptive and inexpensive. If mentors are carefully chosen and well matched to student needs, this service can be an extremely effective program component. There is, however, very little evidence that mentorships are especially appropriate for more able children.

Implications for Action

Despite her categorization of mentorships as "adjunct" activities, B. Clark (1988) stressed that they deserve to be a part of the school program, not after school or during the summer. "Mentorships are not displaced classrooms but unique learning experiences" (Runions & Smyth, 1985, p. 132). Fox (1979b), Harding and Berger (1979), and Higham and Navarre (1984) emphasized the particular value to gifted girls in the establishment of role models, which are more important to them than to boys who are more commonly motivated by achievement. Kerr (1985) stated:

> Mentoring provides the important link between education and a career for eminent women. A good mentor is a model sharing trade secrets and protecting the protegé from sex discrimination. (p. 73)

L. Beck (1989) pointed out the shortage of female mentors in most programs. B. S. Miller and Price (1981) and Sanborn (1979a) suggested the particular utility of mentorships for minorities as well, to which Lambert and Lambert (1982) added the gifted handicapped.

General advice on implementing various types of mentorships, and examples, are offered at some length by Coutant (1983), Cox et al. (1985), Dettmer (1980), and, with a particular but not exclusive emphasis on gifted girls, Rodenstein, Pfleger, and Colangelo (1979), and Shamanoff (1985). Too brief a summary would not do this work justice, but a critical part of all the advice is attention to the careful selection of mentors (e.g., screening interviews to avoid persons motivated by various proselytizing objectives) and matching with children on the basis of a shared interest and objective.

Gray (1984) has shown that mentors benefit from direct training in how to do their job well, and so, in turn, do the children. This should also be part of program planning.

Needed Research

There is no need for more studies that demonstrate that mentorships can generate the positive outcomes noted above in gifted children. On the other hand, some "fine tuning" of the knowledge base is needed.

What are some of the subtleties of the interactions among child's and mentor's gender and various types of internship experiences? For whom are career- and esteem-related outcomes more important and salient, and for whom are achievement outcomes most appropriate? How can a mentorship system manage these assignments well?

Mentorships match the novice with the expert. As research shows the potential of gifted children to think in ways similar to experts (see recommended practice No. 37), can mentorships improve intellectual skills at these levels, for example, metacognitive processes and flexibility in problem solving? To what degree is this a function of the nature of the tasks undertaken in the mentorship, the interaction, or the characteristics of the participants? What is the role of mentor training in aiding such outcomes? These questions might help to answer how internships are especially suitable for highly able students.

Finally, what are the limits of applicability of various forms of mentorships? Apprenticeships, for example, are widely used in special education. In other words, we require elaboration of either the special suitability of mentorships for the gifted or the special adaptation of mentorships as a general strategy for the gifted. Might their widespread adoption in gifted programs assist in their broader use?

56 | Less Teacher-Centered Pedagogy Is Suitable

> Learning environments for gifted children must (a) be student-centered rather than teacher-centered, (b) encourage independence rather than dependence. (Maker, 1982a, p. 85)

> Programs for the gifted must above all else be learner centered, flexible, open-ended, and replete with options and alternatives. (Clendening & Davies, 1980, p. 42)

Conant (1958), echoed by others, pointed out the need for student centeredness to be under teacher guidance: "The teacher serves as stimulator, questioner, listener, and positive reinforcer, but not as the source of knowledge" (Cushenbery & Howell, 1974, p. 30).

Current Knowledge

Freehill (1961/1982) noted that student-centered pedagogy may be observed in many fine schools, but all would be hard-pressed to defend the practice in terms of research. Student centeredness is compatible with the idea of the student's becoming an independent learner and contributor to knowledge. Personal, religious, or state ideology might not favor such a goal.

Gallagher (1985) pointed out the potential of the open education (not open classroom—the architecture is irrelevant) approach to working with gifted children. An outgrowth of trend-setting British infant schools (early elementary grades), the idea of child-centered pedagogy came to gifted education from general education. The suitability of the approach was widely debated in the 1970s and briefly reviewed by Shore (1981). A major study by Bennett (1976) charged that the most able students were ill served by nontraditional elementary education because he observed they often performed less well on academic tests. Such test performance is a major focus of traditional schooling, which judges its success by how well learners do on standard achievement tests. His research did not compare the two groups of children on the goals that were particular to the open model, for example, personal initiative in setting appropriate learning goals, independent questioning and study skills, peer teaching, and so on. Bennett's research was also criticized on methodological grounds, but these criticisms are less important to the present argument than its having missed the point on the nontraditional goals. Whitener's (1989) meta-analysis also examined only testable achievement, and she also concluded that high-achieving students fare better in structured environments and differ less from low achievers when instruction is self-paced.

Shore's (1981) study compared gifted and other children in a crossed design of architecturally and pedagogically open versus traditional classes, on measures of students' liking school, academic self-concept, and school performance. Architecture was not related to any differences. Ability was, and gifted children were pleased with school and thought at least as well of themselves as did the others. There were no evidence that they were in any way ill served. Treffinger and Barton (1979) offered a partial report of a study by Barton that found that children could easily make the switch to a child-centered environment while displaying adequate or better academic growth; even the control children gained in academic independence. Indeed, regarding this approach as suitable for all students meant that "gifted students could function more effectively without seeming vastly 'different' from their peers" (p. 84).

So, why is this recommended practice needed? Perhaps there are voices in the field who consider an appropriate education for the gifted to be a high-pressure, discipline-based, competitive, carefully evaluated, expert-teacher-driven school. The recommended practice counterbalances such outside counsel.

Implications for Action

What little evidence exists supports the advice that child-centered pedagogy has a place. Minges, Gats, and Kresser (1978) suggested the following:

> Allow the student to engage in the organization and planning of his own learning activities. Provide real life learning experiences and simulations that call for active participation. Be a resource for learning rather than a dispenser of information. Encourage exploration, inventiveness, originality and inquisitiveness. Allow a child to arrive at his own solution making his own mistakes, unless there is some danger in his particular decision. (p. 51)

Treffinger and Barton (1979) advised teachers that all children have some ability in this regard. Teachers must convey a positive attitude about self-directed learning and themselves learn new classroom management skills, including new ways to react to student initiatives. Maker (1982a) offered a large number of detailed suggestions for modifying the learning environment in the direction of this recommended practice. She especially advised a great reduction in teacher talk.

Needed Research

First, a great many studies should be undertaken that compare more and less able pupils in well-regarded student- and teacher-centered environments, on variables that are important to both educational perspectives. Personnel of both sets of programs must accept the goals on which students will be evaluated as valuable educational objectives, even though school time may be biased one way or the other in each case. A study that intentionally includes a traditional setting that rejected the student-centered objectives could be interesting, too. A meta-analysis based on a large number of these studies would be helpful. Achievement, cognitive, and affective variables should be evaluated.

Case studies of successful implementations would be useful, if enough were accumulated. These should probably be reported as program evaluations and refer explicitly to the attainment of benefits claimed in the models they have adopted (e.g., is there less teacher talk observed?).

Difficult but desirable research would follow children who have attended teacher- and student-centered programs to ascertain if they bore any relation to later activities, talents, or careers in adulthood. One must, in all cases, be alert to the possibility that self or family selection might influence initial program choice, where such choice is available.

Finally, to what extent is student-centered pedagogy especially suitable to or necessary for exceptionally able students? Suitability has some support already; there is less evidence available for the necessity and for the unique or different application to the gifted.

57 Gifted Children Should Learn by Teaching Each Other

"Programs that provide opportunities for students to teach fellow pupils can extend the possibilities for developing potential" (Passow, 1975, p. 408). These students might instruct their peers (defined by both age and ability) and also teach younger gifted children. Although the terms *peer teaching* and *peer tutoring* are often used interchangeably, we prefer the former because it implies regular learning, not remediation: The tutors "teach their peers those aspects of the subject in which they are especially proficient" (Conant, 1958, p. 112).

Peer teaching has socioemotional as well as academic benefits, as noted by Wolf and T. M. Stephens (1985):

> Allowing secondary students to serve as peer counselors gives them a chance to provide a service and enhance their self-perception. Tutors feel their knowledge and expertise are useful and appreciated. . . . Peer counselors and tutors should not be assigned busy work. (p. 75)

The value of peer support in the socioaffective domain was endorsed by Blanning (1977), who addressed peer teaching as a useful pedagogical option for rural or other isolated schools.

Current Knowledge

Testimonials and case studies abound to the effect that gifted children regard learning from peers very highly (Torrance & Reynolds, 1979), and extremely successful projects have been "organized and taught by students with unusual interests, energy and skills" (Johnsen-Harris, 1983, p. 81). Many report the benefits of gifted adolescents' teaching younger, bright children ("Gifted Students as Teachers," 1981; Kingsley, 1986; Masterson, 1979; Speed, 1982). To have bright children teach and help other bright children can be a positive experience for both partners.

These observations are consistent with the general benefits of peer teaching, reported by pioneers in its formal study (Zacharias, 1966) and by reviewers of the field (Gartner, Kohler, & Riessman, 1972; Schermerhorn, Goldschmid, & Shore, 1976). This challenges unique applicability of this recommended practice to high-ability students. Ward (1961/1980) anticipated one side of this when he observed that,

> In the classroom, the use sometimes made of gifted children in the aid of less apt in academic situations would seem particularly appropriate. . . . The superior individual can profit from the opportunity to perceive that even with effort and interest some people do not learn readily. He can also profit from the opportunity to gain deeper insights for himself through the process of organizing and explaining certain ideas and skills to others. (p. 96)

In an unreported experience, Winston Emery of McGill University in Montreal found that a group of able elementary school students were well instructed in winter camping techniques by intellectually handicapped schoolmates who had prior experience with this activity.

Peer teaching offers learning and social benefits to the participants, leads to appreciated learning, and is, in part, easy to implement. It is not clear that it offers special benefits to the gifted, however, either in the teaching or learning role. All children learn especially well from the experience of teaching other children; this observation is consistent with Piaget's theory (cf. Kamii, 1985, 1989) and with research that examines social origins of intellectual processes (Vygotsky, 1978). The major risk is to overgeneralize and exploit bright students as assistant teachers.

Implications for Action

Peer instruction offers promise across wide levels of ability. Peer counseling is more complex, but it is worth exploring in gifted programs. Peer counseling should be an adjunct of a professional counseling program until we know more about it (also see recommended practice Nos. 30 and 73).

Peer teaching and counseling may be useful points of contact between a gifted program and the regular program, but this point goes beyond bright children teaching other bright children.

Do not consume an unreasonable portion of any student's time in remediation with other pupils, nor so engage students without their mutual consent. To do so would create an unequal (hence not peer) relationship between the participants and may limit the more capable partner's opportunity for new learning.

Needed Research

The first question is the special appropriateness of peer teaching for the gifted. Comparisons should be made within and across levels of ability, on more outcomes than satisfaction and factual learning, especially the enhancement of self-concept and the participants' learning skills. The impact on high-level learning strategies (see recommended practice No. 46) should also be studied.

The level of peer instruction has not yet been explored. It is not as relevant if the only benefits are on low-level factual teaching and learning. The risks of remedial tutoring between students who are not intellectual peers also need to be explored; at the moment these risks are primarily conjecture.

Peer counseling has not been studied adequately, nor how peer teaching and counseling programs might be effective bridges between the gifted and regular programs, both for children and adults.

58 | Creative Abilities Should Be Nurtured

Cushenbery and Howell (1974) stated simply that "creativity must be encouraged at every level" (p. 6). Feldhusen (1985a) cited Stein's (1981) overview of the subject and urged us "to assess creativity as a component of giftedness and to nurture it as a major concern in educational programs for the gifted and talented" (p. 10).

Creativity and its encouragement are, of course, central to Renzulli's (1977) widely adopted model of giftedness and curricular adaptation. Khatena (1979) reminded us of the roles of other professionals, parents, and teachers.

Current Knowledge

The literature on creativity, divergent thinking, and their other manifestations is enormous. It is replete with arguments about which of the versions really represent creativity, and how they may be related to giftedness. We will not examine those.

We accept as given that there are qualities of the human intellect properly called creativity (see Milgram, 1984). There is no doubt that, when discovered, they should be nurtured. Parke (1985) and Torrance (1986) have cited evidence that creativity (in the selected forms) can be taught, or at least enhanced, and that people can become more creative in areas where they have some beginning competence. This research is controversial, because the more likely it is empirical and demonstrates measurable gains, the more likely it uses measures of divergent thinking whose validity as measures of creativity is, indeed, debatable. B. Clark (1988) helped delimit the discussion by stating that "we can teach some of the aspects of creative behavior" (p. 72). Davis (1981) pointed out that creativity includes the notions of creative problem solving and innovation. We therefore suggest that the discussion of recommended practice No. 36 be examined in this context. Tannenbaum (1981) suggested that curricula that extend beyond the usual enable the gifted to make original contributions to knowledge.

Essentially, this recommendation is based on societal values, not psychology or pedagogy. Despite the problems encountered by creatively gifted persons (see recommended practice No. 189), creative products are highly valued in Western society at least. On that basis alone the recommendation is acceptable. It is not suitably subject to empirical verification.

Even if creatively or otherwise gifted persons are in the most favored position to benefit from educational experiences that promote the enhancement of creative thinking, there is every indication that this guiding principle is an essential ingredient of contemporary educational practice for all children.

Implications for Action

A myriad of specific and general practices are available from which teachers and others may draw. B. Clark (1988) provides a good overview. Many appropriate models for use with the gifted are offered by Maker (1982b), Parke (1985), and Renzulli (1986a).

Although the recommended practice should be observed, one should not pretend that it has special status in gifted education.

Needed Research

It would be useful to assemble and add to the literature that demonstrates gains in creative performance following intervention and to compare these effects among gifted students and others under different educational regimes. When sufficient studies are available, meta-analysis would be an appropriate technique to apply.

Can gifted programs act as models for innovation and improvement in general education? Where creativity has not been especially emphasized, are there any resulting deficits at the individual or school level?

---

59 | Include Inquiry, Discovery, and Problem Solving

These approaches are characterized by their involving learners in the process of creating new knowledge, not merely accumulating it (also see recommended practice No. 37). Advocates include Barbe and Frierson (1975), Kamii (1985, 1989), Maker (1982b), Parnes (1979), Polette (1982—especially see pp. 15–16), Stewart (1985), Taba (1975), and Woodliffe (1977). Martinson (1976) wrote:

> The independence, ability, interests, and initiative of the gifted underscore the right of the gifted to play a major role in the determination of their learning agenda. In learning from their own quest and search for resolution, they extend their knowledge, talents and skills, perceptiveness, and curiosity about the environment. (p. 65)

However, de Bono and Maier (1983) cautioned that problem solving can be misdirected into artificial, excessively logical tasks: This

> is dangerous to the child with an above average ability. . . . The questionable transference between the ability to solve hypothetical situations or complex mind puzzles, and the ability to think effectively in real life situations, must be circumvented. (p. 442)

Getzels (1979) moderated de Bono's severest criticism by pointing out that problem solving and problem finding are on a continuum; a problem may be changed during its solution.

Traditional study skills may underpin higher level creative activities. Freehill (1961/1982) suggested the importance of "library skills—the ability to read graphic materials, take notes, summarize, and present conclusions in a clear and understandable fashion" (p. 249). Polette (1982) argued that "any process-oriented program must rely heavily on the basics of reading, writing, and research to be successful" (p. 16).

Current Knowledge

We located virtually no formal research in support of this recommended practice other than that reported with No. 37. The literature is replete with testimonials and reports of use. Most journal articles are either general endorsements (Dirkes, 1985; Flack & Feldhusen, 1985; VanTassel-Baska, M. Landau, & Olszewski, 1985) or guides to implementation in science (Yager, 1982), social and future studies (Reis & Hébert, 1985; Subotnik, 1984), and mathematics (Friesen, 1980; Gibney, 1982; Wheatley, 1983). Major science curricular projects have been designed according to such principles, and the National Research Council (1989) in the United States has proposed such an approach to the teaching of mathematics to all students.

Callahan (1985) has pointed out that inquiry and similar approaches "closely parallel the principles of gifted education" (p. 193), but no study has shown that they are differentially appropriate for the gifted.

Implications for Action

Inquiry, discovery, and problem solving are consistent with most of what we are learning about the nature of giftedness and creativity in learning. Rawl and O'Tuel (1983) reminded us to make the tasks challenging, not frustrating, and Montgomery (1983) suggested that teachers be taught to function in these modes. This seems to highlight the weak link in the process, because we doubt that new teachers are taught to work this way, that student teachers are encouraged to do so, or that most classrooms actually function in this manner. Treffinger (1980) recommends that teachers share the process with the learners; this raises the question about the need for teachers themselves to be able to think in these ways. Teacher in-service is crucial.

Effective implementation of this pedagogy with bright children could be an important basis for improved communication between gifted and general education.

Needed Research

It would be useful to have a small number of reviews of the literature on this topic, which assemble the supporting literature in general and include advice for implementation by subject matter or level. The advice could then be validated.

It is very important to learn why such a popular idea is not widely implemented and what training and incentives teachers need to bring it about. Is teachers' subject-matter expertise related to their ability or willingness to teach with such methods? What about their own ability to learn by such means and to use them in independent learning? Other potentially related variables also need to be identified and studied. Another issue that warrants study is the relevance of traditional study skills as foundations for these kinds of activities.

60 | Investigate Real Problems and Solutions

In gifted education, this practice has its most direct origins in Renzulli's Enrichment Triad and the creative problem-solving models inspired by Osborn and applied to education in programs such as the Future Problem-Solving Program developed by Torrance. Renzulli (1979) posed the practice in the context of a defensible program objective:

> The primary role of each teacher in the program for gifted and talented students will be to provide each student with assistance in (1) identifying and structuring realistic solvable problems that are consistent with the student's interests, and (2) acquiring the necessary methodological resources and investigative skills that are necessary for solving these particular problems. (p. 114)

This recommended practice on real problems is related to suggestions for independent study (No. 65) and to professional level products (No. 37).

Current Knowledge

In general education, solving real problems was advocated by John Dewey (1938). In gifted education, real problems imply that students take on the role of firsthand inquirers (Renzulli, 1977; Reis & Renzulli, 1985).

The practice has been espoused and implemented by practitioners (see McCauley, 1984, for an example); however, the issue is difficult to investigate empirically because what makes a problem "real" is neither always clear, nor universally accepted, nor implemented similarly. Maker (1982a) explained that *real* means the student has gone beyond merely summarizing or recapit-

ulating information to transforming information or producing a creative solution. Renzulli (1982) suggested four characteristics of a real problem:

1. A real problem must have a personal frame of reference, since it
   involves an emotional or affective commitment as well as an intellectual or cognitive one.
2. A real problem does not have an existing or unique solution.
3. Calling something a problem does not necessarily make it a real
   problem for a given person or group.
4. The purpose of pursuing a real problem is to bring about some
   form of change and/or to contribute something new to the sciences,
   the arts, or the humanities. (p. 149)

Most research on the use of real problems has been done as a part of
the Triad/Revolving Door Model (Olenchak & Renzulli, 1989; Reis, 1981;
Starko, 1988). The numbers of Type III (independent or small group) investigations initiated and completed, and their accompanying product assessments, serve as outcome variables. However, Starko (1988) used involvement in Type III investigations to predict productivity outside school and
self-efficacy. Students reported they believed their participation in Type III
investigations influenced them in many ways, ranging from their career
choices to study skills. This definition is compatible with the idea of children's learning best when they construct their own realities (see recommended practice No. 59), which applies to all children.

Social and technological problems are part of the curriculum associated with the Future Problem-Solving Program, inspired by Torrance's
work on the images bright children had about the future (cf. Torrance,
Bruch, & Goolsby, 1976). In recent years, students have suggested or voted
on the problems they wish to examine (Crabbe, 1982).

Implications for Action

Educators can implement this practice to encourage active, problem-
centered learning for gifted students. The most difficult aspect of the practice
is determining which problems are "real." At the moment, we perhaps know
best what is not real—namely, contrived problems, such as most workbook
exercises, simply to be solved at the student's desk.

Providing students with opportunities to select learning experiences
on the basis of interest, to develop topics into researchable issues or problems, and to develop and implement a plan of action increases the likelihood
of involving real problems and solutions. Inserting real problems does not

remove the need to prepare students intellectually and motivationally to deal with them.

Needed Research

Because Renzulli Type III investigations (of which real problems are an integral part) have been asserted as an enrichment component unique to gifted students, some investigation into the "lower bound" is necessary to substantiate the claim. Are there differences in the levels of ability, skills, or prior knowledge required for problems differing in scope? Do children perform differently when the real problem is fighting on the playground as compared with national or global real problems of pollution, pestilence, or war?

Discussion is needed in the field to define a "real" problem more clearly. Some empirical data could assist this consideration: Do experts in given disciplines agree on what constitutes a real problem? Is it possible to infer from a student product that the problem under investigation was real for the student?

Do bright students or others learn more or better with real versus contrived problems? What are the differences in these outcomes?

Research is also needed on the pedagogical adaptations required to address real problems in the curriculum and how these methods might be adapted suitably for bright students, if such problems can be shown to be especially appropriate.

---

61 | Gifted Historical Figures Should Be Studied

This recommended practice refers to the study of life stories of notable historical figures. Khatena (1982) envisioned the practice more broadly:

> Eminent creators as role models for emulation appear to be very important to the emergence of other eminent creators, and more predictable if emulation occurs in the same discipline and especially during the developmental period of genius. (p. 180)

The practice is also recommended by Stewart (1985), who emphasized it in the context of social studies:

> Looking at history through biographies and autobiographies of famous people can help students see the connections between their own experiences and the larger world. (p. 253)

Barbe and Malone (1985) suggested that such study may be interesting to bright students in a language-arts curriculum.

Current Knowledge

We located no studies that examined this practice or its impact. Some descriptions of instructional programs or activities are found in the study of heroes (Blanning, 1978) or in the use of biographies of gifted persons in bibliotherapy (Frasier & McCannon, 1981).

Implications for Action

The study of eminent individuals may provide inspiration and hope to many. Although gifted children may indeed benefit from the study of historical role models, other children may also do so.

The study of historical figures may help high-ability youth with some of the difficulties they face in society. Maker (1982b) elaborated several useful ideas for the study of people as one means of differentiating curriculum content:

> There should be a definite focus on problems unique to gifted or creative individuals and how they have resolved these situations. Some issues worthy of study are lack of social recognition of the value of creative products, defining success in a personal vs. a social sense, resolving conflicts between self-expectations for success and the expectations of others, coping with the perception of being different or abnormal, and many others that can be identified by the students through their own personal experiences or through their relationship to the lives of others. (p. 33)

Learning to cope with society's indifference or hostility to creative ideas might be a lesson well taught through the study of gifted persons (historical or living) who have experienced similar difficulties, but care must be taken not to inflame pessimism. We also caution anyone developing such curricular ideas to be alert to racial, gender, or other stereotypes, because history is not always a model of equal opportunity.

Needed Research

Some well-documented case studies of historical figures serving as role models in a program of bibliotherapy would be useful. Do students cite these persons as powerful influences on their lives? If they do, what messages are most important? Does the area of endeavor need to be shared by the student and the historical figure, or do students take away more generalized messages of triumph over adversity?

If lack of recognition for creative products were perceived as a problem by some bright children, the effects of discussing how famous historical people dealt with this could be assessed experimentally. Care should be taken in these discussions: Abraham Lincoln's views of nationhood and slavery and Galileo's model of the universe led to personal tragedy, even though their ideas prevailed.

Because claims are made for the effect of this practice on productivity, level of aspiration, and personal adjustment, some investigations of these long-term outcomes are in order, although they would be limited by the nature of self-report data.

62 | **Rapid Pacing Should Be Provided**

Rapid pacing is a form of acceleration, but it takes place on a lesson-to-lesson basis, and within lessons. It was popularized by J. C. Stanley's Study of Mathematically Precocious Youth (SMPY) (cf. W. C. George, 1976; W. C. George & Denham, 1976). It is one of the key elements in program design, according to Feldhusen (1985a; recommended practice Nos. 29, 31, and 64 present the others), and is endorsed by Passow (1980b) as an appropriate way to adapt education for bright students. Reis and Renzulli's (1985) notion of curriculum compacting is somewhat related.

> Lessons must be paced quickly so that students are always reaching and being challenged by new ideas. Since gifted students can assimilate new ideas rapidly, slowly paced classes soon become classes where the students grow bored and their minds tend to wander. (G. A. Fleming, 1982, p. 32)

This advice is sometimes offered with qualifications. Stewart (1985) suggested that fast pacing was appropriate if it "does not cause undue stress or emotional problems for the child" (p. 235). Passow (1980b) stated: "Which modifications should be adopted to ensure appropriate experiences for gifted students will depend, then, on the goals to be attained" (p. 25). Fast pacing is not always the most appropriate for particular content and particular learners. Does fast pacing mean fewer detailed explanations, fewer examples, more homework, faster talking teachers, less discussion, less review? Nowhere does advocacy of this practice make its classroom application clear, except SMPY for mathematically highly precocious children. The absence of specificity in the advice is accompanied by a perplexing observation about the above balance from Cox, Daniel, and Boston (1985), in the course of their continental survey of exemplary programs: "The goal we have in mind is not fully realized in any system we examined during the course of our study" (p. 143).

Current Knowledge

There is no doubt that fast pacing has worked in the SMPY situation. High school mathematics was completed in one-fifth the usual amount of class time (W. C. George, 1976); however, not all the children kept up in the fast-paced classes. Problems were encountered by students who fell behind in the large homework load of "several hours per week" (p. 257). Nearly half the original group of 28 students withdrew from the originally planned program; these students were given a more socially interactive learning situation in smaller classes.

Both groups were then successful. One question not answered by the data presented is the ratio of homework time in the fast-paced classes versus the regular course. The full five-to-one advantage appears to have been somewhat reduced by the independent study time of the fast class and by the extra class time needed by the maverick group. The question remains as to what extent fast pacing is home-study rather than a real curricular change.

Fox (1981a) described several studies in which early SMPY students were followed up. About 70% considered the SMPY experience to have been more stimulating than their regular classes, but only 48% found it more enjoyable; only 1 of 29 students failed to complete the curriculum, however. Despite the resounding academic success of SMPY-type programs and their appropriateness to large numbers of mathematics students, some students need other kinds of services.

The SMPY studies themselves have provided some insight into who these may be, namely, students whose preferred learning situations are more social and interactive. Kersh and Reisman (1985), G. A. Fleming (1982), and the numerous SMPY reports suggest strongly that fast pacing is most suitable when the objective is mastery of known content and processes. It does make sense for gifted students who are comfortable with a teacher-centered, performance-oriented learning situation to move as quickly through such content as might interest them so as to get on with the creative part of study in the discipline as soon as possible. However, it is important to recall the dilemma discussed in recommended practice No. 31: It is not clear to what extent a great mastery of disciplinary content is necessary to engage in creative production within a domain. That question is open.

Callahan (1985) argued against rapid pacing in science for the very reasons implied here:

> Rapid progression through a structured curriculum also tends to inhibit the opportunity for in-depth study of a self-selected science topic as well as the development of independent and self-directed study skills. Topics and activities tend to be teacher-selected and directed. . . . There will also be little opportunity to develop complex, abstract, and/or higher-level thinking skills or to encourage open-ended tasks where the student can use creativity. (p. 197)

Callahan's points at least constitute hypotheses that require investigation. In fairness to the SMPY studies, they were conducted before contemporary cognitive views of learning began to be noticed in the literature on giftedness in the 1980s. We do not know whether or not some of the potential losses cited by Callahan are in fact realized in quickly paced classes; her concerns need to be checked.

The universality of the fact-pace advice is challenged by Lajoie and Shore (1986), who noted that high-IQ students were not always the fastest mental processors. Accuracy was a better predictor of performance than speed of processing, but this was on the Matching-Familiar-Figures test, not curricular material. Dover and Shore (1991) examined these differences in speed of processing on another laboratory task, water-jars combination puzzles, though a degree of algebraic thinking underlies the solutions. In that study, gifted students who showed greater cognitive flexibility, that is, who used an alternative (and simpler) solution strategy when it was merely available and not required, were faster and had more sophisticated insights into their own problem-solving strategies than did less flexible gifted students or average-ability pupils. These differences were more pronounced than differences in arithmetic success with the tasks. We may therefore ask if more flexible, more metacognitively skilled pupils—those better able to monitor, evaluate, and regulate their own thinking processes—might be able to cope better with fast pacing. The matter remains open, on other criteria, as to whether or not they would or should be encouraged to elect it. Lajoie and Shore's (1986) concluding suggestion was that gifted students should strive for accuracy in their work, at whatever speed they find comfortable (also see recommended practices Nos. 46 and 59).

There appear to be no studies dealing with potential stress and emotional problems resulting from fast pacing.

Implications for Action

The argument for fast pacing is most convincingly made for highly selected students in mathematics, but we do not know what they miss in terms of cognitive or creative development in the subject. They will miss nothing, of course, if regular mathematics programs are generally as bad as mathematics education experts claim they are (National Research Council, 1989). If an accelerated course were the best available in a school, it would be a worthwhile contribution to the repertoire of available options. If high-quality regular and enriched programs were available, programs that addressed the intellectual skills and creative processes leading to creative mathematical thinking, for example, the advantage of rapid pacing might be more limited. Concepts such as more selective curriculum compacting might become more viable, using such simple strategies as not teaching what a child already knows (VanTassel-Baska, 1981). Until quality curricula are available, some rapid pacing, at least compacting, is defensible.

Needed Research

Does rapid pacing provide the gains in intellectual skills that are important to high-level thinking? Are creative and interdisciplinary thinking enhanced?

What are the stresses or emotional problems that may accompany rapid pacing? Are gifted children necessarily bored by a slow pace? Is this boredom a function of what is happening at a slow pace rather than of the pace itself—for example, excessive attention to mastery of known facts and processes, which, it is clear, most bright people can learn quickly?

How should rapid pacing be implemented with different goals? What is the contribution available from curriculum compacting and other established proposals? Does the added homework burden deplete the time advantage to the child and cancel part of the gain in class time? Does it reduce opportunities for play or cultural or athletic education that appeals to the child or family? What do some gifted children not like about fast pacing?

For what curricular goals and what types of gifted students is fast pacing especially appropriate? How fast is fast? How fast is too fast and for whom? To what extent are homogeneous, teacher-paced classes needed? What pace do children with different abilities and previous learning experiences in the subject set for themselves under optimal conditions? What might be those optimal conditions? Research on such questions across ages, social and economic conditions, and subject matter, among other variables, would strengthen our understanding of the role of rapid pacing and provide guidelines for its implementation.

63 | **Teach Gifted Children to Complete Their Tasks**

> Many gifted children will complete and check work only if pressured to do so. Because they lack the persistence required to complete a task, their achievement rarely matches their ability. (Woodliffe, 1977, p. 9)

This concern underlies the interest in persistence and task commitment among bright children. On the other hand, partially contrary advice was offered by B. Clark (1988):

> Don't insist that every project have closure before other things can happen. Often, what the child wanted or needed to learn from an experience occurs before the project is "finished." Sometimes other fascinating areas just have to be explored before the project can be finished properly. Otherwise you may end up with a few finished projects and a turned-off child. (p. 571)

Current Knowledge

Woodliffe's suggestion was based on her years as a teacher of the gifted. Other teachers' reports mention the same lack of follow-through on the part of some gifted children (e.g., Lince & Meel, 1980). Task commitment and persistence are addressed at considerable length in the literature on giftedness (Haensly, Shiver, & Fulbright, 1980; Renzulli & Reis, 1985).

Attempts to improve such perseverance appear to have been generally successful (Oxley, 1980; Stedtnitz & Speck, 1986). The suggestion that completion also includes checking and revising one's work fits well with gifted students' thinking skills, metacognitive processes, and functioning with a high level of expertise (see recommended practice Nos. 37 and 46).

The published research base is largely anecdotal. Although many successful adults may have been scholastically persistent children, it does not follow that all or most such children achieve the same success as adults.

We found one supportive empirical study. Scott (1979) correlated measures of convergent and divergent thinking with achievement motivation in Grade 9 high-IQ students. No significant correlations were found with convergent thinking, but this is an artifact of the restricted IQ range. On the other hand, higher divergent scores were related to willingness

> to work long hours towards distant goals and maintenance of high standards. They want to understand many areas of knowledge to satisfy their intellectual curiosity. Boys value perseverance even in the face of great difficulty; girls value logical thought. (p. 5296)

The reported gender difference in the nature or absence of perseverance is unique, but Scott's data do hint at support for the links among creativity, task commitment, and the general idea of giftedness.

Finally, a note of caution. A classic study in psychology (Zeigarnik, 1922) found that interrupted learning tasks were better remembered than those carried to completion. The nature of the problem and the processes required to solve it, as opposed to the right answer, might be better served by noncompletion under some circumstances. We need to know why different children do not finish many or particular tasks. If the learning goal addresses the process and general principles of the material, might noncompletion be an advantage? If such cognitive control is being exercised by bright students on their own, could this be less of a deficit than thought? This supports B. Clark's (1988) suggestion that the imperative to complete tasks should be enforced with discretion. There is, however, no implication that completion of tasks is irrelevant.

Implications for Action

Persistence and checking probably lead to higher grades and more scholarships and, if one is not obsessive about them, they may be quite defensible.

Nearly all the references cited above suggest ways to encourage such behavior. A guiding principle seems to be to ensure a good match between the task and the student's abilities, the former being slightly ahead of the latter but within reach (Foster, 1985). There will be times when it is unnecessary or even undesirable to complete a particular task, especially if the objective in undertaking it has been satisfied or if forcing its completion has unwanted consequences. It follows that bright children should learn to make and share increasingly in the exercise of the discretion.

Needed Research

It is not established clearly that gifted children are less likely to complete tasks than others; all we really know is that some gifted children are in a hurry to get on to another task. Is this a more serious liability for the gifted than for others? Are there personality and gender correlates of nonpersistent behavior? It would also be useful to examine task completion behavior specifically in relation to metacognitive performance, including students' awareness of and possible reasons for noncompletion.

Longitudinal studies are needed to examine what happens to children, and bright children in particular, who are not scholastically persistent and do not finish their work. One might begin by interviewing teachers for the names of such students and observing whether or not this leads to any deficits in performance or thinking processes in the short or long term.

Studies of how to improve the performance in question are less important until the nature and extent of the problem (if a problem exists) are elucidated.

64 | Emphasize In-Depth Investigation of Subject Matter

"Develop intellectual depth and thinking ability, rather than concentrating on the mere imparting of knowledge" (Butler & Butler, 1979, p. 244).

> To extend the "core-curriculum" for the gifted, one can take a subject in greater depth or breadth, either pouring over the same problem in finer and finer detail or relating it to other subjects outside the basics. (Freeman, 1985a, p. 16)

The phrase "in depth" recurs frequently (cf. Barbe & Malone, 1985; Feldhusen, 1985a; Gowan, Khatena, & Torrance, 1979b). Students' interest may be the key to such study (Cushenbery & Howell, 1974; Massé & Gagné, 1983; Tempest, 1974—also see recommended practice No. 39) and student choice the vehicle to tapping that interest (Callahan, 1985). Gallagher (1985) and Goldberg, Passow, and Lorge (1958/1980) advised that factual knowledge is less important on its own than as a stepping stone to higher level thinking skills and the interrelating of ideas. In-depth study therefore refers to a variety of specific activities: examination of fine details, the development of related thinking skills, and establishing relationships among ideas (also see recommended practice No. 31).

Current Knowledge

VanTassel-Baska (1985) claimed that gifted children "crave depth" (p. 48) and Freeman (1985a) suggested they "often have a natural desire for detail, to get to know all there is about a subject" (p. 16). Even if they like it, is it good for them?

Renzulli (1979), Woodliffe (1977), and Gallagher (1985) all advised a balance between indulging in such deep studies and broadening one's horizons at a more general level.

Overall, the recommended practice is the advice of experts in the field, neither supported nor refuted by systematic data.

Implications for Action

It is appropriate to observe this recommended practice, certainly in areas of identified student interest and choice, though the defense for doing so is implicit at this stage. The practice is attractive in that it answers, in part, how gifted education can differ from the usual variety.

Barbe and Malone (1985) give an example of in-depth study based on the lives of famous persons. Students also studied individuals who actually interacted with the famous persons in their own lives; these mutual influences could then be explored beyond the details local to each individual. Khatena (1982) suggested several examples, including phonetics, philology, and etymology as a part of language arts, or higher arithmetic, numerical analysis, permutation and combination, and statistics in elementary mathematics. Feldhusen and Reilly (1983) noted the use of seminars in the Purdue Model to encourage the process of in-depth study, and VanTassel-Baska (1985) suggested the use of Socratic techniques and learning materials designed for adults.

Recall that this recommended practice primarily addresses the academic goals of a gifted program. Excessive attention to the depth or rigor of subject-matter content might interfere with the attainment of other key goals (e.g., self-esteem for a gifted underachiever).

Needed Research

When should this goal be given priority and for whom? Can such study aid in the development of high-level thinking skills? To what extent is success with in-depth study limited by student interests and the exercise of student choice?

65 | Include Independent Study Under Competent Supervision

Independent study is recommended by almost everyone (B. Clark, 1988; Davis & Rimm, 1989; Feldhusen, VanTassel-Baska, & Seeley, 1989; Gallagher, 1985; J. P. Parker, 1989; Swassing, 1985b; Treffinger, 1986). Ward (1975) summarized the issue:

> The unique characteristics of gifted children make possible a "reversed ratio" of teaching to learning. For this reason independent (individual) study is particularly suited to the needs of gifted students. (p. 300)

B. Clark (1988) made the teacher's responsibility and role more explicit. Bright students

> often have the curiosity, the interest, and the motivation to pursue a study of their own choosing; but all too often they do not have the skills, skills such as how they can search for primary sources, use professional methods of inquiry, collect and organize raw data, analyze and evaluate data, and form conclusions. These skills often need to be taught if the student is to be successful. (p. 158)

Independent study redefines the role of the teacher, especially increasing its sophistication.

Current Knowledge

The literature on independent study for gifted students is primarily prescriptive and descriptive. It has been recommended as one means of self-directed learning (Treffinger, 1986) and as individualized instruction (Jeter & Chauvin, 1982; Swassing, 1985b). It is a major component of several models of gifted education at the elementary level (Feldhusen & Kolloff, 1978; Renzulli, 1977; Treffinger, 1986) and at the secondary level (Betts, 1986; Feldhusen & Robinson, 1986; Reis & Renzulli, 1985), in rural settings (Caudill, 1977; Lupkowski, 1984) and in art (A. Gregory, 1982), computers (Glaser, 1978), mathematics (Fox, 1974), and science (Brandwein, 1955/1981; Cooke, 1980).

The empirical literature supporting independent study is spotty but consistent. Studies of the learning styles of gifted students (see recommended practice No. 35) indicate that they prefer independent projects (Stewart, 1981) or independent approaches to learning (Dunn & Griggs, 1985). McCormick and Swassing (1982) surveyed reading provisions for the gifted in 149 school districts from 44 states; 16% of the districts reported extra-classroom programs and stated that one of the most important components of their programs was the opportunity for independent study. Dole and Adams (1983) surveyed experts in gifted education and in reading. Both groups reported that independent study was the most important means of differentiating reading instruction for the gifted. In a survey of general gifted program goals, Hickey (1988) used the Delphi technique to establish what priorities experts, administrators, teachers, and parents identified for students; although independent study was not identified as the most important, it was considered "very important" by all of them.

Evidence of the effectiveness of independent study is embedded in evaluations of materials, specialized programs, or general enrichment models (cf. Starko, 1988). Parke (1983) investigated the use of programmed materials in mathematics with students in kindergarten, first, and second grades. When compared with high-achieving and randomly selected control groups, students in the self-instructional group mastered more skills. Fox (1974) also reported that fast-paced independent study of mathematics was a frequently used provision in the development of the Study of Mathematically Precocious Youth, whose success has been widely documented. Independent study has been shown to have positive effects on creative productivity as defined by Renzulli-inspired enrichment programs.

Implications for Action

Independent study is easy and inexpensive to implement and benefits students with intense curiosity about a particular topic. It should be conducted under competent supervision and not be used as a dumping ground for a pesky, bright child. Neither should it relegate a child unwillingly to private study.

A growing list of commercially available materials make independent study more easily implemented in the classroom. These materials attest to the caution that bright children need to be taught prerequisite skills for independent study. One promising scheme for doing so is the nine-step Independent Study Process (ISP) formulated by Doherty and Evans (1981a, 1981b).

1. Select a topic.
2. Establish a schedule.
3. Develop five or more questions to direct the research.
4. Secure references or data.
5. Research the topic.
6. Develop five final objectives using Bloom's Taxonomy.
7. Have an evaluative conference with the teacher.
8. Make a product.
9. Display the product.

Needed Research

The need for independent study and its general usefulness to serve gifted students does not need much additional research attention unless one is uncomfortable with the notion that it is widely applicable in general education. Is it less desired and successful with a broader range of students?

Most needed now are finer examinations of the best ways of conducting independent study. What skills beyond library and reference techniques are necessary for successful independent study? Which skills should be the responsibility of regular classroom teachers, which of gifted specialists? What is the nature of appropriate supervision? Do students in resource-room programs do better than gifted students served in self-contained or regular classrooms? A comparison of product ratings by a blind jury would be a reasonable means of studying the issue.

Does independent study influence continuing motivation? Is it predictive of later productivity?

Finally, what competencies are needed by teachers to implement independent study with their gifted students? How may these competencies best be imparted?

66 | Prepare Students for High-Level Occupations

On one hand, the gifted have been urged to prepare for high-level occupations because they represent society's talent "capital." On the other, high-level occupations have been viewed as a part of self-actualization for the multitalented individual. Tannenbaum (1979) summarized the manpower issue:

> To some extent, the eagerness among educators to increase the nation's talent supply was inspired by politicians and economists who had worried about our diminishing reservoir of high-level manpower in science and technology even before Sputnik dramatized the problem. . . . Only six of ten in the top 5 percent and only half of the top 25 percent of high school graduates went on to earn college diplomas. At the more advanced levels, a mere 3 percent of those capable of earning the Ph.D. actually did so. (p. 8)

Care is needed not to overgeneralize from these figures, because college diplomas are not the only paths to occupational success and status for an individual, despite their value overall to society. Entrepreneurs and artists, for example, have varied educational backgrounds.

> Although some current rhetoric extols the merits of giftedness across disciplines—gifted mechanics, for example, or talented plumbers—the career tendency for bright youngsters remains, as always, towards professional occupations. (Delisle, 1985b, p. 370)

Feldhusen (1983b) included the recommended practice in a list of needs basic to talented youth.

Current Knowledge

Numerous references on occupational preferences and career aspirations of young people (see recommended practice Nos. 49 and 90) concern college undergraduates, many of whom are gifted and talented. Longitudinal studies of career-related outcomes among high school students reported that 70% of them ultimately enrolled in graduate study (Sanborn, 1979a). Similar high-level occupational aspirations were reported by Marshall (1981) and Tidwell (1980a).

There are two main concerns about high-level occupations for the gifted. First, several persons have cautioned against pressuring the gifted into long and expensive training programs for professions that may not suit them (Frederickson, 1979; E. L. Herr & Watanabe, 1979; Sanborn, 1979a). Conversely, some students (usually girls or disadvantaged youth) need encouragement to raise the level of their expectations (Callahan, 1979; Frasier, 1979; Kerr, 1983).

Relevant research comes from Terman and Oden (1959) and Willings (1983b, 1985, 1986). Both document cases of highly gifted adults who experienced problems in the workplace, including, for example, not getting along with supervisors. Although the authors did not concentrate on the choice of high- or low-level occupations as a contributing factor to the discontent, several of the individuals were functioning in less challenging jobs than they were capable of doing. Willings suggested that guidance could help bright persons, especially the creatively gifted, deal more effectively with their occupational choices and situations.

There is some anecdotal evidence that the gifted individual has an "elaborate and complex work value system" that can be fulfilled through work (Jepsen, 1979). Case studies of gifted adults indicate that challenging work is an important expression of their identity (Bloom, 1985).

Implications for Action

Raising the career aspirations of girls and economically disadvantaged youth is a reasonable objective. Frasier (1979) alerts counselors that upward mobility for economically disadvantaged youths may be painful.

Any adoption of this practice should be managed with care. Career and occupational choice is a complex and developmental process. Exhortations for high-level occupations may miss the mark unless accompanied by thoughtful educational and vocational counseling that respects personal and cultural values.

Needed Research

What do "high-level occupations" mean to highly able children and to adults? High paying? High status? Power wielding? Intellectually and creatively challenging? For example, are some often low-paying but highly creative professions in the performing arts (e.g., acting, dancing) or community service considered high-level occupations? Which occupations on occupational reference lists are rated as high level by bright students, their parents, teachers, potential employers, and others? Is there agreement?

Second, an investigation of gifted individuals in both high- and low-level occupations would provide comparative descriptions of career and life satisfaction related to occupational choice. Although it would be difficult to determine causality, studies that examine the contribution of underemployment to dissatisfaction in gifted adults would help to establish the possible danger of not encouraging gifted youngsters to aim occupationally high.

Third, it would be useful to explore what prompts the high-level dropouts mentioned by Tannenbaum (1979).

Fourth, particular attention could be addressed to women in high-level occupations, and especially to why more bright women than men have more limited ranges of occupational preferences. Are different strategies needed to attract women and men to these occupations? Do they rate the same occupations as high level?

Chance life events may influence occupational outcomes and life satisfaction enough to mask effects of the practice on groups of gifted individuals. Thus, investigating the practice empirically from the orientation of self-actualizing the gifted person will be difficult and probably inconclusive. From society's self-serving point of view, it is a truism that the most talented individuals are desired for the most important jobs. The issue is likely to be decided on the basis of values as much as on a well-researched knowledge base.

CHAPTER FIVE

Advice to Parents

<table>
<tr><td>67</td><td>**Emotional Support From Parent Groups and Counselors Should Be Available**</td></tr>
</table>

There are two major themes in the parent literature. The first emphasizes the role of parents in facilitating their children's intellectual, social, and emotional development. This recommended practice concerns the second major theme, which is what kind of support parents need to cope with their own emotional reactions to dealing with a gifted child. There is widespread endorsement of parent counseling to respond to these emotional strains (Kaufmann & Castellanos, 1986; A. O. Ross, 1979; Webb, Meckstroth, & Tolan, 1982).

> A most important aspect of our work is to run a voluntary counseling service, because parents of gifted children experience difficulties strangely similar to those experienced by parents of handicapped children—strains on family relationships, educational problems, and the dilemma of how much time, money, and resources to spend. (J. C. Williams, 1981, p. 150)

Current Knowledge

The first of two major deficits in the research literature is empirical studies that directly test the hypothesis that parents of high-ability children need emotional support. In contrast, there is considerable research on the excellent family environments of high-ability children (Colangelo & Dettman, 1983; Cornell & Grossberg, 1987; Olszewski, Kulieke, & Buescher, 1987), which contradicts the notion that their parents are under special stress or in need of counseling. There may, of course, be subgroups of parents who do experience these needs. We found no studies that attempted to identify those parents most at risk for emotional difficulties that would justify counseling.

Similarly, we were unable to locate empirical studies that demon-

174

strated that parent counseling or parent groups are effective sources of emotional support for parents of high-ability children. Many authors recommend specific counseling approaches or report the success of their own counseling work (Braggett, Ashman, & Noble, 1983; Congdon, 1980; Conroy, 1987; Dettman & Colangelo, 1980; Gowan & Bruch, 1971; R. L. Harris & Bauer, 1983; A. O. Ross, 1979; Webb et al., 1982; J. C. Williams, 1981; Wolf & Stephens, 1983). None offered objective evidence for these claims.

Implications for Action

One of the frustrations of reviewing the literature is to encounter such striking agreement among authorities about the value of a particular practice but a virtual absence of research in its support. The literature identifies some parent problems and describes several counseling models. However, there is no empirical basis (e.g., surveys, accumulated case studies) for favoring any one counseling approach or strategy (e.g., support groups, workshops, individual counseling) over another. Educators and counselors are advised to follow their own judgment in deciding when and how to implement a parent-counseling program, which should be tailored to the specific needs or concerns of the parents in question.

Needed Research

A reasonable program of parent-counseling research might begin with surveying the incidence of various complaints and emotional difficulties parents experience in raising high-ability children. The oft-repeated claim that such problems are similar to those experienced by parents of handicapped children needs verification. How serious are these problems and what impact do they have on child and family?

A standardized means of assessing typical problems faced by parents of high-ability children would be a useful methodological as well as practical contribution to the field. Are there common constellations of problems or general types of parent reactions? For example, is it possible to identify objectively those parents who are intimidated by their child's abilities? Do they tend to discourage the child or fail to provide adequate support for his or her developmental needs? Can they be discerned from those who are overindulgent, or, as Congdon (1980, cf. p. 151) put it, who "pressurize" their child?

A next step might be to examine correlates of particular parent problems or constellations of problems. Are less well-educated parents more intimidated by the child's abilities, and are better educated parents more likely to pressure the child?

Given a means of identifying types of parent problems and perhaps a preliminary theory of etiological factors associated with these problems, the groundwork would be laid for intervention research. What kinds of counseling approaches are most effective with what kinds of parent problems?

68 Participate in and Lobby for Programs

The call for parent participation is nearly universal in the literature. Parents of children with disabling characteristics have clearly been in the forefront of parental involvement, at least in advocacy. Parent participation in general is now widely accepted as a goal in all public education, and even private schools claim parental involvement as part of their raison-d'être. It remains to be seen how much of all this is rhetoric.

Here is an example of the general advice from the literature on giftedness: "If parents wish to contribute most effectively in their children's education, they must actively interact with those who administer and staff the gifted program" (P. A. Alexander & Muia, 1982, p. 193).

The most frequently mentioned form of involvement is advocacy and lobbying for good-quality programs; this partly overlaps recommended practice No. 2. B. Clark (1988) also suggested direct teaching with small groups, providing or organizing materials, and conferences for planning and evaluation with the child and teacher. Khatena (1979) proposed that the main contribution was to do their best as parents in the home and related environment. Identification of giftedness was frequently mentioned.

Current Knowledge

There seems to be no evaluation of the effectiveness of this advice but rather a combination of expressions of the importance of parental involvement and many lists of ways to accomplish this. Dettman and Colangelo (1980) described the recommended practice as a "premise" (p. 158), but Bogue and Wolf (1985) implied that parental involvement was a consequence of good program planning, not a cause: "An important benefit of the enrichment program was its ability to provide opportunities for parents to be involved in classes with their children" (p. 114). Cassidy (1981) noted that some professionals resent what is perceived as parental interference.

Lacking from all the writing on this topic is any systematic presentation of evidence supporting the advice. We have, in this recommended practice, an excellent example of the oracular origins of a sizable part of the knowledge base on educating and raising exceptionally able children.

Implications for Action

Parental involvement in schools is not a new idea, certainly not in North America where voluntary organizations such as Home and School or Parent-Teacher Associations abound. Some jurisdictions have made such general involvement a legal part of the school administrative structures, such as the School Committees in Quebec. The critical point, at this time, is to limit one's defense of its promotion to the belief that it is a good idea. There is no documented evidence that parent involvement makes a difference in the quality of education of gifted students or that it is particularly important in gifted education.

Needed Research

Direct parental involvement in gifted education has been overlooked as a topic worthy of sustained, systematic study, perhaps even by a center devoted to the question.

Several questions lend themselves to empirical verification through surveys and case studies. How widespread are the different kinds of involvement? How did the involvement come about, as a cause or an effect of the program's creation? A combination of both? What was the attitude of staff toward parental involvement? Did it shift with time? Was parental involvement a premise on the part of parents, teachers, politicians? How important is it to be organized in local, regional, or national organizations? Are there more good programs where such organizations mobilize or represent parental involvement? Most importantly, what are the consequences of parental involvement? Is it correlated with or does it cause better programs? Does it make teachers, children, parents, administrators, or politicians happier? These questions have to be examined separately for the different kinds of involvement, because identifying one's own child's special needs, helping with field trips, and planning curriculum are very different activities and might be perceived very differently.

Other inquiry, largely comparative or part of policy studies, needs to focus on how parental involvement in programs for the highly able is to be differentiated from corresponding advice regarding any other groups of children.

69 | Avoid Stereotypes and Misconceptions About the Gifted Label

Stereotypes and misconceptions about high-ability youth plague parents and teachers alike.

Gifted students have been the victims of debilitating myths and stereotypes. These stereotypes have been prevalent and powerful enough to keep this group of high potential students our most neglected educational minority. (Colangelo, 1979, p. 375)

The perception improves, however, among those who have more direct experience and among those who have had courses aimed at understanding and educating gifted children. (B. Clark, 1988, p. 153)

Current Knowledge

The study of stereotypes and misconceptions is imbedded in a broader literature on attitudes toward giftedness, gifted programs, and high-ability students in general. For example, Colangelo and Kelly (1983) found that parents and teachers rank gifted programs relatively low in importance in comparison with other school activities.

Cornell (1984) found that parents have a wide range of both positive and negative views toward giftedness. Although many parents welcomed the application of the term to their children, other parents, particularly fathers, refused to apply the term even though their child was placed in a gifted program. Over one-third of all parents in the study voiced negative views of giftedness, the most common being that giftedness was associated with social or emotional maladjustment. Other parents opposed the use of the term on grounds that it was élitist, or that others would develop misconceptions about their child.

When asked to define giftedness, interviewed parents typically stressed learning ability over IQ (Cornell, 1984). In a study of written definitions, parents routinely identified at least seven different characteristics of giftedness, with no single characteristic mentioned by more than 40% of the sample. The most frequently noted characteristic was perceptiveness (40%); least often mentioned were precocity (15%) or creativity (13%) (Cornell & Grossberg, 1989). Learning ability and IQ were mentioned by only about one-fourth of these parents. One wonders whether a survey of authorities in the field would yield any greater convergence (e.g., see Sternberg & Davidson, 1986).

Some of the more prevalent (and sometimes conflicting) stereotypes teachers hold about high-ability children include the following:

1. They are odd and bookwormish, with few social interests.
2. They have no emotional difficulties or learning problems and will be successful in any educational environment.
3. They are white and middle class (Kaufmann & Castellanos, 1986; also see recommended practice No. 88).

Teacher attitudes toward giftedness are mixed and may interact with attitudes toward other characteristics (A. Robinson, 1986c). Students perceived as both gifted and studious but nonathletic may be perceived negatively by teachers (Cramond & Martin, 1987). Students who are black (Rubovits & Maehr, 1973) or from working-class backgrounds (Maltby, 1984) also may be subject to less favorable treatment by teachers than other gifted program students. Kaufmann and Sexton (1983) reported that 45% of 98 surveyed parents indicated that they had encountered teachers who were "unsympathetic" to their child's needs.

Gallagher (1985) contended that teachers feel threatened by the exceptional abilities and challenging behavior of high-ability students. Might this be a defensive reaction to the stress of teaching difficult students?

T. Busse, Dahme, Wagner, and Wieczerkowski (1986) compared teacher perceptions of "highly gifted" students in Germany and the United States. Teachers in both countries had very favorable views of these students, emphasizing their reasoning abilities, independence, and good adjustment. The absence of negative stereotypes is heartening, but the study was limited by the use of a teacher-nominated sample. Each teacher selected one student to describe, and if teachers quite understandably described their favorite students, ratings would be biased in a positive direction and not reflect their attitudes toward high-ability students as a group.

Surprisingly, psychologists and counselors may have more negative attitudes toward giftedness than teachers do (Wiener, 1968; Deiulio, 1984). This reflects poorly on the training and preparation of school mental health professionals, despite the available literature on counseling high-ability youth (Colangelo & Zaffrann, 1979; Ziv, 1977).

Implications for Action

As noted by Kaufmann and Castellanos (1986), "Gifted people, contrary to prevalent stereotypes, tend to be an extremely diverse group" (p. 235). There is evidence of stereotypes and misconceptions among both parents and teachers. Education about the diversity of high-ability children and the multidimensionality of current conceptions of giftedness should be an ongoing process, through in-service training, education, or work experience (Dettmer, 1985a; Wiener, 1968; Wiener & O'Shea, 1963; Weiss & Gallagher, 1980). Similar research on parents is not available.

Two sets of proposed standards for training programs in gifted education in the last decade (Seeley, Jenkins, & Hultgren, 1979; Association for the Gifted, 1989) call for gifted program teachers to have specialized advanced training and for all teachers to have information on these students included in their training.

Needed Research

Stereotypic views are inconsistent with definitions of giftedness that stress diversity of talents and interests and the use of multiple identification procedures (see recommended practice No. 14). The origins of stereotypical views are not known.

Studies need to examine educational strategies for altering stereotypes and correcting misconceptions. We do not know how resistant to change various attitudes are. Experience and contact with the diversity of high-ability youth may be useful in remedying some misconceptions, but others are still found even among highly experienced teachers and parents.

| 70 | **Be Aware of How Personal Needs and Feelings Influence the Relationship With the Child** |

The perception of a child as "gifted" can be of great psychological significance to the parent and elicit a wide range of personal feelings and responses. First, and perhaps foremost, the normal hopes and dreams for a child are magnified by the grand possibilities that "giftedness" seems to imply (Greenstadt, 1981; A. Miller, 1981; Webb, Meckstroth, & Tolan, 1982).

> The gifted child can represent an exceptionally powerful source of narcissistic gratification—for example, as reflected in the parent's strong feelings of pride in the child. The parent's identification with the gifted child draws the parent into an especially close attachment to the child. (Cornell, 1984, p. 79)

Some parents are dismayed or react negatively to the idea that their child is exceptionally able. These reactions may range from understandable anxiety over how to "do the right thing" in raising their child to an outright aversion toward having a child who is "too smart." The most commonly noted negative reactions are anxiety and guilt that the parent will not know how to nurture and facilitate the child's talents (Greenstadt, 1981; Webb et al., 1982):

> Parents of gifted children may feel guilty about their inability to provide the child with what they see as necessary intellectual stimulation or educational opportunities. They may feel guilty about giving more attention to the gifted child than to their other children and conflicted about his not participating in the usual social or athletic activities. (A. O. Ross, 1979, p. 406)

A few parents even respond to their children's exceptional abilities with jealousy, resentment, or unconscious rivalry (Cornell, 1984; Greenstadt, 1981):

> They may feel threatened by their gifted child who is more and more frequently demonstrating that he is becoming brighter than they and who, in increasingly frequent situations, can find answers to problems the parents themselves are unable to solve. (A. O. Ross, 1979, p. 406)

Current Knowledge

Most empirical studies have found that parents provide very positive family environments for high-ability children (Colangelo & Dettmann, 1983; Cornell & Grossberg, 1987; Janos & Robinson, 1985a; Olszewski, Kulieke, & Buescher, 1987). Parents tend to be particularly well informed about their children's needs and strive hard to provide them with both appropriately nurturing and educationally stimulating environments. Although most studies compare families of high-ability children with families of less able children, they do not examine differences among families within the gifted group and thus may create the false impression of homogeneity (Cornell & Grossberg, 1987). Few studies have investigated the more problematic parent-child relationships that many counselors and teachers report (Bridges, 1973; Colangelo & Dettmann, 1983; A. O. Ross, 1979).

Numerous case studies describe parents whose emotional overinvestment in their child's giftedness led them to dominate the child's life with constant training and pressure to excel (for examples, see Ehrenwald, 1963; Montour, 1977; Weiner, 1953). Newman, Dember, and Krug (1973) described a syndrome of excessive maternal involvement that resulted in underachievement and superficial intellectualism in 15 high-IQ children. Drawing upon cases she has treated with psychoanalysis, A. Miller (1981) elaborated in compelling detail the consequences of parental narcissism for the child's later adult personality and adjustment.

Beyond the case-study literature, there is only limited systematic research on parental reactions to highly talented children. Cornell (1984) found that parents who perceived their child as gifted described much greater feelings of pride in the child and a much closer relationship with the child than did parents who did not perceive their otherwise able child as gifted. Even within the same family, parents who perceive a child as gifted appear to have a more intense relationship with the child than do spouses who do not perceive the same child as gifted. Moreover, parents know much more about the child perceived as gifted than about nongifted siblings (Hitchfield, 1973).

Most research in developmental psychology stresses the importance of parental involvement for healthy child development (Maccoby & Martin, 1983); however, this body of work focuses on the detrimental effects of underinvolvement. Overinvolvement has not received systematic attention (Maccoby & Martin, 1983).

A direct causal relationship between parental overinvestment in giftedness and adverse effects on the child has not been established, although there are some recent suggestive and provocative findings. Two studies (Cornell, 1989; Cornell & Grossberg, 1989) found that children whose parents use the term "gifted" to describe them are less well-adjusted than are equally able peers whose parents refrain from using the term. Group differences were found on a variety of standard adjustment measures, including measures based on parent report, child self-report, and peer status. Pelton (1989) found a weak negative relationship between a questionnaire measure of parental overinvolvement and child self-concept and peer status.

Unfortunately, there is little research to describe the scope or magnitude of parental anxiety or guilt in raising high-ability children (cf. review by Colangelo & Dettmann, 1983). We also do not know to what extent some parents maintain pejorative, stereotypic attitudes toward the concept of giftedness (see recommended practice No. 69) that influence the parent-child relationship (Colangelo, 1979; Cornell, 1984).

Frierson (1965) suggested that many of the positive responses that parents have to high-ability children are biased by socioeconomic status. There are less favorable attitudes and reactions to high-ability children by parents from lower socioeconomic status groups. Similarly, Cheyney (1962) reported less encouragement and support for high-IQ children's intellectual development by parents of lower socioeconomic status. Finally, Bridges (1973) commented that parents of low socioeconomic status may be excited by the opportunities for advancement open to their high-ability child but also concerned that they cannot provide adequate educational experiences.

Implications for Action

There is no basis for assuming that parents in general will have problematic attitudes and reactions to their child's giftedness. Neither are healthy parental pride and exuberance necessarily signs of overinvolvement! Parents and educators can be aware of the personal significance that giftedness can have for some parents and the ways that parental investment in the child's talents and abilities can influence the parent-child relationship. Such understanding may be useful in presenting information to parents at the time of identification and placement in a gifted program.

Counselors and psychologists who work with highly able youth should be well informed about the various ways that parents may respond to the idea that their son or daughter is gifted. McMann & Oliver (1988) provide a good overview of specific counseling issues with these families (see also Colangelo & Zaffrann, 1979).

Needed Research

Despite numerous case studies and accumulated clinical lore about parental overinvolvement (e.g., the "stage mother" syndrome), the varieties of parental reactions (especially negative ones) to the idea of giftedness in their children are not well charted, and the consequences of these different reactions for the parent-child relationship and for child adjustment are not well understood. (The impact of these relationships on siblings is discussed in recommended practice Nos. 76 and 88.)

We require methods of assessing parental involvement and distinguishing between healthy involvement and overinvolvement. Parental involvement appears to be a multidimensional construct (Pelton & Cornell, 1988), but it is not clear what dimensions or aspects should be the focus of concern. There appears to be no systematic research on effective counseling methods or family therapy with overinvolved parents.

| 71 | **Avoid Excessive Emphasis on Developing the Child's Giftedness** |

This recommendation targets parents who are so obsessed with their child's "giftedness" that it becomes the guiding principle determining their child's activities. Two selections from the literature illustrate the overwhelming advice against this:

> Avoid pressurizing the gifted child. . . . There are parents who assume almost total responsibility for the education of their gifted child. They organize and regiment his life, march him round museums and art galleries crowding impression upon impression. The child becomes absorbed in educational materials and the private acquisition of skills. No expense is spared for the purpose of stimulating and supposedly educating his mind. Such parents need to be reminded that there are times when these children want to play and act like other children and they should be allowed to do so. (Congdon, 1979, pp. 355–356)

> The child may experience excessive parental expectations to achieve at a uniformly high level, resulting in stressful reactions and emotional conflicts (re-

bellious behavior, performance anxiety, neurotic perfectionism, etc.). (Cornell, 1984, p. 74)

Current Knowledge

Most of the parent literature in gifted education addresses ways in which parents can respond to their child's educational and developmental needs (e.g., B. Clark, 1988; B. S. Miller & Price, 1981; Perino & Perino, 1981; Webb, Meckstroth, & Tolan, 1982; Zorman, 1982). Parents are advised how to recognize signs of the child's abilities, promote creativity, develop caring relationships, or provide enriching cultural or educational experiences.

Parents with single-minded devotion to developing their child's abilities are best described in individual case studies or accounts of historical figures such as Mozart or John Stuart Mill (Ehrenwald, 1963; A. Miller, 1981; Montour, 1977; Weiner, 1953). These reports often describe a tyrannic parental dominance of the child's development, with seemingly every moment scheduled for some type of educational activity. Adverse outcomes for these children range from poor social skills and maladjusted behavior in childhood to career disillusionment, depression, and even mental illness in adulthood.

Few studies have systematically examined the kinds of parents depicted in case reports. As noted in recommended practice No. 70, Cornell (1984) described a pattern of idealization of gifted children by some parents, although the parents' emphasis on developing their child's abilities was not assessed directly. In later work, Pelton and Cornell (1988) reported the development of a questionnaire to assess parent overinvolvement. Pelton (1989) found limited evidence that some forms of high parent involvement are associated with poorer self-concept and less favorable peer status in their children.

Bloom (1985) and his colleagues conducted a retrospective interview study of 120 young adults with exceptional achievements in music, art, athletics, or mathematics and science. Parent encouragement and support was critical to the child's talent development, especially during the initial years of study.

> The parents of the talented individuals . . . could be described as child-oriented and willing to devote their time, their resources, and their energy to giving each of their children the best conditions they could provide for them. Almost no sacrifice was too great if they thought it would help their child's development.
>
> In the majority of these homes we found that the parents placed great stress on achievement, on success, and on doing one's best at all times. These

parents were models of the "work ethic" in that they were regarded as hard workers, they did their best in whatever they tried, they believed that work should come before play and that one should work toward distant goals. (Bloom, 1985, p. 510)

Parental involvement decreased after early childhood and the children entered school:

The major role in setting expectations and demands was assumed by the new teacher. The parents helped their children set schedules and plans for the practice, but by this time they did not need to monitor the practice, since the students had already developed the appropriate habits. (Bloom, 1985, p. 521)

Bloom emphasized that parents were strong advocates of their values and work ethic, and they were supportive and encouraging. There is no explicit statement whether some were extremely demanding or personally driven to see their child excel. Also missing from the study is whether the talented individuals were satisfied with their upbringing and how happy or well-adjusted they were as adults.

Elkind (1981, 1987) stimulated considerable controversy with his charge that many parents and educators place too much emphasis on early learning and skill acquisition in young children. From his developmental perspective, children should not be expected to learn material that is too advanced for their cognitive and affective level (see also Kagan & Zigler, 1987). Although some children can be forced to learn at an early age (e.g., preschool reading), they may learn by rote memory or other mechanical processes that are devoid of true understanding. More importantly, Elkind contended that such children might not develop a love of learning and may be impaired by anxiety and neurotic needs for achievement in later grades.

Recent research has produced some support for Elkind's position. A longitudinal study of over 300 preschool children drawn from 22 different schools examined the effects of parent attitudes toward early learning on the child's later school performance and other outcome measures (Hirsh-Pasek, Hyson, Rescorla, & Cone, 1989; Rescorla, Hyson, Hirsh-Pasek, & Cone, 1990). The researchers contrasted parents with high academic expectations for their preschool child with parents with low academic expectations. The children of parents with high expectations scored higher on academic skills, although group differences dissipated after the children entered kindergarten 1 year later. However, congruent with Elkind's concerns, the children of parents with high expectations also tended to be more anxious and less creative and developed a more negative attitude toward kindergarten than the other children did.

The debate and controversy over the merits of formal instruction in academic work at the preschool level are beyond the scope of this book, let alone this recommendation. Clearly, there are conflicting points of view and evidence on both sides of the issue (Kagan & Zigler, 1987). Findings that support early education for disadvantaged preschoolers (e.g., Headstart research) are unlikely to be applicable to the broader population of preschool children and even less likely to apply to high-ability children alone (although undoubtedly some of them fall into the disadvantaged group).

Implications for Action

The distinction between a healthy degree of parental encouragement and excessive demandingness is difficult to specify (A. O. Ross, 1979). Parents should respond to their child's special educational needs; exceptional talent rarely develops without solid parental support. Parents often make considerable personal sacrifices of time and money in order for the child to practice, take lessons, compete, and so on (Bloom, 1985).

The concern that parents can be too devoted to children and demand too much from them is generally not disputed. Nevertheless, only a few studies have started to address this topic, and practical guidelines are so far based on informed opinion more than established fact:

1. Allow the child free time to play or pursue interests that are not necessarily goal-oriented (Hirst, 1981).
2. See that the child's social needs are not neglected in the pursuit of strictly academic ones (Congdon, 1979; Perino & Perino, 1981; see also recommended practice No. 74).
3. Make sure the child feels loved and valued for himself or herself, not because of his or her achievements (B. Clark, 1988; Cornell, 1984; Greenstadt, 1981; see also recommended practice No. 70).
4. Parents should feel free to take time apart from their children and to pursue private interests (Webb et al., 1982).
5. Be cautious about drilling preschool children in academic skills they will learn in kindergarten and first grade. Excessive pressure may produce early skill development but could have adverse side effects, such as a more anxious and negative attitude toward learning and less creativity (Elkind, 1987; Hirsh-Pasek et al., 1989).

Needed Research

The line of research represented by the work of Hirsh-Pasek et al. (1989) should be pursued vigorously by others. The Rescorla Educational

Attitude Scale is an especially promising means of assessing parent academic expectations for their preschool children (Rescorla et al., 1990). The development of analogous instruments for parents of older children would be desirable. Ongoing development of the Parent Involvement Scale (Pelton & Cornell, 1988) is a step in this direction.

The balance between healthy encouragement and excessive parental pressure needs examination. Academic expectations may have to be examined in the context of other factors in the parent-child relationship. Perhaps parental expectations only become "excessive" in the absence of other positive qualities in the parent-child relationship; it is not clear whether relative or absolute levels of emphasis are critical. Finally, Pelton and Cornell's hypothesis (Pelton, 1989; Pelton & Cornell, 1988) that the relationship between parent involvement and child adjustment is curvilinear bears further study. Both very high and very low parent involvement may prove disadvantageous to the child's self-concept and social adjustment.

72 | Discourage Children's Perfectionism and Excessive Self-Criticism

Perfectionism is regarded as a common characteristic of high ability children (B. Clark, 1988; Takacs, 1986; Webb, Meckstroth, & Tolan, 1982; Whitmore, 1985). Parents are advised not only to discourage the child's perfectionism but to be aware of their own expectations and behaviors that tend to reinforce it.

> Don't expect perfection. Speaking of his parents, a young gifted teenager wrote recently, "[They] made me feel inadequate and frustrated if I was not constantly performing at my best." Subtle cues—like the refrigerator displaying only papers marked 100 percent—and blatant comparison—keeping a chart to record each sibling's number of report card A's—are equally destructive to a child's present and future self-worth. . . . Learn to accept outstanding effort as well as accomplishment—from yourself and your children—to avoid the psychological trap of never being quite good enough. (Alvino, 1985, p. 255)

Current Knowledge

Silverman, Chitwood, and Waters (1986) listed perfectionism on their checklist for parents to identify giftedness in their children. What is wrong with being a perfectionist? Perfectionism is by definition an unrealistic attitude, yet its damaging effect on the child's self-concept is most often cited as a critical problem (Webb et al., 1982).

Schneidman (1972) and Delisle (1986) hypothesized that conflict over unattainable perfectionist goals was a major contributing factor to suicide among talented adolescents.

B. Clark (1988) thoughtfully pointed out that perfectionism is not only painful for the child, but also for those around:

> Not only must gifted persons meet high standards and specified levels of performance, but their acceptance of other people is based on the other person's ability to meet these standards. These expectations of others can seriously interfere with interpersonal relationships, the view the gifted have of their world, and certainly how other people view them. Unfortunately, unless someone helps gifted children to understand the dynamics of this problem and provides some alternative behaviors, it can continue throughout their lives. (B. Clark, 1988, p. 142)

Nevertheless, the question "What's wrong with perfectionism?" is not answered readily and unequivocally. The difference between perfectionism and the high standards that drive talented individuals to great accomplishment is difficult to specify. Although authorities unanimously disparage "perfectionism" as a crippling, neurotic trait, many of those same authors extol "task commitment" and "idealism" as virtues of giftedness. Perhaps it is not too provocative to ask whether these are truly different characteristics or just different perspectives on the same thing? When a child succeeds in meeting his or her standards, do we refer to task commitment, but when he or she fails, do we speak of perfectionism? Given the increasing recognition of task commitment (or other similar qualities) as central to a conception of giftedness (Feldhusen, 1986; Renzulli, 1986b; also see recommended practice No. 20), the question deserves further thought and research.

What causes perfectionism? There are at least two implicit theories in the literature about the causes of perfectionism. One theory attributes perfectionism directly to the child's high intelligence and correspondingly high ability to recognize flaws and imperfections in his or her own work (Takacs, 1986; Webb et al., 1982; Whitmore, 1985). Another view is that "parental over-emphasis on achievement can prompt perfectionism" (Webb et al., 1982, p. 19).

> When a child exhibits unusual abilities, others tend to magnify them. They begin to see her as extraordinary, and as able to solve a wide array of problems. Their expectancies of her become exaggerated, and they may begin to expect perfection—that she can solve all problems. The gifted child's performance clearly does not reach this level, and as time passes the disparity

between expectation and performance can be a great source of stress. (Webb et al., 1982, p. 110)

Perino and Perino (1981) declared that parental perfectionism can backfire and result in underachievement:

> Many parents of gifted children are trying to relive their own lives through their children, they push the children to do the things they wish they had done for themselves. This type of behavior frequently alienates the child. (p. 62)

These two theories of perfectionism probably operate in tandem. Pacht (1984) and Sorotzkin (1985) offered much more detailed theories of perfectionism and suggested treatment approaches. There is limited empirical research on perfectionism, but most of it focuses on clinical populations, such as individuals with depression, eating disorders, or compulsive behavior problems (e.g., Hewitt & Dyck, 1986). Morse (1987) presented one of the few studies of perfectionism in young children. She reported counseling techniques used to treat elementary school children who procrastinate in their schoolwork.

Implications for Action

It is not clear how parents can encourage high standards in their children yet discourage perfectionism. Is the difference qualitative or merely quantitative? Certainly parental acceptance of less than perfection and provision of plenty of support when the child fails to meet internal or external standards of performance are strongly advised (B. Clark, 1988; Takacs, 1986; Webb et al., 1982).

Parents are also advised to recognize and avoid the ways in which they might encourage perfectionism in their children (Adderholdt-Elliott, 1987; Alvino, 1985; Perino & Perino, 1981; Sebring, 1983; Takacs, 1986). Prevention is more effective than intervention. Sometimes parents may remove pressure from their children by attending more closely to their own achievement needs (Cornell, 1984; Perino & Perino, 1981). Nevertheless, perfectionism may develop anyway, in which case interventions may range from parent-child discussions to professional counseling. B. Clark (1988) advised parents to draw upon their own experiences:

> One of the best ways to aid a child to handle perfectionism is to discuss some of the problems you have faced and the strategies you have used to work on your own perfectionist need. (p. 169)

Perfectionistic needs and other unrealistic attitudes that result in chronic self-denigration and other neurotic behavior can be treated by several forms of psychotherapy. Two of the most relevant and best known approaches are the rational-emotive therapy of Albert Ellis (Ellis & Harper, 1975) and the cognitive therapy of Aaron Beck (A. T. Beck, Rush, Shaw, & Emery, 1979). Both approaches focus on short-term efforts to help the person identify and alter irrational beliefs and negative self-statements.

Needed Research

There is little research on perfectionism in high-ability children. Although there have been some attempts to measure it as a scale within other instruments (Roehling & Robin, 1986; Hewitt & Dyck, 1986), a standard method of identifying and quantifying perfectionism in youth is needed. Particular attention should be given to distinguishing between perfectionism as a neurotic or maladaptive characteristic and high task commitment, which is generally regarded as healthy and adaptive. Hypotheses about the causes of perfectionism need examination.

Finally, the efficacy of counseling or other treatment approaches must be assessed. Cognitive-behavioral approaches appear to be the best suited to this problem, and researchers may find it possible to apply therapeutic techniques already in use with adolescents and young adults who suffer from depression.

73 | Encourage Social as Well as Academic Development

This advice seems to apply to all children and sounds so plausible as to be undeniable. In fact, the recommendation is merely proxy for more specific concerns that are not amenable to a succinct statement.

One concern is that children with advanced intellectual development do not have similarly advanced social development:

> Gifted children often suffer from a lack of synchronicity in the rates of development of their intellectual, affective, and motor progress, which has its effect in a number of aspects of their lives, and its results in turn produce further psychological problems. (Terrassier, 1985, p. 265)

A related concern is that children with advanced intellectual abilities are simply more vulnerable to problems in relating to others, so that social development is a special need (B. Clark, 1988; Roedell, 1984).

Finally, parents who understandably focus on encouraging a child's intellectual development may overlook social needs:

> Other problems may arise because the gifted child's social judgement and maturity do not develop at the same rate as his curiosity or knowledge about facts. (Webb, Meckstroth, & Tolan, 1982, p. 16)

> Parents should be wary about overemphasizing achievement to the detriment of important social areas. (Perino & Perino, 1981, p. 114)

Current Knowledge

Social and intellectual development are both multidimensional, multicomponential processes, so that a single, straightforward relationship is not possible. There are several bodies of research that address the question from different perspectives.

First, the relationship between intellectual ability and social adjustment is not decidedly negative (inverse). Studies from Terman onward demonstrate that most high-ability children are socially well adjusted (B. Clark, 1988). (Evidence of favorable peer acceptance—a more narrow concept—is discussed in recommended practice No. 74.) There is some suggestion that social adjustment becomes problematic in the extreme upper range of intellectual ability (B. Clark, 1988; Janos & Robinson, 1985a; Roedell, 1984), although the evidence is far from conclusive, and there are some contradictory findings (Grossberg & Cornell, 1988).

Second, there are indeed reports of social adjustment problems found among some high-ability children, as well as detailed recommendations about how to respond to them (e.g., Alvino, 1985; Pringle, 1970; Takacs, 1986). Typically, these problems are judged to be by-products of the child's intellectual abilities. For example, children may be intolerant of less able peers, or unaware that their enthusiasm for expressing their knowledge is seen as showing off. Pursuit of intellectual subjects and hobbies may make it difficult to find friends who share the same interests.

Finally, one of the more intriguing lines of research concerns the investigation of advanced social development, so-called "social giftedness." Abroms (1985) reviewed research on attempts to study "social intelligence." Most research can be grouped into the following categories:

1. Perspective taking—an ability to take the perspective of another person and accurately identify that person's thoughts or feelings
2. Prosocial behavior—relatively altruistic attempts to help or express sympathy for another

3. Moral reasoning—sophistication in reasoning used to identify a behavior as morally good or right
4. Leadership—assuming a role of authority or influence in group interaction

Overall, intellectually able children tend to be rated higher than less able peers in all four areas, although findings appear to be most consistent when measures of social intelligence are based on verbal reasoning rather than observed behavior.

The available evidence indicates that most intellectually able children will not experience social adjustment problems. If anything, their social development will probably be above average, even if not at the same level as their intellectual development. Some problems do occur.

Implications for Action

The above conclusion does not imply that parents need have no concern for their child's social development. Parents of high-ability children tend to be conscientious about their child's social and emotional as well as intellectual development (Colangelo & Dettmann, 1983; Cornell & Grossberg, 1987; Janos & Robinson, 1985a; Olszewski, Kulieke, & Buescher, 1987).

There is also ample documentation that social adjustment problems occur, and expert advice on what to do. There are no systematic studies to demonstrate the effectiveness of specific social interventions for high-ability youth, although there is a growing body of literature on social-skills training and related interventions with children in general (e.g., Conger & Keane, 1981; Kennedy, 1988; Roedell, Slaby, & Robinson, 1977).

Needed Research

Just as with the study of peer relations (see recommended practice No. 74), further research comparing groups of high- and average-intelligence children is of limited value. It is more important to identify highly intelligent youth who have social adjustment problems and to compare them to equally intelligent youth who are socially well adjusted. Are differences in social adjustment associated with social-skills deficits or are there specific behaviors associated with high intelligence? What can be attributed to environmental factors (such as inadequate school programs, negative attitudes toward high ability, family problems) versus individual factors (such as the child's intolerance for others or egotistical behavior)? Of course, intervention outcome studies are needed, too.

Although many authors recognize that there are highly intelligent children who are egotistical, obnoxious, withdrawn, or otherwise fall into redundant categories that Kennedy (1988) and others now delicately term "socially incompetent," few have studied them in a systematic, empirical manner. Is the subject too sensitive or are researchers afraid of reinforcing negative stereotypes? Whatever the objections and inhibitions, research on the topic is worthwhile because it can lend insight into how to help an important subgroup of high-ability children.

74 | Facilitate Social Development Through Ability-Peer Contact

Perino and Perino (1981) articulated this major concern of many parents: "Gifted children need to work with other gifted children" (p. 12). Webb, Meckstroth, and Tolan (1982) offered a more complex view of the child's need for peers:

> An intellectual peer for the gifted child may not be the same person who is a physical peer with skill levels in baseball or hopscotch more in keeping with her age group. Thus the gifted child often needs several different kinds of peers . . . some for sports, different ones for intellectual pursuits, and still others for emotional friendships. (p. 15)

Underlying both views is the common theme that the peer relations of high-ability children pose a serious concern.

Current Knowledge

Peer relations are increasingly recognized as a critical factor in child development. Longitudinal studies have found consistently that the quality of a child's peer relationships are predictive of the child's future social and emotional adjustment (J. G. Parker & Asher, 1987).

There is reasonably consistent evidence of at least average or above-average acceptance by peers in elementary classrooms (Gallagher, 1958; Gallagher & Crowder, 1957; Schneider, 1987; Schneider, Clegg, Byrne, Ledingham, & Crombie, 1989; see also review by Janos & Robinson, 1985a). Austin and Draper (1981) pointed out that classroom studies overlook the fact that high-ability students often have older friends, which would lead to an underestimate of the quality of their peer relations.

Fewer studies have examined the peer status of adolescents, but there is some indication of different findings. High-ability adolescents appear to be no more popular, and perhaps less popular, than their average classmates (Brody & Benbow, 1986; Keisler, 1955; Montemayor, 1984; Schneider et al., 1989).

The finding that high-ability students, as a group, enjoy favorable peer status does not negate the observation that some students do experience peer problems. High-ability students may experience peer problems for the same reasons other students do. Recent research has focused on social-skill deficits in children with peer-relation problems (Kennedy, 1988). We identified no studies comparing unpopular students of high and average ability.

Many authors contend that peer-relations problems in high-ability youth are the result of discrepancies between the child's well-developed intellectual abilities and less well-developed physical and social skills (Webb et al., 1982; Roedell, Jackson, Robinson, 1980; Terrassier, 1985). Intellectually advanced preschoolers also may have advanced social knowledge, but this may not always translate into similarly advanced prosocial behavior (see review of conflicting evidence in Austin & Draper, 1981).

Hollingworth (1926) is generally credited with first emphasizing the special problems faced by children with extremely high intelligence. Based on her observations and case studies, very highly intelligent youth are open to friendship but simply cannot locate peers who share their intellectual interests. Several studies of very highly intelligent youth have produced mixed or equivocal results (Brody & Benbow, 1986; Freeman, 1979; Gallagher, 1958).

Progress in understanding why some high-ability children have peer problems has been limited by the reliance on designs that simply compare high-ability students with less able peers. Future studies must examine individual differences in how equally intelligent students relate to others. For example, one study found a consistent relationship between lower social self-concept and less favorable peer status with classes and social groups composed entirely of high-ability youth (Cornell, Pelton, Bassin, Landrum, Ramsay, Cooley, Lynch, & Hamrick, 1990). Janos, Fung, and Robinson (1985) found that high-ability children who think of themselves as "different" from other children reported more difficulties in their friendships than did equally able children who did not think of themselves as different.

Finally, it is important to consider how placement in a gifted program affects peer relations. This is an unrecognized confounding variable in many studies, because peer attitudes toward high-ability children may be a function of both personal characteristics of the subject and feelings about the subject's status in a special program. Maddux, Scheiber, and Bass (1982) found limited evidence that high-ability students might experience lower peer status during the first year of placement in a segregated gifted program. Does grouping with ability peers improve peer relations? Do peer relations with ability peers differ from those with age peers? Is there a relation between IQ discrepancy and peer acceptance? How do high-ability peers get along with one another?

Implications for Action

Many high-ability children enjoy and benefit from association with peers of similar interests and abilities; parents should facilitate this kind of peer contact if it is not routinely available. But as Webb et al. (1982) pointed out, an individual child will have reason to associate with different peers (singly or in groups) for different reasons, not all of which require that the peers be of comparable ability.

Probably the best guide for parents is whether the child is content and secure in his or her associations with peers. If a child demonstrates poor self-esteem, frequently complains of loneliness or boredom, or has obvious difficulties in getting along with others (e.g., is teased or rejected by peers), then parents should consider some form of intervention. This could mean helping the child identify peers with similar interests; local youth clubs, community programs, and even a change in schools might be considered. Often, parents can arrange informal meetings with potential friends for their child through contacts with other parents in a local gifted association.

Some intellectually able children lack the social skills and interpersonal sensitivity to relate well to others, regardless of their ability level. High intelligence cannot be used as an excuse for rudeness or insensitivity. Takacs (1986) carefully described common social behavior problems exhibited by some high-ability children. These problems included tendencies to interrupt others, criticize and correct what others said, and use mockery and argument to compensate for other perceived social deficiencies or anxiety. Alvino (1985) described the differences between healthy and unhealthy peer relationships in adolescence.

Needed Research

Is social competence enhanced by bringing high-ability youth into contact with other children of similar ability? The consensus of expert opinion is "yes," but empirical support, notably for a causal relationship, is lacking.

Few studies have examined individual differences in peer status within the population of high-ability youth or attempted to identify the correlates of favorable peer relations. Studies of adolescent peer relations are especially needed.

So much effort has concentrated on how high-ability youth get along with less able peers that little is known about how they get along with each other. The experience of being in a group of ability peers has a significant effect on the student's self-concept (see recommended practice No. 84); there may be comparable effects on peer relations, for example, with regard to competition for grades and classroom recognition.

Peer status is closely associated with popularity, but few agree that popularity is the essence of peer relationships or healthy social adjustment in general (Kennedy, 1988). How does one compare the child with several very close friends to the one who is popular with everyone but is not especially close with anyone? What qualities of peer relationships are central to healthy adjustment?

75 | **Foster Potential for Giftedness Through Preschool Intervention**

Whitmore (1986), in the introduction to several papers, acknowledged that:

> A fundamental premise of the authors is that the early educational experiences of gifted children will critically influence the extent to which children with exceptionally high intellectual potential become high achievers or underachievers. (p. 103)

It is not always asserted that the intervention should be conducted in a school. Ehrlich's (1978) Astor Project was a community approach. Adjemovitch (1983), Rowlands (1974), and especially White (1983) stressed the parental role. Most projects have targeted children in the prekindergarten and kindergarten age range. Whitmore's (1980) Cupertino project served children in the early elementary grades. White (1983) emphasized very young children:

> The single key ingredient for the nurturing of the best possible development, is an awful lot of time during the course of the day with somebody who, between the time you are seven to twenty-four months of age, is crazy about you. (This is probably advisable for us at all ages, but in terms of the very young child, it seems especially appropriate.) (p. 23)

We therefore have widespread advocacy of attention to the preschool years to maximize later intellectual and concomitant motivational development.

Current Knowledge

We do not have complete agreement on what the treatment should be, who should provide it, or at what age it should begin.

The main evidence provided by published research on early intervention for very able children is that interventions are highly successful. Roedell, Jackson, and Robinson (1980) were able to advance the scholastic performance of preschoolers by several grades. Ehrlich (1978, 1982) showed that inner-city children could be helped to overcome academic disadvantages that constrained them. Bauer and Harris (1979), Cassidy and Vukelich (1978), and Hanninen (1984), among others, reported specific projects with positive short-term outcomes for children, parents, and teachers. Roedell et al. (1980) drew our attention to an interesting study by Durkin (1966) that reported that "after six years of school instruction in reading, children who had read before entering first grade still maintained their lead in achievement over classmates of the same mental age who did not begin to read until the first grade" (p. 25). This does not imply that the grade-level readers were underachieving or lacked achievement motivation. Neither is there any information about how the children came to be preschool readers, or about artistic, mathematical, or other abilities that might warrant attention under the heading of giftedness. Caldwell (1985), building on Durkin's work, showed several differences between the instructional needs of preschool readers and nonreaders but reported that in her sample the readers were, on average, 15 months older (65.5 versus 50.4). At that age, a year is a lot, and one is not convinced that any of the subsequent differences were not artifacts of the age difference and resulting experience, since there were no significant differences in mental age or Piagetian levels of functioning.

The main extensive evidence of long-term benefit from specific early intervention is White, Kaban, and Attanucci's (1979) work on the Harvard Preschool Project. However, this project examined the development of competence in essentially unselected children, not among those who were particularly endowed or deficient.

Freeman (1979) pursued this very point, in counterpoint to the recommended practice:

> The gifted infant, by virtue of her extra abilities, will be far more able to take advantage of whatever opportunities for learning may arise. A baby with an active mind and body is more likely to search out experience than one who lets life pass by. In this way, a gifted infant does indeed obtain early enrichment, but she also has a continuingly richer life. (p. 87)

The success of late talent searches, such as conducted by J. C. Stanley and his colleagues (Stanley, Keating, & Fox, 1974; and others), suggests that all is not irretrievably lost by the absence of explicit, formal early interventions. This was reinforced by Kitano and Tafoya (1982) who observed links between early and later leadership.

Very few interventions have dealt with extremely young children. Most address kindergarten children (age 5 to 6 in most of North America) or those 1 year younger. Success of such programs can be used just as easily to defend preschool intervention or intervention on arrival.

The one positive thread in the available reports concerns children who might be considered "at risk." Several projects have worked with rural or handicapped (Hanninen, 1984), poor or culturally different (Ehrlich, 1978, 1982) gifted youngsters who, it is shown elsewhere (see Chapter 8), may be particularly prone to underachievement. A preschool head start for these children might indeed put them on a more equal footing with their peers on arrival. The problem with the present state of knowledge is that there is no direct evidence, first, that it is better to attempt to deliver any such services before school age rather than to build them into the early years of schooling, or second, that these types of interventions are any more needed by or useful for highly able children than for all children.

There is considerable evidence that preschool intervention is effective, in other words, sufficient, but little evidence that intervention must occur early to be effective.

Implications for Action

The premise that some children's potential to excel is masked by a variety of conditions is actually reinforced by the success of the many types of interventions. Purposeful search for hidden giftedness is warranted at any age (see recommended practice No. 17).

We do not know that earlier is better, but prudence suggests that this should be the working assumption until we know better. On the other hand, if the resources are available to intervene later, one may do so. Legal constraints on school systems favor the provision of services following school entry.

Useful specific advice is given by additional references such as Abraham and Hartwell (1985) on qualities parents and teachers may observe and guidelines for action, Ehrlich (1980) on identification, Kaplan (1980) on the importance of play, and L. G. Johnson (1983), who advocates an enriched and enriching environment for all children, while watching for children engaged or interested "in activities that required knowledge, skills, and attitudes beyond the normal expectations of preschool children" (p. 14). The paper's title is telling—"Giftedness in Preschool: A Better Time for Development Than Identification."

Needed Research

Ethical and design requirements are critical. One cannot deny services to children identified as being in need just to study what happens to them in comparison with others who receive services. Also, identification is a form of intervention; identified unserved children would not be a true control.

Cross-age studies could examine the incidence and rates of underachievement and negative attitudes to learning in highly able and comparison groups. If early intervention for the gifted is critical, then the rates of these problems should increase with age and ability level. Some secondary analysis may be possible initially, owing to the numbers of studies that have already looked at these issues in single samples.

A second type of useful research would look at the impact of interventions with children of different ages, having identified problems of the types that early interventions are intended to avert. If early intervention is to be supported, these studies should find a declining success rate with increasing age of initial service and decreasing ability level. Again, some secondary analysis of prior reports might be possible.

Detailed longitudinal case studies of specific at-risk children, alone and in groups, could be revealing. Do underachievement and negative attitudes or other precursors of underachievement occur with greater frequency in younger rather than older children, and in more able rather than less able? Are the longer term consequences of earlier interventions better with more able children? Long-term follow-up studies, even of past interventions, would help.

One serious difficulty is that underachievement is essentially a school phenomenon. We therefore need to know more about the developmental precursors of all the positive qualities we might describe as evidence of giftedness. This is unlikely to be achieved rapidly, but it clearly establishes the need for longitudinal case studies in research on high abilities.

Looking at the impact of an enriched and enriching environment on a full range of children would require the curriculum to be aimed at less able pupils. If the more able did not benefit more than the less able who received the same program, then early intervention is not needed specifically for the gifted. It gets rather convoluted!

If it cannot be shown clearly that there are special risks or benefits for the gifted, this recommended practice should be relegated to the category of good general education, important, but not the focus of this volume.

76 | Be Sensitive to Potential Sibling Adjustment Problems

There is strong intuitive appeal to the idea that siblings compare themselves with one another, and that anything that elevates the status of one child may inspire hurt feelings in the other. Many authors (Alvino, 1985; B. Clark, 1988; Cornell, 1984; A. O. Ross, 1979; Sunderlin, 1981; Webb, Meckstroth, & Tolan, 1982) have advised parents to be alert to possible sibling-adjustment problems, from depression and withdrawal to jealousy and anger.

Current Knowledge

Do siblings suffer from adjustment problems? The evidence is equivocal. Cornell (1983, 1984) found that some second-born siblings of gifted program children were less well adjusted than control children of comparable birth order and age. These problems were hypothesized (cf. Cornell & Grossberg, 1986) to occur primarily in families that emphasized a differential view of their children. In contrast, parents who saw their children as having comparable abilities (whatever the school decided), or different abilities of comparable value, were less likely to have children with self-esteem problems. Adversely affected siblings of gifted-program children were socially less mature, less outgoing, and more easily upset and frustrated than siblings of above-average comparison children.

Kaufmann and Sexton (1983) surveyed 98 parents and found that approximately 20% reported sibling problems in reaction to one of their children's being gifted. The 20% figure is hard to interpret in the absence of information on the number and ages of siblings in these families and the parental attitudes toward the relations between the children. Given that some proportion of families would have only one child or very young siblings, it is probably an underestimate.

Cornell and Grossberg (1986) found no clear evidence of adjustment problems in siblings of gifted-program children. However, the subgroup of siblings who were perceived by their parents as less gifted than their brothers or sisters had lower self-esteem and higher anxiety levels. These children were defensive about acknowledging even minor problems and personal shortcomings and tended to internalize or somaticize their problems. Grenier (1985) found no differences between labeled and unlabeled siblings in self-image or perceived parental treatment, but sibling competition and comparison were associated with a favorable self-image in labeled children and an unfavorable self-image in unlabeled siblings.

In a fascinating study, Renzulli and McGreevy (1986) located twins in which one child was included in a gifted program and the sibling was either overlooked or specifically not included. Most of the unselected twins expressed regret over not being in the program but denied that the decision caused problems in their sibling relationship. Parents did report problems with sibling rivalry, and some explicitly encouraged the selected twin to play down his or her enthusiasm for the program. Renzulli and McGreevy surmised that problems were most evident when the twins were closest in academic potential.

In conclusion, although there is some evidence that sibling-adjustment problems exist, we do not really know how serious, pervasive, or long-lasting these problems might be. Moreover, we do not know which siblings (brothers or sisters? older or younger?) are most vulnerable, or how to determine when problems occur. We do not know whether a child is most affected because his or her sibling is superior in ability, or because he or she is denied the special status of the gifted label or placement in a special program, although available evidence favors the latter possibility. Finally, we do not know what interventions are most effective in ameliorating a sibling's self-esteem problems.

How long do sibling effects last? Colangelo and Brower (1987a) found none after 5 years. If anything, the siblings placed in gifted programs were more troubled about family reactions to their placement than were their nonidentified brothers and sisters (Colangelo & Brower, 1987b). However, their cross-sectional and retrospective design could not have detected problems that occurred at the time of labeling of the sibling and that may have dissipated over time. Moreover, the response rate among siblings (19%) was unusually low, so problems may have gone undetected by the researchers.

How and why do problems develop? Cornell (1984) contended that some families idealize gifted children in a way that may adversely affect the family status and self-esteem of siblings not perceived as gifted. Children placed in gifted programs enjoyed higher family status than their siblings in regular school programs, and these siblings were less well adjusted than control children on standard personality measures. Similarly, Ballering & Koch (1984) found that labeled children enjoyed a more favorable relationship with their mothers than did siblings not labeled as gifted. Adjustment problems or poor self-esteem might develop when there is competition, comparison, or unequal status between labeled and unlabeled siblings (Grenier, 1985).

Silverman and Waters (1987) contended that parents with a firstborn gifted child simply may not recognize that their next born is equally able. They invited parents with one previously identified gifted child to bring in a young sibling for IQ testing. Much to the parents' surprise, 91 (61%) of the 148 siblings had Stanford-Binet IQs within 10 points, and only 25 siblings had IQs below 120.

Both Cornell (1984) and Silverman and Waters (1987) theorized that younger children often were not recognized as gifted because parents associated giftedness with the characteristics of their firstborn children. These children were stereotypically achievement-oriented, perfectionistic, and serious-minded. Second-born children were more relaxed and easy-going and seemed less driven to please adults or achieve in school (Pfouts, 1980). Pfouts also found that family relations were relatively harmonious when a firstborn brother was the clear academic achiever in the family. Problems emerged when a second-born brother was the more academically inclined, or when his intellectual abilities rivaled those of his older brother. D. H. Tuttle (1990) examined the impact of maternal labeling of giftedness on the sibling relationship in over 100 pairs of first- and second-born children between the ages of 10 and 16. She found striking birth-order differences in the effect of being labeled gifted. Firstborn children who were labeled gifted by their mothers enjoyed a positive, close sibling relationship, irrespective of how their siblings were labeled. In contrast, second-born children who were labeled as gifted experienced more difficulties in their sibling relationship. These effects were present even after controlling for sibling school placement, academic ability, sex, age, and socioeconomic status. Ballering and Koch (1984) also found that siblings appeared to get along better with one another as the difference in their IQs increased.

Silverman (1987) suggested that second-born children often develop interests and attitudes that are polar opposites to the firstborn child's in order to avoid sibling rivalry. In the broader child development literature, Schachter (1982) theorized that siblings may develop polar-opposite personality traits through a process she termed "deidentification." Tesser (1980) proposed that when siblings have similar values or interests in some area, the less successful sibling may experience a diminution of self-esteem. In contrast, if siblings have divergent values or interests, the less successful sibling may enjoy the success of the other vicariously without loss of self-esteem. A theoretical integration of Schachter's concept of deidentification and Tesser's self-esteem maintenance model may be useful in explaining the reactions that children have to their gifted-program siblings.

In conclusion, the advice receives general support. Parents should indeed be sensitive to adjustment problems in siblings, but it is not certain under what circumstances they will occur or with what consequences.

Implications for Action

Parents may need help in broadening their concept of giftedness because of a tendency to associate the concept with personality characteristics and behaviors of their firstborn. The unique interests and diverse abilities of each child in the family need recognition if children are to avoid unfavorable comparisons with one another.

Schools should be sensitive to sibling issues in their selection process (Renzulli & McGreevy, 1986). When a child is selected for a gifted program, it seems advisable to determine whether there are siblings whose talents were overlooked. Many parents resist the idea of placing a child in a gifted program because they fear the implications of gifted labeling both for the labeled child and siblings. Schools should educate parents about the broader implications and significance of their curricular placement decisions.

Needed Research

The duration, severity, and long-term consequences of sibling problems need more thorough examination. Future research should identify characteristics of siblings and families most at risk for adjustment problems. Likely important factors to consider are sibling birth order, sex, age, and ability level. Parental perceptions of both children's abilities, as well as the value they place on giftedness, may be critical mediating variables in how a sibling responds to a child labeled as gifted.

It might be fruitful to examine the extent to which siblings are able to define and identify with specific roles or personal aspirations that are equally valued in the family. Sibling self-esteem problems may be difficult to detect or measure with standard research methods because family members resist acknowledging them. Parents may be defensive about recognizing that they prefer one child over another. Unlabeled siblings understandably may be reluctant to discuss a topic that makes them feel inferior. Interviews may be more successful than paper-and-pencil measures in engaging family members and encouraging them to express their feelings openly.

The entire question of negative impact on nonselected siblings might be avoided if siblings were routinely offered a place in the services. Such a policy could be supported if a series of studies demonstrated that accepting the sibling of an identified child into a program did more good and caused fewer problems than keeping the sibling out. Such research is necessary, because it might enable schools to avoid exporting problems to the home, or, at least, to particularly susceptible homes.

CHAPTER SIX

Advice to Professionals

| 77 | **Educational and Vocational Counselors Knowledgeable About Giftedness Are Required** |

The emphasis in this recommended practice is on the training required of counselors to satisfy the academic and career counseling needs of the gifted, in contrast to their personal counseling requirements (see recommended practice No. 78).

> There are some special guidance problems which gifted children face, which need specialized attention from counselors who themselves have received specialized training. (Zaffrann & Colangelo, 1979b, p. 145)

Seeley (1985) indicated that one of the problems was that mental health professionals are trained in a medical model to look for deficits in test performance as indices of need for attention. On the other hand, Rothney and Koopman (1958), supported by Sanborn (1979b), suggested that "counseling the gifted does not differ in nature from the counseling of other students, but it does vary in its demands on the counselors" (p. 348). Do academic and vocational counseling of the gifted call upon new skills or new applications of usual skills? Does giftedness demand a specialist counselor or a modicum of knowledge on the part of general counselors?

Current Knowledge

Considerable authority has been given to this recommended practice by its endorsement in the "Marland Report," which provided extensive expert witness that "pupil personnel workers are not equipped for the task of working with the gifted and that they should be given added preparation" (U.S. Commissioner of Education, 1972, p. 34). The assertion remains largely a matter of opinion, though not without some logic and rationale.

Numerous books and articles address special characteristics of gifted students, most notably multipotentiality. Keeping doors open can be a burden. Although some students make lasting career decisions very early, others may have difficulty choosing (cf. Willings, 1980). What special training, if any, do counselors need to assist?

Another unique condition is underachievement coupled with high ability, but as Whitmore (1980) has contended, the academic difficulty is usually a symptom of a personal problem, namely, poor self-image. This may, in some cases, be ameliorated by help in choosing appropriate courses and thinking about careers.

Advice in course taking is one function of academic counseling. It has been especially examined with able girls. Fox (1977b) summarized the special problems of encouraging academic and career paths in mathematics. Counselors were actually negative influences, and, under those circumstances, fortunately ignored by some 80% of the children. Counselors' skills were less influential than role models and other influences on these decisions (Brody & Fox, 1980). Hauck and Freehill (1972) reported several case studies illustrating positive to negative counseling experiences.

Rothney and Koopman (1958, p. 348) proposed that there are three principal differences to be taken into account regarding guidance of the gifted:

1. "Educational and occupational opportunities for the gifted are usually greater than for others."
2. "Gifted pupils become ready for self-appraisal and self-conceptualization at higher levels and at earlier ages."
3. "Gifted children may be subject to unusual pressures by parents, teachers, peers, and others."

Several other ways in which the special training of counselors might be defensible also occur to us:

4. Gifted children are more likely to be accelerated.
5. Highly able students more often face courses that are insufficiently challenging.
6. Bright girls with high achievement motivation face social discouragement.
7. The same may be true for black high-ability children.

8. Culturally different, highly able students may need help integrating their abilities and ethnicity (suggested by Colangelo, 1985).
9. Bright students might have more difficulty than others narrowing diverse career interests.
10. In some schools, especially where few students proceed to outstanding universities or earn important scholarships, very able students may be at a disadvantage owing to inexperience of counselors with such opportunities.

There has been very little formal research on any of these educational aspects of counseling the gifted, though the above paragraphs suggest a strong rationale for the need. Even more seriously, Deiulio (1984) cited the "Marland Report" to support a claim, probably based on Wiener (1968), that "counselors and psychologists more often demonstrated apathy, indifference or hostility toward the gifted than any other personnel groups" (p. 165). These negative attitudes appear to be persistent over time (A. Robinson, 1986c), but counselors' attitudes seem to be more favorable in schools with formal programs for the gifted (Wiener, 1968).

The recommended practice contains a slight ambiguity, allowing a second interpretation to the effect that there is a shortage of counselors knowledgeable about giftedness. This straightforward issue has not been addressed in the literature, the emphasis having been on attitudes rather than knowledge.

Implications for Action

We should be cautious in requiring that academic and vocational counselors for the gifted be specially trained in advance for this task. The 10 areas of possible special need stated above should be considered in relation to student outcomes. Attractive advice and additional references on the counseling of gifted women in particular are offered by Noble (1989).

Ensure that the coordinator of services for highly able students at the school is also empowered to interact with counseling staff, because there is some evidence that familiarity can overcome negative attitudes (Wiener, 1968). Welcome to gifted programs the contributions of educational and vocational counselors who have positive attitudes about and are committed to educational services for highly able students.

Needed Research

There is a definite need to justify and possibly refine this recommended practice. A suitable start could be a needs assessment based on counselors already working with the gifted, children, teachers, and others. Does counseling the gifted call upon unique counseling skills, or does it call upon basic skills in a unique combination or to greater depth? Are the 10 suggested items of unique needs of bright students the essence of such training, in either context? How informed are counselors about giftedness?

It is also essential to compare programs and their outcomes where knowledgeable counselors are in place versus others. Do gifted students in the favored situations receive better academic and career counseling? What is the impact on services of providing in-service training to counselors already in place? Any such studies must do the best job under the circumstances to take account of the counselors' interest and motivation for involvement. There should be long-term follow-up of the above studies, so that career and retrospective data can be obtained. In the interim, graduates (as far back as possible) could be interviewed regarding their earlier experiences with counseling services.

The literature to date does not make a distinction between the academic and vocational parts of this recommended practice. We have done so, because the academic part, course advising and the like, can be very much shared with other school personnel, including teachers.

Finally, research is needed on whether or not specific training for counselors can lead to positive changes in counselors' attitudes or specific benefits for the gifted in areas where educational counseling might help.

78 | Group and Individual Counseling Are Recommended

Personal counseling has long been advocated as an essential part of a program for the gifted (Fichter & Swassing, 1985; Witty, 1951b). The minority status of the gifted and their shared needs and characteristics make group techniques especially suitable (Zaffrann & Colangelo, 1979a) as well as a preventative approach in this format (Wolf & Stephens, 1985). Kerr (1985) suggested that "individual counseling and guidance can help gifted girls and women change their negative attitudes toward themselves and to raise their career goals" (p. 163).

This recommended practice particularly addresses counseling for socioemotional and other personal difficulties. Educational guidance is addressed in recommended practice No. 77, and No. 90 focuses on specific elements of career counseling.

Current Knowledge

The knowledge base on this topic is very anecdotal, consisting of testimonials about the importance of counseling, suggestions about why it is important, and considerable advice on action to take. Bright youngsters need professional support, not in spite of their giftedness but because of it; they also need help with problems of isolation, achievement pressure, self-esteem, careers, and interpersonal difficulties at many levels (cf. Allan & Fox, 1979; Gowan, 1979a; Colangelo & Zaffrann, 1979).

Lajoie and Shore (1981) reviewed the literature and concluded that gifted youth were no less at risk than others to be victims of delinquency, dropping out, or suicide. The potential for preventative group counseling is most attractive. Torrance (1985) has reported on the depth and degree of gifted students' concern for major global issues that affect all of humanity and our planet; some of the associated fears could be quite debilitating. Derevensky and Coleman (1989) have documented bright children's general fears.

Wolf and Stephens (1985) pointed out some of the special concerns of gifted girls, such as career versus maternal tensions and the competitive nature of many male-dominated activities, that merit group counseling. Gifted women also report having needed such help for educational, personal, and vocational goals (Walker & Freeland, 1987). Keeler (1978) reported an experimental study (without a nongifted comparison group). Gifted boys and girls across grade levels benefited from group counseling.

There is, therefore, evidence of differential needs regarding global concerns and fears as well as in the vocational domain. The efficacy of particular counseling solutions remains to be confirmed more adequately.

Implications for Action

It seems reasonable to experiment with individual and group counseling on a variety of topics well described in the literature. Extra benefits for special populations, for example, gifted girls and underachievers, might be found. Although research support is not yet adequate, the anecdotal evidence is uniformly positive.

Needed Research

It is not necessary to show that good counseling can help gifted children (Hauck & Freehill, 1972, present case studies that illustrate positive and negative impact); rather, we need to be shown how such counseling specifically aids the gifted in contrast to two control conditions—other gifted children who are not receiving counseling (for ethical reasons, control groups should receive any potentially helpful treatment at the end of the experiment) and nongifted children who are. Systematically replicated case studies in the tradition of research reporting in the helping professions would be instructive and valid.

Few existing materials on counseling the gifted make specific connections between the particular need it addresses and the therapy offered. Keeler (1978) assessed five different variables, so it is difficult to determine which specific interventions affected what parts of the outcome. A thorough understanding of the application of counseling to the gifted requires good experimental design and controls.

79 | Counselors Should Keep a File of Scholarship Resources

What first appeared to be a trivial recommendation was repeated many times over nearly four decades (Gold, 1965; Khatena, 1982). Many capable students cannot undertake suitable higher or even secondary education because of limited finances.

> Just as early identification of the athletically gifted assures their vocational and educational support, so should the identification of the academic varsity provide for support of college attendance for able scholarship contenders. Counselors ought to keep a current file of such scholarship resources. (Gowan & Bruch, 1971, p. 63, citing Gowan & Demos, 1964, and J. B. Henry, 1965.)

Current Knowledge

Knowledge on this topic consists mostly of firmly held opinion, though defensible on many social grounds. The general point is elaborated with regard to additional discrimination against gifted females in their search for financial assistance (Kerr, 1985; Rodenstein, Pfleger, & Colangelo, 1977) and constraints imposed by parental expectations, social class, and ethnic background (Goldberg, Passow, & Lorge, 1958/1980). The responsibility of counselors for intervening in this process appears to have been suggested first by Witty (1954).

Witty (1951b) cited evidence of the widely accepted relation between the amount of schooling a student completes and family income. We did not encounter any report of the effects of scholarships in remediating this problem nor of the particular competence of counselors to provide the clearing-house.

Implications for Action

> Educators working with other citizens must find ways to identify and offer educational opportunity for many gifted children who, at present, because of financial obstacles, do not acquire an education commensurate with their ability and promise. (Witty, 1951a, p. 8)

The situation has not changed much in 40 years. Counselors are well placed to facilitate this process, though keeping a file is too narrow an expression of the task. One must seek out qualified but needy students and actively recruit support from corporations, service clubs, and other potential sources. Some poor students may need additional motivational support to participate in a special program or further education.

Needed Research

It would be useful to have some updated information on the current need, for example, demographics, socioeconomic conditions, higher education attendance, gender, and dropping out. Studies of economically disadvantaged students might seek to establish the relation (if any exists) between aggressive scholarship counseling and the postsecondary aspirations of these students. Where such scholarships or bursaries might now exist, it would be useful to see if they are related to an improvement in attendance and also to confirm the role or potential role of counselors (and others?) in the process.

A second line of useful research would seek the number of highly able students who avoid higher education for financial reasons and document the need for scholarship or other assistance. The next step would be to examine the role of costs in college choices by highly able students.

80 | Early College Entrants Require Special Attention to Socioemotional Adjustment

A major barrier to the wide use of early college entrance for highly able youth is concern about the student's socioemotional adjustment. Although Daurio (1979) and others (Janos & Robinson, 1985b; Pollins, 1983) point out that most studies have failed to find convincing evidence that early college entrance is harmful to student adjustment, the concern remains widespread in the field (e.g., see Southern, Jones, & Fiscus, 1989).

Established early entrance programs give the socioemotional adjustment of their young college students special attention. H. B. Robinson (1983) described the emphasis placed by the University of Washington Early Entrance Program (EEP) on helping early college entrants (all under age 15) adjust to college life:

> The EEP provides guidance and a home base for these young students, acting far more actively *in loco parentis* than is the custom in colleges today. This is particularly true of the first two years. . . . Group meetings are held twice weekly; at these, attendance is mandatory during the first year and is encouraged during the second. (p. 150)

In recent years the Seattle program has established a transition school within the university to facilitate the early entrants' academic as well as socioemotional adjustment to college (Janos & Robinson, 1985b).

Current Knowledge

There is no reported empirical evidence that early college entrance is harmful to socioemotional adjustment (Daurio, 1979; Pollins, 1983). This optimistic view must be qualified by recognition of the serious limitations of most research in this area (see the review by Cornell, Callahan, Bassin, & Ramsay, 1991). Some studies have examined accelerants prior to college entrance, or at some other single point in time, but not assessed changes after a period of college study (Janos, Sanfillipo, & Robinson, 1986; Pollins, 1983; N. M. Robinson & Janos, 1986). Other studies have used inadequate or inappropriate measures of social and emotional adjustment, such as a few unvalidated questions on a survey or a telephone interview (Brody, Lupkowski, & Stanley, 1988; Pollins, 1983; T. M. Richardson & Benbow, in press).

Much of the evidence of good adjustment for early college entrants is based on case studies and subjective reports of program success (E. H. Gregory & March, 1985; J. C. Stanley, 1985; J. C. Stanley & McGill, 1986). One of the largest and most widely cited studies (Fund for the Advancement of Education, 1953, 1957) contained a number of methodological problems. Although the authors acknowledged many of these limitations, later writers seem to have overlooked them. In one college program, two-thirds of the students dropped out by the end of the first year, and less than half of those who remained participated in the follow-up, so that it seems questionable to generalize from such a biased sample (Fund for the Advancement of Education, 1957; Pressey, 1967).

Cornell, Callahan, and Loyd (1991) found considerable variation in socioemotional adjustment within a sample of adolescent girls enrolled in a residential early college entrance program. Although many girls had no significant problems, over half experienced a period of depression sufficient to warrant staff attention and five engaged in suicidal behavior. Approximately half the girls saw mental health counselors and some 30% dropped out of the program for stress-related reasons. Personality adjustment and family relations measured at the outset of the school year were moderately predictive of a series of adjustment outcomes. This study did not demonstrate that early college entrance itself caused adjustment problems, but it did suggest that students vary widely in their adjustment, and it identified some ways in which adjustment problems might be anticipated.

Recently, Cornell et al. (in press) completed another study of female early college entrants (from the same residential college program) which did address how acceleration might have affected personality adjustment. In this study, 33 first-year accelerants were compared to equally capable agemates who lived at home and attended traditional high schools. Both groups completed a standard personality measure, the California Psychological Inventory, at the beginning and end of one academic year. The findings were striking. Although accelerants and non-accelerants had fairly similar personality profiles at the beginning of the school year, the accelerants underwent significant, positive changes by the end of the year, while non-accelerants made few changes. As a group, the accelerants became more independent, self-assured, and accepting of both themselves and others. They became less stereotypically "feminine," and much more non-conformist and self-directed in their attitudes. In contrast, the few changes made by the non-accelerants suggested less independence and self-assertiveness, combined with a stronger sense of being different from others.

The two studies by Cornell, Callahan, and Loyd (1991, in press) present a complex picture of how adolescent girls fare in an early college entrance program. There is considerable variability, with some experiencing adjustment problems and dropping out. However, first-year students who remained in the program generally did quite well. These findings support the need for careful selection of candidates for early college entrance. Also it is important for future studies to pinpoint what factors in the early college entrance experience, or in the students' personal backgrounds, are critical to their adjustment.

Implications for Action

It would be unreasonable for educators and counselors to conclude that early college entrants do not have special needs or do not have some risk of developing adjustment problems. Unfortunately, the literature does not help very much in specifying what kinds of special needs or problems.

A number of established early college-entrance programs provide special counseling and support services to early college entrants (Cornell, Callahan, & Loyd, 1991; E. H. Gregory & Stevens-Long, 1986; H. B. Robinson, 1983). These students have two advantages, special services and a peer group of other accelerants. Colleges should maintain contact with early matriculants and monitor their need for support and intervention.

Needed Research

It is critical that researchers employ more rigorous research designs and more appropriate methods for assessing the socioemotional adjustment of early college entrants. Although a randomized experiment is probably impractical, a prospective, quasi-experimental design with repeated measures is possible. A reasonable study would examine student adjustment with an array of standard social and personality adjustment measures. Students should be studied prior to program entrance and at regular intervals afterwards. Accelerants should be compared with equally capable students who do not choose to enter college early. Every effort should be made to include those early entrants who later drop out of college, because they may be the ones most likely to have experienced adjustment problems. Postgraduation surveys especially miss these dropouts.

Finally, emphasis should shift from the global question of whether early college entrants do or do not experience socioemotional problems. Attention should focus on identifying ways to predict which students are best suited for early college entrance, what variables such as age or elements of a student's background might be related to socioemotional adjustment problems, and which variables or experiences help these students avoid such problems.

81 | Take Account of Early Developing Intrinsic Motivation

Ward (1961/1980) commented forcefully upon the lack of role for individuals in the design of their own education:

> The role of the individual in the process of his own education is by far more ignored than acknowledged. . . . Even the concept of "intrinsic motivation" usually assumes the guise, "How can the teacher conduct the teaching so that

intrinsic motivation will be developed?" . . . This irony of omitting the individual's capacity for self-determination is crucial enough when the education of the *average* student is accomplished (or attempted) through a pattern of majors, minors, and electives which are independent of the judgment of the person himself. Where the intellectually gifted child is concerned, the irony approaches the magnitude of immorality. (p. 91)

Even if motivation is intrinsic, it is not necessarily automatically or appropriately applied. Ziv (1977) concurred that "the gifted child's eagerness to learn is his most salient characteristic" (p. 36). Feldhusen (1985b, 1986) and B. Clark (1983—in the earlier editions of her text) also noted early development of intrinsic motivation.

Current Knowledge

Little direct evidence has been brought to bear on this recommended practice, but opinion has shifted. B. Clark (1988) did not repeat her earlier claim of early development. Goldberg (1958) discerned that achievement motivation was not uniformly distributed across the Terman sample that, viewed otherwise, partly served as an inspiration for Ward's concern. White and his colleagues (White, 1983; White, Kaban, & Attanucci, 1979) disseminated the results of the Harvard Preschool Project in which a striving for competence was widely observed in all healthy infants, and C. W. Williams (1958) described a program that had the very goal of developing achievement motivation, therefore not presuming its ubiquity. Hill (1967/1983) pointed out that students' so-called intrinsic motivation is nevertheless dependent on the attractiveness of the learning materials, and Short (1985) described her own experience to show how motivation was seriously dissipated during school years. Perrone and Male (1981) suggested one mechanism by which this decline might happen: "High achieving children, particularly those who are well behaved, may be recipients of so much praise and reward that they do not acquire the capacity for either self-motivation or self-reward" (p. 53). Alternatively, they may lose it and become addicted to external reinforcement (a testable hypothesis).

Takacs (1982) drew our attention to an observation by Feldman (1979) that "the remarkable feats of highly gifted children have not been achieved in the absence of intense, prolonged educational experience" (p. 43). Renzulli (1977) was one of the first to give importance to such experience while acknowledging intrinsic motivation as a characteristic of eminent persons. This view has been reinforced by Bloom's (1985) and Feldman's (1986) overviews of prodigies and the development of eminence. Early development of intrinsic motivation is not automatic.

One study that directly addressed early learning of motivation was done by Moss (1986, 1990), working with Shore at McGill University in Montreal. High- and average-IQ preschoolers were videotaped on a series of structured gamelike tasks while interacting with their mothers. Detailed analysis of the dialogue and actions showed that the interactions between the mothers and high-IQ children were characterized by prompts from the parent that directed the children to principles that might help them solve problems (e.g., attending to the matching of colors in a jigsaw puzzle, or to prior instances) and encouraged much freer choice of constructions to create, whereas the mothers of the less able children more often gave direct suggestions or correct answers. Causality was not established in this study, but the more able children clearly operated in an environment more conducive to the reinforcement or development of self-directed problem solving and, as well, to metacognitive thinking.

High intrinsic motivation is a characteristic of high-achieving gifted children. Given the nature of past (and present!) selection criteria for most of the programs in which bright children have been observed, it is easy to understand how it must have seemed that high levels of intrinsic motivation were virtually innate. The hereditary connotations of the concept of giftedness in much of the early literature would have predisposed observers to this view; however, there may be no intrinsic motivation in some very gifted children, perhaps especially underachievers or those who have experienced various forms of trauma (physical, personal, economic, etc.). Intrinsic motivation can be present early, but it may be a fragile commodity, lost more easily than gained.

There is an inherent logic in the suggestion that an individual's level of intrinsic motivation is important information for educators; this is explored further in our discussions of recommended practice Nos. 39 (on the assessment of interests), 40 (on the provision of broad curriculum choice), 25 (on grading practices), and others that deal with individualization. The main problem with the recommendation is that it needs updating.

There is insufficient explanation of how attention to intrinsic motivation might be different for the gifted compared with others. The implication in much of the literature that gifted children have more of it, or a superior kind, is not supported. Newland (1976) anticipated the present state of affairs with remarkable insight:

> We just don't know . . . whether very young children early manifest marked intrinsic motivation as the result of some inherent characteristic, or whether they merely learn very quickly to progress from extrinsic to intrinsic motivation, or whether their parents only accede more fully when they independently undertake some line of endeavor. (p. 109)

Implications for Action

Intrinsic motivation should certainly be used to advantage. It is as much to be developed in all children as preserved in those who have it. One way to utilize this advantage is to involve children in planning their own educational experiences to varying degrees. Cushenbery and Howell (1974) suggested that awareness of learning goals is a first step in this direction.

Needed Research

First, does the development or appearance of intrinsic motivation in very able children occur differently from the way it does in others? Second, how, and in what ways uniquely, does the development or erosion of intrinsic motivation differ for more and less able students? Third, in what ways, at different levels of development of intrinsic motivation, might one best take advantage of its presence or compensate for its absence?

These questions differ from much previous research on giftedness by asking for the examination of the interactions among levels of motivation and abilities, and other variables. Past studies frequently limited themselves to descriptions of the motivational characteristics of gifted and other groups; such studies have little explanatory power.

82 The Limitations of Gifted Students' Physical, Social, and Emotional Development Should Be Taken Into Account

Sellin and Birch (1980) summarized earlier advice to conclude "that chronological age is not a sufficient index for grouping talented pupils in performance areas. Account must also be taken of physical, emotional, and social factors" (p. 102). B. Clark (1988) regarded the unevenness in intellectual and physical growth as a challenge in providing a well-integrated educational plan for able students. Hill (1967/1983), Robb (1976), and C. W. Williams (1958) have made similar observations. Exceptional abilities in some domains magnify the apparent unevenness. High expectations that are appropriate in an area of advanced development, such as the intellectual, should not be overgeneralized to other areas of performance.

Current Knowledge

Although the underlying observation of uneven growth is widely reported and certainly true, it is based largely on the accumulated wisdom of teachers, psychologists, and others who observe children. Many case studies in textbooks are composites or fictional characters. Real cases are available but not usually focused on this issue. Nevertheless, reports by Altman (1983) and Freeman (1985b) lend credence to the advice. Gowan and Bruch (1971) observed,

> The general picture of development in gifted children is that of advancement through developmental sequences at a faster rate than the average. Notable exceptions may be found in individual cases, for sometimes the mental, physical, social, and emotional aspects of development do not move at the same pace. (p. 5)

Tannenbaum (1983) observed that some children enter differentiated programs with psychosocial problems already extant. Terrassier (1981) noted that some consequences of uneven development can be very anomalous, such as high reading ability but serious writing difficulties in some individuals.

Janos, Fung, and Robinson (1985) noted that some gifted children themselves "tend to overgeneralize the domains of superiority, and focus on differences from, rather than similarities to, other children" (p. 81). Manaster and Powell (1983) echoed this same observation, with an interesting insight: "The gifted must be seen as average with gifts, not superior with faults" (p. 73).

Implications for Action

The obvious implications are academic, but one must also take into account the effects of this advice on the child's emotional state. Arent (1979) reminded us to remember that we are dealing with a child, not an adult, and Buescher (1985) suggested that gifted adolescents can get frustrated as a result of their own overgeneralization.

> All but the most sophisticated of educators continue to believe the myth that giftedness implies the interpersonal ability to deal effectively with life's struggles and goals. (Delisle, 1985a, p. 4)

The creation of suitable products such as classwork, special projects, and presentations can be a source of great satisfaction to any child; the lack of balance is a threat. Freeman (1985a) noted how crucial it is to "avoid giving overwhelming stress to the intellectual aspects of their development, to the detriment of their emotional and physical needs" (p. 5).

Perez (1980) suggested that adults' sense of humor and sensitivity to children's perfectionism are important in implementing this recommended practice. Schilling (1986) noted that self-image suffers if such care is not taken. Page (1983) focused her advice on parents and emphasized the development of a well-rounded child. Parental and school expectations should respect wide variation in intellectual, physical, social, and emotional development, especially when one of these is notably advanced.

Needed Research

There is a need to examine the literature thoroughly and gather together references to all the genuine case studies of uneven development and its consequences. These should then be classified according to their contribution to the understanding of this and other recommended practices. Some gaps may be found, to which additional cases might contribute.

Second, a new question is arising as a result of the growth of cognitive research on giftedness. From a psychometric perspective, J. C. Hagen (1981) offered useful insight:

> Gifted children cannot be expected to perform as well on previously learned tasks—for example in testing situations—as older children of the same mental age. Even though the gifted have learned the task equally well, such factors as physical maturity and years of experience in school may lead to a significantly superior performance by older, lower IQ children of the same mental age. Educators of gifted children may wish to distinguish between expectations for learning and expectations for test performance. (p. 67)

Working with preschoolers, Kanevsky (1990) and Kanevsky and Rapagna (1990) used such a crossed design of chronological and mental ages to compare generalization of procedures across tasks (two different adaptations of the classic Tower of Hanoi problem) and media (from manipulation to a computer simulation). On quantitative measures, her results confirmed J. C. Hagen's expectation, as the younger children's were slightly inferior to those of older children with equal MAs. However, the younger but more able children were superior on several qualitative assessments. Why were these two different results observed? What different qualities are the two types of assessment tapping? What is the role of the age of the children or the task? Which elements of the curriculum may be more dependent on experience or maturity? Which intellectual processes? What is the nature of the gray zones between these different conditions; where and how might crossovers occur? Are these intellectual differences related in different ways to emotional and social development?

Finally, there is a need for the validation of teacher and parent strategies for satisfying this recommended practice. Are some general approaches better than others? For example, are the children better served in schools where different subjects are taught by different teachers, so strengths are not overgeneralized? What kinds of experiences help the children to maintain a balanced self-image: counseling, group counseling, mentorships? There is a useful role for research that adds validated, specific procedures to the rather general admonitions that presently fill the literature on uneven development.

CHAPTER SEVEN

Social and Emotional Adjustment

| 83 | Develop Independence, Autonomy, and Self-Reliance |

Giving children an increasing measure of independence and self-responsibility is essential for maturation. (Hildreth, 1981, p. 96)

Permit the children their own individuality, and enjoy them for who they are, not who you would like them to be. . . . Allow your children to make lots of decisions, and consult them on issues affecting them whenever you believe they can understand the consequences. (B. Clark, 1988, p. 570)

The virtues of independence, autonomy, and self-reliance are thoroughly inculcated in North American thinking, but other cultures may react differently to this statement.

Current Knowledge

Many studies document that children variously identified as highly intelligent or creative, or accomplished in some achievement area, tend to score high on measures of independence (Bachtold, 1968; Barron & Harrington, 1981; D'Heurle, Mellinger, & Haggard, 1959; Freeman, 1979; Griggs & Price, 1980; Werner & Bachtold, 1969; see also the review by Janos & Robinson, 1985a). It is not clear whether or not there are differences among the terms independence, self-reliance, autonomy, and self-direction.

Family studies reveal that parents of high-ability children encourage independence in a variety of ways (Bloom, 1985; McGillivray, 1964; Norman, 1966; Winterbottom, 1954; see also review by Olszewski, Kulieke, & Buescher, 1987). In contrast, studies with the Family Environment Scale do not find that parents score high on the Independence subscale (Cornell,

1984; Cornell & Grossberg, 1987). A more differentiated analysis of the independence construct may reveal that parents of academically able children primarily emphasize independence in learning and achievement (cf. Moss, 1986, 1990) but not necessarily social or emotional independence. Parents of creatively talented children may emphasize much broader independence (Getzels & Jackson, 1962; Nichols, 1964).

Implications for Action

There is general support for the recommendation that parents should encourage independence in their children. Suggestions for achieving this goal and examples are offered by B. Clark (1988), Perino and Perino (1981), Takacs (1986), and Webb et al. (1982).

Needed Research

Concepts of independence, autonomy, and self-reliance could be subject to further refinement, perhaps analogous to refinements in notions such as self-concept (for example, see Byrne, 1984). What are the necessary and specific ingredients of "independence training," and how are parent attitudes translated into parent-child interaction and subsequent child independence?

There is also a need for longitudinal studies that seek the consequences of independence training, both in terms of character development and intellectual or creative productivity.

Independence is seen as a hallmark of high-ability children and is often emphasized as a defining characteristic of creative children (Franks & Dolan, 1982; Olszewski, Kulieke, & Buescher, 1987). The extent to which this is a culturally determined value is not often recognized in the research literature. The stereotypic ideal image of the independent artist or scientist who achieves greatness while working alone may influence attitudes and expectations held by parents of the potential artist or potential scientist. It might also cause parents and teachers to devalue social experiences for bright children. It would be useful to examine the contrasting role of cooperation and mutual dependence as alternative strategies for achievement and accomplishment. Some recent attention has been focused on this approach (Slavin, 1983, 1987b).

84 | Develop Positive Self-Concept

A positive self-concept is widely recognized as a hallmark of healthy personal adjustment as well as a key ingredient in academic achievement (Colangelo & Pfleger, 1979; B. Clark, 1988; Feldhusen, 1986; Silvernail, 1985; Tannenbaum, 1983). Accordingly, it should not be surprising that a multitude of authors have endorsed the importance of self-concept for high-ability youth:

> It does a person no good to be incredibly bright if at the same time she is also incredibly miserable or has such emotional impairment that she functions destructively. . . . A major key is in helping gifted children develop understanding of themselves, a positive self-concept. (Webb, Meckstroth, & Tolan, 1982, pp. 26–27)

Current Knowledge

Groups of high-ability youth tend to be better adjusted than control groups of less able youth, despite differences in how such groups may be defined or how self-concept is measured (Colangelo & Pfleger, 1979; Kelly & Colangelo, 1984; Ketcham & Snyder, 1977; A. D. Ross & Parker, 1980; Tidwell, 1980b). Such findings are useful in refuting the negative stereotype that high-ability youth are generally or inherently maladjusted. However, a positive stereotype could divert attention from the self-concept problems faced by some high-ability students (Alvino, 1985; Webb et al., 1982).

Self-concept has become more narrowly defined in recent years, as a hierarchical and multifaceted construct (Byrne, 1984; Marsh, Byrne, & Shavelson, 1988). There is consistent empirical support for distinguishing academic self-concept from other facets of self-concept, such as social and athletic. Even academic self-concept is divisible into components related to different academic subjects, for example, mathematics (Byrne, 1984). Self-concept is considerably more complex than whether "it" is positive or negative.

There is some evidence that the superior adjustment of bright students is limited to specific facets of self-concept, but the pattern of findings is not consistent. A. D. Ross and Parker (1980) reported that high-ability youth have much higher academic than social self-concepts. Kelly and Colangelo (1984) found that students in gifted programs scored higher than general students on both academic and social self-concept measures, although it is not clear if there were significant academic versus social differences within the gifted group.

Mönks, van Boxtel, Roelofs, and Sanders (1986) found no significant differences in general self-concept between Dutch students in gifted and non-gifted programs, but that multiply talented gifted-program students had superior social self-concepts. Underachieving gifted-program students manifested academic self-concept deficits relative to control students and both academic and social deficits relative to gifted-program achievers.

High-ability youth may experience self-concept problems for a number of reasons. First, some may be adversely affected by the same stressful life events and circumstances (poverty, family discord, child abuse, etc.) that beset others. Second, they may experience conflicts arising from a poor fit with their social or academic environment, as, for example, when they are denied adequate educational programs or do not have social contact with peers of comparable ability (B. Clark, 1988). Third, they may respond negatively to parental pressure or expectations for high achievement (Alvino, 1985; Webb et al., 1982). All of these factors need research attention. The latter two reasons imply self-concept problems specific to high-ability youth, even if their incidence is unclear.

Phillips (1984, 1987) examined students whose self-perceptions drastically underestimated their actual high abilities. She found support for the theory that children's perceptions of their academic competence may be influenced more strongly by parent appraisals than by objective evidence and achievement.

Several studies have found a drop in academic self-concept when students enter a gifted program (J. Coleman & Fults, 1982, 1985; Olszewski, Kulieke, & Willis, 1987). This decline may be an artifact of how self-concept was assessed. Self-concept instruments explicitly or implicitly ask students to compare themselves with their classmates, so that it is only natural for students to rate themselves less highly when they compare themselves with students of similar ability. In these cases, a slight decline in self-concept scores may simply reflect a realistic perception of their peers and a healthy respect for their abilities. In a study of two summer programs for academically talented junior high students, Olszewski, Kulieke, and Willis (1987) found that students in both programs experienced such decline in academic self-concept but an increase in social and athletic self-concepts over a 3-week period.

Self-concept is not an end in itself. It stands in a reciprocal, interactive relationship with behavior (B. Clark, 1988; Marsh et al., 1988). In this vein, Cornell et al. (1990) examined the relationship between multiple facets of student self-concept at the beginning of a summer enrichment program and peer status near the end of the 2-week program. Social self-concept was consistently predictive of peer status in both classroom and social group settings; other facets of self-concept played subsidiary roles in different age and sex groups.

Implications for Action

Some high-ability youth do experience self-concept problems that merit attention by educators and parents, but the self-concepts of bright children are not generally at risk. The relationship between self-concept and high ability is complex, and facile generalizations must be avoided. Self-concept problems are not necessarily caused by the youth's high ability, but high ability provides no guarantee of protection from self-concept problems. Careful evaluation of each case is necessary.

There is an identifiable group of highly competent youth who consistently underestimate their own abilities. This reflects a self-concept problem with serious negative implications for future achievement. In these cases, parent beliefs and attitudes should be examined closely. Surprisingly, parental expectations may have the greatest effect on the child's self-concept.

It is important to distinguish the perceptions of academic ability from social, athletic, or other aspects of self-concept. A favorable academic self-concept does not indicate a favorable social self-concept, and overemphasis on academic success may be associated with less favorable self-perceptions of social competence. There may be some benefit to a student's social and athletic self-concept in associating with peers of similar academic ability. In all cases of self-concept problems, it seems important to determine the reference group the student is using as a basis for comparison, as well as the relative value placed on academic success by the student and his or her parents.

Needed Research

We need to identify the individual differences and specific factors (e.g., parent influences, social comparison processes) that affect the development of self-concept and produce the kinds of self-concept problems some high-ability youth experience. The possibility of social self-concept deficits in students who overemphasize academic success should be considered.

Although many studies report a relationship between self-concept and academic achievement (see reviews in Byrne, 1984, and Tannenbaum, 1983), the influence of self-concept on other behavioral outcomes needs examination.

Existing self-concept instruments are designed for a general student population and may not tap the specific problems or concerns of high-ability youth. Also, none of the major instruments (see review by Hughes, 1984) addresses problems of excessive self-concern or inflated self-esteem, although educators report such problems in some high-ability students.

We need to understand more about the development of self-concept over time and in response to different gifted programs. What kinds of interventions or treatment programs are effective at sustaining or improving self-concept? There is widespread interest in improving the self-concept of all students (Silvernail, 1985), but many claims of treatment effectiveness are unjustified, given the methodological difficulties in studying self-concept change (Scheirer & Kraut, 1979).

Research indicating a drop in academic self-concept but a possible increase in nonacademic self-concept after entrance into a gifted program needs follow-up. Are these short-term or long-term changes? Does a drop in academic self-concept have adverse implications for the student's adjustment, or does it reflect a healthy accommodation to peers of comparable ability?

85 | Identify and Develop Leadership Ability

The relationship between leadership and giftedness was made explicit in the "Marland Report" (U.S. Commissioner of Education, 1972) federal definition of giftedness.

> Children capable of high performance include those with demonstrated achievement and/or potential ability in any of the following areas, singly or in combination: 1) general intellectual ability, 2) specific academic aptitude, 3) creative or productive thinking, 4) leadership ability, 5) visual or performing arts, 6) psychomotor ability. (p. ix)

This was something of a surprise to many in the field, because leadership had never received the attention given to other ability areas. Nevertheless, this federal standard has become the prototype for definitions adopted by most states (Gallagher, Weiss, Oglesby, & Thomas, 1983).

A number of authors have taken up the challenge of identifying and developing leadership abilities as part of a comprehensive approach to gifted education (Bleedorn, 1979; Foster & Silverman, 1988; W. B. Richardson & Feldhusen, 1986). A succinct introduction to the place of leadership in gifted education was provided by B. Clark (1988):

> We shall discuss it as a set of skills that enable a group to reach its goals to maintain itself with mutual satisfaction, and to adapt to environmental change; and that allow individuals within the group to attain self-fulfillment. . . . The characteristics found commonly among gifted children can, if given opportunity to develop, enhance any leadership role. (p. 526)

Current Knowledge

Is leadership an ability or a set of interrelated skills? There have been numerous attempts to define, operationalize, or measure leadership potential in high-ability youth (Foster, 1981; Friedman, Jenkins-Friedman, & Van-Dyke, 1984; F. A. Karnes & D'Ilio, 1988a, 1988b; Khatena & Morse, 1987; Kitano & Tafoya, 1984; Lamb & Busse, 1983; Plowman, 1981; Renzulli, Smith, White, Callahan, & Hartman, 1976; W. B. Richardson & Feldhusen, 1986; Taylor & Ellison, 1983; Willings, 1983a). As illustrated by Davis and Rimm (1989), however, one finds lists of qualities of individuals who display leadership, not of the construct itself.

Self-ratings may be more valid measures of leadership performance than teacher ratings (Friedman et al., 1984; F. A. Karnes & D'Ilio, 1988b). Students identified as leaders typically display high general intelligence, but there does not appear to be an established personality profile of young leaders (F. A. Karnes, Chauvin, & Trant, 1984b; Tannenbaum, 1983).

Despite so many attempts, there is general agreement that leadership has never been satisfactorily defined or measured (B. Clark, 1988; Gallagher, 1985; Sheive & Schoenheit, 1987; Stodgill, 1974). This has led some critics to reject leadership as a simple construct and call for a multifaceted approach (cf. Khatena, 1982).

Even advocates of leadership training question whether it represents a form of giftedness:

> We do not assume that there is a special "gift" called leadership; rather, we take the position that gifted learners, like all students in a democratic society, need to know the rudiments of leadership. (Foster & Silverman, 1988, p. 357)

The search for an appropriate definition of leadership may be just as elusive as the search for a definition of giftedness. Both are exceedingly broad rubrics. Leadership is a social category, not a scientific one. There may be different qualities needed or sufficient to lead different groups toward different goals. This has led to attempts to categorize types of leaders or styles of leadership (Burns, 1978; Willings, 1983a). Moreover, this observation imposes a priori and practical limits on the effectiveness of any single type of leadership training.

Can leadership be taught? *Roeper Review* has devoted considerable attention to leadership issues over the years (e.g., Friedman et al., 1984; Hensel & Franklin, 1983; Huckaby & Sperling, 1981; Lamb & Busse, 1983; Lindsay, 1981b; Plowman, 1981; Willings, 1983a). Most of the reports concentrated on a general conception of leadership and outlined a basic teaching approach. The much needed next step is for the authors to present more objective evidence documenting the success of their leadership programs. For example, Hensel and Franklin (1983), as well as Lamb and Busse (1983), reported that their programs improved students' leadership skills but offered no concrete evidence for these claims.

F. A. Karnes, Chauvin, and colleagues have taken a lead role in the field. They have developed a *Leadership Skills Inventory* (F. A. Karnes & Chauvin, 1984b) and have undertaken systematic research on its psychometric properties (Chauvin & Karnes, 1982, 1983, 1984; F. A. Karnes & D'Ilio, 1988a, 1988b). The *Leadership Skills Inventory* (LSI) can be used in conjunction with the authors' one-week Leadership Studies Program (F. A. Karnes, Meriweather, & D'Ilio, 1987). On the basis of an LSI profile of skills in 9 areas (such as speech communication skills, values clarification, group dynamics skills, planning skills), students can select relevant training activities from an accompanying *Leadership Skills Inventory Activities Manual* (F. A. Karnes & Chauvin, 1984a).

F. A. Karnes et al. (1987) reported that their program was effective in improving leadership skills of students in Grades 6 through 11. This research was based on a single group, pretest-posttest design using the LSI. More rigorous and confirming evidence is needed. Students in the program should be compared with control groups of students undergoing no training or an alternative approach. In addition, it is important to demonstrate change on more than the LSI alone. Effects of using the LSI as both a diagnostic and outcome measure need to be ruled out. It would be useful to demonstrate that students in leadership training are more effective leaders on a group task, or that they are more successful in future leadership positions.

Should leadership ability be identified and developed? Although definitions of leadership may vary according to cultural priorities, in general the answer is probably yes, but there is weak or nonexistent evidence that special attention is more effective than incidental, that gifted students are especially deficient in this area or show greater potential, that leadership training needs to be especially adapted for the gifted, or that the critical variables in effective leadership training for any youth resemble those qualities that particularly define giftedness. These are tempting hypotheses, so far supported by a very small amount of generalizable research, some creative program ideas for leadership development, and perhaps a large amount of wishful thinking in the direction of meritocracy.

Implications for Action

There are two main approaches to leadership training. The first is to identify students with high leadership potential ("gifted leaders") and provide special training or educational experiences. Though the materials might be useful on a broader basis, this is the orientation of W. B. Richardson and Feldhusen's (1986) program for secondary students.

The second approach is to incorporate leadership training as a component of a general curriculum for high-ability (or perhaps all) students. The F. A. Karnes and Chauvin (1984a, 1984b) program addresses slightly younger children as well and takes this slightly broader approach, as does Magoon's (1981) program.

The most important question, however, is whether or not leadership skills should be a formal part of special provisions for highly able children. The literature does not answer that question adequately. It may be a more defensible element if pursued as a formal part of education in general. Leadership and participation in decision-making processes may differ in democratic and meritocratic societies or contexts.

Needed Research

There is a clear need to integrate practices in gifted education with research on leadership. Most general research on leadership concerns adults in leadership positions in politics or business. One can anticipate some problems in transfer of knowledge from an adult-oriented field to child-oriented applications. Nevertheless, adults well regarded for their leadership in a variety of domains would be useful subjects in studies that asked them to reflect upon how their leadership talents emerged. The reports might be somewhat romanticized, but they would alert researchers to useful variables to attend to.

It might be interesting, while many of the contributors to the "Marland Report" are still active in the field, to document how and why leadership was included.

How can leadership be reconciled with the calls for additional attention to more traditional areas (e.g., science and mathematics, languages, art, and music) and the development of creativity in the already crowded gifted program curriculum? Is it too expensive or time-consuming relative to other choices (Wood, 1985)?

The first research priority must be to demonstrate that leadership constitutes an array of abilities or skills and knowledge that can be identified; and second, that leadership can be developed or taught. Without training, how do extremely able students compare with others in various leadership skills or abilities? Can or should leadership training be especially adapted for the gifted? Are critical leadership variables those that particularly define giftedness? Does leadership training affect children's political thinking? Finally, a question more philosophical than empirical, would special leadership training opportunities for the highly able, rather than for all students, be consistent with democratic ideals?

86 | Encourage the Broadening of Interests

Tannenbaum (1983) advised, "It is important to prevent children from being narrowly focused in their educational experience, spending most of their time on one or two subjects and virtually neglecting others" (p. 447). His concern was that children may develop handicapping gaps in their knowledge and basic academic skills. Renzulli (1986b), for example, would concur: "Type I enrichment consists of general exploratory experiences that are designed to expose students to new topics, ideas, and fields of knowledge not ordinarily covered in the regular curriculum" (p. 77). Tempest (1974) recommended that

> teachers of clever children must be prepared for the emergence of unexpected interests and allow time for their pursuit, even if, as is very likely, they prove to be transitory. While they last, the child is able to enrich his experience by pursuing in depth something he sees as worth while and he should be encouraged to do so. (p. 31)

Current Knowledge

High-ability students typically have a wide range of interests (W. H. Clark & Hankins, 1985; Janos & Robinson, 1985a; Lu, 1982; Renzulli, Hartman, & Callahan, 1971; Terman, 1925; Terman & Oden, 1947; Whitmore, 1985). W. H. Clark and Hankins (1985) found that gifted program students were far more interested in educational matters and world affairs and international relations as well.

Probably the best known approach to broadening student interests is Renzulli's Triad Enrichment Model (e.g., see Renzulli, 1976, 1986b). The Triad Model emphasizes giving students maximum freedom in selecting areas of personal interest and then assisting them in developing the necessary skills to pursue those interests in depth. This and other approaches to enrichment are widely applicable across ages and subjects, and so variable in curricular content that they still require validational research (Tannenbaum, 1983).

Nevertheless, a few studies support some specific applications. Stedtnitz (1986) found that enrichment activities based on the Renzulli model effectively increased both the number and range of interests of 4- to 6-year-old children. Another study found beneficial effects of an astronomy enrichment program for fifth- to seventh-grade students (Reis, Atamian, & Renzulli, 1985). Tannenbaum (1983) reviewed additional research and provided a detailed plan for evaluating enrichment programs.

Talented females may require special encouragement to broaden their interests beyond conventional sex-role stereotypes (Callahan, 1979; Eccles, 1985; Hollinger, 1984; and see recommended practice No. 90). Fox (1978) suggested that otherwise capable females may avoid careers in science and mathematics because of conflicting interest patterns.

The recommendation that students should broaden their interests must be qualified when it comes to career selection. In contrast, counselors typically find that high-ability students have so many interests that they cannot choose among multiple potential career paths (Gowan, 1979b; Roper & Berry, 1986; Zaffrann & Colangelo, 1979b; see also recommended practice Nos. 87 and 90). They should be helped to understand more clearly the link between various interest areas and specific careers (e.g., see Post-Kammer & Perrone, 1983).

Implications for Action

The natural curiosity and multiple aptitudes of many bright youngsters make it relatively easy to stimulate their interests in many areas. Two concerns require special attention. First, female students may need special intervention to broaden their interest in traditionally male-oriented subjects and careers. Such intervention should probably start early and continue throughout the school years (Callahan, 1979; Eccles, 1985). Second, the emphasis on broadening interests should be replaced gradually by a narrowing of interests sometime during adolescence, allowing plenty of opportunity for normal adolescent indecision about career options. By the time students reach college age, overly broad interests can start to become a career-counseling problem (see recommended practice No. 90).

Needed Research

Program evaluation research on enrichment programs and other efforts to broaden student interests are needed. How long do students retain interests after the enrichment program is over? What are the factors that discriminate students who retain their interest from those who do not? Are there positive (or negative) outcomes associated with retaining broad interests? At what point should students begin to narrow their interests, at least as they relate to career choice?

There is an anomaly. On one hand, bright students respond well to interest-broadening educational activities. On the other, many studies show their interests already to be broader. How do some bright children come to have this head start? Do interest-broadening interventions increase the gap between the highly able and others? Do they benefit less able children to a greater, equal, or lesser degree, in absolute or relative terms? Do less able children need different kinds of interventions in this context? What role does gender play?

87 | Focus on Excellence in a Few Areas

That high-ability youth should focus their interests seems to stand in opposition to the previous recommendation (No. 86) to broaden their interests. We will describe support for the present recommendation and later suggest some means of reconciliation between the two.

Feldhusen (1986) emphasized specialized learning as preparation for later achievement:

> Our general faith is that gifted and talented youth should receive tutelage of some kind and should become knowledgeable in some discipline or area of study as a prelude to creative achievement. (pp. 117–118)

At what point should exceptionally able students begin to narrow their interests and specialize their education? Will early specialization give students a head start on their future careers and increase their adult productivity, or will it prematurely foreclose more promising lines of talent development, limit creativity, or dampen later enthusiasm (also see recommended practice No. 71)?

Recommendations for early specialization are pervasive, even though often implicit, in writings urging the use of acceleration and other programs of advanced coursework (J. C. Stanley & Benbow, 1983; W. C. George, Cohn, & Stanley, 1979; Horne & Dupuy, 1981; Mercurio, Schwartz, & Oesterle, 1982; Mezynski, J. C. Stanley, & McCoart, 1983).

Current Knowledge

Empirical studies and case reports of outstanding individuals in diverse fields consistently reveal a pattern of focused attention and devotion to a specific field of study early in life (Bloom, 1985; V. Goertzel & Goertzel, 1962; M. G. Goertzel, Goertzel, & Goertzel, 1978; Roe, 1953). Summarizing studies of outstanding pianists, sculptors, swimmers, tennis players, mathematicians, and research neurologists, Bloom (1985) reported that parents begin to encourage specialization at an early age. Among teenagers, pursuit of the talent field began to infringe on many other activities.

Studies of eminent or outstanding individuals are necessarily retrospective and are vulnerable to biases in recall or selective reporting. It is difficult to infer a causal relationship between early specialization and later outstanding performance when other influences, for example, natural talent or ability, family environmental characteristics, and quality of teachers, cannot be distinguished and controlled. The issue is what weight to give to early specialization and the accompanying sacrifice of other interests and pursuits.

Are there benefits to early specialization? Talent-search programs identify highly able students in a specific area and then offer a variety of educational experiences designed to encourage excellence in that area. Probably the best known talent search associated with gifted education in the U.S.A. is the Study of Mathematically Precocious Youth (SMPY) program, which originated at The Johns Hopkins University (J. C. Stanley, Keating, & Fox, 1974). The talent-search concept has been employed at several other universities (J. C. Stanley & Benbow, 1983; VanTassel-Baska, 1986) and is widely practiced in professional sports, the arts, and other domains. They have expanded their efforts beyond mathematics to include natural and physical sciences, literature, languages, and humanities.

Follow-up studies and case reports indicate clear academic advantage to acceleration by highly talented youth (J. C. Stanley, 1985; J. C. Stanley & Benbow, 1983; J. C. Stanley & McGill, 1986). These studies do not specifically isolate the effects of early specialization. It would be useful to investigate how students "settled" on their specialized interests as well as to examine changes in the students' interests and activities (social as well as academic).

Adams (1985) reviewed the efforts of the British Association for the Advancement of Science, which include a young scientist organization, science fairs, and competitive awards. Mentoring is a widely recommended strategy, too (Edlind & Haensly, 1985; see recommended practice No. 55). Students can help design and implement their course of studies as a means of encouraging in-depth pursuit of special topics or issues that interest them (Dubner, 1984).

Implications for Action

In some ways the contrast between broadening and narrowing interests parallels the conflict between enrichment and acceleration as educational strategies (see Maker, 1982a). Enrichment often entails broadening interests, whereas acceleration (at least within subjects) usually involves specialization. Of course, enrichment and acceleration are not necessarily mutually exclusive (Feldhusen, 1983a; see recommended practice No. 8), and enrichment can stimulate study in great depth. In turn, this can accelerate learning. There is always the likelihood of some conflict between goals of enrichment and acceleration when it comes to the decision to broaden or narrow interests. Eventually, most students must narrow their interests and focus on a specific career. Whether this best occurs early in childhood, in adolescence, or even in early adulthood is not clear. The timing may differ across students or careers.

The success of specialized or advanced (not necessarily curricularly accelerated) work with bright students, and the ability of capable youth in many parts of the world to succeed in highly specialized secondary schools, indicates that the greatest risk might be to fail to make such opportunities available to those for whom they are appropriate. Another danger, however, is to require such specialization, or to make it the only path to a university education or other valuable opportunity; much would be gained by case studies and survey research of bright students who did not specialize early, and, in the tradition of American liberal arts colleges, might not do so until after the completion of a bachelor's degree. Do such students achieve more, less, or the same for themselves or society?

There are also some very bright people whose career or other interests cannot be reduced to the singular. Whether they pursue these varied interests and talents simultaneously or in sequence (such as through career change), the important observation—perhaps speculation—may be that these individuals do not need to specialize their interests. Alternatively, they might specialize in more than one domain. These are researchable questions.

It is difficult to offer definitive general advice. There are some individuals for whom early specialization is suitable.

Needed Research

Several research questions have been alluded to above. It is important to study the factors that influence the development of special interests and that lead some students to begin the pursuit of excellence at an early age. This research should look at people who specialize in single areas as well as those who pursue excellence in more than one domain. The relative value of enrichment and acceleration still needs clarification, although it is unreasonable to expect an either-or outcome.

Some specific questions worthy of research include:

1. When can specialization optimally be introduced?
2. Is it meaningful to consider levels of specialization?
3. What are the effects, good or bad, of encountering early specialization?
4. What are the consequences of avoiding it?
5. What are the consequences of its being required?

6. How can the best outcomes of early specialization and broadening of interests be combined (e.g., focus on career versus general knowledge)?

7. What are the causal relations amongst the myriad variables?

Ultimately, this recommendation speaks to one of the most fundamental questions in all gifted education. What are the ingredients of school and family environments that promote student excellence? At what ages should students begin to specialize in their interests? Because of the risks perceived in attempting extremely early specialization, an experimental study of its effects is ethically difficult, but it does happen on its own and the cases need to be documented. What are the signposts that indicate that parents and teachers should begin encouraging individual students to narrow their interests and pursue excellence in a specific area? Or should they?

88 | Gifted Children Should Not Be Labeled

Labeling means assigning a categorical descriptor to a child primarily to secure needed educational services. In this context, labeling is more than stereotyping: It implies that some sort of differential treatment, assistance, or adaptation of the system occurs once the child has been identified as gifted.

Cox, Daniel, and Boston (1985) stated the practice clearly: "Avoid labeling any group of children as *the gifted*. To do so implies that some are gifted in every area and other children in none" (p. 154). Feldhusen and Baska (1985) linked labeling and programming: "Identification systems that merely enable us to label or categorize 'gifted' youth are of no value, and potentially even harmful. The sole purpose of identification is to guide the educational process and serve youth" (p. 70). Willings (1980) warned that labeling narrows the horizons of the creative individual who may be steered away from expressing talent in one area owing to being labeled exceptional in another. Sanborn (1979c) and Cornell (1983) added a family perspective, urged avoidance of the label, and voiced concern for unlabeled siblings.

Current Knowledge

Hobbs (1975) and his associates investigated labeling in handicapped and delinquent populations. They identified key concerns for the study of giftedness as well: Does the label do the child harm or good? How does it affect siblings, parents, teachers, and friends?

The literature includes policy arguments and empirical studies. The former question labeling children as gifted on economic and ethical grounds (Fenstermacher, 1982; Jacquard, 1983; Sapon-Shevin, 1984). Using the gifted label is presumed to be potentially harmful or unfair to other children. Some object to identifying and serving the gifted because the term gifted is negatively value-laden. Others hesitate about labeling primarily because, even though the label may be accurate or lead to services, it may disrupt the home and school lives of the labeled children (B. Clark, 1988; Cox et al., 1985).

The empirical literature on labeling is small and exploratory but growing rapidly. Studies have investigated the effects of labeling on the labeled child, the family, peers, and school personnel (see A. Robinson, 1986a, 1986c, for reviews). Adolescents are positive about being labeled as gifted (Guskin, Zimmerman, Okolo, & Peng, 1986), or more likely to respond favorably to the label joined to other powerful adolescent labels such as athlete (Tannenbaum, 1962). The gifted child holds high status in the family (Cornell, 1983). Parents report feeling closer to and prouder of a child labeled gifted, but in some cases unlabeled siblings suffer adjustment difficulties (Cornell, 1983, 1984, 1989). Although other studies report fewer sibling difficulties (Chamrad & Robinson, 1989; Cornell & Grossberg, 1986, 1989), Grenier (1985) noted that gifted siblings' self-esteem was enhanced by competition and positive comparison. The opposite was true for an unlabeled sibling. Parental treatment was positively related to self-esteem for all. The negative effects decreased when the sibling age gap was over 3 years. Gifted children do express concern about the impact of the label on their family members (Colangelo & Brower, 1987a), but negative effects may not persist over years (Colangelo & Brower, 1987b).

Several studies have investigated the effects of the label on teachers. Teachers engaged in graduate studies reacted negatively to the gifted label (Craven, 1980), but most were neutral (A. Robinson, 1983) or more likely to respond to other variables as they interacted with the gifted label, for example, race (Rubovits & Maehr, 1973) or level of motivation (A. Robinson, 1986b). Fewer studies have investigated other school personnel, but some evidence suggests that psychologists and counselors react negatively to the gifted label (Deiulio, 1984; Wiener, 1968) and school administrators are slightly positive (Wiener & O'Shea, 1963) or neutral (Griffen, 1984).

Should gifted children be so labeled? The philosophical debate has not been won on either side; there are advocates and adversaries, roughly divided between the need for the label to assure services and concern for the inherent dangers in the label or the process of labeling.

Although the literature is too undeveloped to strongly support or refute the avoidance of labeling children as gifted, there is little support for the assertion of harm to the labeled child, resulting from either isolation or hostility. Families accord labeled children high status, teachers are more likely to respond to other characteristics, and labeled students report positive feelings. No studies have yet examined whether counselors' unsympathetic views can be changed, either by exposure or training.

The strongest evidence in support of the recommended practice comes from family studies in which some negative effects of labeling have been documented. Their severity, longevity, and uniqueness to families with gifted children need to be investigated. Subsequently, these effects need to be weighed against the benefits of special educational programming for the gifted in order to assess the recommended practice fully.

Implications for Action

To minimize "pockets of concern" (A. Robinson, 1990), school personnel can take several actions.

First, schools should inform parents by conference when a child is first labeled for programming. For parents of younger children, information is best disseminated by individual conferences rather than sending a letter home or scheduling "gifted parent" meetings. The professional responsible for parent liaison should give the working definition of giftedness, briefly describe the identification process, refer parents to reading material, and answer their questions. Some training in the education and upbringing of the gifted is desirable.

Second, schools can minimize the public nature of labeling by using the term sparingly. Special classes need not be labeled "g/t." They might be more descriptively and accurately titled and publicized as enrichment classes, independent study, labs, or seminars. "Talented" evokes less emotion than "gifted," but some people may object to using the terms interchangeably.

It is important not to confuse different concerns that have become associated with labeling. The entire identification process may be regarded as an exercise in labeling and categorization, but identification and service can be endorsed while trying to minimize the risks of labeling. One might use different labels, or educate parents and teachers about potential risks. Research is needed to confirm the effectiveness of either approach.

Research Needed

There is always a risk that providing appropriately differentiated educational services will, on its own, lead to labeling. Research is therefore needed to explore the efficacy of interventions intended to help families to deal positively with perceived differences among siblings, and particularly with labeling. Research on the prevention of the negative impact of labeling is important at a broader level: If the negative effects are real, they will not go away by being ignored, and they could seriously undermine advocacy for bright children. This is a delicate topic. Care and sensitivity—to the individuals and to the field—are needed in dealing with the public, schools, and research subjects.

Family dynamics and self-concept are important to further understanding the impact of the "gifted" label at home and school. Studies are needed that control for the salience of the label (does the child perceive himself or others to be labeled and what does the child think that means?) in relation to self-concept. For example, studies of children who are screened for programs but not finally selected or labeled are also needed. Initial disappointment is predictable, but the intensity and longevity of such effects should be examined. Such studies would help establish the relative roles of the identification and programming processes in the creation of the label.

Future researchers need to be aware that labeling effects are not always overt and easy to identify (could we study racial prejudice by asking people if they have it?). Self-report instruments are susceptible to bias and defensiveness. An adolescent in a gifted program may be snubbed by others without recognizing that it arises from labeling effects. Siblings are reluctant to discuss how a gifted sibling makes them feel, and those who feel the worst have the most trouble talking about it. Some parents may say they treat their children equally, but their observable behavior may indicate otherwise.

The suggestion that programs, not children, be labeled (Cox et al., 1985) also requires exploration. Such cosmetic approaches may have the same effects as labeling the child. Does functional labeling of the program avoid labels based on characteristics of the students? An advanced Chinese course could be called just that. This may be more difficult to conceive at the elementary level where most students still spend the majority of their time in fixed groups.

More controlled attitudinal studies are also in order. We cannot hope to get a clear picture of the attitudes of others toward the labeled child unless we can determine what those others are responding to: the gifted label independently of the child, the idea of differentiated or specialized education, the child served by such a program, or some other associated characteristic. The persistence of the negative effects also requires further study.

Finally, more detailed explorations of relations of labeling effects to age, birth order, age gap, gender, and so on, are needed to be able to make precise statements about labeling, its advantages, and its risks. Comparisons with the effects of known positive labels related to athletics, physical appearance, and general behavior, among others, would be very helpful to placing these effects in context.

89   Social or Curricular Conformity Should Not Be Forced on Creatively Talented Children

Creatively talented children are often seen to be at odds with conventional school systems, public or private, which stress conformity and uniformity in learning and behavior. Khatena (1982) wrote:

> We are also well aware of the pressures exerted by education on children to conform to prearranged educational experiences, with consequent press and its ill effects on their mental health (Gowan & Bruch, 1971; Torrance, 1962). These pressures can cause stunting of the creative development of gifted children. (p. 179)

Landau (1979) succinctly wrote, "Education towards conformity is the arch enemy of creative development" (p. 151). Takacs (1986) included social conformity as well: "The creatively gifted child is often a minority of one who must cope with the sanctions of social groups against that divergence" (p. 100).

Current Knowledge

Many studies of creative individuals confirm the relationships among creative ability and qualities associated with nonconformity, such as independence (see recommended practice No. 83), autonomy, and lack of concern for social norms (see reviews by Barron & Harrington, 1981; Dellas & Gaier, 1970; and Janos & Robinson, 1985a).

The distinction between high creativity and high intelligence is also well known (Getzels & Jackson, 1962; see reviews by Barron & Harrington, 1981, and Janos & Robinson, 1985a). High intelligence is more strongly associated with conventional measures of academic success (grades, test scores, etc.) than high creativity (Nichols, 1964; C. E. Schaefer, 1970; E. Schaefer & Bell, 1958; Wallach & Kogan, 1965; Weisberg & Springer, 1961). Thus, adverse effects of any pressures toward conformity in the educational system are specific to children with creative abilities rather than the broader population of students identified for gifted and talented programs.

The critical issue for this recommendation is whether or not creatively talented children experience some deleterious effect as a result of their school experiences. Although many educators can describe instances of creatively talented children who come into conflict with standard curricula and conventional school practices that frustrate their originality and drive to pursue independent interests (cf. several clinical case studies reported by Willings, 1980, 1983a), systematic research is largely unavailable. This is a curious deficit, given the extensive research on creativity in general.

Implications for Action

Creatively talented students may be prone to some degree of frustration in a conventional educational environment. From these students come the artists, researchers, and problem solvers and finders of all types in our society. The severity of this problem and whether it can truly result in a loss of creative ability, loss of motivation, or both, remain to be established.

There are two logical ways to avoid exacerbating the situation. One approach is to individualize instruction as much as possible by offering enrichment opportunities and providing the creative student with options that allow him or her to pursue independent projects consistent with personal interests, preferred learning pace, and style.

The second approach is to help the creative student become more tolerant of restrictions encountered. These may be general, such as disciplinary codes enforced in military or religious schools and colleges. They may be specific, imposed by certain teachers in the course of their work, or necessitated by the presence of hazardous items in laboratories or shops. Counseling might emphasize finding ways to resist pressures to conform to others' expectations or to minimize conflict with them while pursuing creative ideas. There are practical limits on how far the schools can accommodate individual differences, and some schools have decidedly different objectives in this regard. More importantly, school provides a preview of the world of work in this regard, and the exceptionally creative student is likely to encounter similar problems there, too (cf. Willings, 1980). Takacs (1986) recommends teaching "creative conformity" (p. 102), a practice that involves selective conscious conformity when it seems necessary to achieve personal goals.

Probably the most important issue for young persons presented with this recommendation is to maintain a sense of personal integrity while working within the system.

Needed Research

Educational practices that are excessively restrictive or conformist need to be specified, and their effects on creatively talented children need to be investigated. A study demonstrating that a group of children experienced a negative effect on their creativity from a specific educational practice would be extremely powerful and persuasive. We are not proposing that the restrictive environments of which we speak are created for the express purpose of limiting creativity and potential or are directed maliciously at particular children. Aside from matters of safety, where the child must adjust (perhaps with help), we are discussing the consequences of school climates and teaching practices that are deemed to be in the interests of all or most students but that, to the surprise of some, are counterproductive.

When there are concerns about the adverse effects of some educational (or other) practice on a group of children, those adverse effects should be carefully documented in the most rigorous manner possible. This will provide a basis for insisting that concerns be taken seriously and that the educational practice be changed. Instead, current practice frequently is to criticize but not to follow through with careful documentation and evidence. Under these circumstances, it is understandable if educational practices are slow to change. Moreover, the cumulative result of criticisms without evidence is that future concerns are taken even less seriously.

Note that it is not as difficult to conduct research of this nature as it may seem. The usual ethical and practical barriers to conducting research on an educational practice thought to be harmful to children do not apply in the same way when the practice is the status quo and the burden of proof lies with the challenger. A researcher need only study the status quo practice with a pre-post design, gathering data on the functioning of children before and after involvement in the allegedly deleterious classroom or program. The researcher may want to contend that the practice is only deleterious to certain children (e.g., highly creative or individualistic children), but this can be incorporated into the design by a priori definition of high- and low-risk groups.

One might begin to plan such studies by reviewing clinical claims of instances where highly creative children have been harmed by conventional circumstances. This would isolate the variables that should be examined in further research. An open mind should also be kept to the possibility that harmful effects ascribed to less than perfect school circumstances might be effects of home and other circumstances that children encounter, or to medical, psychological, or other characteristics of the children. Such variables need to be controlled carefully.

Finally, research on this topic should examine the extent to which potentially harmful environments need to be ameliorated, or to which their risks can be mitigated by the addition of positive elements (a suitable mentor, a part-time resource room activity, etc.) in the creative child's life. Takac's idea of building resistance to or tolerance of selective unsatisfactory conditions may, for its success, depend at least in part on the presence of these positive elements at least as much as the absence of the negative.

90 | Career Counseling Is Needed, Especially for Girls

The ultimate importance of career guidance was underscored by Willings (1983b):

> We could profitably look into ways of helping gifted children anticipate and work out strategies to overcome the problems they will encounter in the world of work. . . . The last thing we want is for the significant work we have done and will continue to do on behalf of the gifted child to be rendered useless when that child reaches adult life. (pp. 68–69)

The first and most often noted problem is that a single career or line of work may not draw upon all of their interests and abilities nor provide sufficient fulfillment of all their needs to achieve or create.

> Some problems of career development are common to nearly all young people, but there are some which seem to be special problems of the gifted and talented. The fact that the gifted usually possess many potentialities and varied interests complicates their selection of a career. Expectations of parents, teachers, friends, and society in general operate to restrict their range of career choices and to pressure them to achieve high levels. (Sanborn, 1979a, pp. 284–285)

The second group of problems consists of negative attitudes toward exceptional ability and a social system or institutional bureaucracy that often does not accommodate, much less encourage, creativity, innovation, or insightful thinking (Willings, 1983b).

The potential for career problems is especially acute for women (Sanborn, 1979a). Their needs include:

1. "Realistic expectations, either of themselves or of the world in which they will be functioning after they get out of school" (Harding & Berger, 1979, p. 134)
2. "Access to skilled counselors who will provide them with the emotional support, with comprehensive information about career education, and with the specialized strategies that can help raise and maintain high aspirations" (Kerr, 1985, p. 168)
3. "Test biases should be identified, occupational counseling needs to be broadened, and counselors need to be sensitized to the needs of gifted females" (Callahan, 1979, p. 423)

Talented women may also encounter gender-related bias against recognition of their potential and advancement for their achievements. They may experience conflict over their career and family aspirations, and their self-concepts may not reflect true ability and potential.

This practice addresses career guidance counseling; No. 78 addresses socioemotional difficulties more directly.

Current Knowledge

To the naïve observer (or devil's advocate, as the case may be), high-ability youth should be least likely to have career problems. The specific kinds of career problems faced by high-ability individuals require documentation and study.

The Research and Guidance Laboratory for Superior Students at the University of Wisconsin has provided career counseling to thousands of high-ability youth (Sanborn, 1979a; Sanborn, Pulvino, & Wunderlin, 1971; Post-Kammer & Perrone, 1983). Their work represents a valuable source of rich information about the varied counseling needs of high-ability youth.

Perrone (1986) and Post-Kammer and Perrone (1983) reported that many academically talented individuals graduate from high school feeling unprepared to make career decisions. To prevent this from happening, Delisle (1982b) outlined a guidance program that begins in grade school. Frederickson (1986) emphasized strategies to deal with the problems faced by multitalented youth who may be overwhelmed by too many options and alternatives in pursuing a career. Similarly, Willings (1986) advocated a career-examination program tailored to the needs of multitalented students. He reported several successful case histories. Systematic research is still needed.

A noteworthy program for high school seniors provided formal career education in three phases (Borman, Nash, & Colson, 1978; Nash, Borman, & Colson, 1980): learning about different types of careers, observing and learning from a university mentor, and participating in a working internship. Although participants responded positively, longitudinal follow-up on future career benefits of this program would be useful.

Only a few studies have compared different counseling approaches with high-ability youth. Kerr (1986) found that students preferred a test battery consisting of the Self-Directed Search and the Edwards Personal Preference Schedule. Students also preferred same-sex to mixed-sex career counseling groups. Kerr used random group assignment in her experimental design, a rarity in this area.

Kerr and Ghrist-Priebe (1988) conducted one of the few controlled studies that examined the effects of a counseling workshop on high-ability students. Attendees (talented high school seniors) were more likely than wait-list control subjects to discuss career development with their counselors within 2 months of the program. Longer term studies of similar counseling approaches are needed.

Future progress in career-counseling research may hinge on the ability to identify types of counseling approaches especially suitable for different student needs. Toward this end, based on previous ideas raised by Kerr (1981) and Marshall (1981), Roper and Berry (1986) classified students along two dimensions: diverse career interests (underspecialized) versus narrow interest (overspecialized), and academically talented (conformist) versus creatively talented (nonconformist).

The career problems experienced by talented students in general are compounded in the case of talented females (Callahan, 1979; Eccles, 1985; Hollinger & Fleming, 1988).

K. D. Noble (1987) detailed the psychological and social barriers faced by talented women seeking leadership positions. She endorsed a wide array of possible interventions, including early education on psychological issues, feminist-oriented psychotherapy, career counseling that encourages females to study mathematics and science (see recommended practice No. 101), support groups, and education and in-service for parents and teachers. V. S. Garrison, Stronge, and Smith (1986) also advocated a career-education program designed specifically for high-ability females.

Post-Kammer and Perrone (1983) conducted a follow-up study of 648 adults who had previously participated in Wisconsin programs noted above. There were few sex differences, indicating some success in the interventions. There were no differences on most questions concerning ability to make career choices, although males recalled feeling better prepared than females to know where to train for a career. Both sexes ranked work second in importance to marriage and family relationships. Also, both sexes felt that challenge and skill development were the most important factors in their work, although males placed relatively greater emphasis on pay and women placed relatively greater emphasis on relationships with others in the workplace.

Harding and Berger (1979) described a career-education seminar for high-ability female adolescents. The program presented young adult women in a variety of different occupations who spoke about their careers and how they integrated work and family obligations. The program was well received by students, but other outcome data were not collected.

Kerr (1983) examined the occupational goals of 11th-grade males and females before and after a counseling program designed to raise career aspirations. The females showed an increase in career aspirations, although males did not. Male aspirations were already high. The mean score for females after counseling was still lower than for the males.

Schroer and Dorn (1986) examined sex differences in the effects of a group counseling program on talented undergraduates. There were increases in career decisiveness for both males and females, and important sex differences on other measures. Males experienced a decline in personal conflict and perceived external barriers to career decision making, but, surprisingly, females experienced an increase in both. The authors suggested that this unexpected result may have been due to an increase in awareness of career options among the women, which brought them into conflict with personal and social influences that discouraged career achievement.

In summary, the need for career counseling for bright students, especially girls, is primarily gleaned from clinical reports that vary widely in their style of reporting. Some program evaluations have also shown that interventions do work. This recommended practice is widely endorsed and enjoys modest but consistently replicated research support.

Implications for Action

Career counseling for high-ability students is warranted, at least as a form of insurance. As Willings (1983b) reminded us, the best educational programs are of no ultimate value if their graduates fail to make good career decisions or are unable to function effectively in their future work environments. Little comparative work has been done, so educators and counselors can only be advised to select programs that best match their available resources and anticipated student needs.

Talented women experience special problems. Early intervention and preventive efforts are defensible, in order to minimize the expected adverse effects of societal expectations and pressures. It is important to recognize that talented women are likely to experience intrapersonal and interpersonal conflicts in their career decision making, and that counseling may stimulate thinking and inquiry that bring potential or actual conflicts to the surface.

Needed Research

Most research on career guidance counseling has focused on ways to help students make informed career choices. Less often have researchers examined problems high-ability adults actually experience in their careers. Such work would provide a compelling basis for designing preventive programs at the high school and college level. Work on the career guidance needs of disadvantaged and minority students of exceptional ability has also been relatively neglected (B. A. Moore, 1978).

Only a few researchers have conducted follow-up studies to examine the effectiveness of their career education or guidance efforts. Although it is useful to know what kinds of guidance procedures students prefer and whether the students report a subjective sense of increased decisiveness about their career choices, it is more important to know what careers students actually pursue, and how they fare.

Efforts to encourage and develop the talents of high-ability females, especially in science and mathematics, are receiving increasing attention. This, in part, reflects awareness that high-ability females do experience both internal and external conflicts that discourage them from developing their intellectual abilities. In addition, it also reflects increasing societal acceptance of women who pursue high-level careers and the recognition that, in addition to the personal impact, these women represent an important and often underutilized world resource. Research that demonstrates the effectiveness of various programs to facilitate educational and career development of talented females is essential.

CHAPTER EIGHT

Special Groups of Gifted Children

<table>
<tr><td>91</td><td>

Respect Cultural and Social Differences

</td></tr>
</table>

Social justice and cultural pluralism shape this recommended practice. Bernal (1979) stated that, for highly able students,

> gifted programs must be suited to them, not merely offered on a take-it-or-leave-it basis, and not designed and implemented with only little deliberation about their psychological, cultural, and linguistic characteristics. (p. 397)

Cox, Daniel, and Boston (1985—see p. 46) expanded the issue to include international cultural differences. The discussion of this practice focuses on appropriate and effective interventions for gifted minority students. (Regarding the identification of culturally diverse populations, see recommended practice No. 23; programmatic adaptations for economically disadvantaged gifted students are discussed in No. 92).

Current Knowledge

The research base on socially and culturally diverse gifted students is small and uneven. For example, more empirical studies exist on blacks than on American Indians, and the academic successes of Asian and Jewish students have been examined often. Sensitivity to the cultural heritage of students is defensible on philosophical grounds alone. It is inconceivable to depend on research to support or refute the suggestion, but it is important that abuses and their human costs are well documented as a constant reminder. The experiences of exceptionally successful minority groups also offer the prospect, so far largely unrealized, for understanding social and cultural contributions to excellence. One benefit that has been achieved from the study of socially and culturally diverse gifted youth has been an increased awareness of the values contributed by each group. Some of these points are conveyed below in the overview of Maker's (1989) compendium of practices on this topic.

Most of the empirical work on gifted minority students is descriptive and related to the difficulty in identifying them; the literature on interventions offers primarily recommendations, program descriptions, reports, and evaluations (Alamprese, Erlanger, & Brigham, 1989; Blanning, 1977; Frasier, 1989; K. George, 1983; C. R. Harris, 1985; S. T. Johnson, Starnes, Gregory, & Blaylock, 1985; Maker, 1989; A. Robinson, Bradley, & Stanley, 1990; Scruggs & Cohn, 1983; Mulcahy, Wilgosh, & Crawford, 1985). Maker (1983) has characterized the issue as confusion over cultural pluralism. To what degree do programs for gifted minority students promote skills and attitudes that increase the likelihood of students' success in the mainstream culture to the detriment of ethnic identification? The issue is particularly volatile because some cultural groups are perceived to have values that conflict with mainstream success. Maker attempted to reconcile the issue by suggesting that a bicultural view or one that develops potential in both environments is best. However, her admirable sentiment is quite difficult to translate into guidance for educators.

Maker (1989) has edited a book that assembles and reviews recommendations for defensible programs for culturally diverse gifted students. From the position statements and reaction papers of over 30 authors, she summarized recommendations both within and across cultural groups. For example, adaptations for gifted Hispanic students include bilingualism, the frequent expression of physical warmth and touching in the classroom, and an awareness of traditional sex roles (Udall, 1989). American Indians present a wealth of diversity among themselves, but including content that preserves tribal identity is important. Because American Indians often identify giftedness as excellence in singing, dancing, chanting, and various visual arts, curricula that include opportunities to develop these talents are recommended as part of gifted programs (Tonemah, 1985). Further, K. George (1989) reported that program activities are most effective when shared with the tribal community.

Maker's summary of programmatic recommendations for gifted Asian students were less consistent, a reflection of substantial differences among the many subgroups of Asians, which include second-generation Cantonese as well as the children of immigrant Montanards. Hasegawa (1989) and Wong and Wong (1989) observed that the frequent pattern of achievement in mathematics and science and the reputation as the "successful minority" may inadvertently cause problems among Asian students by steering talented writers, musicians, or artists away from those fields.

For gifted Hispanic, American Indian, and Asian students, cooperative learning situations are recommended (L. Garrison, 1989; Kitano, 1989; Tanaka, 1989; Wong & Wong, 1989). In addition, several educators mentioned the particular problems of gifted girls from among cultural groups that remain male-dominated (Kirschenbaum, 1989; Tanaka, 1989; Udall, 1989).

Overall, there are two kinds of relevant prescriptions in the literature. First, those that apply to a broad range of culturally diverse groups, particularly as they relate to the problems of oppressed peoples. A second type of prescription is suited to a specific group. The use of counseling strategies to enhance the development of ethnic identity (Exum & Colangelo, 1981) is an example of a programmatic prescription relevant to any ethnic group. The use of quiet observation without verbal instructions before a child practices a skill is, for example, particularly appropriate for American Indian children (L. Garrison, 1989).

Finally, recommendations for black students often overlap with program modifications recommended for economically disadvantaged students (see recommended practice No. 92). However, there is the specific recommendation that the major purpose of a program for gifted black students should be the development of positive self-concept (Baldwin, 1989). The infusion of black history and culture is recommended by almost everyone (Cohen, 1989; Frasier, 1988; Grant, 1989; Ronvik, 1989).

Although the impetus to respect differences does not need formal or empirical defense, we have not yet gained all the benefit available that sociological and anthropological studies of gifted minority students might provide.

Implications for Action

Programs that infuse multicultural objectives into the curriculum and that acknowledge cultural differences as strengths are a highly desirable course of action for schools.

The tougher issue of how to resolve the rather widespread cultural values of male superiority with ways to help culturally diverse gifted girls has no easy answer. A supportive, counseling component may help.

Needed Research

Because there are so few programs that target gifted minorities, comparative studies of programs that serve minority students as a part of the "regular" gifted program versus programs that serve minority students exclusively would be informative. To what extent does program success depend on having a minimum number of participants? Some groups view being singled out as antithetical to their group cohesiveness. Are programs with heavy infusion of cultural traditions more acceptable?

Documentation of effective strategies for parental involvement would be welcome. Relevant outcome variables might be as straightforward as numbers of school contacts initiated by parents and numbers of hours volunteered by family members in service to the school.

Finally, attention to cultural differences is rightly the business of general education as well. However, gifted education is uniquely suited to offer leadership on viewing cultural differences as strengths rather than deficits served by remedial and compensatory fare in efforts to meet minimum competencies. This effort might be aided by the involvement of researchers and research techniques in sociology, anthropology, social work, ethnography, and other areas wherein resides expertise about social and cultural minorities.

| 92 | **Specially Attend to Gifted Disadvantaged Children** |

Special intervention for gifted disadvantaged children implies two issues: (1) Services for the gifted disadvantaged student are different from the usual services provided to gifted students, and (2) services for the gifted disadvantaged student are different from the usual services provided to disadvantaged students. Passow (1986a) elaborated:

> The goals are the same; the standards are the same for advantaged and disadvantaged. It is the strategies and program structure which differ because individualization and differentiation must take into account the personal and cultural characteristics of the student and the milieu in which he/she functions. (pp. 160–161)

Educating the disadvantaged is made more difficult in gifted education, as it is in all of education, by lack of consensus and a clear definition of disadvantaged. Passow (1986a) brought some clarity to the problem of definition:

> While there is considerable overlap between minorities and disadvantaged populations, the two are not synonymous. Even the term *disadvantaged* has two aspects with respect to compensatory education efforts: *economic disadvantage* which is operationally defined in terms of poverty and *educational*

disadvantage which is operationally defined in terms of below-average academic achievement. There are minority children who achieve academically
and whose families do not live below the poverty level and who, consequently, are neither economically nor educationally disadvantaged. The term
disadvantaged gifted represents a melding of two concepts, each of which has
many different definitions. (p. 149)

This discussion focuses on the economically disadvantaged. Recommended practice No. 23 examines the issue of identifying the gifted in socially and culturally different groups, and No. 91 addresses the special programmatic considerations recommended for gifted students of varying
ethnicity.

Current Knowledge

The development of talent among the disadvantaged has a substantial
history in gifted education. There are poor children who succeed against all
odds (A. Robinson, 1988), and there are educational programs that increase
their chances of doing so. For example, in the 1960s, the National Merit
Scholarship Program initiated a special competition for black students, the
National Achievement Scholarship Program. In New York City, the Higher
Horizons program was initiated following the positive evaluation of a pilot
program that indicated that a curriculum of remedial services, cultural enrichment, group guidance, and parental involvement increased achievement,
lowered the dropout rate, and increased college attendance (Passow, 1986a).
In Israel, a longitudinal study of economically disadvantaged and culturally diverse gifted students documented the outcomes of the Boarding
School Fostering Project. The initial cohort, 78 students sharing a boarding
facility but attending different secondary schools, was compared with two
groups, one consisting of 78 students of comparable socioeconomic and ability levels not residing at the boarding school, and the other comprising 300
students of higher socioeconomic backgrounds attending the same schools.
In a 4-year follow-up, 83.4% of the boarding school group as compared with
60% of the comparable SES group graduated from high school. In terms of
their matriculation exams, the disadvantaged gifted students served in the
boarding school scored similarly to or slightly higher than their more advantaged schoolmates (Smilansky & Nevo, 1979). Also, the low SES boarding
school groups were distributed among the various levels of social acceptance,
as measured by sociograms, much as were their more advantaged peers.
In a recent study commissioned by the United States Department of
Education, Office of Planning, Budget and Evaluation, case-study evaluations of nine programs serving high proportions of economically disadvan-

taged gifted youth were evaluated (Alamprese, Erlanger, & Brigham, 1989). Five of the nine programs were secondary, two were K–12, one was fourth grade only, and one was a teacher-preparation project. All focused on mathematics, science, or both. Programs included in the study provided effectiveness data in one or more of (1) student achievement, (2) above-average student-enrollment figures for participation in mathematics or science courses, and (3) numbers of students participating in academic contests exceeding the district average, student selection of a mathematics or science major in college, or both. Successful programs were characterized by the use of multiple selection criteria, activity-based assessment, and the use of a preselection enrichment program designed to help disadvantaged students meet admission criteria. These programs also offered accelerated classes, enrichment experiences extended beyond the school day and year, and opportunities for independent study. The programs were also characterized by "support structures" in the form of explicit goal setting, professional role models, counseling, and parental involvement.

A recent review of programs that "break the cycle of disadvantage" have indicated the importance of early intervention (Schorr & Schorr, 1988), but most of these studies do not attempt to address the issue of performance or ability differences.

Perhaps the most relevant of the early environmental studies are those of Werner (1989), who examined the home, school, and personological variables that characterized children from impoverished circumstances who succeeded by mainstream standards. She labeled these children as "resilient," echoing the more familiar psychological use of the term to refer to children who thrive emotionally, socially, or academically in an adverse psychosocial climate. Werner followed a multiracial cohort of 698 individuals living on the island of Kaui, Hawaii, for 30 years in an attempt to determine the protective factors that allow children from poverty-stricken environments to flourish. Of the cohort, 72 children were identified as resilient, those who successfully adapted to stressful life events. Although she described her resilient children as "not especially gifted" (the basis for this was not clear, perhaps their excellent but not overall top-of-the-class school performance), many of their characteristics and the family environments reported in the study are similar to those found in the literature on giftedness. For example, as toddlers these children tended to seek out novel experiences. As they grew older they had many interests and hobbies that were not sex-role typed. As adolescents, they developed an internal locus of control. In terms of their family and school environments, resilient children had emotional support from at least one individual within the family and often had a favorite teacher who served as a role model. Girls tended to be assertive, achievement-oriented, and independent. Both sexes reported that participation in school-based extracurricular activities was especially important to them. By age 32, approximately 75% of these resilient youth went on to college. It does appear that gifted disadvantaged children are well served by specially adapted combinations of program elements.

Implications for Action

Given the evidence of underrepresentation of poor children in gifted programs (Alamprese et al., 1989), educators should adopt aggressive recruitment policies: extended tryout periods and preselection preparatory programs, talent-find programs in conjunction with kindergarten screening, and providing enriching experiences in extended-care programs at school.

The research also supports counseling and parental involvement programs for gifted disadvantaged youth. Thus, districts should consider the use of home-school visitors with this group of students and their families. Early and concrete goal setting and educational and career planning are important components of such outreach.

Finally, a school climate that acknowledges that giftedness exists in children of the poor will promote increased service to the economically disadvantaged gifted student. Staff in-service on identifying and nurturing talent, as well as examples of academically successful students from poor homes, is an integral part of special interventions for economically disadvantaged gifted students.

Needed Research

VanTassel-Baska (1989) asserts that little research has been done recently on existing in-school programs for gifted disadvantaged students. Thus, additional program-effectiveness studies that extend the investigations to students below secondary grade levels and beyond mathematics and science outcomes would be useful.

Closer examination of the instructional strategies and curricular organization used with gifted disadvantaged students is necessary. What is the content of the preselection program? What procedures are most effective for teachers using a diagnostic-prescriptive approach with disadvantaged students served in gifted programs? Some attempt to reconcile the frequent recommendation of highly structured learning environments for the disadvantaged with the recommendations for increased classroom freedom for gifted students would contribute to the knowledge base.

Studies of program effectiveness should include social outcomes as well as academic ones—for example, effects of labeling poor children as gifted.

In terms of the students themselves, descriptive studies that extend the work of R. Clark (1983) and Foster and Seltzer (1986) would be helpful. For example, disadvantaged students are often assumed to have skill deficits and to come from unsupportive homes. To what degree is this borne out? Is deficient school performance of these children, more so than in general, an outcome of a self-fulfilling prophecy? Empirically based descriptions of this special population would be helpful.

Finally, are resiliency and the factors that affect it the mediating forces that account for talent development among the impoverished, any gifted children, or any children, who successfully contend with a variety of shifting and unstable situations in their development? Attempts to integrate the extensive literatures on children at risk through economic deprivation and giftedness would be welcome.

93 | Rural Gifted Programs Require Special Consideration

Gifted-child education in sparsely populated areas is a matter of identifying and placing children in appropriate learning situations. The key concepts are identification, placement, access, involvement, motivation, acquiring higher aspirations, and receiving individualized instruction and opportunities for independent learning. (p. 73)

Birnbaum (1977) observed that families in small communities may not wish to have their children identified because they become too conspicuous, the opportunity for interaction with a group of gifted peers is reduced, access to human and cultural resources is limited, and school personnel may lack training in gifted education.

Current Knowledge

Plowman (1977) stated, "There are practically no research [studies] and almost no guidelines relevant to the provision of special education programs for youth in geographic areas characterized by great space and few people" (p. 73). Descriptions of several programs have appeared in the literature and do provide guidelines for serving rural gifted youth.

The few data-based studies focus on teachers. Witters (1979) surveyed 53 rural teachers and their greatest needs were:

1. Knowledge of the needs and problems of the gifted
2. Competencies with identification instruments

3. Preparation of curriculum materials and activities
4. Evaluation of teaching skills and student achievement
5. The development of instructional skills and activities for use with the gifted underachiever

Two studies reported the effectiveness of teacher training in the rural setting. Goodrum and Irons (1981) reported improved attitudes toward gifted education following in-service that included Bloom's Taxonomy and demonstrations of instructional activities. A. Robinson (1985) reported gains in teacher knowledge on gifted education following a 3-week summer institute for educators in rural Illinois.

Hamrin (1981) investigated rural schools in Maine and concluded that effective programs were usually characterized by an innovative and devoted teacher.

The literature also contains descriptions of rural programs for the gifted (cf. Witters & Vasa, 1981). Some report the use of cooperative programs among school districts (Caudill, 1977), resource centers (Cox & Daniel, 1983) or university outreach (Glidden-Flickinger, 1982; Spicker & Southern, 1983) to overcome geographic and cultural isolation.

A second theme of rural gifted education is the need for programs that allow students to be transported either at regular intervals (Silverman, 1980) or by attending residential schools and programs (Cox & Daniel, 1983; Glidden-Flickinger, 1982).

Finally, the literature stresses communications technology. Spicker and Southern (1983) discussed electronic bulletin boards; Caudill (1977), satellite programming; and Lupkowski (1984), Wide Area Telephone Systems (WATS) lines.

A strong case for rural gifted education's being substantially different in principle from any other is not sustained. Some urban gifted children attend residential schools and use electronic media. The importance of teachers and their ability to affect students' knowledge and attitudes is not unique. The strong implication is that rural schools should be limited to a subset of possibilities for serving highly able students.

Implications for Action

Given the resources, the rural educator should pursue cooperative ventures, opportunities for intellectual and social interaction among isolated gifted youngsters (e.g., in exchanges), and improved technology.

Based on experience, Pitts (1986) has offered several suggestions for program development in rural areas. These include garnering support for the program by including a school board member on the planning committee and using a blind identification process to encourage objectivity and prevent favoritism in small, closely knit communities.

Needed Research

Rural districts rarely have the resources to employ an external evaluator; therefore, there is a need for well-designed program evaluations, particularly those that investigate differentially the components or elements that are more crucial than others to rural program effectiveness.

In addition, this practice would benefit from an investigation of assumptions about rural gifted youth. Plowman (1977) stated that "the gifted child in a rural or low-density populated area . . . may be (1) isolated from intellectual stimulation and from learning resources; (2) unsophisticated— uninformed, lacking in social and learning skills; and (3) deprived culturally and educationally" (p. 73). Birnbaum's (1977) assumptions about the role of community climate and particularly rural attitudes beg verification.

Studies of the availability of and access to resources by rural gifted youth would be welcome. The literature would benefit from a simple inventory of which practices, such as those presented in this volume, might be fruitfully applied or adapted in rural areas, and which not, in comparison with other settings. Another useful comparison would be between rural possibilities and successful within-school programs in any setting. Studies are needed that address student outcome variables, both short and long term, and the specific content of the curriculum, especially with regard to an important consideration: Does gifted education serve rural communities or create a "brain drain"?

| 94 | **Education of the Gifted Handicapped Must Recognize Strengths and Handicaps** |

The need for this recommended practice arose from the absence of services for persons with dual exceptionalities or the inadequacy of such services when they did exist. As L. J. Coleman (1985) observed,

> Even in programs for the mildly handicapped, the attention to the remediation of weaknesses with little regard for the strengths works against the interests of children with handicaps. (pp. 92–93)

P. A. Alexander and Muia (1982) provided a good early review of the issues and readily gleaned advice:

What should be considered is the handicapped individual's demonstrated strengths and needs and how the behaviors reflect these strengths and needs. . . . Treating the disability is not enough and should not become the main objective of the student's educational program. The main objective should be optimal growth. . . . Essential, however, in a program designed to work with strengths is the understanding that the outcomes for the gifted handicapped in using such abilities or strengths will be different than those of typical gifted learners. (pp. 48–50)

Gowan and Bruch (1971) helped define *handicapped* in this context, namely, deficits in vision, hearing, or speech, or physically crippling conditions, be they birth defects, gross motor clumsiness, results of accidents or diseases. Handicaps are regarded as different from learning disabilities, which are intellectual and related to mental processing (see recommended practice No. 95). This recommended practice is also supported by B. Clark (1988), Maker (1977), and Whitmore and Maker (1985).

Current Knowledge

The validity of this recommended practice is best demonstrated by (1) confirmation of the existence of the group in question, (2) evidence of their systematic underserved state, and (3) showing that education can improve their state.

The existence of gifted handicapped people is well documented. Porter (1982) offered a brief historical sketch of interest in the field and noted that some 211 of 700 eminent persons in two major historical surveys (V. Goertzel & Goertzel, 1962; M. G. Goertzel, Goertzel, & Goertzel, 1978) could be labeled gifted handicapped. The fact that they are hardly mentioned as a group in the literature until the 1970s, though the formal literature on giftedness has grown rapidly since the 1920s, confirms the underservice.

Can intervention help? The prognosis is good from two points of view. First, gifted handicapped people are not intellectually handicapped, and except for some delays among the blind and the physical limitations their specific handicaps might impose on movement or perception, the gifted handicapped can function intellectually with other gifted people (B. Clark, 1988; M. B. Karnes, Schwedel, & Lewis, 1983). Three researchers have shown that interventions can work very well: M. B. Karnes (1979, 1984), in the pioneer intervention program begun in the late 1960s; Eason, Smith, and Steen (1978), working with gross motor handicapped; and Hanninen (1984), working with sight- and hearing-handicapped and cerebral-palsied children.

Maker (1977) and Blacher-Dixon and Turnbull (1978) noted that services for the gifted handicapped should be conceived as individualization,

not group programming, because there would be low numbers of any combination of dual exceptionalities. The large numbers of cases reported in the
Goertzels' work seem at first glance to contradict this expectation of low
numbers, but their reports of famous persons do not address a population
easily generalized to classrooms. Also, the role of mentors or others who
might have provided critical individualization in these people's lives is not
explored in relation to overcoming the handicaps. Corn and Bishop's (1984)
survey of teacher education of the gifted found that "IEP writing for the
gifted-handicapped is *not* emphasized in teacher training programs which
include coursework in the gifted-handicapped" (p. 144). Such individualization seems clearly, however, to have been a part of successful programs.

Identification must be adjusted so as not to be biased by the handicapping condition (Greene, Malley-Crist, & Cansler, 1978).

Mention is made in several instances of the special situation of parents
of gifted handicapped children. M. B. Karnes et al. (1983) found that parent
involvement was needed at specific points in their children's schooling, for
example, identification, supplementing the intervention at school and home.
They found that parents needed special training to assist with these roles.
Blacher-Dixon and Turnbull (1978) engaged a full-time social worker in
their project "to focus particularly on bridging the gap between the educational program and family needs" (p. 21). M. B. Karnes (1979) noted the
additional benefit of parents' becoming more accepting of their children's
handicaps when they were aware of their strengths.

Although the research literature is not extensive, the recommended
practice that gifted handicapped learners will be well served if identified and
taught on the basis of dual exceptionalities holds up to scrutiny.

Implications for Action

The recommended practice can help avoid double jeopardy in identification—ignoring of the child's handicap because he or she is thought to be
so smart and ignoring of the giftedness because of an overgeneralized response to the handicap.

Many of the demonstration projects address preschool children. It is
less clear what can be accomplished in later interventions.

For specific examples of services that might be offered and principles
for their design, see especially B. Clark (1988), Maker (1977), M. B. Karnes
(1979, 1984), Porter (1982), and Whitmore and Maker (1985).

Needed Research

Validated approaches to identification, specific service, teacher education, and parent involvement are needed. Some of the case studies noted

above were noteworthy in offering more than anecdotal reports of satisfaction. Hard data on satisfaction and learning are presented. These case studies need to be assembled and examined further.

There is also a need to study the timing of interventions, and the extent to which group services are feasible.

95 | Gifted Learning-Disabled Children Need Special Services

Learning-disabled gifted children show evidence of exceptionally high ability, realized or potential, in one or more areas, and exhibit at least one specific learning disability. Two complete volumes have been devoted to this highly specific group of children (P. Daniels, 1983; Whitmore & Maker, 1985). Major portions of both books are devoted to case studies and examples of interventions. Whitmore and Maker stated, "Of all the categories of intellectually gifted persons with some handicapping condition, those with learning disabilities are most vulnerable to neglect and unintentional abuse" (p. 196). VanTassel-Baska (1981) made the same assertion. The vulnerability could exist because the learning disability may be more evident and divert attention away from strengths, it may foster lowered self-esteem in the individual, and counterbalancing positive experiences may not be provided.

Current Knowledge

Whitmore and Maker (1985) suggested that learning disabilities among the gifted are essentially related to school learning and often surface only after a couple of years at school. Learning-disabled gifted children differ from the handicapped in this regard. Teachers are the key to identification.

Most of our knowledge is anecdotal, based on rather brief case presentations (e.g., Baum, 1984; French, 1982; Mindell, 1982; Steeves, 1980; and the numerous examples in the two main texts). It appears that the gifted learning disabled are as capable as other gifted youngsters in memory, problem-solving skills (but rarely in written form), curiosity and drive to know, and creativity (Whitmore & Maker, 1985). They are notably deficient (relative to their giftedness) in some aspect of scholastic performance. Steeves (1980) suggested the underlying problem may not be in the area of poor performance; for example, some mathematical dysfunction may actually be a reading or writing problem spilling over. One of the most interesting observations, first raised by Baum (1984), was that a portion of gifted learning-disabled students' partial successes in school and beyond might be due to their compensating for specific weaknesses. Whitmore and Maker (1985) called it the child's "ability to adapt by devising creative strategies to cope with the psychological conflict and the school demands" (p. 197).

The first experimental study of the possible links among learning disabilities, specially adaptive cognitive strategies, and awareness and control of such strategies through metacognition has been done by Hannah with Shore (cf. Hannah, 1989, for a preliminary report). Gifted, gifted learning-disabled, learning-disabled, and average Grade-6 and Grade-12 pupils in West Virginia were presented with excerpts of Quebec colonial history in which some French terms were retained. These words were entirely unfamiliar to all the children. Detailed protocols and interviews were used to study each child's strategies to figure out what the terms meant and how they monitored their own performance. The gifted and gifted learning-disabled children functioned alike and used metacognitive skills to discern the meanings. Nongifted learning-disabled and the younger, nonexceptional children did not monitor as effectively. The study concluded that gifted learning-disabled children have underlying problem-solving strategies that are more characteristic of their giftedness than their handicaps, and that they do indeed create alternative routes to understanding, with a noticeable degree of self-awareness and control over their thinking. This study also confirmed the distinctiveness of gifted learning-disabled students, because it is their giftedness that is most salient. They are different from other learning-disabled people in learning process, though both may lack confidence.

Another recurring idea is that these students, like the handicapped, should be addressed through their strengths. Maker (1979) summarized studies that demonstrated that weak areas improved when strengths were addressed. Whitmore and Maker (1985) suggested this was a benefit of improved self-concept.

Although the necessary interventions in part resemble those needed for other categories of gifted children, one suggestion in particular sets this group apart. Steeves (1980) reiterated that these students require a multisensory approach to help them circumnavigate their specific deficits. This idea is so far supported only with general reports of its applicability.

Implications for Action

There is support for the need to attend especially to the gifted learning disabled, but additional and more direct evidence is needed. More detailed case studies, with reference to the variables mentioned in the research (e.g., age and grade level, underlying nature of the disability, compensating strengths, learning strategies, and self-concept), are required.

Specific action to take in addressing these children's needs still requires research, but it would be worthwhile to explore multisensory input, direct teaching of coping strategies, even metacognitive training, and working from strengths. All the references contain suggestions for implementation; professional discretion and knowledge of each child allow for cautious attempts to help these children.

Needed Research

It is important to clarify the unique educational needs of the gifted learning disabled and to tie these needs to cognitive and motivational theory relevant to giftedness. With these in mind, validation of proposed interventions should be undertaken in systematic, empirical studies.

The possibility that high-ability learning-disabled children may help us better serve all learning-disabled children is an exciting idea. The applicability of creative adaptation to learning-disabled people other than the highly able deserves attention as does the possibility of locating indicators among preschool children of later learning disabilities. Early intervention strategies could then be explored so as to increase children's resistance to the frustrations that are a great part of the school and later experiences of these young people.

96 | Gifted Delinquent Children Need Special Intervention

There are three conceptually distinct notions about delinquency in high-ability youth. One is that there is an excessively high delinquency rate among high-ability youth. The second is that delinquency arises for different reasons in children of high ability than in others. Third, it is suggested that high-ability youth who are delinquent should be treated with methods different from those used with other delinquent youth.

> The treatment response to gifted children who lapse into delinquency should not be restricted to the traditional concept of security-oriented convenience but be aimed towards capitalizing on their inherent strengths of which their very delinquency is evidence. (Brooks, 1985, p. 303)

Current Knowledge

Seeley (1984) was correct in succinctly stating, "There has been a good deal of conjecture about the relationship between giftedness and juvenile delinquency among adolescents. Many unfounded claims have been sensationalized and much of the research has been ignored" (p. 59).

Mahoney (1980) articulated two competing theories about the relationship. One holds that bright children are vulnerable to delinquency because of their exceptional sensitivity and strong reaction to adverse environmental circumstances. The other counters that high intelligence should be a protective factor, leading to superior judgment and coping abilities that obviate delinquent acting out. Her review of four longitudinal studies supported the latter view.

Exhortations about the "gifted delinquent" are often accompanied by assertions that there are either excessive numbers of delinquents among high-ability youth or disproportionate numbers of high-ability youth among delinquents (M. Parker, 1983). Complicating the picture, M. Parker (1983) reported a high incidence of high-ability youth among "potential delinquents" (p. 184), whereas King (1983) referred to "gifted delinquent prone subjects" (p. 190).

Careful review of the research literature reveals the claim of excessive delinquency among able youth to be a myth (Lajoie & Shore, 1981; Mahoney, 1980; Seeley, 1984). Delinquents are most likely to have below-average abilities; highly intelligent youth are consistently underrepresented in the delinquent population (Hirschi & Hindeland, 1977). Of 663 delinquents with Wechsler IQ testing, Gath, Tennent, and Pidduck (1971) found that delinquents with an IQ above 115 occurred less than half as frequently as would be expected by the normal distribution. This does not imply that gifted delinquents do not exist but merely that delinquency is not apparently more prevalent among bright students than among others (also see Gath et al., 1970a, 1970b).

Evidence supporting distinctive characteristics of high-ability delinquents is limited. Brooks (1985) found a higher incidence of father absence among high-IQ than among average-IQ delinquents, but few other differences. Harvey and Seeley (1984) examined the factor structure of intelligence and creative test scores in a large sample of delinquents. They found few distinctive features of high-ability delinquents, except for a pattern of comparatively high fluid intelligence but poor achievement test performance among them.

All too often, authors have stretched their results into firm conclusions that are not supported by their data. For example, Gath et al. (1971) reported a "marked tendency for more bright boys to have committed offences which seemed predominantly psychologically determined" (p. 278). This conclusion was based on interviews in which psychiatrists concluded that 18 of 50 high-IQ delinquents, as opposed to 8 of 50 average-IQ delinquents, committed psychologically determined offenses. Quite apart from the many sources of bias in this study, this difference is not statistically significant. Unfortunately, subsequent authors (e.g., Brooks, 1985; Mahoney, 1980) now cite this study and repeat its unjustified claim.

The recommendation that high-ability delinquents should receive differential treatment was implemented most thoroughly in a special correctional facility in England, Kneesworth Hall (Brooks, 1972, 1980). This residential program provided comprehensive psychological and educational services in the 1950s to several hundred high-IQ youth convicted primarily of larceny. Unfortunately, a 10-year follow-up (Brooks, 1972) revealed a high recidivism rate and a relatively consistent pattern of underachievement in both education and occupation (see also Tennent & Gath, 1975). Without a control group, it is not possible to conclude how these youth would compare either to ordinary delinquents receiving the same treatment or to high-IQ delinquents not receiving such treatment.

Tremblay (1983) compared high- and average-IQ delinquents in their response to a comprehensive, well-designed, residential treatment program. Both groups responded positively to treatment, and there were no differences between high- and average-IQ delinquents on 22 psychological variables either at the time of admission or after treatment. His conclusions present the most direct and forceful challenge to the recommended practice. With regard to several criteria for program success, Tremblay noted,

> Boys with above average IQ are not different from boys with average IQ on these characteristics at the start of treatment, at the end of treatment and at one year follow up after the end of treatment, although the treatment in question seemed to be better adapted to their needs than to average or below average IQ boys. Creating a separate group of juvenile delinquents based on IQ for residential treatment purposes does not only seem unnecessary but could also be harmful since treatment of juvenile delinquents is based largely on the use of group living. (p. 204)

Implications for Action

High-ability delinquents are an anomaly, despite the attention they receive in the literature. High-ability adolescents are, in fact, at low risk for delinquency.

There is widespread agreement that treatment for all delinquents must be individualized to some degree in order to take into account each youth's pattern of personal strengths and weaknesses (Tremblay, 1983). From this perspective, it is reasonable to consider high intelligence as a factor in planning the individual component of treatment. There is no justification for treatment approaches designed categorically and specifically for high-ability delinquents.

Needed Research

Delinquency researchers may find it illuminating to investigate youth who are delinquent despite superior abilities that are commonly regarded as protective factors against antisocial attitudes and behavior. Research to date has focused almost entirely on bright delinquents who commit offenses such as larceny; it may be of interest to differentiate violent and nonviolent juvenile offenders of differing ability. Also, future research should control for socioeconomic status and other background factors in contrasting high- and average-IQ youth (Gath et al., 1971).

The incidence of criminality among young gifted persons is only one issue and less important than the question about what to do about the ones who are identified. Tremblay's (1983) conclusions are uncommonly clear in gifted education: Separating gifted delinquents on the basis of IQ does not make much difference.

97	**Gifted Underachievers Need Early Intervention and Special Identification**

The distinct needs of the underachieving gifted are acknowledged (see recommended practice No. 98), but this group is often not served by gifted programs (Golicz, 1982). Most districts screen out gifted underachievers (Richert, Alvino, & McDonnel, 1982).

> Early identification (kindergarten, grades one and two) and appropriate programming prevent the establishment of chronic patterns of underachievement or negative attitudes toward school; it also allows early intervention with underachievers, which is much more successful than later efforts at remediation or correction. (Whitmore, 1980, p. 406)

Current Knowledge

The diversity of definitions of underachieving gifted has created a wide assortment of identification procedures. Most of these employ standardized measures (Barbe & Malone, 1985), teacher perceptions, parent perceptions, and self-perceptions. Dowdall and Colangelo (1982) found that the most common method of identifying underachieving gifted was to compare achievement test scores with intelligence test scores. This method seriously strains the versatility of IQ test data.

In contrast, there is much agreement on when remediation should begin (B. Clark, 1988; Dowdall & Colangelo, 1982; Golicz, 1982; Hall, 1980; Pirozzo, 1982; Rimm, 1984; Whitmore, 1979a, 1979b). By far, the studies reporting interventions that were successful in producing long-term gains were conducted at the elementary school level (see recommended practice No. 98). This result was explained by Whitmore (1980), who views underachievement as a behavior supported by negative or apathetic attitudes toward self and school; early identification and remediation would make change easier because it occurs at the beginning of the conflicts leading to underachievement (Pirozzo, 1982; Whitmore, 1980). Most earlier studies on remediation were done at the secondary level, and these attempts were not very successful (Gold, 1965).

Implications for Action

Districts should use multiple identification procedures that do not have an overreliance on standardized measures. The identification method must also be consistent with the district's definition of underachieving gifted. The Estes Attitude Scale (Golicz, 1982) has shown some promise in such identification.

The current literature is clear that identification and remediation must be done as early as possible in the elementary years in order to have long-term successful results, but secondary programs should not ignore underachieving gifted students. They require identification and remediation, but long-term success at this level may be difficult to achieve.

Interventions that showed the most success were not short term. They involved a long-term commitment to helping the underachieving gifted (Dowdall & Colangelo, 1982).

Needed Research

Studies that document economically feasible identification procedures for underachieving gifted students would be helpful. One might locate school districts that have an explicit component for serving this special population and investigate both student outcome measures and identification costs in order to determine the extent of the resources needed to effectively identify underachieving gifted.

If early school intervention is more helpful than later, preschool preventative intervention might be even better still. Research on intervention for bright underachievers needs to examine early childhood development, high risk circumstances, and intervention in general. Children whose parents were involved in parent-effectiveness training courses, or who attended high-quality day care or nursery schools, for example, would be interesting subjects for follow-up. Particular attention might also be paid to the kindergarten and early grade experiences of children.

Other studies that extend Whitmore's work in Cupertino (Whitmore, 1980) are also necessary to uncover any differences in remediation strategies recommended for all underachieving students in contrast to underachievers identified as gifted.

98 | Programs for Gifted Underachievers Should Be Within Gifted Programs

> The evidence available is that positive movement for the underachiever is a difficult matter at best. They would be better off by far in a special program designed for their own needs. (Gallagher, 1985, p. 424)

Should such special services be part of regular gifted programs, separate programs for gifted underachievers, or programs for underachievers of all ability levels?

Current Knowledge

The gifted underachiever first appeared in Terman and Oden's 1947 study. Nonetheless, as Dowdall and Colangelo (1982) stated in their review, "the last twenty years of research on underachieving gifted has produced more confusion than clarity and direction" (p. 182).

The confusion begins with the definition. Dowdall and Colangelo (1982) cited 14 different definitions; however, a common theme was a difference between high potential or expected performance and average or lower actual performance (also see Gallagher, 1985; Shoff, 1984). Terman and Oden (1947) described four shared characteristics that distinguish the achieving from underachieving gifted: (1) lack of integration of goals and self-direction, (2) lack of self-confidence, (3) inability to persevere, and (4) inferiority feelings. Dowdall and Colangelo (1982) observed (1) social immaturity, (2) emotional problems, (3) antisocial behavior, (4) low self-concept, and (5) an unstable family environment. Together, these support the conclusions drawn by Whitmore (1984), Rimm (1985), and Delisle (1982a) that underachievement in gifted students can be ameliorated by appropriate interventions. As suggested by Whitmore (1984) and Davis and Rimm (1989), gifted underachievers are a distinct population with particular needs that require special attention. However, Richert, Alvino, and McDonnel (1982) found many districts use identification procedures that regularly screen out gifted underachievers.

The most common interventions have been personal counseling and special programming, often in the form of homogeneous grouping (Dowdall & Colangelo, 1982; Pirozzo, 1982). Research into the effects of including gifted underachievers in the regular gifted program has produced varied results. Significant improvement in the performance of this group has been reported in studies conducted at the elementary level that provided specific interventions designed for the special needs of underachievers and involved the parents (Hojnacki, 1979; R. H. Jackson, Cleveland, & Mirenda, 1975; Whitmore, 1984). In particular, the importance of a flexible and caring teacher is underscored by Whitmore (1980).

At the secondary level, fewer significant results have been reported. In their 2-year study of the effects of homogeneous grouping, M. B. Karnes, McCoy, Zehrbach, Wollersheim, and Clarizio (1963) found greater gains among the underachievers when they were placed with achieving peers rather than other gifted underachievers. However, the gains were attributed to the stimulating content and teaching strategies of the advanced class rather than to the grouping.

Another secondary-level study by Raph, Goldberg, and Passow (1966) found that special classes for underachieving gifted did not result in a significant change in grade-point average of the group as a whole. There were some benefits to individual students, and, in a class where the teacher provided differentiated methods and demonstrated a caring attitude, students made short-term gains. These gains were lost when the students moved to another teacher. These findings are supported and explained by conclusions drawn by Goldberg, Passow, Justman, and Hogue (1965) that grouping students according to ability without changing the curriculum or teaching methods cannot be expected to produce positive results. In fact, negative results from merely grouping underachievers together were reported by H. V. Perkins (1969): Students reinforced each others' negative behaviors.

Two other studies offered support for serving underachieving gifted pupils within general programming for the gifted. Ziv, Ramon, and Doni (1977) found that when underachieving gifted students were placed in a special program for the gifted, along with achieving gifted students, they increased their self-concepts more than the high achievers did. Martinson (1973) demonstrated the negative effects upon gifted students of placement in a regular class. Whether they were achieving or underachieving gifted, their performance regressed to a lower level. Some developed discipline problems, whereas others withdrew into themselves. The practice of attending to the special needs of underachieving gifted pupils from a base within the regular gifted program does seem to be modestly supported by the current literature.

Implications for Action

The knowledge base for this practice permits several actions with confidence. First, identification procedures need to be instituted in districts so that the gifted underachiever can be identified properly as gifted and served by a gifted program.

Second, identification needs to be done at an early age so that intervention can occur before high school, where, as Gold (1965) concluded, it is often too late.

Third, parental involvement is important in a program for underachieving gifted pupils, especially at the elementary level.

Finally, one must consider the nature of secondary programs one might encounter. If they consist of or include Advanced Placement or honors classes, then underachieving gifted students may have problems because they often lack academic skills.

Needed Research

The confusion and lack of consensus about the definition of underachievement and, therefore, the kinds of underachieving students suggests what is needed in order to clarify the qualified support for this practice in the literature.

Because the causes and correlates of underachievement (e.g., poor self-concept, learning disabilities, or lack of challenging curriculum) are apparently quite varied and often outside the school, the kinds of "treatments" or programs (regular, regular gifted, or specialized for underachieving gifted) that best serve these students also vary. Perhaps the most obvious studies to be done are those that explore which kinds of underachieving students' achievement are positively affected by "regular" gifted programming. Such studies should carefully describe both the "regular" gifted program and the etiology of the underachievement in the students served, in attempts to clarify which kinds of underachieving gifted students improve in which kinds of "regular" gifted programs. Where underachieving students are denied participation in gifted programs, or where other provisions are made, comparative studies of the progress of these students would be very valuable, because there is good evidence that "regular programs" are appropriate but no clear evidence that they are more appropriate than other alternatives. Neither is it clear that solutions appropriate for gifted underachievers are suitable for less able (or any) underachievers whose overall performance might be at a very low level.

99	**Especially Develop Positive Self-Concept in Gifted Underachievers**

The notion that underachievers suffer from poor self-concepts is well entrenched in gifted education. Based on her review of literature, Whitmore (1980) concluded,

> All studies comparing the characteristics of the achiever with those of the underachiever indicate that negative self-concepts are the central trait distinguishing underachievers from those who are achieving commensurate with their ability. (p. 178)

Gallagher (1985) pointed out that counseling of underachievers "should enable them (the argument goes) to reorganize their self-concepts and perceptions into constructive channels, and this, in turn, will result in better school performance" (p. 420).

Eccles (1985), Fox (1979b), and Khatena (1982) contended that poor self-concept plays a special role in the underachievement of high-ability females: They underestimate their own abilities.

Current Knowledge

Underachievement is one of the most prevalent and perplexing problems of high-ability youth (B. Clark, 1988; Pirozzo, 1982; Whitmore, 1980). The topic was so heavily researched 25 years ago that some authors called for a moratorium (Gallagher & Rogge, 1966; Whitmore, 1980). In part, this was due to the large number of poorly designed, often inconclusive studies.

Although many studies found some correlations, it was not established whether poor self-concept was a cause, an effect, or a mere concomitant of underachievement (Tannenbaum, 1983; Whitmore, 1980). Moreover, attempts to change self-concept had no consistent or substantial effect on achievement, so that many reviewers were openly pessimistic (Dowdall & Colangelo, 1982; Gowan, Demos, & Kokaska, 1972; Tannenbaum, 1983; Whitmore, 1980). A central problem with underachievement research is the emphasis on identifying "the" underachiever. As Patterson (1972) noted,

> Underachievement is a problem with a variety of causes, ranging from inadequate preparation or instruction on through deliberate efforts not to achieve at a high level because of fear of being considered a grind or an "egghead,"

through preoccupation with family problems, to emotional disturbances and lack of recognition of potentiality. (p. 126)

The search for underlying commonalities remains a holy grail: In its pursuit, textbooks list characteristics of "the" gifted underachiever (e.g., Davis & Rimm, 1989). Unrecognized learning disabilities may be a factor in many cases of underachievement otherwise assumed to have a basis in the child's personality or family relations. Bow (1988) reported neuropsychological deficits in a sample of high-ability male students underachieveing in reading.

More recent research has raised some promising leads on how to help some kinds of underachieving students, with group counseling (Bland, Melang, & Miller, 1986; Cooper & Robinson, 1987), the opportunity to tutor younger children, and participation in a psychology course on personal and human development (Zeeman, 1982). Several authors have proposed family therapy with underachievers (Thiel & Thiel, 1977; Zuccone & Amerikaner, 1986). This approach needs testing.

Socialization (e.g., parent expectations, peer pressure, teacher attitudes) plays a major role in female underachievement (Callahan, 1979; Eccles, 1985; Kerr, 1985; see also recommended practice No. 90). Able young women need to become aware of their abilities as well as the factors that prevent them from achieving their potential (Reis, 1987).

Underachievement and poor self-concept are common companions, but there is no solid evidence that one causes the other.

Implications for Action

Efforts focused solely on improving self-concept are unlikely to have substantial effect on achievement. Most treatment approaches do attend to self-concept issues in one way or another, but counseling is usually broader in scope, attending to possible family, peer, and teacher relationships as well. Group counseling with emphasis on peer support appears to be promising (Bland, Melang, & Miller, 1986; Cooper & Robinson, 1987). In addition to counseling, more recent approaches emphasize the need to modify the underachiever's classroom environment and make it more rewarding and conducive to learning (Gallagher, 1985; Pirozzo, 1982; Whitmore, 1980). Specific educational skill deficits must be identified and remedied (cf. Crittenden, Kaplan, & Heim, 1984).

There are multiple types of underachievers, so that it is unreasonable to posit a single causal explanation (Gallagher, 1985; Gonzalez & Hayes, 1988; Khatena, 1982; Tannenbaum, 1983). This would imply that no single treatment approach could be effective in all cases (Tannenbaum, 1983).

Several reasonably comprehensive treatment approaches have been described in some detail (Rimm, 1986; Whitmore, 1980). Although proponents of various approaches report success in their work, there are no comparative studies to help determine which, if any, is more effective, or which is most effective with what type of underachieving student.

Needed Research

There is no need to continue documenting relationships between self-concept and underachievement. Instead, the field needs a definitive typology of underachievers, so that research on underachievement can become more differentiated. Close attention to the literature on learning disabilities should be part of this specialization. Failure to distinguish among types of underachievers may explain the often disappointing and conflicting results of research on various treatment approaches (Khatena, 1982; Tannenbaum, 1983). Efforts to distinguish different causal pathways to underachievement, with correspondingly different treatment implications, are needed.

Research on the self-concept of underachievers should take into consideration more sophisticated conceptualizations of self-concept (see recommended practice No. 84). In addition, such studies need to be more specific about the counseling techniques they employ to influence the student's self-concept (Tannenbaum, 1983). Comparisons of different intervention approaches are needed, with attention to both short- and long-term outcomes.

| 100 | **Attend Specially to the Identification of Gifted Girls** |

The sources for this practice refer to underrepresentation by girls in mathematics and to socialization, but it is not difficult to generalize the concern.

> Girls, much more than boys, are reluctant to accelerate their education by grade-skipping, taking college courses, or participating rigorously in special accelerated mathematics programs. These girls seem to be afraid to try things that might make them appear different in relationship to their peers. (Fox, 1976c, pp. 186–187)

> The search for untapped talent should be extended to include not only the differently cultured but also the female child population. Furthermore, it seems that the search for talent should be coupled with efforts toward achieving a significant change in social behavior toward achievement by women. (Butler-Por, 1983, p. 267)

Until society values the accomplishments of women more highly, fewer gifted girls will want to be identified as such.

Three questions regarding the identification of gifted girls seem to require answers. Are gifted girls less likely than gifted boys to be identified? If so, why? And, if so, what can be done to promote the identification of gifted girls?

Current Knowledge

Strong voices have pointed out the difficult position of gifted women (Blaubergs, 1980; Callahan, 1980; Carrelli, 1982; B. Clark, 1988; Ernest, 1978; Fox, 1981b; Fox & Tobin, 1988; Horner, 1972; Kerr, 1985; Navarre, 1979; Noble, 1987; Reis, 1987; Rekdal, 1984; Roeper, 1978; Schmitz & Galbraith, 1985; Schwartz, 1980; Wells, 1985), but little has been said or researched regarding the need for special efforts to identify gifted girls.

A few applicable studies have been summarized by F. B. Tuttle, Becker, and Sousa (1988), who reported that girls develop at a faster rate than boys and have higher IQ scores (Maccoby, 1966), a greater incidence of early admission to school (Callahan, 1979), and a lower dropout rate (Maccoby, 1966). More males are identified for gifted programs than females at the middle and high school level when mathematical skill is crucial (Fox & Turner, 1981), but no preschool or primary study has been done. Alvino, McDonnel, and Richert (1981) studied identification procedures and reported girls to be disadvantaged in many school districts. Dweck and Bush (1976) and Dweck, Davidson, Nelson, and Enna (1978) reported that females hide their giftedness because the educational system teaches them to view themselves as less capable than males.

Horner's (1972) study, replicated by Winchel, Fenner, and Shaver (1974), confirmed the avoidance of success by highly able women. Butler-Por (1983) studied the educational values of different cultures in Israel and found social success was valued more for girls by their parents and by the girls, in contrast to intellectual achievement for boys. Fifty percent of the boys valued material success and status, but none of the girls did. L. W. Hoffman (1972) also studied female achievement motives and found that girls underestimated their abilities and were less likely to explore independently, both of which may mask their giftedness. Gilligan and Phelps (1988) studied adolescents' feelings about themselves and found females motivated by a "voice of caring" whereas boys responded to justice. Some 90% of interviewed females identified failure in terms of relationships, whereas boys more often identified a failure in an activity.

Callahan (1980) stated that gifted girls are a subgroup of the population such as the gifted handicapped, culturally different gifted, or very young gifted who because of their "unique characteristics . . . warrant the consideration of alternative means of identification and program planning if the full spectrum of gifted and talented children are to be served" (p. 16). Silverman (1986b) suggested that the "necessity of finding gifted girls early in life is underscored by the fact that their advanced abilities, observable before they enter school, may be diminishing as a consequence of the educational process" (p. 59). She complained that repeated IQ tests used for identification work against females:

> New proofs of giftedness are demanded at each successive level in order to qualify for services. . . . All practices that eliminate once-qualified students from receiving services have their most devastating effects on the self-concepts of females, undermining their beliefs in their capabilities. (pp. 61–62)

Highly able girls do seem less likely to be identified, partly because of differences in socialization as well as biases in selection procedures.

Implications for Action

The primary implication would be to make competitive achievement and femininity more compatible to prevent gifted girls from masking their giftedness and thereby avoiding identification. Socialization is one of the objectives of schooling, and such matters can and should be addressed. Silverman (1986b) suggested identifying the gifted in preschool or primary grades and, when using IQ, using the highest IQ score possible (rather than the latest score) to find more gifted females. Fox (1976c) suggested interventions that include an emphasis on the social interests of girls.

Other, less direct, interventions may make gifted girls easier to identify. Parents can raise girls from birth trying to avoid sexist toys, clothing, attitudes, and language (Espeland & Galbraith, 1988; Fox, 1981b; Fox & Tobin, 1988; Kerr, 1985; Navarre, 1979). Several school-based suggestions have also been made, including counseling (Grau, 1985). Kirschenbaum (1980) suggested a nonsexist unit on careers in the preschool years. Callahan (1980) pointed out the need for early practice at visual-spatial problem solving for gifted females. Gifted girls should also be encouraged to continue mathematics and science classes throughout high school to combat the "math filter" (B. Clark, 1988; Fox & Tobin, 1988; Kerr, 1985).

Needed Research

The apparent underrepresentation of bright girls in school programs needs to be studied over grade levels but within districts, to determine incidence rates by gender for both screening and selection. Which of the criteria considered together as a regression model, or singly, best predict the identification of gifted girls? Do some constellations of multiple criteria do a better job than others?

A second kind of needed study is the evaluation of interventions or policies on behalf of gifted girls. Does the availability of single-sex classes increase the numbers of nominated and selected girls? Will a career or personal counseling program affect the numbers and kinds of girls identified for gifted programs?

Studies of the ways girls fare in both screening and selection are important for establishing the extent of the problem this recommended practice implies.

101 Secondary Mathematics and Advanced Science Should Be Part of the Curriculum for Gifted Girls

This practice is a response to sex-role stereotyping and the underrepresentation of women in mathematics and science careers.

> In Britain too few girls are encouraged to pursue careers in the sciences, engineering, mathematics, or management. . . . If this situation was reversed it could result in the introduction of different methods of thought and expression to these areas and their value might be better appreciated by the taxpayer. (Congdon, 1986, p. 157)

Congdon's comment is interesting because it anticipates that the greater involvement by women in mathematics and science not merely provides women with something they lack. Women may also bring different interests and thinking styles to these subjects.

Fox (1979b) identified several barriers to the achievement of gifted women:

> Sex-role stereotypes held by educators . . . lead them to discourage rather than encourage intellectual risk-taking and the taking of advanced courses in mathematics and science. (p. 372)

Current Knowledge

Though women comprise more than 50% of the world's population, they make up only 40% of the labor force (Fox, 1981b). Even though the participation rate by women in the paid work force has increased in the last decade, females remain conspicuously absent from the ranks of leadership and underrepresented in jobs of high prestige or salary, many of which have a mathematical or technical training prerequisite. Of the 56,000 U.S. individuals receiving undergraduate engineering degrees during 1977–78, only 4,000 (7%) were women (Wells, 1985). In 2 years this number increased to only 10% (J. Armstrong, 1980). Furthermore, only 3.4% of the doctoral degrees in the physical sciences including mathematics and science were awarded to women in 1968–69 (Centra, 1974). Eleven years later, women represented only 1/10 of 1% of the total number of engineers in the U.S. and only 2% of the physicists (J. Armstrong, 1980). The cause may be rooted in the early education of young gifted females. Fox (1976a) attributed it to the fact that girls are not as eager as boys to skip grades or enroll in high school mathematics or college courses such as computer science.

Furthermore, young gifted girls are not likely to receive encouragement from counselors and teachers in mathematics and science classes (Fox, 1976a). Not only do teachers believe that boys are better than girls at mathematics (Ernest, 1978), but data also indicate that teachers view gifted male students as more competent in critical and logical thinking skills and creative problem-solving skills (Cooley, Chauvin, & Karnes, 1984). Thus, girls may not be noticed, let alone encouraged.

The factors that lead to differential achievement and interest in these subject areas must be considered. The literature appears, on the surface, to support the premise that boys are truly better performers in the areas of mathematics and science. Ernest (1978) reported that boys and girls do not appear to differ greatly during their elementary years in achievement; however, sex differences in achievement begin to appear after age 11 and become more pronounced during adolescence (M. Waters, 1980). Many more males than females are mathematically precocious as early as Grade 7 (Fox, 1976c). Differences were also found between gifted girls and their male counterparts regarding their eagerness to accelerate in mathematics and science (J. C. Stanley, 1973; Fox, 1975), and boys were more advanced than girls in mathematics course taking by the end of the 10th grade (Fox, 1976a).

Socialization pressures faced by adolescent girls might account for the discrepancy in the mathematical ability of males and females (Fox, 1981a; Waters, 1980), but Fox, Brody, and Tobin (1979) reported that some scientists and educators feel that the difference in achievement of males and females in mathematics, science, leadership, and professional positions is a result of innate differences between the sexes. Because there are major factors related to sex differences in achievement, particularly course taking in mathematics and science among gifted students (Fox, 1976b), the conclusion might be drawn that more girls can be successfully encouraged to participate in these areas.

Much of the empirical literature does not deal directly with the recommended practice; it concentrates on the reasons behind the smaller numbers of girls involved in advanced mathematics and science programs. How young gifted girls can become successfully involved in these areas is also the focus of several studies. Within this literature is support for the recommended practice.

Although fewer girls than boys have been identified as precocious mathematical reasoners (Fox, 1976a; J. C. Stanley, 1973), many girls do exhibit considerable potential for development (Fox, 1975). However, methods of educational facilitation in mathematics appear to be differentially successful for gifted boys and girls. Women have typically been found to be more academically predictable than men (Seashore, 1962; J. C. Stanley, 1967), but despite high aptitude scores on tests such as the SAT-M, girls do not behave as predictably as boys with regard to special accelerative educational experiences (Fox, 1975).

Relationships have been found between sex-role identification, masculine interest, and specific mathematical aptitude or problem-solving ability, respectively (Carey, 1958; Elton & Rose, 1967; Milton, 1957). Also, there appears to be a strong correlation between career interest and mathematical aptitude in young women (Astin, 1974; Astin & Myint, 1971). Haven (1972) found that girls who pursued advanced mathematics and science courses in high school were those who saw these courses as instrumental to their educational plans and career goals. There is a good chance that many jobs in the years 2000 + will be related to mathematics and science. Cox and Daniel (1983) stressed that educators must alert these girls at a very early age to the fact that mathematics and science will be crucial keys needed to unlock their future career opportunities.

Fox (1976c) observed that girls who desire to accelerate face conflict because their underlying values are not consistent with their intellectual talents. Most women (including gifted girls) in any sample tend to score higher than men on measures of social values and lower on theoretical values. The reverse is characteristic of gifted boys.

Implications for Action

Females who have not taken advanced mathematics and science courses in high school may find themselves at a disadvantage relative to their male counterparts when pursuing college level studies in these areas. Regardless of the type of occupation that interests them, young girls should realize that most high-level professions are enhanced by proficiency in the areas of advanced mathematics and science (Higham & Navarre, 1984).

Teachers should actively recruit girls for advanced courses. The effort needs to begin in the primary grades by programming differentially for precocious girls. This will result in advanced courses as a natural sequence in the curricula. This programming should attend to the social interests of girls by providing opportunities for cooperation as well as competition.

Assisting girls to connect mathematics and science to later career choices is also a reasonable action to take. This may be accomplished by an examination of competencies required for many high-level occupations and by the investigation of the lives of highly successful adult women.

Needed Research

Most of the research to date concentrates on why there are fewer females than males involved in advanced mathematics and science programs. Career and professional studies have documented the underrepresentation problem, though updated data would be useful to plot trends. Now we need studies that evaluate the best ways to enroll and sustain girls in advanced mathematics and science courses. For example, case studies of schools comparing those that have difficulty enrolling girls with those that have above-average enrollment and retention of girls in such courses would be useful.

Certainly, studies of the factors that best predict girls' course-taking behavior, achievement, and satisfaction with mathematics and science study would have practical value. Using career achievement as the criterion, it would be useful to undertake a multivariate analysis that includes groups of girls with rigorous secondary preparation and those without.

Finally, do women make different kinds of contributions to the advancement of knowledge, especially mathematics and science? Are these true gender differences, or the outcomes of selectively encouraged talents? Gifted education itself provides a useful testing ground, as the proportion of women in research positions has risen dramatically.

Conclusion

The principal conclusions of this report are contained in Chapters 1 through 8. Our purpose here is to offer general observations about the overall results of our analysis of research support for recommended practices in gifted education and to explore briefly some implications of this work.

Overview of Research Support for the Recommended Practices

We identified 101 recommended practices in gifted education from 100 textbooks in the field. As we added new editions and original works to those previously reviewed, we noted a remarkable absence of new practices. Indeed, we found more eloquent and refined statements but few new recommendations. One of the reasons for this may be found in the References, wherein we have marked with an asterisk the instances in which an author was cited in the opening section of a particular recommended practice. In other words, such an author was a spokesperson for the practice rather than—or as well as—the author of a research or critical work on the topic. There is a very high concentration of asterisks among a subgroup of authors who are cited as sources of many practices and who might therefore be described as influential in guiding practice in the field. Notable among these are such familiar names as Barbara Clark, June Cox, John Feldhusen, James Gallagher, John Gowan, Milton Gold, Joe Khatena, June Maker, Harry Passow, Joseph Renzulli, Abraham Tannenbaum, James Webb, Joanne Whitmore, and their frequent coauthors. Many of the cited authors, including some of these, have played a dual role, having done or supervised original research as well. Every professional field needs its codifiers, creative synthesizers who assemble the best ideas and present them in a useful and usable way, and often supplement them with new insights. Every professional field also requires a corpus of research to validate these practices, and this is where we fall short. There is no sign of an abatement in the publishing of books

277

giving advice on gifted education; nor is there much sign of the major programmatic research necessary to validate educational practice in this field and
to generate new ideas for practice (an observation supported by Passow,
1989). Such research is the substance on which our synthesizers must base
their work.

A good sign is that some authors' work tends to be concentrated on
clusters of recommended practices. Some are working on parental roles, others on identification, still others on the needs of special populations of bright
students. This is to be encouraged, because so much of the research that
needs to be done requires career specialization, not one-shot studies. A more
disturbing quality of the same reference list is the number of people whose
names appear only once or twice. To a small extent this is an artifact of our
seeking widely for supporting research and the brevity of our discussions,
but in most instances we have cited all the research we could find. The authors have often done valuable research or analysis, but for some reason they
have not made a continuing commitment to scholarship on giftedness and
gifted education. The field needs to consider ways to attract and retain the
research talents of the hundreds of scholars who have contributed to the
present literature.

The above commentary about the fragmentation of scholarship in the
field provides a context for our overall assessment of research support for
recommended practices in the education and upbringing of the gifted. *Such
support is largely lacking.* Approximately 40% of the recommended practices
are supported, most of them marginally, and few of these directly address
curriculum, programming, or pedagogy. A similar number are neither refuted nor supported, or are supported only in some circumstances. A sizable
number enjoying some support are not differentiated in their applicability to
exceptionally able students. To arrive at these conclusions, we used seven
categories to classify the practices:

1. Good research support exists for this practice, both with regard to
   its efficacy and to its differentiated appropriateness for very bright
   children, and it can be advocated with relatively little qualification
   (we caution, however, that this classification omits many important
   details covered in the reviews).
2. Some research support exists; we found evidence for either the
   value of the practice and its differentiation or at least its particular
   applicability to exceptionally able students despite insufficient validation of the actual practice.
3. We found both support and refutation, usually in the form that the
   practice was favorable under some circumstances or for some per-

sons and not others; this may be regarded as a form of highly qualified support.

4. No research appears on the topic.
5. Some or substantial support exists for the practice, but it was found to be appropriate for all children, rendering the practice an application of good-quality general education rather than special education for the highly able.
6. Some evidence suggested that this recommended practice was inappropriate.
7. Good evidence indicated that this practice was inappropriate.

Strongly Supported Practices

A total of seven practices enjoy good support in the research literature on giftedness. They are listed here with their category headings, and brief discussions follow. The total number of recommended practices in each heading is also noted in parentheses beside each. This pattern is repeated for each level of support.

2: Identification and Assessment (2 of 15)

16. IQ is a necessary part of identification.
18. Testing instruments should have high maximum scores.

3: Curricular and Program Policies (2 of 24)

28. Acceleration should be used.
49. Include career education, especially for girls.

7: Social and Emotional Adjustment (1 of 8)

90. Career counseling is needed, especially for girls.

8: Special Groups (2 of 11)

94. Education of the gifted handicapped must recognize strengths and handicaps.
101. Secondary mathematics and advanced science should be part of the curriculum for gifted girls.

It is interesting, and it should not be a surprise, that the best supported practices arise directly from the strong psychometric strand in the foundations of gifted education. IQ is a very defensible part of an identification program, but care is needed not to misinterpret this conclusion. IQ is widely used as the preeminent identification criterion, but the recommended practice that is supported is that it should be used where appropriate, not necessarily for every individual. Gender differences have long fascinated psychometricians, hence the many references to girls' special needs (why not regard the boys' needs as special and the girls' as baseline?).

It is nevertheless very helpful that three widely applicable practices receive strong support, however one might identify the students. Career education and special opportunities in mathematics and advanced science, with special attention to the involvement of girls, can be included in programs with confidence and sought with similar assurance. As well, a relatively new area of study has proved fruitful in directing our attention to the intellectual and creative strengths of the handicapped, not abandoning these students to the limitations of their handicaps.

Recommended Practices with Some Support

Thirty-four practices were so rated, rather evenly distributed across all eight categories. These are priority areas for research because much stands to be gained by the field should it be possible to validate these practices quickly and more adequately. Such validation would strengthen practice and advocacy, because over half of them address alternative identification, curricular, and pedagogical practices.

1: Advocacy and Administration (3 of 10)

1. Continuous government support should be solicited.
6. Early admission is appropriate in specific cases.
8. Acceleration and enrichment should be integrated.

2: Identification and Assessment (6 of 15)

14. Base identification on multiple criteria.
19. Past and present achievements should be used.
20. Affective talents should be assessed.
21. Nominations should be considered.
23. Consider cultural and social differences.
24. Selection should be appropriate to the program.

3: Curricular and Program Policies (7 of 24)

27. Intervention should be adapted to levels of giftedness.
30. Ability grouping is appropriate.
32. Stress affective as well as cognitive growth.
33. Materials should be high in quality and reading level, require complex verbal responses, and avoid repetition.
34. Provide a qualitatively different curriculum, at least part-time.

35. Take learning styles into account.
37. Employ professional end-products as standards.

4: Advice to Educators (5 of 17)

50. Reading should be highly individualized.
57. Gifted children should learn by teaching each other.
60. Investigate real problems and solutions.
65. Include independent study under competent supervision.
66. Prepare students for high-level occupations.

5: Advice to Parents (3 of 10)

69. Avoid stereotypes and misconceptions about the gifted label.
71. Avoid excessive emphasis on developing the child's giftedness.
76. Be sensitive to potential sibling adjustment problems.

6: Advice to Professionals (3 of 6)

78. Group and individual counseling are recommended.
81. Take account of early developing intrinsic motivation.
82. The limitations of students' physical, social, and emotional development should be taken into account.

7: Social and Emotional Adjustment (2 of 8)

83. Develop independence, autonomy, and self-reliance.
87. Focus on excellence in a few areas.

8: Special Groups (5 of 11)

92. Specially attend to gifted disadvantaged children.
95. Gifted learning-disabled children need special services.
97. Gifted underachievers need early intervention and special identification.
98. Programs for gifted underachievers should be within gifted programs.
100. Attend specially to the identification of gifted girls.

A program built around these practices and those more strongly supported, even today, would be solidly defensible. The acceleration versus enrichment argument is replaced with a rationale for integrating the two, and a variety of identification procedures are used, with attention to the diversity in both the program and the student body. Traditional approaches such as ability grouping are accompanied by alternatives that are consistent with contemporary thinking about intelligence, expertise, and knowledge production as a curricular objective. Much more than in the strongly supported practices alone, individualization is a driving principle, and learning and teaching are supported by concerns for the development of values, character, and autonomy. Special attention is extended beyond services for girls to economically disadvantaged, learning-disabled, and underachieving capable children.

We have a very attractive portrait of the "who" and "how" emerging, but the major item that remains absent from this picture of a defensible program is the "what" and, to a lesser extent, "when." The subject-matter content of a defensible curriculum for the gifted so far stresses only mathematics and science, especially at the secondary level. In fairness, career thinking, affective growth, and personal growth are covered in the first two categories of recommended practices, but this is a limited palette from which to complete the picture. Unfortunately, the missing elements are not found among the supported practices. This indicates most clearly where urgent work and the reporting of results are needed in gifted education.

Recommended Practices with Elements of Both Support and Refutation

This was a small group of nine practices with little pattern among them. Some of these topics are widely regarded as controversial, such as the funding base for gifted programs, the social adjustment of early matriculants, and the labeling of gifted children. Their appearance on this list is appropriate. In all cases, the implication is that greater precision is needed in stating the practice, often separating the "dos" from the "don'ts."

1: Advocacy and Administration (1 of 10)

3. Administer and fund gifted programs separately.

2: Identification and Assessment (1 of 15)

15. Use standardized identification instruments.

4: Advice to Educators (1 of 17)

62. Rapid pacing should be provided.

5: Advice to Parents (3 of 10)

70. Be aware of how personal needs and feelings influence the relationship with the child.
73. Encourage social as well as academic development.
75. Foster potential for giftedness through preschool intervention.

6: Advice to Professionals (1 of 6)

80. Early college entrants require special attention to socioemotional adjustment.

7: Social and Emotional Adjustment (2 of 8)

86. Encourage the broadening of interests.
88. Gifted children should not be labeled.

The supportable parts of these practices include such elements as using standardized instruments when they are appropriate to the program goals, using rapid pacing when the curricular activity involves a group of children with similar capabilities and strong background in an area of largely codified and organized content, and avoiding the negative effects of the gifted label on unselected siblings.

On the other hand, using these same examples, standardized instruments are inappropriate to the recognition of unique achievements in independent study; rapid pacing is contrary to the time needed for creative reflections, attention to accuracy, and exploration in depth of an area of interest; and bright children are helped, not hindered, by recognition of their abilities.

Some recommended practices contain an inherent degree of conflict. For example, to encourage the broadening of interests (No. 86) challenges a focus on excellence in a few areas (No. 87), and better support was found for focusing. It is important to remember, however, that the danger in these sweeping statements is to overgeneralize. Our conclusions apply in general; they may not apply to a specific individual. At the program-planning level there is stronger support for the need to provide opportunities to develop depth rather than breadth, yet for some individuals and special groups, breadth is at least of equal concern. This discrimination can be built into a defensible program plan.

Recommended Practices on Which There Is Insufficient Research to Make a Judgment about Support

Thirty-four practices were judged to belong to this category. It is of great concern that some of these are very important. Identification and assessment procedures extended over time fall into this category—these are the sources of data that can provide evidence of the appropriateness of initial selection criteria. Several address key elements of the curriculum such as the arts, world affairs, and the future. Important general and administrative considerations such as advocacy, full-time program coordination, teacher training, and grading practices are among these, as are developmental concerns such as perfectionism, peer contact, and self-concept. We know very little about some crucial topics.

1: Advocacy and Administration (5 of 10)

2. Advocacy is needed to encourage and maintain support.
4. Coordination is required between grade levels.
5. A full-time coordinator is necessary.
7. Participation should be voluntary.
9. Teachers should be specially selected and trained.

2: Identification and Assessment (5 of 15)

11. Systematic identification should be widespread.
12. Identification should be an ongoing process.
13. Identification should be made as early as possible.
17. Include testing for potential giftedness.
25. Fair grading practices should be employed.

3: Curricular and Program Policies (10 of 24)

26. Programs should be part of overall individualization.
31. Curriculum should be multidisciplinary.
36. Gifted children need to set long- and short-term goals.
39. Systematically assess student content interests.
40. Broad curriculum choice should be available.
41. Curriculum should be future-oriented.
42. Emphasize abstract and basic concepts.
43. The arts should be included.
44. Include world affairs and a global perspective.
46. Thinking skills should be taught.

4: Advice to Educators (4 of 17)

51. Extracurricular activities should be encouraged.
52. Continuous program evaluation is necessary.
63. Teach gifted children to complete their tasks.
64. Emphasize in-depth investigation of subject matter.

5: Advice to Parents (4 of 10)

67. Emotional support from parent groups and counselors should be available.
68. Participate in and lobby for programs.
72. Discourage children's perfectionism and excessive self-criticism.
74. Facilitate social development through ability-peer contact.

6: Advice to Professionals (2 of 6)

77. Educational and vocational counselors knowledgeable about giftedness are required.
79. Counselors should keep a file of scholarship resources.

7: Social and Emotional Adjustment (2 of 8)

85. Identify and develop leadership ability.
89. Social or curricular conformity should not be forced on creatively talented children.

8: Special Groups (2 of 11)

93. Rural gifted programs require special consideration.
99. Especially develop positive self-concept in gifted underachievers.

To provide a sense of the scope of those practices for which we do not have adequate research support, consider the following scenario. Imaginary developers of a new program in a school district decide to propose a program with the following elements: a full-time coordinator, special selection and training of teachers, and curricular coordination across grades and between elementary and secondary schooling. Identification will be an ongoing, broadly based activity, beginning at kindergarten or earlier when possible. Reports of the progress and achievements of participating students will indicate their standing in both the regular and special programs. The curriculum will be multidisciplinary, drawing extensively on students' interests with broad choice of subject matter, involving the learners in establishing learning goals and studying subjects in depth. Curriculum will include teaching of thinking and leadership skills and encourage a global perspective. The arts and extracurricular activities will be featured. Parents will be actively recruited as partners in the program, and special attention will be given to developing self-concept and respecting the nonconforming strengths of creatively gifted children.

It sounds absolutely marvelous! Maybe it would be. However, the proposers of such a plan would have very little research on which to base their defense of it as the best choice, or even a good choice, among those available. We are not offering this as a reason to avoid these practices. Empirical research support is not the only criterion for choosing program elements. For example, the arts are important as an expression of cultural values, and that is reason enough to include them. They are a critical part of civilization, and talented people play a special role in the arts, for the benefit of everyone. The critical points here are two. First, empirical evidence, when available, constitutes powerful validation for actions in our culture; therefore such evidence should be sought. Second, in the absence of such evidence, advocates of these recommended practices should take care not to misrepresent their advocacy as research-supported.

If any researchers and reflective teachers are interested in breaking new research ground, these are the practices that demand their attention, as also stressed by Passow (1989). They are the subject of a great deal of thought and writing but not systematic, data-based, replicable study. The largest number of these practices are in the crucial category of curricular and program policy; several practices in other sections overlap in their applicability to program or pedagogy. This part of our results points out, more strikingly than any other, that although we already have an evolving psychology and sociology of giftedness, and those are both interesting and important to the development of pedagogy and policy, the education of able children remains a fledgling science. Here are found some of the priority questions that may be addressed. It is important for researchers in the field to ensure that the widest possible array of these topics are explored. Communication among researchers is essential to assure this kind of broad research coverage.

Recommended Practices Applicable to All Children

Gifted education is occasionally accused of being good-quality general education reserved for an élite group of students. From one perspective, we were pleased to discover that this group of practices contained only 14 of our 101 items, implying that bright students do seem to have some educational needs that can be addressed over and above the important general issue of high-quality educational opportunities for all students. Another perspective is that gifted education must indeed be seen and practiced according to that very principle: high-quality educational experiences for all children. In that context, it is also good that some practices that are espoused in gifted education, and that have some research support for their effectiveness, suffer only in that no case can be made for their special applicability to highly able students. It is appropriate that these are drawn almost entirely from curricular and program policies and advice to educators. These practices are as follows:

3: Curricular and Program Policies (5 of 24)

29. Enrichment should be a program component.
38. Combine individual programming with a common curriculum.
45. Microcomputers should be included.
47. Communication skills should be taught.
48. Humanistic values should be developed.

4: Advice to Educators (7 of 17)

53. A variety of teachers is needed.
54. Use a variety of school and community resources.
55. Mentor or apprenticeship programs should be used.
56. Less teacher-centered pedagogy is suitable.
58. Creative abilities should be nurtured.

59. Include inquiry, discovery, and problem solving.
61. Gifted historical figures should be studied.

7: Social and Emotional Adjustment (1 of 8)

84. Develop positive self-concept.

8: Special Groups (1 of 11)

91. Respect cultural and social differences.

These are important practices that gifted education should continue to promote. Further research remains necessary, but the evidence is positive in each case. The link to general education should be acknowledged. Gifted education provides exceptional opportunities to demonstrate and refine these practices, with little risk, for the ultimate benefit of all learners.

In order to have this effect, it might be important to report research on these practices in more general publications than those devoted exclusively to giftedness. As noted in the Introduction, there is still insufficient communication between the literatures (and their authors). Research on the practices noted here is more likely to be of interest to the readers of general educational and psychological journals. Furthermore, these might offer especially useful opportunities for collaboration with educational researchers and teachers with more general interests, which could extend support for gifted education.

Recommended Practices For Which There Is Some Evidence That They Are Inappropriate

Only two recommended practices were so judged, and both may be regarded as somewhat minor. The roles of consultants for teachers and psychologists in identification are expensive items in a program budget. In addition to concerns about their intrinsic merit and special applicability to the education of the gifted, they need to pass the test of cost-effectiveness. At what point in the development of programs should tens or hundreds of thousands of dollars be spent, if at all, on these recommended practices?

1: Advocacy and Administration (1 of 10)

10. Provide consultant services for teachers.

2: Identification and Assessment (1 of 15)

22. Psychologists should participate in identification.

It has not been shown that teachers do not want or need help; rather, the argument lies in how to provide this assistance and what kinds of help are made available. Concerning identification, psychologists are not the only people who can provide the services advocated, though they may well have a defensible role within individual testing. In contrast, concerns were raised in Chapters 2 (see recommended practice No. 22) and 6 (No. 77) about the attitudes of psychologists (and counselors) toward gifted education and bright students. Many of the key studies here require updating, but the present state of the art is that these practices are contradicted by the little research that is available. Better evidence could, as in all cases, change this conclusion.

A Recommended Practice Strongly Refuted

We found but one:

8: Special Groups (1 of 11)
96. Gifted delinquent children need special intervention.

Caution is once again in order. The conclusion is not that gifted delinquent children do not require attention, but rather that their giftedness and delinquency do not appear to interact so as to require special consideration of their giftedness and criminality together. The two elements can be dealt with independently: The giftedness and delinquency can be addressed separately, using acceptable practices from both fields in tandem. This contrasts, for example, with advice about gifted underachievers and gifted learning-disabled persons, where there is some support for uniqueness of the combination and calling upon specially adapted services. Rejection of the practice also does not imply that gifted delinquents do not exist; anecdotal evidence is strong on that point. The contention concerns what one should do about it.

The Interaction of Some Practices

Our analysis of the state of knowledge in the field and the research we reviewed examined each practice separately. This exposes some interpretive risks, because the recommended practices do bear upon each other. Any real program must necessarily address more than one practice at a time. Are there pairs or groups of recommended practices that should not be advocated simultaneously, even if one or more of the points is supported individually? An answer to this question about interactions is important to the development of general program standards or guidelines.

For example, a decision about separating the funding or administration of a gifted program from those for other exceptional children (No. 3, with conflicting evidence) may prove incompatible with the search for governmental fiscal support (No. 1, with some support), for even the most creative administrator. An identification plan for kindergarten through Grade 2 or 3 (No. 13, insufficient research) could be incompatible with insistence on using IQ tests with high maximum scores (No. 18, strongly supported), since the degree of test difficulty required to generate very high-IQ scale scores can lead to a test that might be a frustrating or discouraging experience for young children. Not forcing conformity (No. 89, no research) on creatively gifted persons provides an interesting contrast with the need to learn to cope with demands in the world of work (in No. 90, strongly supported), where getting along with colleagues and employers is important: Might it be possible to demonstrate the efficacy of encouraging some skills of adaptation that may be seen by others as an acceptable level of conformity? Early intervention for gifted underachievers (No. 97, some support) and being treated as part of a regular or adapted gifted program (No. 98, also some support) require clarification: How can these be accomplished simultaneously?

Support or refutation is not an absolute distinction. None of the recommended practices we have gleaned from the book literature is without basis. The need we are recognizing, however, is that a comprehensive overview reveals the need for both precision and the avoidance of simplistic arguments. Not only is more work needed on the individual recommended practices or on others that other readers may glean from the same or different books or from other sources we did not survey thoroughly (journals, conference reports, ERIC documents, training tapes, expert symposia, etc.—it would be interesting to compare the outcomes); but also research is needed on the various combinations of practices that might be assembled in a program plan. There are interactions among the practices that need consideration. One might get a more accurate impression of the importance of a particular practice not only by looking at its simple presence versus absence with different children but also by examining what happens in an elaborated program when the particular practice is present, removed, or varied. When viewed alone, a practice might appear to be highly related to assorted outcomes. In a fuller program context, other program elements may be contributing to the outcomes of interest. Practices should be shown not only to contribute positively to desired outcomes but also to make an additional unique contribution when added to a set of complementary practices. Only the single-variable studies are done easily in a laboratory setting. The interactional studies require the collaboration of schools with real programs. The "subjects" of such studies are not individual students but the programs themselves.

Summary

Several allusions have been made in the preceding pages about particular strengths or weaknesses of recommended practices in one or the other of the categories. When these results are examined from the perspective of the eight categories of recommended practices and the seven levels of research support, we obtain the following four broad conclusions. These assume that our eight categories usefully or adequately taxonomize our practical knowledge of gifted education.

Our earlier conclusions about the state of knowledge in gifted education are affirmed:

1. None of the categories of recommended practice is distinguished by broad, strong support.
2. The strongest support is for limited-term, specific actions related to the use of intelligence tests and the recognition of special groups; available wisdom in curriculum and pedagogy is less well supported.
3. Some of the advice regarding teaching methodology, as well as program and curriculum planning, is an extension of good-quality general education and has not been shown to be needed uniquely by, or of benefit to, exceptionally able students.
4. Little or no research exists to either support or refute a full third of the available recommended practices in the field, concentrated particularly in the advice regarding administration, the follow-up of identification procedures, curricular and program policies, and advice to parents and professionals (other than teachers); no category of advice is excluded from this research-poor condition.

This is a somewhat disturbing overview given the firmness with which some of the 101 practices have been advocated. However, only three recommended practices are to any extent contradicted, and only one of those with some certainty. This suggests that the major problem facing the field is not malpractice but insufficiently developed and validated curricular and pedagogical alternatives. The strongest research and the best backed practices are, to an unmeasurable but visible extent, artifacts of psychology's preoccupation with IQ in the last 60 years and more. In a way, this shows that we do pay attention to research, if not the most up-to-date research. A third of the practices have some support. Some may require only a few additional research programmes to move into the more strongly supported category. In addition, nine of the practices are characterized by both support and refutation: Contradiction and controversy fuel the research fire. Thus, somewhat over one third of the practices are a rich source of ideas for needed studies.

The needed research that we have emphasized throughout the detailed reviews in Chapters 1 through 8 has a distinctively educational flavor, and it draws on a broader theoretical base than psychometric or differential psychology. We began the text with our observation of an insufficient link between gifted education and theory. Perhaps a more accurate assessment would be that the link has been unbalanced.

It will not be possible to redress the imbalance if all the needed research is left exclusively to differential psychologists or others outside the schools. Research on giftedness and gifted education should not eschew the methodological skills and insights into thinking and learning available from psychology or elsewhere, but, in addition to contributions from other disciplines, teachers and educators must take an active role in addressing the research agenda on gifted education. This can be done by asking some of the questions posed in the conclusion to each review of the recommended practices. Moreover, teachers and other educators should be active members of the research teams that look at these questions.

References

Note: The bracketed numbers concluding each reference refer to the recommended practice numbers, not to page numbers. An asterisk preceding a recommended practice number indicates that the item was cited as a source of a recommended practice in the opening section of the review in question; it may also have been cited elsewhere. References to the Introduction and the Conclusion are indicated as "Intro." or "Concl."

Abraham, W., & Hartwell, L. K. (1985). Early identification of the pre-school child: A study of parent and teacher effectiveness. *Gifted Education International, 3,* 127–129. [75]

Abroms, K. I. (1985). Social giftedness and its relationship with intellectual giftedness. In J. Freeman (Ed.), *The psychology of gifted children* (pp. 201–218). Chichester, England: Wiley. [73]

Adams, H. B. (1985). The British Association and curriculum enrichment in the county of Cleveland. *Gifted Education International, 3,* 57–58. [87]

Adderholdt-Elliott, M. (1987). *Perfectionism: What's bad about being too good?* Minneapolis: Free Spirit.

Adjemovitch, D. (1983). Reaching the unreached: A view from the UNICEF perspective. In B. M. Shore, F. Gagné, S. Larivée, R. H. Tali, & R. E. Tremblay (Eds.), *Face to face with giftedness* (pp. 358–368). New York: Trillium. [*75]

Alamprese, J. A., Erlanger, W. J., & Brigham, N. (1989). *No gift wasted: Effective strategies for educating highly able, disadvantaged students in mathematics and science: Vol. I. Findings, Final Report* (Contract No. 300-87-0152). Washington, DC: U.S. Department of Education, Office of Planning, Budget and Evaluation. [91, 92]

Alexander, P. A., & Muia, J. A. (1982). *Gifted education: A comprehensive roadmap.* Rockville, MD: Aspen. [*1, *35, *47, *52, *68, *94, Intro.]

Alexander, P. J., & Skinner, M. E. (1981). The effects of early entrance on subsequent and academic development: A follow-up study. *Journal for the Education of the Gifted, 3,* 147–150. [6]

Allan, S. D., Fox, D. K. (1979). Group counseling the gifted. *Journal for the Education of the Gifted, 3,* 83–92. [78]

Allen, H. D. (1983). Extracurricular mathematics: Incentive for the gifted. In B. M.

Shore, F. Gagné, S. Larivée, R. H. Tali, & R. E. Tremblay (Eds.), *Face to face with giftedness* (pp. 448–459). New York: Trillium. [*51]

Altman, R. (1983). Social-emotional development of gifted children and adolescents: A research model. *Roeper Review, 6,* 65–67. [82]

Alvino, J. J. (1985). *Parents' guide to raising a gifted child.* New York: Ballantine. (Also Boston: Little, Brown.) [*72, 73, 74, *76, 84, Intro.]

Alvino, J. J., McDonnel, R. C., & Richert, E. S. (1981). National survey of identification practices in gifted and talented education. *Exceptional Children, 48,* 124–132. [11, 14, 100]

Ambach, G. M. (1984). Guest editorial: Excellence and equity in education—implications for gifted education. *Gifted Child Quarterly, 28,* 3–5. [37]

Ambrose, I. M. (1980). Gifted programs and community resources. *Roeper Review, 3,* 18–19. [54]

American Association for Gifted Children. (1978). *On being gifted.* New York: Walker. [*55, Intro.]

Anderson, M. A., Tollefson, N. A., & Gilbert, E. C. (1985). Giftedness and reading: A cross-sectional view of differences in reading attitudes and behaviors. *Gifted Child Quarterly, 29,* 186–189. [50]

Archambault, F. X., Jr. (1983). Measurement and evaluation concerns in evaluating programs for the gifted and talented. *Journal for the Education of the Gifted, 7,* 12–25. [52]

Arent, R. P. (1979). The gifted child and feelings. *G/C/T,* No. 9, 69–70. [82]

Armstrong, D. C. (1987, August). *A consumer validation study: What do gifted children report about the match between their ideal and actual gifted programs.* Paper presented at the 7th World Conference on Gifted and Talented Children, Salt Lake City, UT. [Intro.]

Armstrong, D. C. (1988). *Appropriate programming for the gifted: A Q-analysis of gifted sixth grade students' perceptions of present and ideal teaching strategies.* (Unpublished doctoral dissertation, The Union for Experimenting Colleges and Universities, 1987.) *Dissertation Abstracts International, 49*(4), 709A. [Intro.]

Armstrong, D. C. (1989). Appropriate programming for the gifted: An analysis of gifted elementary students' perceptions. *Journal for the Education of the Gifted, 12,* 277–292. [Intro.]

Armstrong, J. (1980). *Achievement and participation of women in mathematics: An overview.* Denver: Education Commission of the States. [*101]

Association for the Gifted. (1989). *Standards for programs involving the gifted and talented.* Reston, VA: The Council for Exceptional Children. [69, 74, Intro.]

Astin, H. S. (1974). Sex differences in mathematical and scientific precocity. In J. C. Stanley, D. P. Keating, & L. H. Fox (Eds.), *Mathematical talent: Discovery, description, and development* (pp. 70–86). Baltimore: Johns Hopkins University Press. [101]

Astin, H. S., & Myint, T. (1971). Career development and stability of young women during the post high school years. *Journal of Counseling Psychology, 19,* 369–394. [101]

Aubrecht, L. (1981). Organizing for advocacy: Making it work on the state and local level. In P. B. Mitchell (Ed.), *An advocate's guide to building support for gifted* *and talented education* (pp. 31–41). Washington, DC: National Association of State Boards of Education. [*2]

Austin, A. B., & Draper, D. C. (1981). Peer relationships of the academically gifted: A review. *Gifted Child Quarterly, 25,* 129–133. [74]

Bachtold, L. M. (1968). Interpersonal values of gifted junior high school students. *Psychology in the Schools, 5,* 368–370. [83]

Baldwin, A. Y. (1975). Instructional planning for gifted disadvantaged children. In B. O. Boston (Ed.), *Developing elementary and secondary school programs* (pp. 13–20). Reston, VA: Council for Exceptional Children. [23]

Baldwin, A. Y. (1981). Effect of process oriented instruction on thought processes in gifted children. In A. H. Kramer, D. Bitan, N. Butler-Por, A. Evyatar, & E. Landau (Eds.), *Gifted children: Challenging their potential—New perspectives and alternatives* (pp. 178–188). New York: Trillium.

Baldwin, A. Y. (1989). The purpose of education for gifted black students. In C. J. Maker & S. W. Schiever (Eds.), *Critical issues in gifted education: Defensible programs for cultural and ethnic minorities: Vol. 2* (pp. 237–245). Austin, TX: Pro-Ed. [91]

Ballering, L. D., & Koch, A. (1984). Family relations when a child is gifted. *Gifted Child Quarterly, 28,* 140–143. [76]

Barbe, W. B., & Frierson, E. (1975). Teaching the gifted: A new frame of reference. In W. B. Barbe & J. S. Renzulli (Eds.), *Psychology and education of the gifted* (2nd ed., pp. 435–438). New York: Irvington. [*59]

Barbe, W. B., & Malone, M. M. (1985). Reading and writing. In R. H. Swassing (Ed.), *Teaching gifted children and adolescents* (pp. 276–313). Columbus, OH: Merrill. [*33, *61, *64, 97]

Barbe, W. B., & Renzulli, J. S. (Eds.). (1975). *Psychology and education of the gifted* (2nd ed.). New York: Irvington. [21, Intro.]

Barron, F., & Harrington, D. (1981). Creativity, intelligence, and personality. *Annual Review of Psychology, 32,* 439–476. [83, 89]

Baska, L. (1989). Standardized testing for minority students: Is it fair? In C. J. Maker, *Critical issues in gifted education: Vol. II. Defensible programs for cultural and ethnic minorities* (pp. 226–236). Austin, TX: Pro-Ed. [21, 23, 88]

Baskin, B. H., & Harris, K. H. (1980). *Books for the gifted.* New York: Bowker. [33]

Bauer, H., & Harris, R. L. (1979). Potentially able learners (P.A.L.s): A program for gifted pre-schoolers and parents. *Journal for the Education of the Gifted, 2,* 214–219. [75]

Baum, S. (1984). Meeting the needs of learning disabled gifted students. *Roeper Review, 7*(1), 16–19. [95]

Bayley, N. (1969). *Manual for the Bayley Scales of Intellectual Development.* New York: Psychological Corporation. [20]

Bear, G. G. (1983). Moral reasoning, classroom behavior, and the intellectually gifted. *Journal for the Education of the Gifted, 6,* 111–119. [48]

Beasley, W. A. (1985). The role of microcomputers in the education of the gifted. *Roeper Review, 7,* 156–159. [45]

Beck, A. T., Rush, A. J., Shaw, B. F., & Emery, G. (1979). *Cognitive therapy of depression.* New York: Guilford. [72]

Beck, L. (1989). Mentorships: Benefits and effects on career development. *Gifted Child Quarterly, 33,* 22–28. [55]

Becker, J. (1982). Global studies for the gifted. *Roeper Review, 5*(2), 44–45. [44]

Bennett, N. (1976). *Teaching styles and pupil progress.* London: Basic. [56]

Bernal, E. M., Jr. (1979). The education of the culturally different gifted. In A. H. Passow (Ed.), *The gifted and the talented: Their education and development. Seventy-eighth yearbook of the National Association for the Study of Education: Part 1* (pp. 395–400). Chicago: University of Chicago Press. [*23, *91]

Betts, G. T. (1986). The autonomous learner model for the gifted and talented. In J. S. Renzulli (Ed.), *Systems and models for developing programs for the gifted and talented* (pp. 27–56). Mansfield, CT: Creative Learning Press. [65]

Betz, N. E., & Fitzgerald, L. F. (1987). *The career psychology of women.* New York: Academic. [49]

Biersdorf, M. P. (1979). Further adventures in language arts. *Roeper Review, 1*(4), 19–20. [50]

Birch, J. W. (1975). Early school admission for mentally advanced children. In W. Barbe & J. S. Renzulli (Eds.), *Psychology and education of the gifted* (pp. 303–309). New York: Irvington. [*6]

Birch, J. W. (1984). Is *any* identification procedure necessary? *Gifted Child Quarterly, 28,* 157–161. [21]

Birnbaum, M. J. (1977). Educational problems of rural education for the gifted. In J. M. Blanning (Ed.), *Ideas for urban/rural gifted/talented: Case histories and program plans* (p. 69). Ventura, CA: Office of the Ventura County Superintendent of Schools for the National/State Leadership Training Institute for the Gifted and Talented. [*93]

Birns, B., & Golden, M. (1972). Prediction of intellectual performance at 3 years from infant tests and personality measures. *Merrill-Palmer Quarterly, 18*(1), 53–58. [20]

Bishop, W. E. (1968). Successful teachers of the gifted. *Exceptional Children, 34,* 317–325. [9]

Bishop, W. E. (1981). Characteristics of teachers judged successful by intellectually gifted high achieving high school students. In W. B. Barbe & J. S. Renzulli (Eds.), *Psychology and education of the gifted* (3rd ed., pp. 449–459). New York: Irvington. [*9]

Blacher-Dixon, J., & Turnbull, A. F. (1978). A preschool program for gifted-handicapped children. *Journal for the Education of the Gifted, 1,* 15–23. [94]

Bland, M., Melang, P., & Miller, D. (1986). The effect of small-group counseling on underachievers. *Elementary School Guidance and Counseling, 20,* 303–305. [99]

Blanning, J. M. (1977). Gifted adolescents in an urban independent study program. In J. M. Blanning (Ed.), *Ideas for urban/rural gifted/talented: Case histories and program plans* (pp. 1–66). Ventura, CA: Office of the Ventura County Superintendent of Schools for the National/State Leadership Training Institute for the Gifted and Talented. [17, *57, 91, Intro.]

Blanning, J. M. (1978). High school students undertake study of controversial heroes. *G/C/T,* No. 4, 35–36. [61]

Blaubergs, M. S. (1980). Sex-role stereotyping and gifted girls' experience and education. *Roeper Review, 2*(3), 13–15. [100]

Bleedorn, B. B. (1979). Strategies and resources for creative encounters with the future: Developing gifted thinking and leadership. In J. J. Gallagher (Ed.), *Gifted children: Reaching their potential* (pp. 119–133). New York: Trillium. [*41, *85]

Bloom, B. S. (Ed.). (1985). *Developing talent in young people.* New York: Ballantine. [13, 20, 43, 55, 66, 71, 81, 83, 87, Intro.]

Bogue, K. L., & Wolf, J. S. (1985). School and community in action. *Roeper Review, 8,* 112–114. [54, 68]

Bonds, C. W., & Bonds, L. T. (1983). Teacher, is there a gifted reader in first grade? *Roeper Review, 5*(3), 4–5. [50]

Booth, L. (1980). Motivating gifted students through a shared-governance apprentice/mentor program. *Roeper Review, 3*(1), 11–13. [55]

Boothby, P. (1980). Creative and critical reading for the gifted. *The Reading Teacher, 33,* 674–676. [50]

Borland, J. H. (1978). Teacher identification of the gifted: A new look. *Journal for the Education of the Gifted, 2,* 22–32. [9, 21]

Borland, J. H. (1986). IQ tests: Throwing out the bathwater, saving the baby. *Roeper Review, 8,* 163–167. [16]

Borland, J. H. (1989). *Planning and implementing programs for the gifted.* New York: Teachers College Press. [9]

Borman, C., Nash, W. R., & Colson, S. (1978). Career guidance for gifted and talented students. *Vocational Guidance Quarterly, 27,* 72–76. [90]

Boston, B. O. (Ed.). (1975a). *Developing elementary and secondary school programs.* Reston, VA: Council for Exceptional Children, ERIC Clearinghouse on Handicapped and Gifted Children. [Intro.]

Boston, B. O. (1975b). Starting a gifted program. In B. O. Boston (Ed.), *Developing elementary and secondary school programs* (pp. 21–28). Reston, VA: Council for Exceptional Children, ERIC Clearinghouse on Handicapped and Gifted Children. [5, 55]

Boston, B. O. (1976). *The sorcerer's apprentice: A case study in the role of the mentor.* Reston, VA: Council for Exceptional Children. [Intro.]

Boultinghouse, A. (1984). What is your style? A learning style inventory for lower elementary grades. *Roeper Review, 6,* 208–210. [35]

Bow, J. N. (1988). A comparison of intellectually superior male reading achievers and underachievers from a neuropsychological perspective. *Journal of Learning Disabilities, 21,* 118–123. [99]

Bracey, G. W. (1987). The social impact of ability grouping. *Phi Delta Kappan, 68,* 701–702. [30]

Braggett, E. J., Ashman, A., & Noble, J. (1983). The expressed needs of parents of gifted children. *Gifted Education International, 1,* 80–83. [67]

Brandwein, P. F. (1981). *The gifted student as future scientist.* Ventura, CA: Office of the Ventura County Superintendent of Schools for the National/State Leadership Training Institute for the Gifted and Talented. (Original work published 1955) [19, 65, Intro.]

Breiter, J. C. (1988, November). *Text selection for graduate courses in gifted education.* Paper presented at the meeting of the National Association for Gifted Children, Orlando, FL. [Intro.]

Breiter, J. C. (1989). Texts currently used in graduate level courses in gifted education. *Journal for the Education of the Gifted, 12,* 311–319. [Intro.]

Bridges, S. (1973). *IQ—150.* New York: Crane, Russak. [70, 76]

Bristow, W. H., Craig, M. L., Hallock, G. T., & Laycock, S. R. (1951). Identifying gifted children. In P. Witty (Ed.), *The gifted child* (pp. 10–19). Boston: Heath. [*20]

Brody, L. E., & Benbow, C. P. (1986). Social and emotional adjustment of adolescents extremely talented in verbal and mathematical reasoning. *Journal of Youth and Adolescence, 15,* 1–18. [74]

Brody, L., & Fox, L. H. (1980). An accelerative intervention program for mathematically gifted girls. In L. H. Fox, L. Brody, & D. Tobin (Eds.), *Women and the mathematical mystique* (pp. 164–178). Baltimore: Johns Hopkins University Press. [28, 53, 77]

Brody, L. E., Lupkowski, A. E., & Stanley, J. C. (1988). Early entrance to college: A study of academic and social adjustment during freshman year. *College and University, 63,* 347–359. [80]

Brooks, R. (1972). *Bright delinquents: The story of a unique school.* London: The National Foundation for Educational Research in England and Wales. [96]

Brooks, R. (1980). *Bright delinquents.* Brighton, England: Brighton Polytechnic. [96]

Brooks, R. (1985). Delinquency among gifted children. In J. Freeman (Ed.), *The psychology of gifted children: Perspectives on development and education* (pp. 297–308). Chichester, England: Wiley. [*96]

Brown, P. P. (1987). The role of the school psychologist in gifted education. *Roeper Review, 4*(4), 28–29. [22]

Brown, W., & Rogan, J. (1983). Reading and young gifted children. *Roeper Review, 5*(3), 6–9. [50]

Bruner, J. S. (1963). *The process of education.* New York: Vintage. (Original work published 1960). [37]

Brunswik, E. (1955). The conceptual framework of psychology. In O. Neurath, R. Carnap, & C. Morris (Eds.), *International encyclopedia of unified science: Vol. 1* (pp. 655–752). Chicago: University of Chicago Press. [33]

Buescher, T. M. (1985). A framework for understanding the social and emotional development of gifted and talented adolescents. *Roeper Review, 8,* 10–15. [82]

Burns, J. (1978). *Leadership.* New York: Harper & Row. [85]

Busse, T., Dahme, G., Wagner, W., & Wieczerkowski, W. (1986). Teacher perceptions of highly gifted students in the United States and West Germany. *Gifted Children Quarterly, 30,* 55–60. [69]

Butler, N., & Butler, R. (1979). Parents' and children's perception of classes for highly gifted children. In J. J. Gallagher (Ed.), *Gifted children: Reaching their potential* (pp. 223–245). New York: Trillium. [*64]

Butler-Por, N. (1983). Giftedness across cultures. In B. M. Shore, F. Gagné, S. Larivée, R. H. Tali, & R. E. Tremblay (Eds.), *Face to face with giftedness* (pp. 250–270). New York: Trillium Press. [*100]

Butler-Por, N. (1985). Gifted children in three Israeli cultures. In J. Freeman (Ed.), *The psychology of gifted children: Perspectives on development and education* (pp. 309–323). Chichester, England: Wiley. [23]

Byrne, B. M. (1984). The general/academic self-concept nomological network: A review of construct validation research. *Review of Educational Research, 54,* 427–456. [83, 84]

Caldwell, S. T. (1985). Highly gifted preschool readers. *Journal for the Education of the Gifted, 8,* 165–174. [50, 75]

Callahan, C. M. (1978). *Developing creativity in the gifted and talented.* Reston, VA: Council for Exceptional Children. [Intro.]

Callahan, C. M. (1979). The gifted and talented woman. In A. H. Passow (Ed.), *The gifted and talented: Their education and development. Seventy-eighth yearbook of the National Society for the Study of Education: Part I* (pp. 401–423). Chicago: University of Chicago Press. [66, 86, *90, 99, 100]

Callahan, C. M. (1980). The gifted girl: An anomaly? *Roeper Review, 2*(3), 16–20. [100]

Callahan, C. M. (1985). Science. In R. H. Swassing (Ed.), *Teaching gifted children and adolescents* (pp. 276–313). Columbus, OH: Merrill. [31, *46, 59, 62, *64]

Callahan, C. M., & Caldwell, M. (1983). Using evaluation results to improve programs for the gifted and talented. *Journal for the Education of the Gifted, 7,* 60–74. [52]

Callow, R. (1980). Recognizing the gifted child. In R. Povey (Ed.), *Educating the gifted child* (pp. 109–119). London: Harper & Row. [*12, *13]

Carey, G. L. (1958). Sex difference in problem-solving performance as a function of attitude differences. *Journal of Abnormal and Social Psychology, 56,* 256–260. [101]

Carrelli, A. O. (1982). Sex equity and the gifted. *G/C/T,* No. 25, 2–6. [100]

Carter, K. R., & Hamilton, W. (1985). Formative evaluation of gifted programs: A process and model. *Gifted Child Quarterly, 29,* 5–11. [52]

Carter, K. R., & Swanson, H. L. (1990). An analysis of the most prominent gifted journal articles since the Marland Report: Implications for researchers. *Gifted Child Quarterly, 34,* 116–123. [Intro.]

Cassidy, J. (1981). Parental involvement in gifted programs. *Journal for the Education of the Gifted, 4,* 284–287. [50, 68]

Cassidy, J., & Vukelich, C. (1978). Providing for the young academically talented: A pilot program for teachers and children. *Journal for the Education of the Gifted, 1,* 70–76. [75]

Caudill, G. (1977). Program implementation and programming for rural gifted students. In J. M. Blanning (Ed.), *Ideas for urban/rural gifted/talented: Case histories and program plans* (pp. 89–93). Ventura, CA: Office of the Ventura County Superintendent of Education for the National/State Leadership Training Institute for the Gifted and Talented. [*40, 65, 93]

Centra, J. A. (1974). *Women, men and the doctorate.* Princeton, NJ: Educational Testing Service. [101]

Chambers, J. A., Barron, F., & Sprecher, J. W. (1980). Identifying gifted Mexican-American students. *Gifted Child Quarterly, 24,* 123–128. [23]

Chamrad, D. L., & Robinson, N. M. (1989, April). *Sibling relationships in school-age pairs with 0, 1, or 2 "gifted" members*. Paper presented at the annual meeting of the Society for Research on Child Development, Kansas City, MO. [88]

Chauncey, H. (1958). Measurement and prediction—tests of academic ability. In J. B. Conant (Ed.), *The identification and education of the academically talented student in the American secondary school* (pp. 27–35). Washington, DC: National Education Association. [*15]

Chauvin, J. C., & Karnes, F. A. (1982). Reliability of a leadership inventory used with gifted students. *Psychological Reports, 51,* 770. [85]

Chauvin, J. C., & Karnes, F. A. (1983). A leadership profile of secondary gifted students. *Psychological Reports, 53,* 1259–1262. [85]

Chauvin, J. C., & Karnes, F. A. (1984). Perceptions of leadership characteristics by gifted elementary students. *Roeper Review, 6,* 238–240. [85]

Chen, A. W. (1981). Brain hemispheric functions as a basis for giftedness. *Roeper Review, 4,* 9–11. [35]

Cheyney, A. B. (1962). Parents view their intellectually gifted children. *Peabody Journal of Education, 40,* 98–101. [70]

Ciha, T., Harris, R., Hoffman, C., & Potter, M. (1974). Parents as identifiers of giftedness, ignored but accurate. *Gifted Child Quarterly, 18,* 191–195. [9]

Clark, B. (1983). *Growing up gifted: Developing the potential of children at home and at school* (2nd ed.). Columbus, OH: Merrill. [*25, *81]

Clark, B. (1985). Giftedness: The integration of brain function. *Gifted International, 3*(1), 23–30. [35]

Clark, B. (1988). *Growing up gifted: Developing the potential of children at home and at school* (3rd ed.). Columbus, OH: Merrill. [*5, *25, 27, *28, *29, *30, *38, *44, 48, *49, *55, 58, *63, *65, *68, *69, 71, *72, *73, *76, 81, *82, *83, *84, *85, 88, *94, 97, 99, 100, Intro.]

Clark, G., & Zimmerman, E. (1983). At the age of six, I gave up a magnificent career as a painter: Seventy years of research about identifying students with superior abilities in the visual arts. *Gifted Child Quarterly, 27,* 180–184. [43]

Clark, G., & Zimmerman, E. (Eds.). (1984). *Educating artistically talented students.* Syracuse, NY: Syracuse University Press. [43]

Clark, R. (1983). *Family life and school achievement: Why poor black children succeed or fail.* Chicago: University of Chicago Press. [92, 97]

Clark, W. H., & Hankins, N. E. (1985). Giftedness and conflict. *Roeper Review, 8,* 50–53. [25, 86]

Clendening, C. P., & Davies, R. A. (1980). *Creating programs for the gifted: A guide for teachers, librarians and students.* New York: Bowker. [*5, 54, *56, Intro.]

Clendening, C. P., & Davies, R. A. (1983). *Challenging the gifted.* New York: Bowker. [44]

Cohen, L. (1989). What the children taught me: Comments on "The purpose of education for gifted black students." In C. J. Maker & S. W. Schiever (Eds.), *Critical issues in gifted education: Defensible programs for cultural and ethnic minorities: Vol. 2* (pp. 246–254). Austin, TX: Pro-Ed. [91]

Coker, H. A. (1983). The gifted in a developing society: The Nigeria case. In B. M. Shore, F. Gagné, S. Larivée, R. H. Tali, & R. E. Tremblay (Eds.), *Face to face with giftedness* (pp. 328–345). New York: Trillium. [2]

Colangelo, N. (1979). Myths and stereotypes of gifted students: Awareness for the classroom teacher. In N. Colangelo, C. H. Foxley, & D. Dustin (Eds.), *Multicultural nonsexist education: A human relations approach* (pp. 375–381). Dubuque, IA: Kendall/Hunt. [*69, 70, Intro.]

Colangelo, N. (1985). Counseling needs of culturally diverse gifted students. *Roeper Review, 8,* 33–35. [77]

Colangelo, N., & Brower, P. (1987a). Gifted youngsters and their siblings: Long-term impact of labeling on their academic and personal self-concept. *Roeper Review, 10,* 101–103. [76, 88]

Colangelo, N., & Brower, P. (1987b). Labeling gifted youngsters: Long term impact on families. *Gifted Child Quarterly, 31*(2), 75–78. [76, 88]

Colangelo, N., & Dettman, D. (1983). A review of research on parents and families of gifted children. *Exceptional Children, 50,* 20–27. [67, 69, 70, 73]

Colangelo, N., & Kelly, K. R. (1983). A study of student, parent, and teacher attitudes toward gifted programs and gifted students. *Gifted Child Quarterly, 27,* 107–110. [69]

Colangelo, N., & Pfleger, L. R. (1979). Academic self-concept of gifted high school students. In N. Colangelo & R. T. Zaffrann (Eds.), *New voices in counseling the gifted* (pp. 188–193). Dubuque, IA: Kendall/Hunt. [*84, Intro.]

Colangelo, N., & Zaffrann, R. T. (Eds.). (1979). *New voices in counseling the gifted.* Dubuque, IA: Kendall/Hunt. [69, 70, 78, Intro.]

Coleman, E. B., & Shore, B. M. (in press). Problem-solving processes of high and average performers in physics. *Journal for the Education of the Gifted.* [47]

Coleman, J., & Fults, B. (1982). Self-concept and the gifted classroom: The role of social comparisons. *Gifted Child Quarterly, 26,* 116–120. [84]

Coleman, J., & Fults, B. (1985). Special class placement, level of intelligence, and the self-concepts of gifted children: A social comparison perspective. *Remedial and Special Education, 6,* 7–12. [84]

Coleman, L. J. (1985). *Schooling the gifted.* Menlo Park, CA: Addison-Wesley. [39, *94, Intro.]

Colon, P. T., & Treffinger, D. J. (1980). Providing for the gifted in the regular classroom—Am I really MAD? *Roeper Review, 3,* 18–21. [35]

Colson, S. (1980). The evaluation of a community-based career education program at Texas A&M University for gifted and talented high school senior students as an administrative model for an alternative program. *Gifted Child Quarterly, 24,* 101–106. [54]

Compton, M. F. (1982). The gifted underachiever in the middle school. *Roeper Review, 4*(4), 23–25. [51]

Conant, J. B. (1958). *The identification and education of the academically talented student in the American secondary school.* Washington: National Education Association. [*56, *57, Intro.]

Congdon, P. (1979). Helping gifted children: Some suggestions for parents. In J. J. Gallagher (Ed.), *Gifted children: Reaching their potential* (pp. 347–363). New York: Trillium. [*71]

Congdon, P. (1980). Helping gifted children: Some suggestions for parents. In R. Povey (Ed.), *Educating the gifted child* (pp. 143–157). London: Harper & Row. [51, 67, *101]

Conger, J., & Keane, S. P. (1981). Social skills intervention in the treatment of isolated or withdrawn children. *Psychological Bulletin, 90,* 478–495. [73]

Conroy, E. H. (1987). Primary prevention for gifted students: A parent education
group. *Elementary School Guidance and Counseling, 22,* 110–116. [67]

Cooke, G. J. (1980). Scientifically gifted children. *G/C/T,* No. 12, 17–18. [65]

Cooley, D., Chauvin, J. C., & Karnes, F. A. (1984). Gifted females: A comparison of
attitudes by male and female teachers. *Roeper Review,* 6(3), 164–167. [101]

Cooper, S. E., & Robinson, D. A. (1987). The effects of a structured academic support group on GPA and self-concept of ability. *Techniques, 3,* 260–264. [99]

Corn, A. L., & Bishop, V. E. (1984). Educating teachers of the gifted-handicapped:
A survey of teacher education programs. *Journal for the Education of the Gifted,
7,* 137–145. [94]

Cornell, D. G. (1983). Gifted children: The impact of positive labeling on the family
system. *American Journal of Orthopsychiatry, 53,* 322–335. [76, 88]

Cornell, D. G. (1984). *Families of gifted children.* Ann Arbor, MI: UMI Research
Press. [69, *70, *71, 72, *76, 83, *88, Intro.]

Cornell, D. G. (1989). Child adjustment and parent use of the term "gifted." *Gifted
Child Quarterly, 33,* 63–64. [70, 78, 88]

Cornell, D. G., Callahan, C. M., Bassin, L. E., & Ramsay, S. G. (1991). Affective
development in accelerated students. In W. T. Southern & E. D. Jones (Eds.),
Academic acceleration of gifted children (pp. 74–101). New York: Teachers College Press. [6, 28, 80]

Cornell, D. G., Callahan, C. M., & Loyd, B. (1991). Socioemotional adjustment of
adolescent girls enrolled in a residential acceleration program. *Gifted Child
Quarterly, 35,* 58–66. [80]

Cornell, D. G., Callahan, C. M., & Loyd, B. H. (in press). Personality growth of
female early college entrants: A controlled, prospective study. *Gifted Child
Quarterly.* [80]

Cornell, D. G., & Grossberg, I. N. (1986). Siblings of children in gifted programs.
Journal for the Education of the Gifted, 9, 253–264. [76, 88]

Cornell, D. G., & Grossberg, I. N. (1987). Family environment and personality adjustment in gifted program children. *Gifted Child Quarterly, 31,* 59–64. [67,
70, 73, 83]

Cornell, D. G., & Grossberg, I. N. (1989). Parent use of the term "gifted": Correlates with family environment and child adjustment. *Journal for the Education
of the Gifted, 12,* 218–230. [69, 70, 88]

Cornell, D. G., Pelton, G. M., Bassin, L. E., Landrum, M., Ramsay, S. G., Cooley,
M. R., Lynch, K. A., & Hamrick, E. (1990). Self-concept and peer status of
gifted program youth. *Journal of Educational Psychology, 82,* 456–463. [74,
84]

Cornfield, R. J., Coyle, K., Durrant, B., McCutcheon, C., Pollard, J., & Stratton, W.
(1987). *Making the grade: Evaluating student progress.* Toronto: Prentice-Hall.
[25]

Cornish, R. L. (1968). Parents', pupils', and teachers' perception of the gifted child's
ability. *Gifted Child Quarterly, 12,* 14–17. [9]

Coutant, M. F. (1983). A constituency for the gifted and talented. In A. H. Roldan

(Ed.), *Talented and gifted children, youth and adults: Their social perspectives and culture* (pp. 142–143). Manila: Reading Dynamics (Monroe, NY: Trillium). [*26, 55]

Cox, J., & Daniel, N. (1983). Special problems and special populations: Identification. *G/C/T*, No. 30, 54–61. [93, 101]

Cox, J., & Daniel, N. (1984). Comprehensive programs: The role of the state agency and other partners in education. *G/C/T*, No. 33, 57–60. [5]

Cox, J., & Daniel, N. (1985). The Richardson survey concludes. *G/C/T*, No. 37, 33–36. [5, 23, 52]

Cox, J., Daniel, N., & Boston, B. (1985). *Educating able learners: Programs and promising practices.* Austin: University of Texas Press. [*4, 5, 8, 17, 29, *35, 43, *44, *53, *54, *55, *62, *88, *91, Intro.]

Crabbe, A. B. (1982). Creating a brighter future: An update on the future problem solving program. *Journal for the Education of the Gifted, 5,* 2–9. [60]

Cramond, B., & Martin, C. E. (1987). Inservice and preservice teachers' attitudes toward the academically brilliant. *Gifted Child Quarterly, 31,* 15–19. [69]

Craven, C. J. (1980). The effect of the stimulus term "mentally gifted" on the formation of impressions of experienced educators who are advanced graduate students. *Dissertation Abstracts International, 41*(12), Section A, 5055. [88]

Criscuolo, N. P. (1986). 15 effective ways to challenge gifted readers. *G/C/T, 9*(2), 39–40. [50]

Crittenden, M. R., Kaplan, M. H., & Heim, J. K. (1984). Developing effective study skills and self-confidence in academically able adolescents. *Gifted Child Quarterly, 28,* 25–30. [99]

Crutsinger, C. (1980). Together we are learning. *G/C/T*, No. 14, 50–57. [5]

Cushenbery, D. C., & Howell, H. (1974). *Reading and the gifted child: A guide for teachers.* Springfield, IL: Thomas. [*33, *36, *50, 51, *56, *58, *64, 81, Intro.]

Daniels, P. (1983). *Teaching the gifted learning-disabled child.* Rockville, MD: Aspen. [2, *95, Intro.]

Daniels, R. R. (1986). The SOI-LA test for elementary school. *G/C/T, 9*(2), 15–17. [35]

Dar, Y., & Resh, N. (1986). Classroom intellectual composition and academic achievement. *American Educational Research Journal, 23,* 357–374. [30]

Daurio, S. P. (1979). Educational enrichment versus acceleration: A review of the literature. In W. C. George, S. J. Cohn, & J. C. Stanley (Eds.), *Educating the gifted: Acceleration and enrichment* (pp. 13–63). Baltimore: Johns Hopkins University Press. [6, 28, *80]

Davidson, J. E., & Sternberg, R. J. (1984). The role of insight in intellectual giftedness. *Gifted Child Quarterly, 28,* 58–64. [45]

Davis, G. A. (1981). Personal creative thinking techniques. *Gifted Child Quarterly, 25,* 99–101. [58]

Davis, G. A., & Rimm, S. B. (1989). *Education of the gifted and talented* (2nd ed.). Englewood Cliffs, NJ: Prentice-Hall. [10, *16, *65, 85, 98, 99, Intro.]

Dawkins, B. (1978). Do gifted junior high school students need reading instruction? *Journal for the Education of the Gifted, 2,* 3–9. [50]

Dearborn, P. (1979). Will you come and join the dance: An invitation to gifted writers. *Journal for the Education of the Gifted, 2*, 173–180. [47]

de Bono, E. (1982). *de Bono's thinking course*. London: British Broadcasting Corporation. [46]

de Bono, E., & Maier, N. (1983). Teaching thinking to the gifted. In B. M. Shore, F. Gagné, S. Larivée, R. H. Tali, & R. E. Tremblay (Eds.), *Face to face with giftedness* (pp. 438–447). New York: Trillium. [*59]

DeBrun, J. E., & Schaff, J. F. (1982). Community-based science research program for gifted and talented high school students. *Roeper Review, 5*, 12–14. [54]

DeHaan, R., & Wilson, R. (1958). Identification of the gifted. In N. B. Henry (Ed.), *Education for the gifted: Fifty-seventh yearbook of the National Society for the Study of Education: Part II* (pp. 166–192). Chicago: University of Chicago Press. [11, *12, *14]

Deiulio, J. M. (1984). Attitudes of school counselors and psychologists toward gifted children. *Journal for the Education of the Gifted, 7*, 164–169. [22, 69, 77, 88]

DeLeon, J. (1983). Cognitive style differences and the underrepresentation of Mexican Americans in programs for the gifted. *Journal for the Education of the Gifted, 6*, 167–174. [23]

Delisle, J. R. (1982a). Learning to underachieve. *Roeper Review, 4*(4), 16–23. [98]

Delisle, J. R. (1982b). Reaching towards tomorrow: Career education and guidance for the gifted and talented. *Roeper Review, 5* (2), 8–11. [49, 90]

Delisle, J. R. (1984). The biased model of career education and guidance for gifted adolescents. *Journal for the Education of the Gifted, 8*, 95–106. [49]

Delisle, J. R. (1985a). Counseling gifted persons: A lifelong concern. *Roeper Review, 8*, 4–5. [82, *98]

Delisle, J. R. (1985b). Vocational problems. In J. Freeman (Ed.), *The psychology of gifted children: Perspectives on development and education* (pp. 367–378). Chichester, England: Wiley. [*49, *66]

Delisle, J. R. (1986). Death with honors: Suicide among gifted adolescents. *Journal of Counseling and Development, 64*, 558–560. [72]

Dellas, M., & Gaier, E. (1970). Identification of creativity. *Psychological Bulletin, 73*, 55–73. [89]

Delp, J. L., & Martinson, R. A. (1975). *The gifted and talented: A handbook for parents*. Ventura, CA: Ventura County Superintendent of Education for the National/State Leadership Training Institute for the Gifted and Talented. [Intro.]

Denton, C., & Postlethwaite, K. (1984). A study of the effectiveness of teacher-based identification of pupils with high ability in the secondary school. *Gifted Education International, 2*, 100–106. [21]

Derevensky, J. L., & Coleman, E. B. (1989). Gifted children's fears. *Gifted Child Quarterly, 33*, 65–68. [78]

Dettman, D. F., & Colangelo, N. (1980). A functional model for counseling parents of gifted students. *Gifted Child Quarterly, 24*, 158–161. [67, 68]

Dettmer, P. (1980). The extended classroom: A gold mine for gifted students. *Journal for the Education of the Gifted, 3*, 133–143. [55]

Dettmer, P. (1985a). Attitudes of school role groups toward learning needs of gifted students. *Roeper Review, 7*, 253–257. [69]

Dettmer, P. (1985b). Gifted program scope, structure and evaluation. *Roeper Review,* 7, 146–152. [52]

Dewey, J. (1938). *Experience and education.* New York: Macmillan. [60]

D'Heurle, A., Mellinger, J., & Haggard, E. (1959). Personality, intellectual, and achievement patterns in gifted children. *Psychological Monographs, 73* (No. 483). [83]

Dickson, W. P. (1985). Thought-provoking software: Juxtaposing symbol systems. *Educational Researcher, 14*(5), 30–38. [45]

Diessner, R. (1983). The relation between cognitive abilities and moral development in intellectually gifted children. *G/C/T,* No. 28, 15–17. [48]

Dirkes, M. A. (1981). Only the gifted can do it. *Educational Horizons, 59*(3), 138–142. [44]

Dirkes, M. A. (1985). Metacognition: Students in charge of their thinking. *Roeper Review, 8*(2), 96–100. [59]

Dishart, M. (1983). Psychosocial facilitators, enhancers, and inhibitors of gifted children. In B. M. Shore, F. Gagné, S. Larivée, R. H. Tali, & R. E. Tremblay (Eds.), *Face to face with giftedness* (pp. 27–38). New York: Trillium. [27]

Doherty, E., & Evans, L. (1981a). Help! Need direction in independent study? *G/C/T,* No. 16, 43–46. [65]

Doherty, E., & Evans, L. (1981b). Independent study process: They can think, can't they? *Journal for the Education of the Gifted, 4,* 106–111. [65]

Dole, J. A., & Adams, P. J. (1983). Reading curriculum for gifted readers: A survey. *Gifted Child Quarterly, 27*(2), 64–72. [50, 65]

Dolny, C. (1985). University of Toronto Schools' gifted students' career and family plans. *Roeper Review, 7*(3), 160–162. [49]

Donald, J. G. (1983). Knowledge structures: Methods for exploring course content. *Journal of Higher Education, 54*(1), 31–41. [31]

Dorn, C. M. (1984). The arts as academic education. *Art Education,* 16–19. [43]

Dover, A. (1983). Computers and the gifted. *Gifted Child Quarterly, 27,* 81–85. [45]

Dover, A., & Shore, B. M. (1991). Giftedness and flexibility on a mathematical set-breaking task. *Gifted Child Quarterly, 35,* 99–105. [62]

Dowdall, C. B., & Colangelo, N. (1982). Underachieving gifted students: Review and implications. *Gifted Child Quarterly, 26,* 179–184. [97, 98, 99]

Dubner, F. S. (1984). IMPACT: A high school gifted program that works. *Roeper Review, 7,* 41–43. [87]

Dunn, R., & Griggs, S. (1985). Teaching and counselling gifted students with their learning style preferences. Two case studies. *G/C/T,* No. 41, 40–43. [35, 65]

Dunstan, J. (1978). *Paths to excellence and the Soviet school.* Windsor, Berks., England: NFER Publishing. [2]

Dunstan, J. (1983). *Attitudes to provision for gifted children.* In B. M. Shore, F. Gagné, S. Larivée, R. H. Tali, & R. E. Tremblay (Eds.), *Face to face with giftedness* (pp. 290–327). New York: Trillium. [2]

Durkin, D. (1966). *Children who read early.* New York: Teachers College Press. [75]

Dweck, C. S., & Bush, C. S. (1976). Sex differences in learned helplessness: I. Differential debilitation with peer and adult evaluators. *Developmental Psychology, 12,* 147–156. [100]

Dweck, C. S., Davidson, W., Nelson, S., & Enna, B. (1978). Sex differences in learned helplessness: II. The contingencies of evaluative feedback in the classroom and III. An experimental analysis. *Developmental Psychology, 14,* 268–276. [100]

Eason, B. L., Smith, T. L., & Steen, M. F. (1978). Perceptual motor programs for the gifted-handicapped. *Journal for the Education of the Gifted, 2,* 10–21. [94]

Ebmeier, H., Dyche, B., Taylor, P., & Hall, M. (1985). An empirical comparison of two program models for elementary gifted education. *Gifted Child Quarterly, 29,* 15–19. [9]

Eccles, J. S. (1985). Why doesn't Jane run? Sex differences in educational and occupational patterns. In F. D. Horowitz & M. O'Brien (Eds.), *The gifted and talented: Developmental perspectives* (pp. 251–295). Washington, DC: American Psychological Association. [86, 90, *99]

Edlind, E. P., & Haensly, P. A. (1985). Gifts of mentorships. *Gifted Child Quarterly, 29,* 55–60. [55, 87]

Ehrenwald, J. (1963). *Neurosis in the family and patterns of psychosocial defense.* New York: Norton. [70, 71]

Ehrlich, V. Z. (1978). *The Astor program for gifted children: PreKindergarten through grade three.* New York: Columbia University, Teachers College. [*75]

Ehrlich, V. Z. (1980). Identifying giftedness in the early years: From three through seven. In S. N. Kaplan (Ed.), *Educating the preschool/primary gifted and talented* (pp. 3–22). Ventura, CA: Office of the Ventura County Superintendent of Schools for the National/State Leadership Training Institute for the Gifted and Talented. [75]

Ehrlich, V. Z. (1981). A philosophy of education of the gifted in early childhood. In A. H. Kramer, D. Bitan, N. Butler-Por, A. Evyatar, & E. Landau (Eds.), *Gifted children—Challenging their potential: New perspectives and alternatives* (pp. 217–221). New York: Trillium. [*40]

Ehrlich, V. Z. (1982). *Gifted children: A guide for parents and teachers.* Englewood Cliffs, NJ: Prentice-Hall. [Reissued by Trillium, Monroe, NY] [75]

Elkind, D. (1981). *The hurried child: Growing up too fast too soon.* Newton, MA: Addison-Wesley. [6, 13, 71]

Elkind, D. (1987). *Miseducation: Preschoolers at risk.* New York: Knopf. [6, 71]

Ellis, A., & Harper, R. (1975). *A new guide to rational living.* Englewood Cliffs, NJ: Prentice-Hall. [72]

Elton, C. F., & Rose, H. A. (1967). Traditional sex attitudes and discrepant ability measures in college women. *Journal of Counseling Psychology, 14,* 538–543. [101]

Enzmann, A. M. (1963). A comparison of academic achievement of gifted students enrolled in regular and separate curriculums. *Gifted Child Quarterly, 7,* 176–179. [30]

Ernest, J. (1978). Mathematics and sex. *The American Mathematical Monthly, 83,* 595–614. [100, 101]

Espeland, P., & Galbraith, J. (1988). Watch your language. *Challenge, 7*(1), 13–14. [100]

Evans de Bernard, A. (1985). Why Jose can't get in the gifted class: The bilingual child and standardized reading tests. *Roeper Review, 8,* 80–82. [23]

Evertson, C. M., Anderson, C. W., Anderson, L. M., & Brophy, J. E. (1980). Relationships between classroom behaviors and student outcomes in junior high mathematics and English classes. *American Educational Research Journal, 17,* 43–60. [42]

Exum, H. A., & Colangelo, N. (1981). Culturally diverse gifted: The need for ethnic identity development. *Roeper Review, 3*(4), 15–17. [91]

Fantini, M. D. (1981). A caring curriculum for gifted children. *Roeper Review, 3*(4), 3–4. [48]

Fatouros, C. (1986). Early identification of gifted children is crucial . . . but how should we go about it? *Gifted Education International, 4,* 24–28. [13]

Fearn, L., & Owen, J. J. (1984). The individual educational plan for gifted and talented students. *Roeper Review, 7,* 80–83. [38]

Feldhusen, J. F. (1983a). Eclecticism: A comprehensive approach to education of the gifted. In C. P. Benbow & J. C. Stanley (Eds.), *Academic precocity: Aspects of its development* (pp. 192–204). Baltimore: Johns Hopkins University Press. [87]

Feldhusen, J. (1983b). Multiple resources of multiple talents. In A. H. Roldan (Ed.), *Talented and gifted children, youth and adults: Their social perspectives and culture* (pp. 209–214). Manila: Reading Dynamics (Monroe, NY: Trillium). [*55, *66]

Feldhusen, J. (1985a). An introduction. In J. Feldhusen (Ed.), *Toward excellence in gifted education* (pp. 1–14). Denver: Love. [*31, *58, *62, *64, 80]

Feldhusen, J. F. (1985b). Summary. In J. F. Feldhusen, *Toward excellence in gifted education* (pp. 177–182). Denver: Love. [*4, *28, *47, *81]

Feldhusen, J. (1985c). The teacher of gifted students. *Gifted Education International, 3,* 87–93. [9, *31]

Feldhusen, J. (Ed.). (1985d). *Toward excellence in gifted education.* Denver: Love. [9, *55, Intro.]

Feldhusen, J. F. (1986). A conception of giftedness. In R. J. Sternberg & J. E. Davidson (Eds.), *Conceptions of giftedness* (pp. 112–127). Cambridge: Cambridge University Press. [*20, 72, *81, *84, *87]

Feldhusen, J. F., Asher, J. W., & Hoover, S. M. (1984). Problems in the identification of giftedness, talent, or ability. *Gifted Child Quarterly, 28,* 149–151. [24]

Feldhusen, J. F., & Baska, L. (1985). Identification and assessment of gifted and talented. In J. F. Feldhusen (Ed.), *Toward excellence in gifted education* (pp. 69–84). Denver: Love. [*21, *88]

Feldhusen, J. F., & Hoover, S. M. (1984). The gifted at risk in a place called school. *Gifted Child Quarterly, 28,* 9–11. [47]

Feldhusen, J. F., & Kolloff, G. (1978). A three stage model for gifted education. *G/C/T,* No. 4, 3–5 and 53–57. [8, 65]

Feldhusen, J. F., & Reilly, P. (1983). The Purdue Secondary Model for gifted education: A multi-service program. *Journal for the Education of the Gifted, 6,* 230–244. [64]

Feldhusen, J. F., & Robinson, A. (1986). The Purdue Secondary Model for gifted and talented youth. In J. S. Renzulli (Ed.), *Systems and models for developing programs for the gifted and talented* (pp. 153–179). Mansfield Center, CT: Creative Learning Press. [*43, 65]

Feldhusen, J. F., VanTassel-Baska, J., & Seeley, K. R. (1989). *Excellence in education of the gifted.* Denver: Love. [*65]

Feldman, D. H. (1979). The mysterious case of extreme giftedness. In A. H. Passow (Ed.), *The gifted and talented: Their education and development. Seventy-eighth yearbook of the National Society for the Study of Education: Part II* (pp. 335–351). Chicago: University of Chicago Press. [81]

Feldman, D. H. (1986). *Nature's gambit: Child prodigies and the development of human potential.* New York: Basic. [81]

Fenstermacher, G. D. (1982). To be or not to be gifted: What is the question? *Elementary School Journal, 82*(3), 229–303. [88]

Fichter, G. (1987). Special education for gifted children is a good idea. *Journal for the Education of the Gifted, 10,* 79–86. [3]

Fichter, G., & Swassing, R. H. (1985). Program implementation and evaluation. In R. H. Swassing (Ed.), *Teaching gifted children and adolescents* (pp. 402–430). Columbus, OH: Merrill. [*78]

Flack, J. D., & Feldhusen, J. F. (1983). Future studies in the curricular framework of the Purdue Three-Stage Model. *G/C/T,* No. 27, 2–9. [59]

Flack, J. D., & Lamb, P. (1984). Making use of gifted characters in literature. *G/C/T,* No. 34, 3–11. [50]

Fleming, E. S. (1985). Career preparation. In R. H. Swassing (Ed.), *Teaching gifted children and adolescents* (pp. 340–374). Columbus, OH: Merrill. [*36, *41, *49, *53, 54, *55]

Fleming, E. S., & Hollinger, C. L. (1981). The multidimensionality of talent in adolescent young women. *Journal for the Education of the Gifted, 4,* 188–197. [14]

Fleming, G. A. (1982). Mathematics. In N. E. A. Maier (Ed.), *Teaching the gifted: Challenging the average* (pp. 25–34). Toronto: University of Toronto Guidance Centre. [*62]

Flowers, J. V., Horsman, J., & Schwartz, B. (1982). *Raising your gifted child: How to determine, develop, and nurture your child's special abilities.* Englewood Cliffs, NJ: Prentice-Hall. [Intro.]

Foster, W. H. (1979). The unfinished task: An overview of procedures used to identify gifted. In N. Colangelo & R. T. Zaffrann (Eds.), *New voices in counseling the gifted* (pp. 63–75). Des Moines, IA: Kendall/Hunt. [*24]

Foster, W. H. (1981). Leadership: A conceptual framework for recognizing and educating. *Gifted Child Quarterly, 25,* 17–25. [85]

Foster, W. H. (1985). Helping a child toward individual excellence. In J. F. Feldhusen (Ed.), *Toward excellence in gifted education* (pp. 135–161). Denver: Love. [*53, 63]

Foster, W. H., & Seltzer, A. (1986). A portrayal of individual excellence in the urban ghetto. *Journal of Counseling and Development, 64,* 579–582. [92]

Foster, W. H., & Silverman, L. (1988). Leadership curriculum for the gifted. In J. VanTassel-Baska, J. Feldhusen, K. Seeley, G. Wheatley, L. Silverman, & W. H. Foster (Eds.), *Comprehensive curriculum for gifted learners* (pp. 356–373). Boston: Allyn & Bacon. [*85]

Fox, L. H. (1974). Facilitating educational development of mathematically precocious youth. In J. C. Stanley, D. P. Keating, & L. H. Fox (Eds.), *Mathematical talent: Discovery, description and development* (pp. 47–69). Baltimore: Johns Hopkins University Press. [65]

Fox, L. H. (1975, August). *Values and career interest of mathematically precocious youth.* Paper presented at the annual meeting of the American Psychological Association, Montreal. [101]

Fox, L. H. (1976a, August). *Changing behaviors and attitudes of gifted girls.* Paper presented at the annual meeting of the American Psychological Association, Washington, DC. [101]

Fox, L. H. (1976b). Identification and program planning: Models and methods. In D. P. Keating (Ed.), *Intellectual talent: Research and development* (pp. 32–54). Baltimore: Johns Hopkins University Press. [101]

Fox, L. H. (1976c). Sex differences in mathematical precocity: Bridging the gap. In D. P. Keating (Ed.), *Intellectual talent: Research and development* (pp. 183–214). Baltimore: Johns Hopkins University Press. [4, *18, *100, 101]

Fox, L. H. (1977a). Sex differences: Implications for program planning for the academically gifted. In J. C. Stanley, W. C. George, & H. C. Solano (Eds.), *The gifted and the creative: A 50 year perspective* (pp. 113–139). Baltimore: Johns Hopkins University Press. [*6]

Fox, L. H. (1977b). The effects of sex role socialization on mathematics participation and achievement. In L. H. Fox, E. Fennema, & J. Sherman, *Women and mathematics: Research perspectives for change* (pp. 1–77). Washington, DC: U.S. Department of Health, Education and Welfare, National Institute of Education. (NIE Paper in Education and Work: No. 8) [77]

Fox, L. H. (1978). Interest correlates to differential achievement of gifted students in mathematics. *Journal for the Education of the Gifted, 1,* 24–36. [86]

Fox, L. H. (1979a). Career education for gifted preadolescents. In W. C. George, S. J. Cohn, & J. C. Stanley (Eds.), *Educating the gifted: Acceleration and enrichment* (pp. 89–97). Baltimore: Johns Hopkins University Press. [*49]

Fox, L. H. (1979b). Changing times and the education of gifted girls. In J. J. Gallagher (Ed.), *Gifted children: Reaching their potential* (pp. 364–381). New York: Trillium. [55, *99, 101]

Fox, L. H. (1979c). Programs for the gifted and talented: An overview. In A. H. Passow (Ed.), *The gifted and talented: Their education and development. Seventy-eighth yearbook of the National Society for the Study of Education: Part I* (pp. 104–126). Chicago: University of Chicago Press. [54]

Fox, L. H. (1981a). Instruction for the gifted: Some promising practices. *Journal for the Education of the Gifted, 4,* 246–254. [62, 100, 101]

Fox, L. H. (1981b). Preparing gifted girls for future leadership roles. *G/C/T,* No. 17, 7–10. [100, 101]

Fox, L. H., Brody, L., & Tobin, D. (1979). *Women and mathematics: The impact of early intervention programs upon course-taking and attitudes in high school.* Baltimore: Johns Hopkins University, Intellectually Gifted Child Study Group. [101]

Fox, L. H., Brody, L. E., & Tobin, D. (1980). *Women and the mathematical mystique.* Baltimore: Johns Hopkins University Press. [Intro.]

Fox, L. H., & Tobin, D. (1978). Broadening career horizons for gifted girls. *G/C/T,* No. 4, 18–22, 45. [49]

Fox, L. H., & Tobin, D. (1988). Broadening career horizons for gifted girls (reprinted from Jan/Feb 1978). *Gifted Child Today, 11*(1), 9–13. [100]

Fox, L. H., & Turner, L. D. (1981). Gifted and creative female: In the middle school years. *American Middle School Education, 4,* 17–23. [100]

Franks, B., & Dolan, L. (1982). Affective characteristics of gifted children: Educational implications. *Gifted Child Quarterly, 26,* 172–178. [83]

Frasier, M. M. (1979). Counseling the culturally diverse gifted. In N. Colangelo & R. T. Zaffrann (Eds.), *New voices in counseling the gifted* (pp. 304–311). Dubuque, IA: Kendall/Hunt. [66]

Frasier, M. M. (1988). The gifted can be poor and minority, too. *Educational Leadership, 46*(6), 16–18. [91]

Frasier, M. M. (1989). Identification of gifted black students: Developing new perspectives. In C. J. Maker (Ed.), *Critical issues in gifted education: Vol. II. Defensible programs for cultural and ethnic minorities* (pp. 213–225). Austin, TX: Pro-ed. [23, 91]

Frasier, M. M., & McCannon, C. (1981). Using bibliotherapy with gifted children. *Gifted Child Quarterly, 25,* 81–85. [61]

Frederickson, R. H. (1979). Career development and the gifted. In N. Colangelo & R. Zaffrann (Eds.), *New voices in counseling the gifted* (pp. 264–276). Des Moines, IA: Kendall/Hunt. [*49, 66]

Frederickson, R. H. (1986). Preparing gifted and talented students for the world of work. *Journal of Counseling and Development, 64,* 556–557. [90]

Freehill, M. F. (1982). *Gifted children: Their psychology and education.* Ventura, CA: Office of the Ventura County Superintendent of Schools for the National/State Leadership Training Institute for the Gifted and Talented. (Original work published 1961) [18, 26, *38, *42, *46, *47, *54, 56, *59, Intro.]

Freeman, J. (1979). *Gifted children: Their identification and development in a social context.* Lancaster, England: MTP Press. [16, 74, 75, 83, Intro.]

Freeman, J. (1983). The IQ as a measure of intellectual giftedness. In B. M. Shore, F. Gagné, S. Larivée, R. H. Tali, & R. E. Tremblay (Eds.), *Face to face with giftedness* (pp. 91–96). New York: Trillium. [16]

Freeman, J. (1985a). A pedagogy for the gifted. In J. Freeman (Ed.), *The psychology of gifted children: Perspectives on development and education* (pp. 1–20). Chichester, England: Wiley. [46, *64, 82, Intro.]

Freeman, J. (1985b). Emotional aspects of giftedness. In J. Freeman (Ed.), *The psychology of gifted children* (pp. 247–264). Chichester, England: Wiley. [*51, 82]

French, J. N. (1982). The gifted learning disabled child: A challenge and some suggestions. *Roeper Review, 4*(3), 19–21. [95]

Friedman, P. G., Jenkins-Friedman, R., & Van Dyke, M. (1984). Identifying the leadership gifted: Self, peer, or teacher nominations? *Roeper Review, 7,* 91–94. [21, 85]

Frierson, E. C. (1965). Upper and lower status gifted children: A study of differences. *Exceptional Children, 32,* 83–90. [70]

Friesen, C. D. (1980). Problem solving: Meeting the needs of mathematically gifted students. *School Science and Mathematics, 80*(2), 127–130. [59]

Fuchs, D., & Fuchs, L. S. (1989). Effects of examiner familiarity on black, Caucasian, and Hispanic children: A meta-analysis. *Exceptional Children, 55,* 303–308. [17]

Fund for the Advancement of Education. (1953). *Bridging the gap between school and college. Evaluation Report No. 1.* New York: Author. [80]

Fund for the Advancement of Education. (1957). *They went to college early. Evaluation Report No. 2.* New York: Author. [80]

Gagné, F. (1985). Giftedness and talent: Reexamining a reexamination of the definitions. *Gifted Child Quarterly, 29,* 103–112. [*17]

Gagné, F. (1986). *Douance, talent et accélération du préscolaire à l'université.* Montréal: Centre Éducatif et Culturel. [6, 28]

Galbraith, B. W. (1985). Interlochen Arts Academy: Its guidelines for success. *Journal for the Education of the Gifted, 8,* 199–210. [43]

Gallagher, J. J. (1958). Peer acceptance of highly gifted children in elementary school. *The Elementary School Journal, 58,* 465–470. [74]

Gallagher, J. J. (1976). Needed: A new partnership for the gifted. In T. Gibson & P. Chennels (Eds.), *Gifted children: Looking for their future* (pp. 57–72). London: Latimer. [35]

Gallagher, J. J. (Ed.). (1979a). *Gifted children: Reaching their potential.* New York: Trillium. [Intro.]

Gallagher, J. J. (1979b). Issues in education of the gifted. In A. H. Passow (Ed.), *The gifted and talented: Their education and development. Seventy-eighth yearbook of the National Society for the Study of Education: Part I* (pp. 28–44). Chicago: University of Chicago Press. [5]

Gallagher, J. J. (1985). *Teaching the gifted child* (3rd ed.). Boston: Allyn & Bacon. [*9, 16, *27, 28, *42, *44, 56, *64, *65, 69, 85, *98, *99, Intro.]

Gallagher, J. J., Aschner, M. J., & Jenne, W. (1967). *Productive thinking of gifted children in classroom interaction.* Washington, DC (now Reston, VA): Council for Exceptional Children. [Intro.]

Gallagher, J. J., & Crowder, T. (1957). The adjustment of gifted children in the regular classroom. *Exceptional Children, 23,* 306–312, 317–319. [74]

Gallagher, J. J., & Rogge, W. (1966). The gifted. *Review of Educational Research, 36,* 37–54. [99]

Gallagher, J. J., Weiss, P., Oglesby, K., & Thomas, T. (1983). *The status of gifted/talented education: United States survey of needs, practices, and policies.* Los Angeles: National/State Leadership Training Institute for the Gifted and Talented. [*85]

Ganapole, S. J. (1982). Program evaluation: Measuring the educational outcomes of gifted programs. *Roeper Review, 5,* 4–7. [52]

Gardiner, B. (1983). Stepping into a learning styles program. *Roeper Review, 6,* 90–92. [35]

Gardner, H. (1983). *Frames of mind: The theory of multiple intelligences*. New York: Basic. [14, 27, Intro.]

Gardner, H., & Hatch, T. (1989). Multiple intelligences go to school: Educational implications of the theory of multiple intelligences. *Educational Researcher, 18*(8), 4–10. [46, Intro.]

Garrison, L. (1989). Programming for the gifted American Indian student. In C. J. Maker (Ed.), *Critical issues in gifted education: Defensible programs for cultural and ethnic minorities* (pp. 116–127). Austin, TX: Pro-Ed. [91]

Garrison, V. S., Stronge, J. H., & Smith, C. R. (1986). Are gifted girls encouraged to achieve their occupational potential? *Roeper Review, 9,* 101–104. [90]

Gartner, A., Kohler, M., & Riessman, F. (1972). *Children teach children*. New York: Harper & Row. [57]

Gath, D., Tennent, G., & Pidduck, R. (1970a). Educational characteristics of bright delinquents. *Journal of Educational Psychology, 40,* 216–219. [96]

Gath, D., Tennent, G., & Pidduck, R. (1970b). Psychiatric and social characteristics of bright delinquents. *British Journal of Psychology, 116,* 515–516. [96]

Gath, D., Tennent, G., & Pidduck, R. (1971). Criminological characteristics of bright delinquents. *British Journal of Criminology, 11,* 275–279. [96]

Gear, G. (1978). Effects of training on teachers' accuracy in the identification of gifted children. *Gifted Child Quarterly, 22,* 90–97. [9]

Geffen, L. (1989). Recent doctoral dissertation research on gifted. *Roeper Review, 11,* 173–174. [Intro.]

Genesee, F. (1987). *Learning through two languages: Studies of immersion and bilingual education*. Cambridge, MA: Newbury House. [47]

Gensley, J. (1979). Parent perspective: Only the learner can learn. In J. C. Gowan, J. Khatena, & E. P. Torrance (Eds.), *Educating the ablest: A book of readings on the education of gifted children* (2nd ed., pp. 261–262). Itasca, IL: Peacock. [*55]

George, K. (1983). Native American Indian: Perception of gifted characteristics. In B. M. Shore, F. Gagné, S. Larivée, R. H. Tali, & R. Tremblay (Eds.), *Face to face with giftedness* (pp. 223–238, 246, 247). New York: Trillium. [23, 91]

George, K. (1989). Imagining and defining giftedness. In C. J. Maker (Ed.), *Critical issues in gifted education: Defensible programs for cultural and ethnic minorities* (pp. 107–112). Austin, TX: Pro-Ed. [91]

George, P. G., & Gallagher, J. J. (1978). Children's thoughts about the future: A comparison of gifted and non-gifted students. *Journal for the Education of the Gifted, 2,* 33–42. [41]

George, W. C. (1976). Accelerating mathematics instruction for the mathematically talented. *Gifted Child Quarterly, 20,* 246–261. [*62]

George, W. C., Cohn, S. J., & Stanley, J. C. (Eds.). (1979). *Educating the gifted: Acceleration and enrichment*. Baltimore: Johns Hopkins University Press. [8, 24, *87, Intro.]

George, W. C., & Denham, S. A. (1976). Curriculum experimentation for the mathematically gifted. In D. P. Keating (Ed.), *Intellectual talent: Research and development* (pp. 103–131). Baltimore: Johns Hopkins University Press. [*7, *62]

Getzels, J. W. (1979). The art student to fine artist: Potential problem finding and performance. In A. H. Passow (Ed.), *The gifted and the talented: Education and development. Seventy-eighth yearbook of the National Society for the Study of Education: Part I* (pp. 372–387). Chicago: University of Chicago Press. [*59]

Getzels, J. W. (1981). Problem finding and the nature and nurture of giftedness. In A. H. Kramer, D. Bitan, N. Butler-Por, A. Evyatar, & E. Landau (Eds.), *Gifted children: Challenging their potential* (pp. 1–20). New York: Trillium. [*48, 59]

Getzels, J. W., & Csikszentmihalyi, M. (1976). *The creative vision: A longitudinal study of problem finding in art.* New York: Wiley. [43, 45]

Getzels, J. W., & Jackson, P. W. (1962). *Creativity and intelligence: Explorations with gifted students.* New York: Wiley. [83, 89]

Ghatala, E. S., Levin, J. R., Pressley, M., & Lodico, M. G. (1985). Training cognitive strategy-monitoring in children. *American Educational Research Journal, 22,* 199–215. [46]

Gibney, T. (1982). The gifted as problem solvers in elementary schools. *Roeper Review, 4*(4), 13–14. [59]

Gibson, J., & Chennells, P. (Eds.). (1976). *Gifted children: Looking to their future.* London: Latimer. (Also available from Trillium Press, NY) [Intro.]

Gifted students as teachers (1981). *Gifted Children Newsletter, 2*(11), 7. [57]

Gilligan, C., & Phelps, E. B. (1988). *Seeking connection: New insights and questions for teachers. A paper based on the research studies of adolescents and of schools conducted by the Center for the Study of Gender, Education and Human Development, 1983–1988.* Cambridge, MA: Harvard Graduate School of Education. [100]

Glaser, D. (1978). Computers . . . are all dinosaurs dead? *G/C/T,* No. 4, 14–17, 46–50. [65]

Glazer, S. P., & Shore, B. M. (1984). *The social and academic success of younger-than-average aged students at McGill University.* Montreal: McGill University, Centre for Teaching and Learning Services (now Centre for University Teaching and Learning). [6, 51]

Glidden-Flickinger, G. (1982). Gifted and talented education summer institute. *Journal for the Education of the Gifted, 5,* 209–212. [93]

Goertzel, M. G., Goertzel, V., & Goertzel, T. G. (1978). *300 eminent personalities.* San Francisco: Jossey-Bass. [87, 94]

Goertzel, V., & Goertzel, M. G. (1962). *Cradles of eminence.* Boston: Little, Brown. [87, 94]

Gold, M. J. (1965). *Education of the intellectually gifted.* Columbus, OH: Merrill. [*4, *17, 19, *26, 29, *40, *51, *79, 97, 98, Intro.]

Gold, M. J. (1979). Teachers and mentors. In A. H. Passow (Ed.), *The gifted and the talented: Their education and development. Seventy-eighth yearbook of the National Society for the Study of Education: Part I* (pp. 272–288). Chicago: University of Chicago Press. [*9]

Goldberg, M. L. (1958). Motivation of the gifted. In N. B. Henry (Ed.), *Education for the gifted: Fifty-seventh yearbook of the National Society for the Study of Education: Part I* (pp. 87–107). Chicago: University of Chicago Press. [81]

Goldberg, M. L. (1986). Issues in the education of gifted and talented children: Part II. *Roeper Review, 9,* 43–50. [35, 39]

Goldberg, M. L., & Passow, A. H. (1980). The effects of ability grouping. In A. H. Passow (Ed.), *Education for gifted children and youth: An old issue—A new challenge* (pp. 77–81). Ventura, CA: Office of the County Superintendent of Schools for the National/State Leadership Training Institute for the Gifted and Talented. (Original work published 1962) [30]

Goldberg, M. L., Passow, A. H., Camm, D. S., & Neill, R. D. (1966). *A comparison of mathematics programs for able junior high school students: Vol. 1. Final report.* Washington, DC: U.S. Office of Education, Bureau of Research. (Project No. 3-0381) [8]

Goldberg, M. L., Passow, A. H., Justman, J., & Hogue, G. (1965). *The effects of ability grouping.* New York: Teachers College Press. [98]

Goldberg, M. L., Passow, A. H., & Lorge, I. (1980). Issues in the social education of the academically talented. In A. H. Passow (Ed.), *Education for gifted and talented children and youth: An old issue—A new challenge* (pp. 45–59). Ventura, CA: Office of the Ventura County Superintendent of Education for the National/State Leadership Training Institute for the Gifted and Talented. (Original work published 1958) [31, *47, *64, 79]

Goldman, N. T., & Rosenfeld, S. (1985). Meeting the needs of preschool gifted children. In R. H. Swassing (Ed.), *Teaching gifted children and adolescents* (pp. 92–133). Columbus, OH: Merrill. [23]

Golicz, H. J. (1982). Use of Estes attitude scales with gifted underachievers. *Roeper Review, 4*(4), 22–23. [*97]

Gonzalez, J., & Hayes, A. (1988). Psychosocial aspects of the development of gifted underachievers: Review and implications. *Exceptional Child, 35,* 39–51. [99]

Goodrum, S., & Irons, V. (1981). Monitoring programmed inservice preparation of teachers for rural gifted students. *Journal for the Education of the Gifted, 4,* 270–277. [93]

Gowan, J. C. (1979a). Differentiated guidance for the gifted: A developmental view. In J. C. Gowan, J. Khatena, & E. P. Torrance (Eds.), *Educating the ablest: A book of readings on the education of gifted children* (2nd ed., pp. 190–199). Itasca, IL: Peacock. [*53, 77, 78, 86]

Gowan, J. C. (1979b). Guiding the creative development of the gifted and talented. In N. Colangelo & R. T. Zaffrann (Eds.), *New voices in counseling the gifted* (pp. 210–224). Dubuque, IA: Kendall/Hunt. [86]

Gowan, J. C. (1979c). The education of disadvantaged gifted youth. In J. C. Gowan, J. Khatena, & E. P. Torrance (Eds.), *Educating the ablest: A book of readings on the education of gifted children* (2nd ed., pp. 329–341). Itasca, IL: Peacock. [*53]

Gowan, J. C. (1984). Art and music as stimulants to right hemisphere imagery and creativity. In A. B. Crabbe, G. A. Davis, J. C. Gowan, J. Khatena, R. Sakai, M. I. Stein, J. L. Steinberg, S. N. Tara, C. W. Taylor, & E. P. Torrance, *New directions in creativity research* (pp. 81–84). Ventura, CA: Office of the Ventura County Superintendent of Schools for the National/State Leadership Training Institute for the Gifted and Talented. [43]

Gowan, J. C., & Bruch, C. B. (1971). *The academically talented student and guidance.* Boston: Houghton Mifflin. [*10, *25, 67, *79, 82, *89, *94, Intro.]

Gowan, J. C., & Demos, G. D. (1964). *The education and guidance of the ablest.* Springfield, IL: Thomas. [*79]

Gowan, J. C., Demos, G. D., & Kokaska, C. J. (Eds.). (1972). *The guidance of exceptional children: A book of readings* (2nd ed.). New York: McKay. [99]

Gowan, J. C., Khatena, J., & Torrance, E. P. (Eds.). (1979a). *Educating the ablest: A book of readings on the education of gifted children.* Itasca, IL: Peacock. [Intro.]

Gowan, J. C., Khatena, J., & Torrance, E. P. (1979b). Introduction to chapter 4: Curriculum. In J. C. Gowan, J. Khatena, & E. P. Torrance (Eds.), *Educating the ablest: A book of readings on the education of gifted children* (pp. 128–130). Itasca, IL: Peacock. [*64]

Grant, C. (1989). Black students and education: Points for consideration. In C. J. Maker & S. W. Schiever (Eds.), *Critical issues in gifted education: Defensible programs for cultural and ethnic minorities: Vol. 2* (pp. 275–280). Austin, TX: Pro-Ed. [91]

Grau, P. N. (1985). Counseling the gifted girl. *G/C/T,* No. 38, 8–11. [100]

Gray, W. A. (1984). Mentoring gifted talented creative students on an initial student teaching practicum: Guidelines and benefits. *Gifted Education International, 2,* 121–128. [55]

Greene, J. W., Malley-Crist, J., & Cansler, P. (1978). Chapel Hill services to the gifted handicapped. *G/C/T,* No. 4, 29–33. [94]

Greenstadt, W. M. (1981). Parents of gifted children: Coping with anxieties. In B. S. Miller & M. Price (Eds.), *The gifted child, the family, and the community* (pp. 77–82). New York: Walker. [*70, 71]

Gregory, A. (1982). Applying the Purdue Three-Stage Model for gifted education to the development of art education for students. *G/C/T,* No. 25, 23–26. [65]

Gregory, E. H., & March, E. (1985). Early entrance program at California State University, Los Angeles. *Gifted Child Quarterly, 29,* 83–86. [80]

Gregory, E. H., & Stevens-Long, J. (1986). Coping skills among highly gifted adolescents. *Journal for the Education of the Gifted, 9,* 147–155. [80]

Grenier, M. E. (1985). Gifted children and other siblings. *Gifted Child Quarterly, 29,* 164–167. [76, 88]

Griffen, L. (1984). Attitudes of public school administrators toward gifted, gifted-handicapped, handicapped and normal students and relationship to administrator belief system. *Dissertation Abstracts International, 45*(05), Section A, 1342. [88]

Griffin, W. M. (1975). Schedules, bells, groups, and independent study. In W. Barbe & J. Renzulli (Eds.), *Psychology and education of the gifted* (2nd ed., pp. 330–335). New York: Irvington. [25]

Griggs, S., & Price, G. (1980). A comparison between the learning styles of gifted versus average suburban junior high students. *Roeper Review, 3,* 7–9. [83]

Grossberg, I. N., & Cornell, D. G. (1988). Relationship between personality adjustment and high intelligence: Terman versus Hollingworth. *Exceptional Children, 55,* 266–272. [27, 73]

Guilford, J. P. (1967). *The nature of human intelligence.* New York: McGraw-Hill. [27]

Guilford, J. P. (1977). *Way beyond the IQ.* Buffalo, NY: Creative Education Foundation. [27]

Guskin, S. L., Zimmerman, E., Okolo, C., & Peng, C. Y. J. (1986). Being labeled gifted or talented: Meanings and effects perceived by students in special programs. *Gifted Child Quarterly, 30*(2), 61–65. [88]

Gutteridge, H. D. (1984). A learning environment. In N. Maier (Ed.), *Teaching the gifted, challenging the average* (pp. 111–122). Toronto: University of Toronto Guidance Centre. [*28]

Haensly, P. A., & Roberts, N. M. (1983). The professional productive process and its implications for gifted students. *Gifted Child Quarterly, 27,* 9–12. [37, 67]

Haensly, P. A., Shiver, D., & Fulbright, M. (1980). Task commitment and giftedness. *Roeper Review, 3*(1), 21–24. [63, 67]

Hagen, E. P. (1980). *Identification of the gifted.* New York: Teachers College Press. [*15, *18, *19, Intro.]

Hagen, J. C. (1981). Concept formation in average gifted and highly gifted children. In A. H. Kramer, D. Bitan, N. Butler-Por, A. Evyatar, & E. Landau (Eds.), *Gifted children: Challenging their potential—New perspectives and alternatives* (pp. 56–70). New York: Trillium. [82]

Hall, E. G. (1980). Knowing who is gifted. *G/C/T,* No. 11, 14–15, 50–51. [97]

Halstead, J. W. (1988). *Guiding gifted readers from preschool through high school: A handbook for parents, teachers, counselors and librarians.* Columbus, OH: Ohio Psychology. [50]

Hamrin, J. M. (1981). *Problems in implementing gifted/talented programs in 11 rural Maine schools.* Biddeford, ME: University of New England. (ERIC Document Reproduction Service No. ED 213 538) [93]

Hannah, C. L. (1989). The use of cognitive methodology to identify, investigate, and instruct learning-disabled gifted children. *Roeper Review, 12,* 58–62. [95]

Hanninen, G. E. (1984). Effectiveness of a preschool program for the gifted and talented. *Journal for the Education of the Gifted, 7,* 192–204. [75, 94]

Hanushek, E. A. (1989). The impact of differential expenditures on school performance. *Educational Researcher, 18*(4), 45–51, 62. [1]

Harding, P. B., & Berger, P. (1979). Future images: Career education for gifted students. In J. J. Gallagher (Ed.), *Gifted children: Reaching their potential* (pp. 134–145). New York: Trillium. [*49, 53, 55, *90]

Harris, C. R. (1985). Tapping creative potential in the multi-cultural gifted underachiever. In A. H. Roldan (Ed.), *Gifted and talented children, youth and adults: Their social perspectives and culture* (pp. 411–433). Manila: Reading Dynamics (Monroe, NY: Trillium). [91]

Harris, R. L., & Bauer, H. (1983). A program for parents of gifted preschoolers. *Roeper Review, 5,* 18–19. [67]

Harvey, S., & Seeley, K. (1987). An investigation of the relationship among intellectual and creative abilities, extracurricular activities, achievement, and giftedness in a delinquent population. *Gifted Child Quarterly, 28,* 73–79. [96]

Hasegawa, C. (1989). The unmentioned minority. In C. J. Maker (Ed.), *Critical issues in gifted education: Defensible programs for cultural and ethnic minorities* (pp. 192–196). Austin, TX: Pro-Ed. [91]

Hauck, B. B., & Freehill, M. F. (1972). *The gifted: Case studies.* Dubuque, IA: Brown. [77, 78]

Haven, E. W. (1972). Factors associated with the selection of advanced mathematics courses by girls in high school. *Educational Testing Service Research Bulletin,* No. 72–12. [101]

Havighurst, R. J. (1958). Community resources in the education of the gifted. In N. B. Henry (Ed.), *Education for the gifted. Fifty-seventh yearbook of the National Society for the Study of Education: Part II* (pp. 386–394). Chicago: University of Chicago Press. [*2]

Haviland, J. (1983). Looking smart: The relationship between affect and intelligence in infancy. In M. Lewis (Ed.), *Origins of intelligence: Infancy and early childhood* (pp. 423–449). New York: Plenum. [20]

Hedges, W. D. (1977). *At what age should children enter first grade: A comprehensive review of research.* Ann Arbor, MI: University Microfilms International. [6, 9]

Heller, K. A., & Feldhusen, J. F. (Eds.). (1986). *Identifying and nurturing the gifted: An international perspective.* Toronto: Hans Huber. [Intro.]

Henry, J. B. (1965). Family financial power and college attendance. *Personnel and Guidance Journal, 43,* 775–779. [*79]

Henry, N. B. (Ed.). (1958). *Education for the gifted. Fifty-seventh yearbook of the National Society for the Study of Education: Part II.* Chicago: University of Chicago Press. [Intro.]

Hensel, N., & Franklin, C. (1983). Developing emergent leadership skills in elementary and junior high students. *Roeper Review, 5,* 33–35. [85]

Herr, E. L. (1976). Career education for the gifted and talented: Some observations. *Peabody Journal of Education, 53,* 98–103. [49]

Herr, E. L., & Watanabe, A. (1979). Counseling the gifted about career development. In N. Colangelo & R. T. Zaffrann (Eds.), *New voices in counseling the gifted* (pp. 251–263). Dubuque, IA: Kendall/Hunt. [66]

Herr, W. A. (1937). Junior high school accelerants and their peers in senior high school: The social factors. *School Review, 45,* 287–299. [51]

Hewitt, P. L., & Dyck, D. G. (1986). Perfectionism, stress, and vulnerability to depression. *Cognitive Therapy and Research, 10,* 137–142. [72]

Hickey, G. (1988). Goals for gifted programs: Perceptions of interested groups. *Gifted Child Quarterly, 32,* 231–233. [65]

Higham, S. J., & Navarre, J. (1984). Gifted adolescent females require differential treatment. *Journal for the Education of the Gifted, 8,* 43–58. [55, 101]

Hildreth, G. H. (1981). The creative child at home. In B. S. Miller & M. Price (Eds.), *The gifted child, the family, and the community* (pp. 92–99). New York: Walker. [*83]

Hill, M. B. (1983). *Enrichment programs for gifted/talented pupils.* Ventura, CA: Office of the Ventura County Superintendent of Schools for the National/State Leadership Training Institute for the Gifted and Talented. (Original work published 1967). [*29, *47, 81, *82, Intro.]

Hirschi, T., & Hindeland, M. J. (1977). Intelligence and delinquency: A revisionist's review. *American Sociological Review, 42,* 571–587. [96]

Hirsh-Pasek, K., Hyson, M., Rescorla, L., & Cone, J. (1989, April). *Hurrying children: How does it affect their academic, social, creative, and emotional development?* Paper presented at the biennial meeting of the Society for Research in Child Development, Kansas City, MO. [71]

Hirst, B. (1981). Private time. In B. S. Miller & M. Price (Eds.), *The gifted child, the family, and the community* (p. 76). New York: Walker. [71]

Hitchfield, E. M. (1973). *In search of promise.* London: Clowes. [70]

Hobbs, N. (1951). Community recognition of the gifted. In P. A. Witty (Ed.), *The gifted child* (pp. 163–184). Boston: Heath. [*19, *54]

Hobbs, N. (1975). *The futures of children.* San Francisco: Jossey-Bass. [88]

Hobson, J. R. (1962). The Brookline, Massachusetts program of early admission to kindergarten. In M. C. Reynolds (Ed.), *Early school admission for mentally advanced children: A review of research and practice* (pp. 19–30). Reston, VA: Council for Exceptional Children. [6]

Hobson, J. R. (1979). High school performance of underage pupils initially admitted to kindergarten on the basis of physical and psychological examinations. In W. C. George, S. J. Cohn, & J. C. Stanley (Eds.), *Educating the gifted: Acceleration and enrichment* (pp. 13–63). Baltimore: Johns Hopkins University Press. (Original work published 1963) [6, 51]

Hoffman, J. L., Wasson, F. R., & Christianson, B. P. (1985). Personal development for the gifted underachiever. *G/C/T,* No. 38, 12–14. [36]

Hoffman, L. W. (1972). Early childhood experiences and women's achievement motives. *Journal of Social Issues, 28,* 129–153. [100]

Hoffman, S. (1977). Intelligence and the development of moral judgment in children. *Journal of Genetic Psychology, 130,* 27–34. [48]

Hojnacki, P. C. (1979). *Implementation of a program for gifted underachievers and gifted students with behavior problems in the primary grades.* (ERIC Document Reproduction Service No. ED 189 778) [98]

Holbrook, S. F. (1962). The early admission program in Minneapolis, Minnesota. In M. C. Reynolds (Ed.), *Early school admission for mentally advanced children: A review of research and practice* (pp. 35–42). Reston, VA: Council for Exceptional Children. [6]

Hollinger, C. L. (1984). The impact of gender schematic processing on the self directed search responses of gifted and talented female adolescents. *Journal of Vocational Behavior, 24,* 15–27. [86]

Hollinger, C. L., & Fleming, E. S. (1988). Gifted and talented young women: Antecedents and correlates of life satisfaction. *Gifted Child Quarterly, 32,* 254–259. [90]

Hollinger, C. L., & Kosek, S. (1984). Early identification of the gifted and talented. *Gifted Child Quarterly, 29,* 168–171. [13]

Hollingworth, L. (1926). *Gifted children: Their nature and nurture.* New York: Macmillan. [27, 30, 74]

Horne, D. L. & Dupuy, P. J. (1981). In favor of acceleration for gifted students. *The Personnel and Guidance Journal, 60,* 103–106. [*87]

Horner, M. C. (1972). Toward an understanding of achievement-related conflicts in women. *Journal of Social Issues, 28,* 157–175. [100]

Horowitz, F. D., & O'Brien, M. (Eds.). (1985). *The gifted and the talented: Developmental perspectives.* Washington, DC: American Psychological Association. [46]

Howley, C. B. (1989). Career education for the gifted. *Journal for the Education of the Gifted, 12,* 205–217. [49]

Hoyt, K. B., & Hebeler, J. R. (1974). *Career education for gifted and talented students.* Salt Lake City, UT: Olympus. [*48, *49, Intro.]

Huckaby, W. O., & Sperling, H. B. (1981). Leadership giftedness: An idea whose time has not yet come. *Roeper Review, 3,* 19–22. [85]

Hudson, L. (1968). *Frames of mind: Ability, perception, and self-perception in the arts and sciences.* London: Methuen. [27]

Hughes, H. (1984). Measures of self-concept and self-esteem for children ages 3–12 years: A review and recommendations. *Clinical Psychology Review, 4,* 657–692. [84]

Jackman, W. D., & Bachtold, L. M. (1969). Evaluation of a seminar for gifted junior high students. *Gifted Child Quarterly, 8,* 163–176. [25]

Jackson, D. M. (1979). The emerging national and state concern. In A. H. Passow (Ed.), *The gifted and the talented: Education and development. Seventy-eighth yearbook of the National Society for the Study of Education: Part I* (pp. 44–62). Chicago: University of Chicago Press. [*1]

Jackson, N. E. (1988a). Precocious reading ability: What does it mean? *Gifted Child Quarterly, 32,* 200–204. [50]

Jackson, N. E. (1988b). The gift of early reading ability. *Understanding Our Gifted, 1*(2), 1, 8–10. [50]

Jackson, N. E., Famiglietti, J., & Robinson, H. B. (1981). Kindergarten and first grade teachers' attitudes toward early entrants, intellectually advanced students, and average students. *Journal for the Education of the Gifted, 4,* 132–142. [6]

Jackson, R. H., Cleveland, J. C., & Mirenda, P. F. (1975). The longitudinal effects of early identification and counseling of underachievers. *Journal of School Psychology, 13,* 119–128. [98]

Jacobs, J. C. (1972). Teacher attitude toward gifted children. *Gifted Child Quarterly, 16,* 23–26. [9]

Jacquard, A. (1983). Highly gifted, or people? In B. M. Shore, F. Gagné, S. Larivée, R. H. Tali, & R. E. Tremblay (Eds.), *Face to face with giftedness* (pp. 79–90). New York: Trillium. [88]

James, W. (1978). *Pragmatism: A new name for some old ways of thinking* (F. Bowers, Ed.). Cambridge, MA: Harvard University Press. (Original work published 1907) [Intro.]

Janos, P. M., Fung, H. C., & Robinson, N. M. (1985). Self-concept, self-esteem, and peer relations among gifted children who feel "different." *Gifted Child Quarterly, 29,* 78–82. [74, 82]

Janos, P. M., & Robinson, N. M. (1985a). Psychosocial development in intellectually gifted children. In F. D. Horowitz & M. O'Brien (Eds.), *The gifted and tal-*

ented: Developmental perspectives (pp. 149–195). Washington, DC: American Psychological Association. [70, 73, 74, 83, 86, 89]

Janos, P. M., & Robinson, N. M. (1985b). The performance of students in a program of radical acceleration at the university level. *Gifted Child Quarterly, 29,* 175–179. [*80]

Janos, P. M., Sanfillipo, S. M., & Robinson, N. M. (1986). "Underachievement" among markedly accelerated college students. *Journal of Youth and Adolescence, 15,* 303–313. [80]

Jarrell, R. H., & Borland, J. H. (1990). The research base for Renzulli's three-ring conception of giftedness. *Journal for the Education of the Gifted, 13,* 288–308. [14, 20]

Jellen, H. G. (1985). Renzulli's enrichment scheme for the gifted: Educational accommodation of the gifted in the American context. *Gifted Education International, 3*(1), 12–17. [14]

Jellen, H. G., & Verduin, J. (1986). *A conceptual handbook for differential education of the gifted.* Carbondale: Southern Illinois University Press. [40, Intro.]

Jenkins-Friedman, R. (1982). Myth: Cosmetic use of multiple selection criteria: *Gifted Child Quarterly, 26,* 24–26. [14, 15]

Jensen, R. A., & Wedman, J. (1983). The computer's role in gifted education. *G/C/T,* No. 30, 10–11. [45]

Jensen, S. (1979). A reading program for gifted high school students. *Roeper Review, 1*(1), 25–27. [50]

Jepsen, D. A. (1979). Helping gifted adolescents with career exploration. In N. Colangelo & R. T. Zaffrann (Eds.), *New voices in counseling the gifted* (pp. 277–283). Dubuque, IA: Kendall/Hunt. [66]

Jeter, J., & Chauvin, J. C. (1982). Individualized instruction: Implications for the gifted. *Roeper Review, 5*(1), 2–3. [26, 65]

Johnsen-Harris, M. A. (1983). Surviving the budget crunch from an independent school perspective. *Roeper Review, 6,* 79–81. [54, 57]

Johnson, L. G. (1983). Giftedness in preschool: A better time for development than identification. *Roeper Review, 5*(4), 13–15. [75]

Johnson, S. T., Starnes, W. T., Gregory, D., & Blaylock, A. (1985). Program of Assessment, Diagnosis, and Instruction (PADI): Identifying and nurturing potentially gifted and talented minority students. *The Journal of Negro Education, 54,* 416–430. [91]

Joseph, E. C. (1983). Expert systems and people amplifiers. In B. M. Shore, F. Gagné, S. Larivée, R. H. Tali, & R. E. Tremblay (Eds.), *Face to face with giftedness* (pp. 138–154). New York: Trillium. [41]

Kagan, S. L., & Zigler, E. F. (1987). *Early schooling: The national debate.* New Haven, CT: Yale University Press. [71]

Kamii, C. K. (1985). *Young children reinvent arithmetic: Implications of Piaget's theory.* New York: Teachers College Press. [57, *59]

Kamii, C. K. (1989). *Young children continue to reinvent arithmetic—2nd grade.* New York: Teachers College Press. [57, *59]

Kanevsky, L. S. (1985). Computer-based math for gifted students: Comparison of cooperative and competitive strategies. *Journal for the Education of the Gifted, 8,* 239–255. [45]

Kanevsky, L. S. (1990). Pursuing qualitative differences in the flexible use of a problem-solving strategy by young children. *Journal for the Education of the Gifted, 13,* 115–140. [82]

Kanevsky, L. S., & Rapagna, S. O. (1990). Dynamic analysis of problem solving by average and high ability children. *Canadian Journal of Special Education, 6*(1), 15–30. [82]

Kaplan, S. N. (1974). *Providing programs for the gifted and talented: A handbook.* Ventura, CA: Office of the Ventura County Superintendent of Schools for the National/State Leadership Training Institute for the Gifted and Talented. [3, 5, *40, Intro.]

Kaplan, S. N. (1979). Language arts and the social studies curriculum in elementary schools. In A. H. Passow (Ed.), *The gifted and talented: Their education and development. Seventy-eighth yearbook of the National Society for the Study of Education: Part I* (pp. 155–168). Chicago: University of Chicago Press. [44]

Kaplan, S. N. (1980). The role of play in a differentiated curriculum for the young gifted child. *Roeper Review, 3*(2), 12–13. [75]

Karnes, F. A., & Chauvin, J. C. (1984a). *The leadership skills activities manual.* East Aurora, NY: Disseminators of Knowledge. [85]

Karnes, F. A., & Chauvin, J. C. (1984b). *The leadership skills inventory.* East Aurora, NY: Disseminators of Knowledge. [85]

Karnes, F. A., Chauvin, J. C., & Trant, T. J. (1984a). Comparison of personality profiles for intellectually gifted students and students outstanding in the fine and performing arts attending self-contained secondary schools. *Psychology in the Schools, 22,* 122–126. [43]

Karnes, F. A., Chauvin, J. C., & Trant, T. J. (1984b). Leadership profiles as determined by the HSPQ of students identified as intellectually gifted. *Roeper Review, 7,* 46–48. [85]

Karnes, F. A., & Collins, E. (1978). Of the productive kind: Community resources and the G/C/T. *G/C/T,* No. 5, 38–39. [54]

Karnes, F. A., & D'Ilio, V. (1988a). Assessment of concurrent validity of the Leadership Skills Inventory with gifted students and their teachers. *Perceptual and Motor Skills, 66,* 59–62. [85]

Karnes, F. A., & D'Ilio, V. (1988b). Assessment of criterion-related validity of the Leadership Skills Inventory. *Psychological Reports, 62,* 263–267. [85]

Karnes, F. A., McCallum, R. S., & Oehler, J. J. (1985). The relationship between learning style preference and personality variables: An exploratory investigation with gifted students. *Gifted Child Quarterly, 29,* 172–174. [35]

Karnes, F. A., Meriweather, S., & D'Ilio, V. (1987). The effectiveness of the leadership studies program. *Roeper Review, 9,* 238–241. [85]

Karnes, M. B. (1979). Young handicapped children can be gifted and talented. *Journal for the Education of the Gifted, 2,* 157–172. [94]

Karnes, M. B. (1984). A demonstration/outreach model for young gifted/talented handicapped. *Roeper Review, 7,* 23–26. [94]

Karnes, M. B., McCoy, G. F., Zehrbach, R. R., Wollersheim, J., & Clarizio, H. F. (1963). The efficacy of two organizational plans for underachieving gifted children. *Exceptional Children, 29,* 438–446. [98]

Karnes, M. B., Schwedel, A. M., & Lewis, G. F. (1983). Long-term effects of early programming for the gifted/talented handicapped. *Journal for the Education of the Gifted, 6,* 266–278. [94]

Kaufman, A. S., & Harrison, P. L. (1986). Intelligence tests and gifted assessment: What are the positives? *Roeper Review, 8,* 154–159. [16]

Kaufmann, F. A., & Castellanos, F. X. (1986). Counseling the gifted child. In A. F. Rotatori, P. J. Gerber, F. W. Litton, & R. A. Fox (Eds.), *Counseling exceptional students* (pp. 232–251). New York: Human Sciences Press. [*67, 69]

Kaufmann, F. A., & Sexton, J. D. (1983). Some implications for home-school linkages. *Roeper Review, 6,* 49–51. [69, 76]

Kaufmann, F. A., Tews, T. C., & Milam, C. P. (1985). New Orleans Center for the Creative Arts: Program descriptions and student perceptions. *Journal for the Education of the Gifted, 8,* 211–219. [43]

Kavett, H., & Smith, W. E. (1980). Identification of gifted and talented children in the performing arts. *G/C/T,* No. 14, 18–20. [14]

Keating, D. P. (1974). The study of mathematically precocious youth. In J. C. Stanley, D. P. Keating, & L. H. Fox (Eds.), *Mathematical talent: Discovery, description, and development* (pp. 23–46). Baltimore: Johns Hopkins University Press. [18]

Keating, D. P. (Ed.). (1976a). *Intellectual talent: Research and development.* Baltimore: Johns Hopkins University Press. [Intro.]

Keating, D. P. (1976b). Discovering quantitative precocity. In D. P. Keating (Ed.), *Intellectual talent: Research and development* (pp. 23–31). Baltimore: Johns Hopkins University Press. [18]

Keating, D. P. (1979). Secondary-school programs. In A. H. Passow (Ed.), *The gifted and talented: Their education and development. Seventy-eighth yearbook of the National Society for the Study of Education: Part I* (pp. 186–198). Chicago: University of Chicago Press. [*3, *8]

Keeler, D. J. (1978). The treatment effects of a group guidance program on selected self-actualization characteristics of gifted secondary age students. *Dissertation Abstracts International, 39*(6-A), 3376. [78]

Keisler, E. R. (1955). Peer group ratings of high school pupils with high and low school marks. *Journal of Experimental Education, 23,* 375–378. [74]

Kelly, K., & Colangelo, N. (1984). Academic and social self-concepts of gifted, general, and special students. *Exceptional Children, 50,* 551–554. [84]

Kennedy, J. H. (1988). Issues in the identification of socially incompetent children. *School Psychology Review, 17,* 276–288. [73, 74]

Kerr, B. A. (1981). Career education strategies for the gifted. *Journal of Career Education, 7,* 318–331. [90]

Kerr, B. A. (1983). Raising the career aspirations of gifted girls. *Vocational Guidance Quarterly, 32,* 37–43. [66, 90]

Kerr, B. A. (1985). *Smart girls, gifted women.* Columbus, OH: Ohio Psychology. [49, 53, 55, *78, 79, *90, 99, 100, 101, Intro.]

Kerr, B. A. (1986). Career counseling for the gifted: Assessments and interventions. *Journal of Counseling and Development, 64,* 602–604. [90]

Kerr, B. A., & Ghrist-Priebe, S. L. (1988). Intervention for multipotentiality: Effects of a career counseling laboratory for gifted high school students. *Journal of Counseling and Development, 66,* 366–369. [90]

Kersh, M. E., & Reisman, F. K. (1985). Mathematics for gifted students. In R. H. Swassing (Ed.), *Teaching gifted children and adolescents* (pp. 137–180). Columbus, OH: Merrill. [31, 62]

Ketcham, R., & Snyder, R. (1977). Self-attitudes of the intellectually and social advantaged student: Normative study of the Piers-Harris children's self-concept scale. *Psychological Reports, 40,* 111–116. [84]

Keys, N. (1938). The underage student in high school and college. *University of California Publications in Education, 7,* 145–271. [51]

Khatena, J. (1979). Parents and the creatively gifted. In J. C. Gowan, J. Khatena, & E. P. Torrance (Eds.), *Educating the ablest: A book of readings on the education of gifted children* (2nd ed., pp. 265–274). Itasca, IL: Peacock. [*21, *58, *68]

Khatena, J. (1982). *Educational psychology of the gifted.* New York: Wiley. [*17, *61, 64, *79, 85, *89, 99, Intro.]

Khatena, J., & Morse, D. T. (1987). Preliminary study of the Khatena-Morse Multitalent Perception Inventory. *Perceptual and Motor Skills, 64,* 1187–1190. [85]

King, M. L. (1983). Environmental availability, giftedness, and delinquency proneness. In B. M. Shore, F. Gagné, S. Larivée, R. H. Tali, & R. E. Tremblay (Eds.), *Face to face with giftedness* (pp. 186–192). New York: Trillium. [48, 96]

Kingsley, R. F. (1986). "Digging" for understanding and significance: A high school enrichment model. *Roeper Review, 9,* 37–38. [54, 57]

Kirschenbaum, R. J. (1980). Combating sexism in the preschool environment. *Roeper Review, 2*(3), 31–33. [100]

Kirschenbaum, R. J. (1983). Let's cut out the cut-off score in the identification of the gifted. *Roeper Review, 5*(4), 6–9. [21]

Kirschenbaum, R. J. (1989). Identification of the gifted and talented American Indian student. In C. J. Maker (Ed.), *Critical issues in gifted education: Defensible programs for cultural and ethnic minorities* (pp. 91–101). Austin, TX: Pro-Ed. [91]

Kitano, M. K. (1989). Critique of "Identification of gifted Asian-American students." In C. J. Maker (Ed.), *Critical issues in gifted education: Defensible programs for cultural and ethnic minorities* (pp. 163–168). Austin, TX: Pro-Ed. [91]

Kitano, M. K., & Kirby, D. (1986). *Gifted education.* Boston: Little, Brown. [44]

Kitano, M. K., & Tafoya, N. (1982). Preschool leadership: A review and critique. *Journal for the Education of the Gifted, 5,* 78–89. [75]

Kitano, M. K., & Tafoya, N. (1984). Preschool children's perceptions of leadership and how it works. *Journal for the Education of the Gifted, 7,* 77–88. [85]

Klausmeier, H. J., Goodwin, W. L., & Tuckla, R. (1968). Effects of accelerating bright older elementary pupils: A second follow-up. *Journal of Educational Psychology, 59,* 53–58. [51]

Klausmeier, H. J., & Ripple, R. E. (1962). Effects of accelerating bright older elementary pupils from second to fourth grade. *Journal of Educational Psychology, 53,* 93–100. [28]

Koetke, W. (1983). Computers and the mathematically gifted. *Mathematics Teacher, 76,* 270–272. [45]

Kohlberg, L. (1978). The cognitive-developmental approach to moral education. In P. Scharf (Ed.), *Readings in moral education* (pp. 36–51). Minneapolis: Winston. (Original work published 1975) [*48]

Kolloff, P. B. (1983). The center for global futures: Meeting the needs of gifted students in a laboratory school. *Roeper Review, 5*(3), 32–33. [44]

Kough, J. (1958). Community agencies and the gifted. In N. B. Henry (Ed.), *Education for the gifted: Fifty-seventh yearbook of the National Society for the Study of Education: Part II* (pp. 377–385). Chicago: University of Chicago Press. [2]

Kramer, A. H., Bitan, D., Butler-Por, N., Evyatar, A., & Landau, E. (Eds.). (1981). *Gifted children: Challenging their potential—New perspectives and alternatives.* New York: Trillium. [Intro.]

Krippner, S., & Blickenstaff, R. (1970). The development of self-concept as part of an arts workshop for the gifted. *Gifted Child Quarterly, 14,* 163–166. [43]

Krutetskii, V. A. (1976). *The psychology of mathematical abilities in schoolchildren.* Chicago: University of Chicago Press. [31]

Kulieke, M. J. (1986). Research design issues in the evaluation of programs for the gifted: A case study. *Journal for the Education of the Gifted, 9,* 193–207. [52]

Kulik, J. A., & Kulik, C. C. (1984). Effects of accelerated instruction of students. *Review of Educational Research, 54,* 409–425. [28]

Kulik, J. A., & Kulik, C. C. (1987). Effects of ability grouping on student achievement. *Equity and Excellence, 23,* 22–30. [30]

Kulik, J. A., & Kulik, C. C. (1991). Ability grouping and gifted students. In N. Colangelo & G. A. Davis (Eds.), *Handbook of gifted education* (pp. 178–196). Needham, MA: Allyn & Bacon. [30]

Lajoie, S. P., & Shore, B. M. (1981). Three myths? The overrepresentation of the gifted among drop-outs, delinquents, and suicides. *Gifted Child Quarterly, 25,* 138–143. [32, 78, 96]

Lajoie, S. P., & Shore, B. M. (1986). Intelligence: The speed and accuracy tradeoff in high aptitude individuals. *Journal for the Education of the Gifted, 9,* 85–104. [45, 62]

Lamb, R. A., & Busse, C. A. (1983). Leadership beyond lip service. *Roeper Review, 5,* 21–23. [85]

Lambert, S. E., & Lambert, J. W. (1982). Mentoring—A powerful learning device. *G/C/T,* No. 25, 12–13. [55]

Landau, E. (1976). Children ask questions about the future of mankind. In J. Gibson & P. Chennells (Eds.), *Gifted children: Looking to their future* (pp. 268–275). London: Latimer. [*41]

Landau, E. (1979). The Young Person's Institute for the Promotion of Art and Science, Museum Ha'aretz, Tel Aviv. In J. J. Gallagher (Ed.), *Gifted children: Reaching their potential* (pp. 146–161). New York: Trillium. [31, *89]

Lanza, L., & Vassar, W. (1975). Designing and implementing a program for the gifted and talented. In W. B. Barbe & J. S. Renzulli (Eds.), *Psychology and education of the gifted* (pp. 316–323). New York: Irvington. [*2, *43]

Lark-Horovitz, B., & Norton, J. A. (1959). Children's art abilities: The interrelations and factorial structure of ten characteristics. *Child Development, 30,* 433–452. [43]

Larkin, J. H., McDermott, J., Simon, D. P., & Simon, H. A. (1980). Expert and novice performance in solving physics problems. *Science, 208,* 1335–1342. [31]

Lasher, M. E. (1986). Differentiating the world history course. *G/C/T, 9*(2), 58–61. [44]

Lawrence, D. (1980). The role of the local education authority. In R. Povey (Ed.), *Educating the gifted child* (pp. 41–52). London: Harper & Row. [*2]

Laycock, F. (1979). *Gifted children.* Glenview, IL: Scott, Foresman. [*12, 13, *18, *30, Intro.]

Lester, F. K., Jr., & Schroeder, T. L. (1983). Cognitive characteristics of mathematically gifted children. *Roeper Review, 5*(4), 26–28. [8]

Lewis, C. L., & Kanes, L. G. (1979). Gifted IEPs: Impact of expectations and perspectives. *Journal for the Education of the Gifted, 2,* 61–69. [38]

Lewis, G. F. (1984). Alternatives to acceleration for the highly gifted child. *Roeper Review, 6,* 133–136. [28]

Lewis, M., & Michalson, L. (1985). The gifted infant. In J. Freeman (Ed.), *The psychology of gifted children* (pp. 35–57). Chichester, England: Wiley. [*20]

Lince, K., & Meel, M. (1980). The middle school teacher's view. *Roeper Review, 3*(1), 25–26. [63]

Lindsay, B. (1981a). Cornerstones and keystones: Humanities for the gifted and talented. *Roeper Review, 4*(2), 6–9. [48]

Lindsay, B. (1981b). The Prometheus perplex: Leadership giftedness and future studies. *Roeper Review, 3*(3), 9–13. [48, 85]

Lindsey, M. (1980). *Training teachers of the gifted and talented.* New York: Teachers College Press. [9, Intro.]

Llanes, J. R. (1980). Bilingualism and the gifted intellect. *Roeper Review, 2,*(3), 11–12. [47]

Lu, C. (1982). A study on the interest development of Chinese school gifted pupils. *Bulletin of Educational Psychology, 15,* 1–17. [86]

Ludlow, B. L., & Woodrum, D. T. (1982). Problem-solving strategies of gifted and average learners on a multiple discrimination task. *Gifted Child Quarterly, 26,* 99–104. [45]

Lupkowski, A. E. (1984). Gifted students in small rural schools do not have to move to the city. *Roeper Review, 7,* 13–15. [65, 93]

Maccoby, E. E. (1966). *The development of sex differences.* Stanford, CA: Stanford University Press. [100]

Maccoby, E. E., & Martin, J. A. (1983). Socialization in the context of the family: Parent-child interaction. In E. M. Hetherington (Ed.), *Handbook of child psychology: Vol. 4* (pp. 1–101). New York: Wiley. [70]

Maddux, C. D. (1983). Early school entry for the gifted: New evidence and concerns. *Roeper Review, 5*(4), 15–17. [6]

Maddux, C. D., & Candler, A. D. (1985). Readability, interest, and coverage of 13 college textbooks on gifted and talented education. *Gifted Child Quarterly, 29,* 12–14. [Intro.]

Maddux, C. D., Scheiber, L. M., & Bass, J. E. (1982). Self-concept and social distance in gifted children. *Gifted Child Quarterly, 26,* 77–81. [74]

Magoon, R. A. (1981). A proposed model for leadership development. *Roeper Review, 3,* 7–9. [85]

Mahoney, A. R. (1980). Gifted delinquents: What do we know about them? *Children and Youth Services Review, 2,* 315–329. [96]

Maier, N. E. A. (Ed.). (1982). *Teaching the gifted, challenging the average.* Toronto: University of Toronto Guidance Centre. [46, Intro.]

Maier, N. E. A., & Shore, B. M. (1989). Begabtenausbildung in Kanada: Individuelle Initiative und institutionelle Mitwirkung (Education of the gifted in Canada: Individual initiative and institutional participation). In H. G. Melhorn & K. K. Urban (Eds.), *Hochbegabtenförderung international (Education of the gifted and talented: International tendencies)* (pp. 74–83). Berlin (DRR): VEB Deutscher Verlag der Wissenschaften. [2]

Mainx, F. (1955). Foundations of biology. In O. Neurath, R. Carnap, & C. Morris (Eds.), *International encyclopedia of unified science: Vol. 1* (pp. 567–654). Chicago: University of Chicago Press. [33]

Maker, C. J. (1975). *Training teachers for the gifted and talented: A comparison of models.* Reston, VA: Council for Exceptional Children. [Intro.]

Maker, C. J. (1977). *Providing programs for the gifted handicapped.* Reston, VA: Council for Exceptional Children. [*9, *17, 23, *40, *47, *94, Intro.]

Maker, C. J. (1979). Developing multiple talents in exceptional children. *Teaching Exceptional Children, 11,* 120–144. [95]

Maker, C. J. (1982a). *Curriculum development for the gifted.* Rockville, MD: Aspen. [*34, 38, *40, 44, *56, 60, 87, Intro.]

Maker, C. J. (1982b). *Teaching models in education of the gifted.* Rockville, MD: Aspen. [25, 26, *37, *42, 46, *48, 58, *59, 61, Intro.]

Maker, C. J. (1983). Quality education for gifted minority students. *Journal for the Education of the Gifted, 6,* 140–152. [23, 91]

Maker, C. J. (Ed.). (1989). *Critical issues in gifted education: Defensible programs for cultural and ethnic minorities.* Austin, TX: Pro-Ed. [91]

Male, R. A., & Perrone, P. (1979). Identifying talent and giftedness: Part II. *Roeper Review, 2*(2), 5–8. [20]

Maltby, F. (1984). *Gifted children and teachers in the primary school.* London: Falmer. [69]

Manaster, G. J., & Powell, P. M. (1983). A framework for understanding gifted adolescents' psychological maladjustment. *Roeper Review, 6,* 70–73. [82]

Mangieri, J. N., & Isaacs, C. W. (1983). Recreational reading for gifted children. *Roeper Review, 5*(3), 11–14. [50]

Mangieri, J. N., & Madigan, F. (1984). Reading for gifted students: What schools are doing. *Roeper Review, 7*(2), 68–70. [50]

Maniatis, E. G. (1983). *An analysis of the differences in problem-solving of gifted and nongifted children using the LOGO programming language.* Unpublished master's thesis, McGill University, Montreal. [45]

Mann, H. (1957). How real are friendships of gifted and typical children in a program of partial segregation? *Exceptional Children, 23,* 199–201. [30]

Marjoram, D. T. E. (1979). The gifted child in the comprehensive school. In J. J. Gallagher (Ed.), *Gifted children: Reaching their potential* (pp. 85–104). New York: Trillium. [5, *22, *40]

Marjoram, D. T. E. (1983). The secondary school curriculum and the gifted child. In B. M. Shore, F. Gagné, S. Larivée, R. H. Tali, & R. E. Tremblay (Eds.), *Face to face with giftedness* (pp. 414–425). New York: Trillium. [*38, *40, *43]

Marsh, H. W., Byrne, B. M., & Shavelson, R. J. (1988). A multifaceted academic self-concept: Its hierarchical structure and its relation to academic achievement. *Journal of Educational Psychology, 80,* 366–380. [84]

Marshall, B. C. (1981). Career decision-making patterns of gifted and talented adolescents: Implications for career education. *Journal of Career Education, 7,* 305–310. [66, 90]

Martin, C. E. (1984). Why some gifted children do not like to read. *Roeper Review, 7*(2), 72–75. [50]

Martin, C. E., & Cramond, B. (1983). Creative reading: Is it being taught to the gifted in elementary schools? *Journal for the Education of the Gifted, 5,* 34–43. [50]

Martinson, R. A. (1972). *Education of the gifted and talented* (Vol. 2). Background papers submitted to the U.S. Office of Education. Washington, DC: U.S. Government Printing Office. [9]

Martinson, R. A. (1973). Children with superior cognitive abilities. In L. Dunn (Ed.), *Exceptional children in the school* (pp. 68–92). New York: Winston. [98]

Martinson, R. A. (1975). *The identification of the gifted and talented.* Reston, VA: The Council for Exceptional Children. (Original work published 1974) [*13, *14, *21, *23, Intro.]

Martinson, R. A. (1976). *A guide toward better teaching for the gifted.* Ventura, CA: Ventura County Superintendent of Education for the National/State Leadership Training Institute for the Gifted and Talented. [59, Intro.]

Martinson, R. A., & Seagoe, M. V. (1967). *The abilities of young children.* Reston, VA: Council for Exceptional Children. [Intro.]

Massé, P., & Gagné, F. (1983). Observations on enrichment and acceleration. In B. M. Shore, F. Gagné, S. Larivée, R. H. Tali, & R. E. Tremblay (Eds.), *Face to face with giftedness* (pp. 395–413). New York: Trillium. [*31, *34, *64]

Masten, W. G. (1985). Identification of gifted minority students: Past research, future directions. *Roeper Review, 8,* 83–85. [23]

Master, D. L. (1984). Writing and the gifted child. *Gifted Child Quarterly, 27,* 162–168. [47]

Masterson, H. (1979). Interage program for critical thinking. *Roeper Review, 2*(2), 31–32. [57]

Matthews, D. (1988). Gardner's multiple intelligence theory: An evaluation of relevant research literature and a consideration of its application to gifted education. *Roeper Review, 11,* 100–104. [14]

Mattson, B. D. (1979). Mentorship for the gifted and talented: Some practical considerations. *G/C/T,* No. 8, 34–35. [2]

McCauley, E. M. (1984). The story of a vacant lot. *Roeper Review, 7,* 11–12. [60]

McCormick, S., & Swassing, R. H. (1982). Reading instruction for the gifted: A survey of programs. *Journal for the Education of the Gifted, 5,* 34–43. [33, 50, 65]

McDonald, J., Moore, M., & Freehill, M. (1982). Discrepant giftedness. *Roeper Review, 5,* 25–28. [*27]

McFarland, S. L. (1980). Guidelines for the identification of young gifted and talented children. *Roeper Review, 3*(2), 5–7. [23]

McGillivray, R. H. (1964). Differences in home background between high-achieving and low-achieving gifted children: A study of one hundred eight pupils in the City of Toronto Public Schools. *Ontario Journal of Educational Research, 6*(2), 99–106. [83]

McMann, N., & Oliver, R. (1988). Problems in families with gifted children: Implications for counselors. *Journal of Counseling and Development, 66,* 275–278. [70]

Meeker, M. (1969). *The structure of intellect: Its interpretation and uses.* Columbus, OH: Merrill. [27, 38, 46]

Meeker, M., & Meeker, R. (1986). The SOI system for gifted education. In J. S. Renzulli (Ed.), *Systems and models for developing programs for the gifted and talented* (pp. 194–215). Mansfield Center, CT: Creative Learning Press. [46]

Mercurio, J., Schwartz, S., & Oesterle, R. (1982). College courses in high school: A four-year followup of the Syracuse University Project Advance class of 1977. *College and University, 58,* 5–18. [*87]

Mezynski, K., Stanley, J. C., & McCoart, R. F. (1983). Helping youths score well on AP examinations in physics, chemistry, and calculus. In C. P. Benbow & J. C. Stanley (Eds.), *Academic precocity* (pp. 86–112). Baltimore: Johns Hopkins University Press. [*87]

Michael, L. S. (1958). Programs in secondary schools. In N. B. Henry (Ed.), *Education for the gifted. Fifty-seventh yearbook of the National Society for the Study of Education: Part II* (pp. 263–315). Chicago: University of Chicago Press. [51]

Miley, J. F. (Ed.). (1975). *Promising practices: Teaching the disadvantaged gifted.* Ventura, CA: Ventura County Superintendent of Education for the National/State Leadership Training Institute for the Gifted and Talented. [Intro.]

Milgram, R. M. (1984). Creativity in gifted adolescents: A review. *Journal for the Education of the Gifted, 8,* 25–42. [58]

Miller, A. (1981). *The drama of the gifted child.* New York: Basic. [*70, 71]

Miller, A. J. (1937). Is the academically able college student socially maladjusted? *School and Society, 45,* 862–864. [51]

Miller, B. S., & Price, M. (1981). *The gifted child, the family and the community.* New York: Walker. [55, 71, Intro.]

Milton, G. A. (1957). The effects of sex role identification upon problem solving skill. *Journal of Abnormal and Social Psychology, 55,* 202–212. [101]

Mindell, P. (1982). The gifted dyslexic: A case study with theoretical and educational implications. *Roeper Review, 4*(3), 22–23. [95]

Minges, N., Gats, J., & Kresser, R. (1978). Don't tie me down. *G/C/T,* No. 4, 6–8, 51–52. [56]

Mitchell, P. B. (1981a). *An advocate's guide to building support for gifted and talented education.* Washington, DC: National Association of State Boards of Education. [Intro.]

Mitchell, P. B. (1981b). *A policymaker's guide to issues in gifted and talented education.* Washington, DC: National Association of State Boards of Education. [Intro.]

Mitchell, P. B. (1981c). Policymaking for gifted and talented education: An analysis of issues and a suggested process for making decisions. In P. B. Mitchell (Ed.), *A policymaker's guide to issues in gifted and talented education* (pp. 8–29). Washington, DC: National Association of State Boards of Education. [2, *14]

Mönks, F. J., van Boxtel, H. W., Roelofs, J. J. W., & Sanders, M. P. M. (1986). The identification of gifted children in secondary education and a description of their situation in Holland. In K. A. Heller & J. F. Feldhusen (Eds.), *Identifying and nurturing the gifted: An international perspective* (pp. 39–65). Toronto: Hans Huber. [84]

Monson, J. A. (1984). An advocate's guide to advocating . . . or a good offence without being offensive. *Journal for the Education of the Gifted, 7,* 224–251. [2]

Montemayor, R. (1984). Changes in parent and peer relationships between childhood and adolescence: A research agenda for gifted adolescents. *Journal for the Education of the Gifted, 8,* 9–23. [74]

Montgomery, D. (1983). Teaching the teachers of the gifted. *Gifted Education International, 2*(1), 32–34. [59]

Montour, K. (1977). William James Sidis, the broken twig. *American Psychologist, 32,* 265–279. [70, 71]

Moore, B. A. (1978). Career education for disadvantaged, gifted high school students. *Gifted Child Quarterly, 22,* 332–337. [90]

Moore, L. P. (1981). *Does this mean my kid's a genius? How to identify, educate, motivate and live with a gifted child.* New York: Plume (New American Library). [Intro.]

Morse, L. A. (1987). Working with young procrastinators: Elementary school students who do not complete school assignments. *Elementary School Guidance and Counseling, 21,* 221–228. [72]

Moss, E. (1986). Interactions mères-enfants et différences intellectuelles individuelles [Mother-child interactions and individual intellectual differences]. *Apprentissage et Socialisation en Piste, 9,* 143–154. [81, 83]

Moss, E. (1990). Social interaction and metacognitive development in gifted preschoolers. *Gifted Child Quarterly, 34,* 16–20. [81, 83]

Mulcahy, R., Wilgosh, L., & Crawford, B. (1985). An experimental on-site program for gifted Inuit youngsters: Problems and issues. In A. H. Roldan (Ed.), *Talented and gifted children, youth and adults: Their social perspectives and culture* (pp. 288–295). Manila: Reading Dynamics (Monroe, NY: Trillium). [91]

Nash, W. R., Borman, C., & Colson, S. (1980). Career education for gifted and talented students: A senior high school model. *Exceptional Children, 46,* 404–405. [90]

National Research Council (U.S.A.). (1989). *Everybody counts: A report to the nation on the future of mathematics education.* Washington, DC: National Academy Press. [59, 62]

Navarre, J. (1979). Is what is good for the gander, good for the goose: Should gifted girls receive differential treatment? *Roeper Review, 2*(3), 21–25. [100]

Nelson, J. B., & Cleland, D. L. (1975). The role of the teacher of gifted and creative children. In W. B. Barbe & J. S. Renzulli (Eds.), *Psychology and education of the gifted* (2nd ed., pp. 439–448). New York: Irvington. [*50]

Nelson, R. G. (1981). Values education for gifted adolescents. *Roeper Review, 3*(4), 10–11. [48]

Neurath, O., Carnap, R., & Morris, C. (Eds.). (1955). *International encyclopedia of unified science: Vol. 1.* Chicago: University of Chicago Press. [33]

Nevitte, N., Gibbins, R., & Coding, P. W. (1988). The career goals of female science students in Canada. *Canadian Journal of Higher Education, 18,* 30–48. [49]

Newland, T. S. (1976). *The gifted in socio-educational perspective.* Englewood Cliffs, NJ: Prentice-Hall. [*5, *6, *10, 26, 81, Intro.]

Newman, J., Dember, C., & Krug, O. (1973). "He can, but he won't": A study of so-called "gifted underachievers." *Psychoanalytic Study of the Child, 28,* 83–129. [70]

Nichols, R. (1964). Parent attitudes of mothers of intelligent adolescents on creativity of their children. *Child Development, 35,* 1041–1049. [83, 89]

Nicol, H. (1983). Restoring a challenge to secondary education. In B. M. Shore, F. Gagné, S. Larivée, R. H. Tali, & R. E. Tremblay (Eds.), *Face to face with giftedness* (pp. 426–437). New York: Trillium. [*40]

Nillissen, L. C. (1987). *International studies and foreign language study in the state of Illinois: An assessment of current status.* Unpublished doctoral dissertation, Loyola University of Chicago. [44]

Noble, K. D. (1987). The dilemma of the gifted woman. *Psychology of Women Quarterly, 11,* 367–378. [90, 100]

Noble, K. D. (1989). Counseling gifted women. *Journal for the Education of the Gifted, 12,* 131–141. [77, 100]

Norman, R. (1966). The interpersonal values of parents of achieving and nonachieving gifted children. *Journal of Psychology, 64,* 49–57. [83]

Oakes, J. (1985). *Keeping track.* New Haven, CT: Yale University Press. [30]

Obrzut, A., Nelson, R. B., & Obrzut, J. E. (1984). Early school entrance for intellectually superior children: An analysis. *Psychology in the Schools, 21,* 71–77. [28]

O'Connell, P. (1985). *The state of the states, gifted and talented education.* Augusta, ME: Council of State Directors of Programs for the Gifted. [3]

Olenchak, F. R., & Renzulli, J. S. (1989). The effectiveness of the schoolwide enrichment model on selected aspects of elementary school change. *Gifted Child Quarterly, 33,* 36–46. [60]

Olson, D. R. (1985). Computers as tools of the intellect. *Educational Researcher, 14*(5), 5–8. [45]

Olson, D. R. (1986). [Letter to the editor in reply to Suhor (1986).] *Educational Researcher, 15*(2), 24. [45]

Olszewski, P., Kulieke, M., & Buescher, T. (1987). The influence of the family environment on the development of talent: A literature review. *Journal for the Education of the Gifted, 11,* 6–28. [67, 70, 73, 83]

Olszewski, P., Kulieke, M., & Willis, G. (1987). Changes in the self-perceptions of gifted students who participate in rigorous academic programs. *Journal for the Education of the Gifted, 10,* 287–303. [84]

O'Shea, H. E. (1975). Friendship and the intellectually gifted child. In W. Barbe &

J. S. Renzulli, *Psychology and education of the gifted* (2nd ed., pp. 220–228). New York: Irvington. [30]

Otey, J. W. (1978). Identification of gifted students. *Psychology in the Schools, 15*(1), 16–21. [11]

Oxley, M. (1980). Task commitment and giftedness a la kindergarten. *Roeper Review, 3*(1), 24. [63]

Pacht, A. R. (1984). Reflections on perfection. *American Psychologist, 39*, 386–390. [72]

Page, B. A. (1983). A parents' guide to understanding the behavior of gifted children. *Roeper Review, 5*(4), 39–42. [82]

Parke, B. N. (1983). Use of self-instructional materials with gifted primary-aged students. *Gifted Child Quarterly, 27*, 29–34. [65]

Parke, B. N. (1985). Methods of developing creativity. In R. H. Swassing (Ed.), *Teaching gifted children and adolescents* (pp. 376–401). Columbus, OH: Merrill. [58]

Parke, B. N. (1989). *Gifted students in regular classrooms.* Boston: Allyn & Bacon. [26]

Parker, J. G., & Asher, S. R. (1987). Peer relations and later personal adjustment: Are low-accepted children at risk? *Psychological Bulletin, 102*, 357–389. [74]

Parker, J. P. (1989). *Instructional strategies for teaching the gifted.* Boston: Allyn & Bacon. [24, *32, 43, *65]

Parker, M. (1975). *The joy of excellence.* Kaslo, British Columbia: Kootenay Centre for the Gifted. [Intro.]

Parker, M. (1983). Bright kids in trouble with the law. In B. M. Shore, F. Gagné, S. Larivée, R. H. Tali, & R. E. Tremblay (Eds.), *Face to face with giftedness* (pp. 179–185). New York: Trillium. [48, 96]

Parnes, S. J. (1979). Creativity: The process of discovery. In J. J. Gallagher (Ed.), *Gifted children: Reaching their potential* (pp. 44–54). New York: Trillium. [*59, *63]

Passow, A. H. (1958). Enrichment of education for the gifted. In N. B. Henry (Ed.), *Education for the gifted. Fifty-seventh yearbook of the National Society for the Study of Education: Part II* (pp. 193–221). Chicago: University of Chicago Press. [29, 30]

Passow, A. H. (1975). The gifted and the disadvantaged. In W. B. Barbe & J. S. Renzulli (Eds.), *Psychology and education of the gifted* (2nd ed., pp. 402–410). New York: Irvington. [23, *57]

Passow, A. H. (1979). A look around and a look ahead. In A. H. Passow (Ed.), *The gifted and the talented: Their education and development. Seventy-eighth yearbook of the National Association for the Study of Education: Part I* (pp. 439–456). Chicago: University of Chicago Press. [12, 26, *38, *40, *53, *54, Intro.]

Passow, A. H. (1980a). *Education for gifted and talented children and youth: An old issue—A new challenge.* Ventura, CA: Ventura County Superintendent of Education for the National/State Leadership Training Institute for the Gifted and Talented. [Intro.]

Passow, A. H. (1980b). Enrichment of education for the gifted. In A. H. Passow (Ed.), *Education for gifted children and youth: An old issue—A new challenge* (pp. 23–40). Ventura, CA: Office of the Ventura County Superintendent of

Schools for the National/State Leadership Training Institute for the Gifted and Talented. [*27, *36, *47, *62]

Passow, A. H. (1981). Nurturing giftedness: Ways and means. In A. H. Kramer, D. Bitan, N. Butler-Por, A. Evyatar, & E. Landau (Eds.), *Gifted children: Challenging their potential* (pp. 94–106). New York: Trillium. [*34]

Passow, A. H. (1983). The four curricula of the gifted and talented: Towards a total learning environment. In B. M. Shore, F. Gagné, S. Larivée, R. H. Tali, & R. E. Tremblay (Eds.), *Face to face with giftedness* (pp. 379–394). New York: Trillium. [38]

Passow, A. H. (1986a). Educational programs for minority/disadvantaged gifted students. In L. S. Kanevsky (Ed.), *Issues in gifted education: A collection of readings* (pp. 147–172). San Diego: San Diego City Schools. [*92]

Passow, A. H. (1986b). Reflections on three decades of education of the gifted. *Roeper Review, 8,* 223–226. [Reprinted (1988) in *Gifted Education International, 5*(2), 79–83.] [Intro.]

Passow, A. H. (1989). Needed research and development in educating high ability children. *Roeper Review, 11,* 223–229. [Intro., Concl.]

Patterson, C. H. (1972). Counseling underachievers. In J. C. Gowan, G. D. Demos, & C. J. Kokaska (Eds.), *The guidance of exceptional children: A book of readings* (2nd ed., pp. 119–127). New York: McKay. [99]

Pegnato, C. W., & Birch, J. W. (1959). Locating gifted children in junior high school: A comparison of methods. *Exceptional Children, 25,* 300–304. [21]

Pelton, G. (1989). *High parental involvement in academically talented youth.* Unpublished doctoral dissertation, University of Virginia, Charlottesville. [70, 71]

Pelton, G., & Cornell, D. G. (1988, April). *Parental involvement and child adjustment in gifted children.* Paper presented at the annual meeting of the Council for Exceptional Children and The Association for the Gifted, Washington, DC. [70, 71]

Pennington, C. R. (1984). Evaluating books for the gifted reader. *G/C/T, 34,* 15–18. [33, 50]

Perez, G. S. (1980). Perceptions of the young gifted child. *Roeper Review, 3*(2), 9–11. [82]

Perino, S. C., & Perino, J. (1981). *Parenting the gifted: Developing the promise.* New York: Bowker. [71, 72, *73, *74, 83, Intro.]

Perkins, D. N., & Salomon, G. (1989). Are cognitive skills context-bound? *Educational Researcher, 18*(1), 16–25. [46]

Perkins, H. V. (1969). *Human development and learning.* Belmont, CA: Wadsworth. [98]

Perrone, P. A. (1986). Guidance needs of gifted children, adolescents, and adults. *Journal of Counseling and Development, 64,* 564–566. [90]

Perrone, P. A., & Male, R. (1981). *The developmental education and guidance of talented learners.* Rockville, MD: Aspen. [34, *47, 81, Intro.]

Petersen, N. M., Brounstein, P. J., & Kimble, G. A. (1988). Evaluation of college-level coursework for gifted adolescents: An investigation of epistemological stance, knowledge gain and generalization. *Journal for the Education of the Gifted, 12,* 46–61. [28]

Pfouts, J. H. (1980). Birth order, age spacing, IQ differences and family relations. *Journal of Marriage and the Family, 42,* 517–521. [76]

Phillips, D. (1984). The illusion of incompetence among academically competent children. *Child Development, 55,* 2000–2016. [84]

Phillips, D. (1987). Socialization of perceived academic competence among highly competent children. *Child Development, 58,* 1308–1320. [84]

Pirozzo, R. (1982). Gifted underachievers. *Roeper Review, 4*(4), 18–21. [97, 98, 99]

Pirozzo, R. (1985). The Peninsula enrichment program: A community-based program for the gifted. *Roeper Review, 8,* 86–89. [54]

Pitts, M. (1986). Suggestions for administrators of rural schools about developing a gifted program. *Roeper Review, 9,* 24–25. [93]

Plese, S. (1982). An application of Triad for gifted enrichment: The organization of a community resource center. *Roeper Review, 5,* 5–8. [54]

Plowman, P. D. (1977). What can be done for rural gifted and talented children and youth? In J. M. Blanning (Ed.), *Ideas for urban/rural gifted/talented: Case histories and program plans* (pp. 71–87). Ventura, CA: Office of the Ventura County Superintendent of Schools for the National/State Leadership Training Institute for the Gifted and Talented. [*93]

Plowman, P. D. (1980). *Teaching the gifted and talented in the social studies classroom.* Washington, DC: National Education Association. [44]

Plowman, P. D. (1981). Training extraordinary leaders. *Roeper Review, 31,* 13–16. [85]

Polette, N. (1982). *3 R's for the gifted: Reading, writing and research.* Littleton, CO: Libraries Unlimited. [26, 33, 46, *59, Intro.]

Pollins, L. D. (1983). The effects of acceleration on the social and emotional development of gifted students. In C. P. Benbow & J. C. Stanley (Eds.), *Academic precocity* (pp. 160–178). Baltimore: Johns Hopkins University Press. [*80]

Porter, R. M. (1982). The gifted handicapped: A status report. *Roeper Review, 4*(3), 24–25. [94]

Post-Kammer, P., & Perrone, P. A. (1983). Career perceptions of talented individuals: A follow-up study. *Vocational Guidance Quarterly, 31,* 203–211. [86, 90]

Povey, R. (Ed.). (1980a). *Educating the gifted child.* London: Harper & Row. [Intro.]

Povey, R. (1980b). Educating the gifted child: An overview. In R. Povey (Ed.), *Educating the gifted child* (pp. 7–24). London: Harper & Row. [*29]

Pressey, S. L. (1955). Concerning the nature and nurture of genius. *Science, 31,* 123–129. [13]

Pressey, S. L. (1967). "Fordling" accelerates ten years after. *Journal of Counseling Psychology, 14,* 73–80. [80]

Pringle, M. L. K. (1970). *Able misfits: A study of educational and behaviour difficulties of 103 very intelligent children (I.Q.s 120–200).* London: Longman. [73]

Rabinowitz, M., & Glaser, R. (1985). Cognitive structure and cognitive processes in highly competent performance. In F. D. Horowitz & M. O'Brien (Eds.), *The gifted and talented: Developmental perspectives* (pp. 75–98). Washington, DC: American Psychological Association. [31]

Rand, D., & Gibb, L. (1989). A model program for gifted girls in science. *Journal for the Education of the Gifted, 12,* 142–155. [53]

Raph, J., Goldberg, M., & Passow, A. H. (1966). *Bright underachievers.* New York: Teachers College Press. [98]

Rawl, R. K., & O'Tuel, F. S. (1983). Information processing theories and the education of the gifted. *Roeper Review, 6*(2), 83–84. [59]

Redfield, D. L., & Rousseau, E. W. (1981). Meta-analysis of experimental research on teacher questioning behavior. *Review of Educational Research, 51,* 237–245. [42]

Reis, S. M. (1981). *An analysis of the productivity of gifted students participating in programs using the Revolving Door Identification Model.* Unpublished doctoral dissertation, University of Connecticut, Storrs. [60]

Reis, S. M. (1987). We can't change what we don't recognize. Understanding the special needs of gifted females. *Gifted Child Quarterly, 31,* 83–89. [99, 100]

Reis, S. M., Atamian, G. C., & Renzulli, J. S. (1985). The effectiveness of a self-instructional curricular unit in the development of advanced level concepts in astronomy. *Gifted Child Quarterly, 29,* 151–154. [86]

Reis, S. M., & Hébert, T. (1985). Creating practicing professionals in gifted programs: Encouraging students to become young historians. *Roeper Review, 8,* 101–104. [37, 59]

Reis, S. M., & Renzulli, J. S. (1985). *The Secondary Triad Model: A practical plan for implementing gifted programs at the junior and senior high school levels.* Mansfield Center, CT: Creative Learning Press. [*25, *37, 60, *62, 65, Intro.]

Reis, S. M., & Renzulli, J. S. (1986). The Secondary Triad Model. In J. S. Renzulli (Ed.), *Systems and models for developing programs for the gifted and talented* (pp. 267–305). Mansfield Center, CT: Creative Learning Press. [*25]

Rekdal, C. K. (1984). Guiding the gifted female through being aware: The math connection. *G/C/T,* No. 35, 10–12. [100]

Renzulli, J. S. (1975a). *A guidebook for evaluating programs for the gifted and talented.* Ventura, CA: Office of the Ventura County Superintendent of Schools for the National/State Leadership Training Institute for the Gifted and Talented. [*52, Intro.]

Renzulli, J. S. (1975b). Identifying key features in programs for the gifted. In W. B. Barbe & J. S. Renzulli (Eds.), *Psychology and education of the gifted* (2nd ed., pp. 324–332). New York: Irvington. [12]

Renzulli, J. S. (1976). The Enrichment Triad Model: A guide for developing defensible programs for the gifted and talented. *Gifted Child Quarterly, 20,* 303–326. [86]

Renzulli, J. S. (1977). *The Enrichment Triad Model: A guide for developing defensible programs for the gifted and talented.* Mansfield Center, CT: Creative Learning Press. [19, 28, *29, *37, *39, 46, *58, 60, 65, 81, Intro.]

Renzulli, J. S. (1979). The Enrichment Triad Model: A guide for developing defensible programs for the gifted and talented. In J. C. Gowan, J. Khatena, & E. P. Torrance (Eds.), *Educating the ablest: A book of readings on the education of gifted children* (pp. 111–127). Itasca, IL: Peacock. [*60, 64]

Renzulli, J. S. (1981). Identifying key features in programs for the gifted. In W. B. Barbe & J. S. Renzulli (Eds.), *Psychology and education of the gifted* (3rd ed., pp. 214–219). New York: Irvington. [*9]

Renzulli, J. S. (1982). What makes a problem real: Stalking the illusive meaning of qualitative differences in gifted education. *Gifted Child Quarterly, 26,* 147–156. [60]

Renzulli, J. S. (1984a). Evaluating programs for the gifted: Four questions about the larger issues. *Gifted Education International, 2,* 83–87. [52]

Renzulli, J. S. (Ed.). (1984b). *Technical report of research studies related to the Revolving Door Identification Model* (2nd ed.). Storrs: School of Education, University of Connecticut. (Also *Addendum,* 1985) [14]

Renzulli, J. S. (1984c). The Triad/Revolving Door system: A research-based approach to identification and programming for the gifted and talented. *Gifted Child Quarterly, 28,* 163–171. [24]

Renzulli, J. S. (1985). A bull's eye on my back: The perils and pitfalls of trying to bring about educational change. *Gifted Education International, 3*(1), 18–23. [14]

Renzulli, J. S. (Ed.). (1986a). *Systems and models for developing programs for the gifted and talented.* Mansfield Center, CT: Creative Learning Press. [26, 58, Intro.]

Renzulli, J. S. (1986b). The three-ring conception of giftedness: A developmental model for creative productivity. In R. J. Sternberg & J. E. Davidson (Eds.), *Conceptions of giftedness* (pp. 53–92). Cambridge: Cambridge University Press. [*20, 72, *86]

Renzulli, J. S., Hartman, R., & Callahan, C. M. (1971). Teacher identification of superior students. *Exceptional Children, 38,* 211–214. [86]

Renzulli, J. S., & McGreevy, A. M. (1986). Twins included and not included in special programs for the gifted. *Roeper Review, 9,* 120–127. [76]

Renzulli, J. S., & Reis, S. M. (1985). *The Schoolwide Enrichment Model: A comprehensive plan for educational excellence.* Mansfield Center, CT: Creative Learning Press. [*21, *29, *35, 38, *39, *40, 63, Intro.]

Renzulli, J. S., Reis, S. M., & Smith, L. H. (1981). *The Revolving Door Identification Model.* Mansfield Center, CT: Creative Learning Press. [14, *19, *21, Intro.]

Renzulli, J. S., & Smith, L. H. (1980). A practical model for designing individual educational programs (IEPs) for gifted and talented students. *G/C/T,* No. 11, 2–8. [38]

Renzulli, J. S., Smith, L. H., White, A. J., Callahan, C. M., & Hartman, R. K. (1976). *Scales for rating the behavioral characteristics of superior students (SRBCSS).* Wethersfield, CT: Creative Learning Press. [85]

Rescorla, L., Hyson, M. C., Hirsh-Pasek, K., & Cone, J. (1990). Academic expectations in mothers of preschool children. *Early Education and Development, 1,* 165–184. [71]

Reynolds, M. C. (1962). *Early school admission for mentally advanced children: A review of research and practice.* Washington, DC: Council for Exceptional Children. [*6, 11, Intro.]

Richardson, T. M., & Benbow, C. P. (in press). Long-term effects of acceleration on the social-emotional adjustment of mathematically precocious youth. *Journal of Educational Psychology.* [80]

Richardson, W. B., & Feldhusen, J. F. (1986). *Leadership education: Developing skills for youth.* New York: Trillium. [*85]

Richert, E. S., Alvino, J. J., & McDonnel, R. C. (1982). *National report on identification: Assessment and recommendations for comprehensive identification of gifted and talented youth* (Contract No. 300-80-0958). Sewell, NJ: Educational Improvement Center-South. [*97, 98]

Rimm, S. B. (1982). Evaluation of gifted programs—As easy as ABC. *Roeper Review, 5,* 8–11. [52]

Rimm, S. B. (1984). The characteristics approach: Identification and beyond. *Gifted Child Quarterly, 28,* 181–187. [21, 23, 24, 97]

Rimm, S. B. (1985). Identifying underachievement: The characteristics approach. *G/C/T,* No. 41, 2–5. [98]

Rimm, S. B. (1986). *Underachievement syndrome: Causes and cures.* Watertown, WI: Apple. [99]

Robb, G. C. (1976). Retrospect and prospect: A British view. In J. Gibson & P. Chennells (Eds.), *Gifted children: Looking to their future* (pp. 140–150). London: Latimer. [*82]

Roberts, S., & Wallace, B. (1980). The development of teaching materials: Principles and practice. In R. Povey (Ed.), *Educating the gifted child.* London: Harper & Row. [*39, *51]

Robinson, A. (1983, April). *The effects of labeling students as gifted.* Paper presented at the annual meeting of the National Association for Gifted Children, Philadelphia. (ERIC Document Reproduction Service No. ED 239 449) [88]

Robinson, A. (1985). Summer institute on the gifted: Meeting the needs of the regular classroom teacher. *Gifted Child Quarterly, 29,* 20–23. [93]

Robinson, A. (1986a). Brave new directions: Needed research on the labeling of gifted children. *Gifted Child Quarterly, 30,* 11–14. [88]

Robinson, A. (1986b, October). *The effects of labeling students gifted on teachers' attributions for classroom achievement.* Paper presented at the Midwest Educational Research Association, Chicago. [88]

Robinson, A. (1986c). The identification and labeling of gifted children. What does research tell us? In K. A. Heller & J. F. Feldhusen (Eds.), *Identifying and nurturing the gifted: An international perspective* (pp. 103–109). Toronto: Hans Huber. [69, 77, 88]

Robinson, A. (1988). *Against all odds: Manifest talent in gifted disadvantaged youth.* Little Rock: Center for Research on Teaching and Learning, University of Arkansas at Little Rock. [92]

Robinson, A. (1990). Does that describe me? Adolescents' acceptance of the gifted label. *Journal for the Education of the Gifted, 13,* 245–255. [88]

Robinson, A., Bradley, R. H., & Stanley, T. D. (1990). Opportunity to achieve: Identifying mathematically gifted black students. *Contemporary Educational Psychology, 15*(1), 1–12. [23, 24, 91]

Robinson, A., & Stanley, T. D. (1989). Teaching to talent: Evaluating an enriched and accelerated mathematics program. *Journal for the Education of the Gifted, 12,* 253–267. [24]

Robinson, H. B. (1983). A case for radical acceleration: Programs of the Johns Hopkins University and the University of Washington. In C. P. Benbow & J. C. Stanley (Eds.), *Academic precocity* (pp. 139–159). Baltimore: Johns Hopkins University Press. [*80]

Robinson, H. B., Roedell, W. C., & Jackson, N. E. (1979). Early identification and intervention. In A. H. Passow (Ed.), *The gifted and the talented: Their education and development. Seventy-eighth yearbook of the National Association for the Study of Education: Part 1* (pp. 138–154). Chicago: University of Chicago Press. [6, *13]

Robinson, N. M., & Janos, P. M. (1986). Psychological adjustment in a college-level program of marked academic acceleration. *Journal of Youth and Adolescence, 15,* 51–60. [80]

Rodenstein, J., Pfleger, L. R., & Colangelo, N. (1977). Career development of gifted women. *Gifted Child Quarterly, 21,* 340–358. [79]

Rodenstein, J., Pfleger, L. R., & Colangelo, N. (1979). Career development of gifted women. In J. C. Gowen, J. Khatena, & E. P. Torrance (Eds.), *Educating the ablest: A book of readings on the education of gifted children* (2nd ed., pp. 383–390). Itasca, IL: Peacock. [*49, 53, 55, 79]

Roe, A. (1953). *The making of a scientist.* New York: Dodd, Mead. [13, 87]

Roedell, W. C. (1984). Vulnerabilities of highly gifted children. *Roeper Review, 6,* 127–130. [*73]

Roedell, W. C., Jackson, N. E., & Robinson, H. B. (1980). *Gifted young children.* New York: Teachers College Press. [52, 74, 75, Intro.]

Roedell, W. C., Slaby, R. G., & Robinson, H. B. (1977). *Social development in young children.* Monterey, CA: Brooks/Cole. [73]

Roehling, P. U., & Robin, A. L. (1986). Development and validation of the Family Beliefs Inventory: A measure of unrealistic beliefs among parents and adolescents. *Journal of Consulting and Clinical Psychology, 54,* 693–697. [72]

Roeper, A. (1978). The young gifted girl: A contemporary view. *Roeper Review, 1*(1), 8–9. [100]

Rogers, B. G. (1983). Metacognition: Implications for training teachers of the gifted. *Roeper Review, 6*(1), 20–21. [46]

Rogers, K. B. (1989). A content analysis of the literature on giftedness. *Journal for the Education of the Gifted, 13,* 78–88. [Intro.]

Roldan, A. H. (Ed.). (1985). *Gifted and talented children, youth and adults: Their social perspectives and culture.* Manila: Reading Dynamics. (Also available from Trillium, Monroe, NY) [Intro.]

Ronvik, R. (1989). Administrative reactions to chapters about programs for gifted black students. In C. J. Maker & S. W. Schiever (Eds.), *Critical issues in gifted education: Defensible programs for cultural and ethnic minorities: Vol. 2* (pp. 281–284). Austin, TX: Pro-Ed. [91]

Roper, C. J., & Berry, K. (1986). College career centers: Reaching out to the gifted and talented. *Journal of Career Development, 3,* 49–60. [86, 90]

Rosenbusch, M. H., & Draper, D. C. (1985). Gifted preschoolers: Learning Spanish as a second language. *Roeper Review, 7,* 209–212. [47]

Ross, A. D., & Parker, M. (1980). Academic and social self-concepts of academically gifted. *Exceptional Children, 47,* 6–10. [84]

Ross, A. O. (1979). The gifted child in the family. In N. Colangelo & R. T. Zaffrann (Eds.), *New voices in counseling the gifted* (pp. 402–407). Dubuque, IA: Kendall/Hunt. [*67, *70, 71, *76]

Rothney, J., & Koopman, W. (1958). Guidance for the gifted. In N. B. Henry (Ed.),

Education for the gifted. Fifty-seventh yearbook of the National Society for the Study of Education: Part II (pp. 347–361). Chicago: University of Chicago Press. [*77]

Rowlands, P. (1974). *Gifted children and their problems*. London: Dent. [*22, *75, Intro.]

Rubovits, P. C., & Maehr, M. L. (1973). Pygmalion black and white. *Journal of Personality and Social Psychology, 25,* 210–218. [69, 88]

Runions, T., & Smyth, E. (1985). Gifted adolescents as co-learners in mentorships. *Journal for the Education of the Gifted, 8,* 127–132. [55]

Sanborn, M. P. (1979a). Career development: Problems of gifted and talented students. In N. Colangelo & R. Zaffrann (Eds.), *New voices in counseling the gifted* (pp. 284–300). Dubuque, IA: Kendall/Hunt. [55, 66, *90]

Sanborn, M. P. (1979b). Counseling and guidance needs of the gifted and talented. In A. H. Passow (Ed.), *The gifted and talented: Their education and development. Seventy-eighth yearbook of the National Society for the Study of Education: Part I* (pp. 428–438). Chicago: University of Chicago Press. [*77]

Sanborn, M. P. (1979c). Working with parents. In N. Colangelo & R. Zaffrann (Eds.), *New voices in counseling the gifted* (pp. 154–164). Des Moines, IA: Kendall/Hunt. [*88]

Sanborn, M. P., Pulvino, C., & Wunderlin, R. (1971). *Research reports: Superior students in Wisconsin high schools*. Madison: University of Wisconsin Press. [90]

Sapon-Shevin, M. (1984). The tug-of-war nobody wins: Allocation of educational resources for handicapped, gifted, and "typical" students. *Curriculum Inquiry, 14*(1), 57–81. [88]

Schacter, F. F. (1982). Sibling deidentification and split-parent identification: A family tetrad. In M. E. Lamb & B. Sutton-Smith (Eds.), *Sibling relationships: Their nature and significance across the lifespan* (pp. 123–151). Hillsdale, NJ: Erlbaum. [76]

Schaefer, C. E. (1970). A psychological study of 10 exceptionally creative adolescent girls. *Exceptional Children, 36,* 431–441. [89]

Schaefer, E., & Bell, R. (1958). Development of a parent attitude research instrument. *Child Development, 29,* 339–361. [89]

Scheirer, M., & Kraut, R. (1979). Increasing educational achievement via self-concept change. *Review of Educational Research, 49,* 131–150. [84]

Schermerhorn, S. M., Goldschmid, M. L., & Shore, B. M. (1975). Learning basic principles of probability in student dyads: A cross-age comparison. *Journal of Educational Psychology, 67,* 551–557. [31]

Schermerhorn, S. M., Goldschmid, M. L., & Shore, B. M. (1976). Peer teaching in the classroom: Rationale and feasibility. *Improving Human Performance Quarterly, 5*(1), 27–34. [57]

Schilling, D. E. (1986). Managing motivational needs of the gifted and talented. *G/C/T, 9*(3), 2–5. [25, 82]

Schlichter, C. L. (1984). Using books to implement Triad activities with elementary students. *Roeper Review, 7*(2), 75–79. [50]

Schmitz, C. C., & Galbraith, J. (1985). *Managing the social and emotional needs of the gifted: A teacher's survival guide*. Minneapolis: Free Spirit. [100]

Schneider, B. H. (1987). *The gifted child in peer group perspective.* New York: Springer. [74]

Schneider, B. H., Clegg, M. R., Byrne, B. M., Ledingham, J. E., & Crombie, G. (1989). Social relations of gifted children as a function of age and school program. *Journal of Educational Psychology, 81,* 48–56. [74]

Schneidman, E. S. (1972). Perturbation and lethality as precursors of suicide in a gifted group. *Life Threatening Behavior, 1,* 23–45. [72]

Schorr, L. B., & Schorr, D. (1988). *Within our reach: Breaking the cycle of disadvantage.* New York: Anchor. [92]

Schroer, A. C., & Dorn, F. J. (1986). Enhancing the career and personal development of gifted college students. *Journal of Counseling and Development, 64,* 567–571. [90]

Schug, M. C. (1981). Using the local community to improve citizenship education for the gifted. *Roeper Review, 4,* 22–23. [54]

Schwartz, L. L. (1980). Advocacy for the neglected gifted: Females. *Gifted Child Quarterly, 24,* 113–118. [100]

Scott, D. L. (1979). An investigation of the association between the value to achieve and modes of thinking in gifted children. *Dissertation Abstracts International, 39*(9-A), 5295–5296. [63]

Scruggs, T. E., & Cohn, S. J. (1983). A university-based summer program for a highly able but poorly achieving Indian child. *Gifted Child Quarterly, 27,* 90–93. [91]

Scruggs, T. E., & Mastropieri, M. A. (1984). How gifted students learn: Implications from recent research. *Roeper Review, 6,* 183–185. [35]

Seashore, H. G. (1962). Women are more predictable than men. *Journal of Counseling Psychology, 9,* 261–270. [101]

Sebring, A. D. (1983). Parental factors in the social and emotional adjustment of the gifted. *Roeper Review, 6,* 97–99. [72]

Seeley, K. (1984). Perspectives on adolescent giftedness and delinquency. *Journal for the Education of the Gifted, 8,* 59–72. [96]

Seeley, K. (1985). Facilitators for gifted learners. In J. F. Feldhusen (Ed.), *Toward excellence in gifted education* (pp. 105–133). Denver: Love. [*9, *22, *77]

Seeley, K. (1989). Arts curriculum for the gifted. In J. VanTassel-Baska, J. F. Feldhusen, K. Seeley, G. Wheatley, L. Silverman, & W. Foster (Eds.), *Comprehensive curriculum for gifted learners* (pp. 300–313). Boston: Allyn & Bacon. [*43]

Seeley, K., Jenkins, R., & Hultgren, H. (1979). Professional standards for training programs in gifted education. *Journal for the Education of the Gifted, 4,* 165–169. [69]

Seif, E. (1981). Futures education for the gifted. *Roeper Review, 4*(2), 24–25. [41]

Seiger, S. D. (1984). Reaching beyond thinking skills to thinking strategies for the academically gifted. *Roeper Review, 6,* 185–188. [46]

Seldman, S., & Spain, M. (1983). A gifted approach to the development of a social studies unit. *Roeper Review, 5*(4), 29–30. [44]

Sellin, D. F. (1988, April). *Understanding voices and choices of gifted and talented.* Paper presented at the annual meeting of the Council for Exceptional Children and The Association for the Gifted, Washington, DC. [Intro.]

Sellin, D. F., & Birch, J. W. (1980). *Educating gifted and talented learners.* Rockville, MD: Aspen. [*47, *82, Intro.]

Shamanoff, G. A. (1985). The women mentor project: A sharing approach. *Roeper Review, 7*(3), 163. [55]

Shavelson, R. J. (1974). Methods for examining representations of a subject-matter structure in a student's memory. *Journal of Research in Science Teaching, 11,* 231–249. [31, 84]

Shavelson, R. J., & Salomon, G. (1985). Information technology: Tool and teacher of the mind. *Educational Researcher, 14*(5), 4. [45]

Shavelson, R. J., & Salomon, G. (1986). Reply to comment on "Information technology: Tool and teacher of the mind." *Educational Researcher, 15*(2), 24–25. [45]

Shaw, M. C., & McCuen, J. T. (1960). The onset of academic underachievement in bright children. *Journal of Educational Psychology, 51,* 103–108. [13]

Sheive, L., & Schoenheit, M. (Eds.). (1987). *Leadership: Examining the elusive.* Reston, VA: Association for Supervision and Curriculum Development 1987 Yearbook. [85]

Shiner, S. M. (1986). Design and implementation of a humanistic, holistic training program for teachers of the gifted. *Gifted International, 3*(2), 64–77. [9]

Shoff, H. G. (1984). *The gifted underachiever: Definitions and identification strategies.* (ERIC Document Reproduction Service No. ED 252 029) [98]

Shore, B. M. (1981). Gifted children's feelings about school and themselves in open and open-area classes. *Journal for the Education of the Gifted, 4,* 112–121. [56]

Shore, B. M. (1986). Cognition and giftedness: New research directions. *Gifted Child Quarterly, 30,* 24–27. [35, 46]

Shore, B. M., & Dover, A. C. (1987). Metacognition, intelligence and giftedness. *Gifted Child Quarterly, 31,* 37–39. [35]

Shore, B. M., Gagné, F., Larivée, S., Tali, R. H., & Tremblay, R. E. (Eds.). (1983). *Face to face with giftedness.* New York: Trillium. [26, 48, Intro.]

Shore, B. M., & Kaizer, C. (1989). The training of teachers for gifted pupils. *Canadian Journal of Education, 14*(1), 74–87. [9]

Shore, B. M., Kanevsky, L. S., & Rejskind, F. G. (1991). Learning and the needs of gifted students. In R. H. Short, L. L. Stewin, & S. J. H. McCann (Eds.), *Educational psychology: Canadian Perspectives* (pp. 372–400). Toronto: Copp Clark Pitman. [*45]

Shore, B. M., & Tsiamis, A. (1986). Identification by provision: Limited field test of a radical alternative for identifying gifted students. In K. A. Heller & J. F. Feldhusen, *Identifying and nurturing the gifted* (pp. 93–102). Toronto: Hans Huber. [14, 21, 22]

Short, D. D. (1985). From the other side of the desk. *G/C/T,* No. 37, 19–21. [81]

Silverman, L. K. (1980). Secondary programs for gifted students. *Journal for the Education of the Gifted, 4,* 30–42. [4, 93]

Silverman, L. K. (1986a). The IQ controversy: Conceptions and misconceptions. *Roeper Review, 8,* 136–139. [13, 16, 100]

Silverman, L. K. (1986b). What happens to the gifted girl? In C. J. Maker (Ed.),

Critical issues in gifted education: Defensible programs for the gifted (pp. 43–89). Rockville, MD: Aspen. [100]

Silverman, L. K. (1987, April). *The second child syndrome.* Paper presented at the annual meeting of the National Association for Gifted Children, New Orleans. [76]

Silverman, L. K., Chitwood, D. G., & Waters, J. L. (1986). Young gifted children: Can parents identify giftedness? *Topics in Early Childhood Special Education, 6,* 23–38. [72]

Silverman, L. K., & Waters, J. L. (1987, April). *Exploding the myth of the nongifted sibling.* Paper presented at the annual meeting of the National Association for Gifted Children, New Orleans. [76]

Silvernail, D. L. (1985). *Developing positive student self-concept* (2nd ed.). Washington, DC: National Education Association. [*84]

Sister Josephina. (1961). Teachers' reactions to gifted children. *Gifted Child Quarterly, 5,* 42–44. [9]

Slavin, R. E. (1983). When does cooperative learning increase student achievement? *Psychological Bulletin, 94,* 429–445. [83]

Slavin, R. E. (1987a). Ability grouping and student achievement in elementary schools: A best-evidence synthesis. *Review of Educational Research, 57,* 293–336. [30]

Slavin, R. E. (1987b). *Cooperative learning: Student teams* (2nd ed.). Washington, DC: National Education Association. [83]

Slavin, R. E. (1988). Synthesis of research on grouping in elementary and secondary schools. *Educational Leadership, 46*(1), 67–76. [30]

Smilansky, M., & Nevo, D. (1979). *The gifted disadvantaged: A ten year longitudinal study of compensatory education in Israel.* London: Gordon & Breach. [92, Intro.]

Solano, C. H. (1979). The first D: Discovery of talent, or needles in a haystack. In N. Colangelo & R. Zaffrann (Eds.), *New voices in counseling the gifted* (pp. 89–106). Dubuque, IA: Kendall/Hunt. [12, 19]

Sorotzkin, B. (1985). The quest for perfection: Avoiding guilt or avoiding shame? *Psychotherapy, 22,* 564–571. [72]

Southern, W. T., & Jones, E. D. (Eds.). (1991). *Academic acceleration of gifted children.* New York: Teachers College Press. [28]

Southern, W. T., Jones, E. D., & Fiscus, E. D. (1989). Practitioner objections to the academic acceleration of gifted children. *Gifted Child Quarterly, 33,* 29–35. [28, *80]

Speed, F. M. (1982). Science. In N. E. A. Maier (Ed.), *Teaching the gifted, challenging the average* (pp. 91–103). Toronto: University of Toronto Guidance Centre. [57]

Speed, F. M., & Appleyard, D. (1985). *The bright and the gifted.* Toronto: University of Toronto Guidance Centre. [*7, Intro.]

Spicker, H., & Southern, W. T. (1983, November). *Curing the undereducated, underserved, rural junior high school gifted blues: A university and local school duet.* Paper presented at the annual meeting of the National Association for Gifted Children, Philadelphia. [93]

Stanley, J. C. (1967). Further evidence via the analysis of variance that women are more predictable academically than men. *Ontario Journal of Educational Research, 10,* 49–55. [101]

Stanley, J. C. (1973). Accelerating the educational progress of intellectually gifted youths. *Educational Psychologist, 10,* 133–146. [101]

Stanley, J. C. (1976). Use of tests to discover talent. In D. P. Keating (Ed.), *Intellectual talent: Research and development* (pp. 3–22). Baltimore: Johns Hopkins University Press. [*18]

Stanley, J. C. (1979a). Identifying and nurturing the intellectually gifted. In W. C. George, S. J. Cohn, & J. C. Stanley (Eds.), *Educating the gifted: Acceleration and enrichment* (pp. 172–180). Baltimore: Johns Hopkins University Press. (Original work published 1976) [7, 29]

Stanley, J. C. (1979b). The case for extreme educational acceleration of intellectually brilliant youths. In J. C. Gowan, J. Khatena, & E. P. Torrance (Eds.), *Educating the ablest: A book of readings on the education of gifted children* (2nd ed., pp. 93–102). Itasca, IL: Peacock. (Original work published 1976) [*28]

Stanley, J. C. (1984). Use of general and specific aptitude measures in identification: Some principles and certain cautions. *Gifted Child Quarterly, 28,* 177–180. [14, 15, 24]

Stanley, J. C. (1985). Young entrants to college: How did they fare? *College and University, 60,* 219–228. [80, 87]

Stanley, J. C , & Benbow, C. P. (1983). Extremely young college graduates: Evidence of their success. *College and University, 58,* 361–371. [*87]

Stanley, J. C., George, W. C., & Solano, C. H. (Eds.). (1977). *The gifted and the creative: A 50 year perspective.* Baltimore: Johns Hopkins University Press. [Intro.]

Stanley, J. C., Keating, D. P., & Fox, L. H. (Eds.). (1974). *Mathematical talent: Discovery, description and development.* Baltimore: Johns Hopkins University Press. [18, 19, 75, 87, Intro.]

Stanley, J. C., & McGill, A. M. (1986). More about "young entrants to college: How did they fare?" *Gifted Child Quarterly, 30,* 70–73. [80, 87]

Stanley, T. D., & Robinson, A. (1986). Regression discontinuity: Integrating research and program design in programs for the gifted. *Journal for the Education of the Gifted, 9,* 181–191. [23, 24, 52]

Starko, A. J. (1988). Effects of the Revolving Door Identification Model on creative productivity and self-efficacy. *Gifted Child Quarterly, 32,* 291–297. [37, 60, 65]

Stedtnitz, U. (1986). The influence of educational enrichment on self-efficacy and interest levels in young children. *Topics in Early Childhood Special Education, 6,* 39–49. [86]

Stedtnitz, U., & Speck, A. (1986). Young children can complete creative, independent projects. *G/C/T, 9*(2), 19–21. [63]

Steeves, J. (1980). My math is all right, what's wrong is my answers. *G/C/T,* No. 12, 52–57. [95]

Stein, M. I. (1981). *Gifted, talented, and creative young people: A guide to theory, teaching, and research.* New York: Garland. [*58, Intro.]

Stephens, R. W. (1986). What is the present status of international education at the sixth-grade level in Ohio public schools? *Dissertation Abstracts International, 47-A,* 2060. [44]

Stephenson, B. (1983). Legislative leadership and the education of the gifted. In B. M. Shore, F. Gagné, S. Larivée, R. H. Tali, & R. E. Tremblay (Eds.), *Face to face with giftedness* (pp. 371–398). New York: Trillium. [*1, 2, 3]

Sternberg, R. J. (1986a). Identifying the gifted through the IQ: Why a little bit of knowledge is a dangerous thing. *Roeper Review, 8,* 143–147. [16]

Sternberg, R. J. (1986b). *Intelligence applied: Understanding and increasing your intellectual skills.* San Diego: Harcourt, Brace, Jovanovich. [46]

Sternberg, R. J., & Davidson, J. E. (Eds.). (1986). *Conceptions of giftedness.* Cambridge: Cambridge University Press. [31, 46, 69, Intro.]

Stevens, K. (1980). The effect of topic interest on the reading comprehension of higher ability students. *Journal of Educational Research, 73*(6), 365–368. [50]

Stewart, E. D. (1981). Learning styles among gifted/talented students: Instructional techniques preferences. *Exceptional Children, 48,* 134–138. [65]

Stewart, E. D. (1985). Social studies. In R. H. Swassing (Ed.), *Teaching gifted children and adolescents* (pp. 233–275). Columbus, OH: Merrill. [*59, *61, *62]

Stoddard, E. P., & Renzulli, J. S. (1983). Improving the writing skills of talent pool students. *Gifted Child Quarterly, 27,* 21–27. [47]

Stodgill, R. (1974). *Handbook of leadership: A survey of theory and research.* New York: Free Press. [85]

Subotnik, R. F. (1984). Emphasis on the creative dimension: Social studies curriculum modifications for intermediate and secondary students. *Roeper Review, 7*(1), 7–10. [59, 63]

Suhor, C. (1986). Comment on "Computers as tools of the intellect." *Educational Researcher, 15*(2), 23–24. [Refers to Olson, 1985] [45]

Sunderlin, S. (1981). Gifted children and their siblings. In B. S. Miller & M. Price (Eds.), *The gifted child, the family, and the community* (pp. 100–106). New York: Walker. [*76]

Swanson, H. L., & Trahan, M. (1986). Characteristics of frequently cited articles in learning disabilities. *The Journal of Special Education, 20,* 167–182. [Intro.]

Swassing, R. H. (1984). The multiple component alternative for gifted education. *G/C/T,* No. 33, 10–11. [24]

Swassing, R. H. (Ed.). (1985a). *Teaching gifted children and adolescents.* Columbus, OH: Merrill. [Intro.]

Swassing, R. H. (1985b). Identification, assessment, and individualization. In R. H. Swassing (Ed.), *Teaching gifted children and adolescents* (pp. 26–58). Columbus, OH: Merrill. [*14, 23, *65]

Swicord, B. (1984). Debating with gifted fifth and sixth graders—Telling it like it was, is, and could be. *Gifted Child Quarterly, 28,* 127–129. [47]

Syphers, D. F. (1972). *Gifted and talented children: Practical programming for teachers and principals.* Arlington (now Reston), VA: Council for Exceptional Children. [*52, Intro.]

Szekely, G. (1981). The artist and the child—A model program for the artistically gifted. *Gifted Child Quarterly, 25,* 67–72. [43]

Taba, H. (1975). Learning by discovery: Psychological educational rationale. In

W. B. Barbe & J. S. Renzulli (Eds.), *Psychology and education of the gifted* (2nd ed., pp. 346–354). New York: Irvington. [42, *59]

Takacs, C. A. (1982). "They don't get gifted until the fourth grade": What parents can do in the meantime. *Roeper Review, 4*(4), 43–45. [81]

Takacs, C. A. (1986). *Enjoy your gifted child.* Syracuse, NY: Syracuse University Press. [*72, 73, 74, 83, *89]

Tanaka, K. (1989). A response to "Are we meeting the needs of gifted Asian-Americans?" In C. J. Maker (Ed.), *Critical issues in gifted education: Defensible programs for cultural and ethnic minorities* (pp. 174–178). Austin, TX: Pro-Ed. [91]

Tannenbaum, A. J. (1962). *Adolescent attitudes toward academic brilliance.* New York: Teachers College Press. [88]

Tannenbaum, A. J. (1979). Pre-Sputnik to Post-Watergate concern about the gifted. In A. H. Passow (Ed.), *The gifted and talented: Their education and development. Seventy-eighth yearbook of the National Society for the Study of Education: Part I* (pp. 5–27). Chicago: University of Chicago Press. [*66]

Tannenbaum, A. (1981). A curricular framework for differentiated education of the gifted. In A. H. Kramer, D. Bitan, N. Butler-Por, A. Evyatar, & E. Landau (Eds.), *Gifted children, challenging their potential* (pp. 155–164). New York: Trillium. [37, 58]

Tannenbaum, A. J. (1983). *Gifted children: Psychological and educational perspectives.* New York: Macmillan. [*12, 24, 30, *32, *34, 37, *55, 82, *84, 85, *86, 99, Intro.]

Taylor, C. W. (Ed.). (1978). *Teaching for talents and gifts: 1978 status. Developing and implementing multiple talent teaching* (Contract NIE-PO-77-0075). Washington, DC: National Institute of Education, U.S. Department of Education, Health and Welfare. [14]

Taylor, C. W., & Ellison, R. L. (1983). Searching for student talent resources relevant to our USOE types of giftedness. *Gifted Child Quarterly, 27,* 99–106. [85]

Tempest, N. R. (1974). *Teaching clever children 7–11.* London: Routledge & Kegan Paul. [*13, *33, *47, *64, *86, Intro.]

Tennent, G., & Gath, D. (1975). Bright delinquents: A three year follow-up study. *British Journal of Criminology, 15,* 386. [96]

Terman, L. M. (1925). *The mental and physical traits of a thousand gifted children.* Stanford, CA: Stanford University Press. [13, 86]

Terman, L. M., & Oden, M. H. (1947). *The gifted child grows up: Twenty-five year's follow-up of a superior group. Genetic studies of genius: Vol. 4.* Stanford, CA: Stanford University Press. [13, 51, 66, 86, 98]

Terman, L. M., & Oden, M. H. (1959). *Genetic studies of genius: The gifted group at mid-life: Vol. 5.* Stanford, CA: Stanford University Press. [13, 66]

Terrassier, J. C. (1981). *Les enfants surdoués ou la précocité embarrassante.* Paris: Éditions ESF. [82, Intro.]

Terrassier, J. C. (1985). Dyssynchrony—uneven development. In J. Freeman (Ed.), *The psychology of gifted children* (pp. 265–274). Chichester, England: Wiley. [*73, 74]

Tesser, A. (1980). Self-esteem maintenance in family dynamics. *Journal of Personality and Social Psychology, 39,* 77–91. [76]

Thelen, H. A. (1967). *Classroom grouping for teachability.* New York: Wiley. [39]

Thiel, R., & Thiel, A. F. (1977). A structural analysis of family interaction patterns, and the underachieving gifted child. *Gifted Child Quarterly, 21,* 267–275. [99]

Thomas, S. B. (1973). Neglecting the gifted causes them to hide talents. *Gifted Child Quarterly, 17,* 193–197. [9]

Tidwell, R. (1980a). A psycho-educational profile of 1,593 gifted high school students. *Gifted Child Quarterly, 24,* 63–68. [66]

Tidwell, R. (1980b). Gifted students' self-images as a function of identification procedure, race, and sex. *Journal of Pediatric Psychology, 5*(1), 57–69. [20, 84]

Tittle, B. (1979). Searching for the hidden treasure: Seeking the culturally different gifted child. *Journal for the Education of the Gifted, 2,* 80–93. [23]

Tonemah, S. (1985). *Tribal-cultural perspectives of gifted and talentedness.* Unpublished manuscript. (Available from D. Montgomery, Elmhurst School, Oklahoma City, OK) [91]

Torrance, E. P. (1962). *Guiding creative talent.* Englewood Cliffs, NJ: Prentice-Hall. [*89]

Torrance, E. P. (1978). Helping your G/C/T child learn about the future. *G/C/T,* No. 1, 5, 28–29. [41]

Torrance, E. P. (1979a). Creativity and its educational implications for the gifted. In J. C. Gowan, J. Khatena, & E. P. Torrance (Eds.), *Educating the ablest: A book of readings on the education of gifted children* (2nd ed., pp. 298–312). Itasca, IL: Peacock. [31, *55]

Torrance, E. P. (1979b). Gifted children of the future: Predictions and proposed solutions. In J. J. Gallagher (Ed.), *Gifted children: Reaching their potential* (pp. 55–84). New York: Trillium. [*41]

Torrance, E. P. (1980). Educating the gifted in the 1980's. *Journal for the Education of the Gifted, 4,* 43–47. [23, 24]

Torrance, E. P. (1985). Future images and characteristics of gifted children around the world. In A. H. Roldan (Ed.), *Gifted and talented children, youth and adults: Their social perspectives and culture* (pp. 102–112). Manila: Reading Dynamics (Monroe, NY: Trillium). [78]

Torrance, E. P. (1986). Teaching creative and gifted learners. In M. C. Whittrock (Ed.), *Handbook of research on teaching* (3rd ed., pp. 630–647). New York: Macmillan. [58, Intro.]

Torrance, E. P., Bruch, C. B., & Goolsby, T. M. (1976). Gifted children study the future. In J. Gibson & P. Chennells (Eds.), *Gifted children: Looking to their future* (pp. 182–204). London: Latimer. [41, 60]

Torrance, E. P., & Reynolds, C. R. (1979). Images of the future of gifted adolescents: Effects of alienation and specialized cerebral functioning. In J. C. Gowan, J. Khatena, & E. P. Torrance (Eds.), *Educating the ablest: A book of readings on the education of gifted children* (pp. 431–445). Itasca, IL: Peacock. [31, 57]

Treffinger, D. J. (1980). Fostering independence and creativity. *Journal for the Education of the Gifted, 3,* 214–224. [59]

Treffinger, D. J. (1986). Fostering effective, independent learning through individualized programming. In J. S. Renzulli (Ed.), *Systems and models for developing* *programs for the gifted and talented* (pp. 429–460). Mansfield Center, CT: Creative Learning Press. [*65]

Treffinger, D. J., & Barton, B. L. (1979). Fostering independent learning. *G/C/T*, No. 7, 3–6, 54. [56]

Treffinger, D. J., & Renzulli, J. S. (1986). Giftedness as potential for creative productivity: Translating IQ scores. *Roeper Review, 8,* 150–154. [16]

Tremaine, C. D. (1979). Do gifted programs make a difference? *Gifted Child Quarterly, 23,* 500–517. [30]

Tremblay, R. E. (1983). Bright juvenile delinquents in residential treatment: Are they different? In B. M. Shore, F. Gagné, S. Larivée, R. H. Tali, & R. E. Tremblay (Eds.), *Face to face with giftedness* (pp. 199–209). New York: Trillium. [48, 96]

Tresize, R. (1978). What about a reading program for the gifted? *The Reading Teacher, 31,* 742–747. [50]

Trifiletti, J. J. (1985). Using computers to teach the gifted. In R. H. Swassing (Ed.), *Teaching gifted children and adolescents* (pp. 316–339). Columbus, OH: Merrill. [*45]

Tuttle, D. H. (1990). Positive labeling and the sibling relationship in families with gifted children. Unpublished doctoral dissertation, University of Virginia. Charlottesville, VA.

Tuttle, F. B., Becker, L. A., & Sousa, J. A. (1988). *Characteristics and identification of gifted and talented students* (3rd ed.). Washington, DC: National Education Association. [100]

Tyerman, M. J. (1985). Gifted children and their identification: The search for culture-fair assessment—a new strategy. In A. H. Roldan (Ed.), *Talented and gifted children, youth and adults: Their social perspectives and culture* (pp. 503–517). New York: Trillium. [23]

Udall, A. (1989). Curriculum for gifted Hispanic students. In C. J. Maker (Ed.), *Critical issues in gifted education: Defensible programs for cultural and ethnic minorities* (pp. 41–56). Austin, TX: Pro-Ed. [91]

U.S. Commissioner of Education. (1972). *Education of the gifted and talented: Report to the Congress* (Document 72-5020). Washington, DC: U.S. Government Printing Office. [14, *17, 43, 77, *85]

Vail, P. L. (1979). *The world of the gifted child.* New York: Walker. (Also Harmondsworth, England: Penguin, 1980) [Intro.]

VanTassel-Baska, J. (1981). *An administrator's guide to the education of gifted and talented children.* Washington, DC: National Association of State Boards of Education. [2, 5, 10, 62, *95, Intro.]

VanTassel-Baska, J. (1985). Appropriate curriculum for the gifted. In J. F. Feldhusen (Ed.), *Toward excellence in gifted education* (pp. 45–67). Denver: Love. [*28, *31, *39, *40, *46, 55, 64]

VanTassel-Baska, J. (1986). Acceleration. In C. J. Maker (Ed.), *Critical issues in gifted education: Defensible programs for the gifted* (pp. 179–196). Rockville, MD: Aspen. [87]

VanTassel-Baska, J. (1989). The disadvantaged gifted. In J. F. Feldhusen, J. VanTassel-Baska, & K. Seeley (Eds.), *Excellence in educating the gifted* (pp. 53–69). Denver: Love. [43, 92, Intro.]

VanTassel-Baska, J., Landau, M., & Olszewski, P. (1985). Towards developing an appropriate math/science curriculum for gifted learners. *Journal for the Education of the Gifted, 8,* 257–272. [59]

Veldman, D. J., & Sanford, J. P. (1984). The influence of class ability level on student achievement and classroom behavior. *American Educational Research Journal, 21,* 629–644. [30]

Vernon, P. E., Adamson, G., & Vernon, D. F. (1977). *The psychology and education of gifted children.* London: Methuen. [14, *16, *18, *22, 23, 26, *38, *70, Intro.]

Vida, L. (1979). Children's literature for the gifted elementary school child. *Roeper Review, 1*(4), 22–24. [50]

Vygotsky, L. S. (1978). *Mind in society: The development of higher psychological processes.* Cambridge, MA: Harvard University Press. [57]

Walker, B. A., & Freeland, T. (1987). Gifted girls grow up. *Journal of the National Association of Women Deans, Administrators and Counselors, 50*(1), 26–32. [78]

Wallach, M. A., & Kogan, N. (1965). *Modes of thinking in young children: A study of the creativity-intelligence distinction.* New York: Holt, Rinehart & Winston. [*89]

Wallis, L. R. (1984). Selective early school entrance: Predicting school success. *Journal for the Education of the Gifted, 7,* 89–97. [6]

Ward, V. S. (1962). *The gifted student: A manual for program improvement.* Atlanta: Southern Regional Education Board. [29]

Ward, V. S. (1975). Program organization and implementation. In W. B. Barbe & J. S. Renzulli (Eds.), *Psychology and education of the gifted* (2nd ed., pp. 295–302). New York: Irvington. [*65]

Ward, V. S. (1980). *Differential education for the gifted.* Ventura, CA: Office of the Ventura County Superintendent of Education for the National/State Leadership Training Institute for the Gifted and Talented. (Original work published 1961) [*31, *33, *34, 40, *48, 57, *81, Intro.]

Ward, V. S. (1981). Basic concepts. In W. B. Barbe & J. S. Renzulli (Eds.), *Psychology and education of the gifted* (3rd ed., pp. 66–76). New York: Irvington. [34]

Ward, V. S. (1985). Giftedness and personal development: Theoretical considerations. *Roeper Review, 8,* 6–10. [31]

Waters, M. (1980). Strategies for teaching children gifted in elementary mathematics. *Arithmetic Teacher, 27*(5), 14–17. [101]

Watson, G., & Glaser, E. (1964). *Appraisal of critical thinking.* New York: Harcourt, Brace, & World. [46]

Webb, J. T., Meckstroth, E. A., & Tolan, S. S. (1982). *Guiding the gifted child: A practical source for parents and teachers.* Columbus: Ohio Psychology. [*27, *36, *67, 69, *70, 71, *72, *73, *74, *76, 83, *84, Intro.]

Weiner, N. (1953). *Ex-prodigy: My childhood and youth.* New York: Simon & Schuster. [70, 71]

Weisberg, P. S., & Springer, K. J. (1961). Environmental factors in creative function. *Archives of General Psychiatry, 5,* 554–564. [89]

Weiss, P., & Gallagher, J. J. (1980). The effects of personal experience on attitudes toward gifted education. *Journal for the Education of the Gifted, 3,* 194–197. [43, 69]

Wells, M. R. (1985). Gifted females: An overview for parents, teachers and counselors. *G/C/T,* No. 38, 43–46. [100, 101]

Wenner, G. C. (1985). Discovery and recognition of the artistically talented. *Journal for the Education of the Gifted, 8,* 221–238. [43]

Werner, E. E. (1989). High-risk children in young adulthood: A longitudinal study from birth to 32 years. *American Journal of Orthopsychiatry, 59*(1), 72–81. [92]

Werner, E. E., & Bachtold, L. (1969). Personality factors of gifted boys and girls in middle childhood and adolescence. *Psychology in the Schools, 2,* 177–182. [83]

Wesolowski, R. J. (1982). Real educational objectives. *Roeper Review, 5*(1), 32–35. [36]

Wheatley, G. H. (1983). A mathematics curriculum for the gifted and talented. *Gifted Child Quarterly, 27,* 77–80. [59]

White, B. L. (1983). The origins of competence. In B. M. Shore, F. Gagné, S. Larivée, R. H. Tali, & R. E. Tremblay (Eds.), *Face to face with giftedness* (pp. 3–26). New York: Trillium. [*75, 81]

White, B. L., Kaban, B. T., & Attanucci, J. (1979). *The origins of human competence: The final report of the Harvard Preschool Project.* Lexington, MA: Lexington. [75, 81]

Whitener, E. M. (1989). A meta-analytic review of the effect of learning on the interaction between prior achievement and instructional support. *Review of Educational Research, 59,* 65–86. [56]

Whitmore, J. R. (1979a). Identifying and programming for highly gifted underachievers in the elementary school. In J. J. Gallagher (Ed.), *Gifted children: Reaching their potential* (pp. 170–207). New York: Trillium. [97]

Whitmore, J. R. (1979b). The etiology of underachievement in highly gifted young children. *Journal for the Education of the Gifted, 3,* 38–51. [97]

Whitmore, J. R. (1980). *Giftedness, conflict, and underachievement.* Boston: Allyn & Bacon. [*1, *5, 13, 16, *75, 77, *97, 98, *99, Intro.]

Whitmore, J. R. (1984). *The challenge: To nurture the full development of potential in all gifted students.* (ERIC Document Reproduction Service No. ED 246 606) [98]

Whitmore, J. R. (1985). New challenges to common identification practices. In J. Freeman (Ed.), *The psychology of gifted children: Perspectives on development and education* (pp. 93–113). Chichester, England: Wiley. [15, 17, *21, *72, 86]

Whitmore, J. R. (Ed.) (1986). *Intellectual giftedness in young children: Recognition and Development.* New York: Haworth. [*75]

Whitmore, J. R., & Maker, C. J. (1985). *Intellectual giftedness in disabled persons.* Rockville, MD: Aspen. [*94, *95]

Wiener, J. L. (1968). Attitudes of psychologists and psychometrists toward gifted children and programs for the gifted. *Exceptional Children, 34,* 354. [10, 22, 69, 77, 88]

Wiener, J. L., & O'Shea, H. E. (1963). Attitudes of university faculty, administrators, teachers, supervisors, and university students toward gifted children and programs for the gifted. *Exceptional Children, 30,* 163–165. [9, 69, 88]

Williams, C. W. (1958). Characteristics and objectives of a program for the gifted. In N. B. Henry (Ed.), *Education for the gifted. Fifty-seventh yearbook of the National Association for the Study of Education: Part II* (pp. 147–165). Chicago: University of Chicago Press. [2, 5, *11, 26, 54, 81, *82]

Williams, F. (1978). A magic circle. *G/C/T,* No. 1, 16–17 and 35–37. [24]

Williams, J. C. (1981). National programs for the gifted. In B. S. Miller & M. Price (Eds.), *The gifted child, the family, and the community* (pp. 144–155). New York: Walker. [*67]

Williams, R. M. (1977, September 3). Why children should draw: The surprising link between art and learning. *Saturday Review,* pp. 11–16. [43]

Willings, D. (1980). *The creatively gifted.* Cambridge: Woodhead-Faulkner. [77, *88, 89, Intro.]

Willings, D. (1983a). Group roles and the gifted child. *Roeper Review, 5,* 18–21. [85, 89]

Willings, D. (1983b). The gifted at work. In B. M. Shore, F. Gagné, S. Larivée, R. H. Tali, & R. E. Tremblay (Eds.), *Face to face with giftedness* (pp. 56–74). New York: Trillium. [66, *90]

Willings, D. (1985). The specific needs of adults who are gifted. *Roeper Review, 8,* 35–38. [66]

Willings, D. (1986). Enriched career search. *Roeper Review, 9,* 95–100. [66, *90]

Wilmeth, F. H. (1979). Age of entrance to kindergarten as related to readiness for first grade. In B. W. Tuckman, *Analyzing and designing educational research* (pp. 35–41). New York: Harcourt, Brace, Jovanovich. [6]

Wilson, F. T. (1951). Evidence about acceleration of gifted youth. *School and Society, 73,* 409–410. [51]

Winchel, R., Fenner, D., & Shaver, P. (1974). Impact of coeducation on "fear of success" imagery expressed by male and female high school students. *Journal of Educational Psychology, 66,* 726–730. [100]

Winne, P. H. (1979). Experiments relating teachers' use of higher cognitive questions to student achievement. *Review of Educational Research, 49,* 13–49. [42]

Winterbottom, M. (1954). *The relation of childhood training in independence to achievement motivation.* Unpublished doctoral dissertation, University of Michigan, Ann Arbor. [83]

Witters, L. A. (1979). The needs of rural teachers in gifted education. *Journal for the Education of the Gifted, 3,* 79–82. [93]

Witters, L. A., & Vasa, S. F. (1981). Programming alternatives for educating the gifted in rural schools. *Roeper Review, 3*(4), 22–24. [93]

Witty, P. A. (1951a). Progress in the education of the gifted. In P. A. Witty (Ed.), *The gifted child* (pp. 1–9). Boston: Heath. [79]

Witty, P. A. (1951b). The education of gifted children and youth—Summary and recommendations. In P. A. Witty (Ed.), *The gifted child* (pp. 267–276). Boston: Heath. [*78, 79]

Witty, P. (Ed.). (1951c). *The gifted child.* Boston: Heath. [Intro.]

Witty, P. A. (1954). Guidance of the gifted. *Personnel and Guidance Journal, 33,* 136–139. [79]

Witty, P. A. (1958). Who are the gifted? In N. B. Henry (Ed.), *Education for the* *gifted. Fifty-seventh yearbook of the National Society for the Study of Education: Part II* (pp. 41–63). Chicago: University of Chicago Press. [*11]

Witty, P. A. (Ed.). (1971). *Reading for the gifted and creative student.* Newark, DE: International Reading Association. [33, 35, 50]

Wolf, J. S., & Stephens, T. M. (1983). Training models for parents of the gifted. *Journal for the Education of the Gifted, 7,* 120–129. [67]

Wolf, J. S., & Stephens, T. M. (1985). Social and emotional development of gifted children and youth. In R. H. Swassing (Ed.), *Teaching gifted children and adolescents* (pp. 60–91). Columbus, OH: Merrill. [24, *32, 48, 54, *55, *57, *78]

Wong, S. Y., & Wong, P. R. (1989). Teaching strategies and practices for the education of gifted Cantonese students. In C. J. Maker (Ed.), *Critical issues in gifted education: Defensible programs for cultural and ethnic minorities* (pp. 182–188). Austin, TX: Pro-Ed. [91]

Wood, C. T. (1985). Policy analysis of California's program for gifted and talented students. *Educational Evaluation and Policy Analysis, 7,* 281–287. [85]

Wooddell, G. D., Fletcher, G. H., & Dixon, T. E. (1982). Futures study for the adolescent gifted: A curriculum evaluation. *Journal for the Education of the Gifted, 5,* 24–33. [41]

Woodliffe, H. M. (1977). *Teaching gifted learners: A handbook for teachers.* Toronto: Ontario Institute for Studies in Education. [*30, 42, *59, *63, 64, Intro.]

Worcester, D. A. (1979). Enrichment. In W. C. George, S. J. Cohn, & J. C. Stanley (Eds.), *Educating the gifted: Acceleration and enrichment* (pp. 98–104). Baltimore: Johns Hopkins University Press. [29]

Wronski, S. P., Fair, J. E., Boyes, R. L., & Fullinwider, R. K. (1987). Global education: In bounds or out? *Social Education, 51*(4), 242–249. [44]

Yager, E. L. (1982). Information from students concerning school science: Implications for instruction of the gifted. *Roeper Review, 4*(4), 9–10. [59]

Yarborough, B. H., & Johnson, R. A. (1983). Identifying the gifted: A theory-practice gap. *Gifted Child Quarterly, 27,* 135–138. [11, 14, 15]

Zacharias, J. R. (1966). Learning by teaching. In W. T. Martin & D. C. Pinck (Eds.), *Curriculum improvement and innovation: A partnership of students, school teachers, and research scholars* (pp. 249–254). Cambridge, MA: Bentley. [57]

Zaffrann, R. T., & Colangelo, N. (1979a). Counseling with gifted and talented students. In J. C. Gowan, J. Khatena, & E. P. Torrance (Eds.), *Educating the ablest: A book of readings on the education of gifted children* (2nd ed., pp. 167–181). Itasca, IL: Peacock. [*78]

Zaffrann, R. T., & Colangelo, N. (1979b). Counseling with gifted and talented students. In N. Colangelo & R. T. Zaffrann (Eds.), *New voices in counseling the gifted* (pp. 142–153). Dubuque, IA: Kendall/Hunt. [*77, 86]

Zeeman, R. D. (1982). Creating change in academic self-concept and school behavior in alienated school students. *School Psychology Review, 11,* 459–461. [99]

Zeigarnik, B. (1922). Über das Behalten von erledigten und unerledigten Handlungen. *Psychologische Forschung, 9,* 1–85. [Cited extensively, pp. 6–21, in K. Lewin (1951), *Field theory in social science: Selected theoretical papers* (D. Cartwright, Ed.). New York: Harper & Row.] [63]

Zeller, C. (1990). Evaluating gifted learners: Some new dimensions. *Guidance and Counselling, 6*(2), 26–32. [25]

Zettel, J. J. (1979). Gifted and talented education over a half decade of change. *Journal for the Education of the Gifted, 3,* 14–37. [1]

Ziv, A. (1977). *Counseling the intellectually gifted child.* Toronto: University of Toronto Guidance Centre. [69, *81]

Ziv, A., Ramon, J., & Doni, M. (1977). Parental perception and self concept of gifted and average underachievers. *Perceptual and Motor Skills, 44,* 563–568. [98]

Zorman, R. (1982). Parents do make a difference. *Roeper Review, 5,* 41–43. [71]

Zuccone, C. F., & Amerikaner, M. (1986). Counseling gifted underachievers: A family systems approach. *Journal of Counseling and Development, 64,* 590–592. [99]

Author Index

Entries following authors' names refer to the Introduction (Intro.), Conclusion (Concl.), or *recommended practice number* (not the text page number).

Abraham, W., 75
Abroms, K. I., 73, 87
Adams, H. B., 87
Adams, P. J., 50, 65
Adamson, G., Intro., 14, 16, 18, 22, 23, 26, 38
Adderholdt-Elliot, M., 72
Adjemovitch, D., 75
Alamprese, J. A., 91, 92
Alexander, P. A., Intro., 1, 35, 47, 52, 68, 94
Alexander, P. J., 6
Allan, S. D., 78
Allen, H. D., 51
Altman, R., 82
Alvino, J. J., Intro., 11, 14, 37, 72, 73, 74, 76, 84, 97, 98, 100
Ambach, G. M., 37
Ambrose, I. M., 54
American Association for Gifted Children, Intro., 55
Amerikaner, M., 99
Anderson, C. W., 42
Anderson, L. M., 42
Anderson, M. A., 50
Appleyard, D., Intro., 7
Archambault, F. X., Jr., 52
Arent, R. P., 82
Armstrong, D. C., Intro.
Armstrong, J., 101
Aschner, M. J., Intro.
Asher, M. J., Intro.

Asher, J. W., 24
Asher, S. R., 74
Ashman, A., 67
Association for the Gifted, The (TAG), Intro., 69, Concl.
Astin, H. S., 101
Atamian, G. C., 86
Attanucci, J., 75, 81
Aubrecht, L., 2
Austin, A. B., 74

Bachtold, L. M., 25, 83
Baldwin, A. Y., 23, 46, 78, 91
Ballering, L. D., 76
Barbe, W. B., Intro., 21, 33, 59, 61, 64, 97
Barron, F., 23, 83, 89
Barton, B. L., 21, 56
Baska, L., 21, 23, 88
Baskin, B. H., 33
Bass, J. E., 74
Bassin, L. E., 6, 28, 74, 80, 84
Bauer, H., 67, 75
Baum, S., 95
Bayley, N., 20
Bear, G. G., 48
Beasley, W. A., 45
Beck, A. T., 72
Beck, L., 55
Becker, J., 44
Becker, L. A., 100

Bell, R., 89
Benbow, C. P., 74, 80, 87
Bennett, N., 56
Berger, P., 49, 53, 55, 90
Bernal, E. M., Jr., 23, 91
Berry, K., 86, 90
Betts, G. T., 65
Betz, N. E., 49
Biersdorf, M. P., 50
Birch, J. W., Intro., 6, 21, 47, 79, 82
Birnbaum, M. J., 93
Birns, B., 20
Bishop, V. E., 94
Bishop, W. E., 9
Bitan, D., Intro.
Blacher-Dixon, J., 94
Bland, M., 99
Blanning, J. M., Intro., 17, 57, 61, 91
Blaubergs, M. S., 100
Blaylock, A., 91
Bleedorn, B. B., 41, 85
Blickenstaff, R., 43
Bloom, B. S., Intro., 13, 20, 42, 43, 55, 66, 71, 81, 83, 87
Bogue, K. L., 54, 68
Bonds, C. W., 50
Bonds, L. T., 50
Booth, L., 55
Boothby, P., 50
Borland, J. H., 9, 14, 16, 20, 21

353

Subject Index

Entries following index items refer to the Introduction (Intro.), Conclusion (Concl.), or *recommended practice number* (not the text page number).

About the Authors

Bruce M. Shore is professor of education at McGill University in Montreal. He is an educational psychologist in the Department of Educational Psychology and Counselling, director of the McGill Giftedness Centre and of the Centre for Research on Instruction. His research is on how bright students think qualitatively differently from others and is moving toward applications of this work on knowledge production as a curricular objective for bright students.

Dewey G. Cornell is assistant professor in the Programs in Clinical and School Psychology at the Curry School of Education of the University of Virginia in Charlottesville. He is a supervising clinical psychologist in the Institute of Law, Psychiatry, and Public Policy, and he heads the Assessment Service in the Center for Clinical Psychological Services. His research interests concern family relations and giftedness as well as juvenile delinquency and applications of clinical psychology to law and public policy.

Ann Robinson is associate professor in the Department of Teacher Education and the Center for Research on Teaching and Learning at the University of Arkansas at Little Rock. She is also director of Project Promise, a federally funded research and service program for gifted middle school students. Her research addresses the social context of giftedness, curriculum, program evaluation, and student-teacher interaction.

Virgil S. Ward is professor emeritus of education at the Curry School of Education of the University of Virginia in Charlottesville. He is an educational epistemologist and was the originator of the concept of "differentiated education for the gifted." He remains devoted to the notion promoted by John Dewey that educational theory and educational practice are mutually interactive and supportive. The Virgil Scott Ward Chair in Differential Education for the Gifted was established in 1990 at the University of Virginia.

Feedback Form

Please feel free to share your comments on this book. You may photocopy this page if you wish. It would be very helpful to us if you would indicate to which of the following your comments apply.

____I wish to suggest a recommended practice you appear to have missed. A reference to this practice is attached or follows:

____You have missed a research study concerning recommended practice number ____. A copy of the text or a reference citation is attached or follows:

____I have just concluded ____or am planning ____a study relevant to recommended practice number ____. A copy of the report ____or the reference ____is enclosed; or please contact me about it ____(name and address please!):

____I have a comment about the book:

Date:

Optional—Your name, address with postal code, telephone number:

Please send your feedback to

> Bruce M. Shore
> McGill University
> 3700 McTavish Street
> Montreal, Quebec, Canada H3A 1Y2
>
> FAX (514) 398–4679